HOW TO BUILD
HONDA
HORSEPOWER

RICHARD HOLDENER

Copyright © 2002 by Richard Holdener

All rights reserved. Photographs by Richard Holdener and Lisa Estrada. All text and photographs in this publication are the property of Richard Holdener, unless otherwise noted or credited. It is unlawful to reproduce – or copy in any way – resell, or redistribute this information without the expressed written permission of the publisher.

All text, photographs, drawings, and other artwork (hereafter referred to as information) contained in this publication is sold without any warranty as to its usability or performance. In all cases, original manufacturer's recommendations, procedures, and instructions supersede and take precedence over descriptions herein. Specific component design and mechanical procedures—and the qualifications of individual readers—are beyond the control of the publisher, therefore the publisher disclaims all liability, either expressed or implied, for use of the information in this publication. All risk for its use is entirely assumed by the purchaser/user. In no event will CarTech®, Inc., or the author be liable for any indirect, special, or consequential damages, including but not limited to personal injury or any other damages, arising out of the use or misuse of any information in this publication.

This book is an independent publication, and the author(s) and/or publisher thereof are not in any way associated with, and are not authorized to act on behalf of any of the manufacturers included in this book. All registered trademarks are the property of their owners. The publisher reserves the right to revise this publication or change its content from time to time without obligation to notify any persons of such revisions or changes.

Edited By: Steve Hendrickson

ISBN-13 978-1-884089-60-2
ISBN-10 1-884089-60-7

Order No. SA71

Printed in China

CarTech® Inc.,
39966 Grand Avenue
North Branch, MN 55056
Telephone (651) 277-1200 • (800) 551-4754 • Fax: (651) 277-1203
www.cartechbooks.com

OVERSEAS DISTRIBUTION BY:

Brooklands Books Ltd.
P.O. Box 146, Cobham, Surrey, KT11 1LG, England
Telephone 01932 865051 • Fax 01932 868803
www.brooklands-books.com

Brooklands Books Aus.
3/37-39 Green Street, Banksmeadow, NSW 2109, Australia
Telephone 2 9695 7055 • Fax 2 9695 7355

Front Cover: *A 200-hp all-motor B16A sits next to the World's Fastest Street Civic, which is equipped with a 500-hp Vortech supercharged B18C.* (Lisa Estrada)

Back Cover, Right: *Supercharging is one of the best ways to add performance to the already capable B18C engine family; this example is fitted with a Jackson Racing supercharger kit.* (Richard Holdener)

Back Cover, Left: *The author drove this 1998 Civic EX (converted to Si specs) to several land speed records at both El Mirage dry lakebed in southern California, and at the Bonneville salt flats. The author was also responsible for building the record-setting B20-based LS/VTEC hybrid power plant.* (Richard Holdener)

TABLE OF CONTENTS

	About the Author	5
	Introduction to Dyno Testing	6

Chapter 1 The Long and Short of Air Intake Systems 8

Test	Engine	Comparison	
1	D16Z	AEM versus RS Akimoto	10
2	B16A	Iceman versus Modified Iceman	12
3	B20 Hybrid	Modified Iceman versus Hosetech	14
4	D16Y	K&N Drop-In Filter versus K&N Air Intake	16
5	D15B7	Stock Air Intake versus APC Toucan	18
6	B16A	Stock Air Intake versus Comptech	20
7	D16Y	Stillen versus K&N versus APC	22
8	B18A	Stock Air Intake versus RS Akimoto	24

Chapter 2 Intake Manifolds and Throttle Bodies 26

Test	Engine	Comparison	
1	B16A & B20	Throttle Body-Stock versus RC Engineering 64.5-mm Throttle Body	28
2	B16A & B20	Del Sol Intake Manifold versus Type R Intake Manifold	30
3	B16A	Stock B16A Intake Manifold versus Extrude Hone ported Del Sol Intake Manifold	32
4	B16A	Del Sol Intake Manifold versus Venom Intake Manifold	34
5	B16A	Del Sol Intake Manifold versus Skunk Intake Manifold	36
6	B16A	Del Sol Intake Manifold versus STR Intake Manifold	38
7	D16Z	Holley 62-mm Throttle Body versus Stock 55-mm (Supercharged)	40
8	B18A	Stock B18A Intake Manifold versus Extrude Hone-Ported B18A Intake Manifold	42
9	B16A	Killer Bee Racing Intake Manifold versus Stock Del Sol Intake Manifold	44

Chapter 3 Heads, Cams, and Sprockets 46

Test	Engine	Comparison	
1	B18C	Type R Cams versus June Stage 3 Cams	48
2	B18A	Stock Cams versus Crane Cams	50
3	B16A	B16A Cams versus Crower 63401 Cams	52
4	B16A	B16A Cams versus Crower 63402 Cams	54
5	B16A	Adjustable Cam Sprockets, Take I	56
6	B16A	Adjustable Cam Sprockets, Take II	58
7	D16Z	Stock D16Z versus Competition Cams 59300	60
8	B18C	Stock B18C (GSR) versus Competition Cams 57200	62
9	B16A	Stock B16A Head versus Extrude Hone-Ported B-16A Head	64
10	B16A	Stock B16A Head versus Milled B16A Head	66

Chapter 4 Headers, Cats, and Performance Exhaust 68

Test	Engine	Comparison	
1	D16Z	MagnaFlow Cat-Back Exhaust and Chikara Header	70
2	B16A	Stock Exhaust Manifold versus APEXi Civic and Integra Type R Headers	72
3	B16A	DC Sports 4-1 Header versus DC Sports Tri-Y Header	74
4	B16A	DC Sports 4-1 Header versus Kamakazi 4-1 Header	76
5	D15B7	Stock versus Greddy Cat-Back Exhaust and Pacesetter Header	78

How to Build Honda Horsepower

Table of Contents

	6	B18A	Thermal Cat-Back Exhaust, Chikara header, and Removed Cat	80
	7	B16A	Stock versus Comptech Cat-Back Exhaust and Header	82
	8	D16Z	Stock versus Stillen Header and No Cat versus Kamakazi Header (Supercharged)	84
	9	D16Y	Stock versus Jackson Racing Header	86

Chapter 5 Superchargers: Big Boost Bolt-Ons 88

Test	Engine	Comparison	
1	B17C & B18A	PowerTrain Dynamics LS and GSR (Powerdyne)	90
2	D16Z	Jackson Racing Supercharger (Effect of Boost)	92
3	B16A	Vortech Supercharged/Intercooled Civic Si	94
4	B16A	Vortech SC Civic Si Big Boost	96
5	B18C	Vortech Supercharged Integra GSR	98
6	H22	Jackson Racing Supercharged Prelude	100
7	B20	Jackson Racing Supercharged CRV	102
8	C30A	Comptech Supercharged NSX	104
9	F20C	Comptech Supercharged S2000	106
10	B18C	Jackson Racing Supercharged GSR	108
11	B16A	Effects of Intake Charge Temp: Ice Water versus Ambient	110

Chapter 6 Turbocharged Terrors 112

Test	Engine	Comparison	
1	B16A	Low-Buck B16A Turbo	114
2	B16A	Boost Wars: 12 psi versus 15 psi	116
3	B16A	.48 A/R Housing versus .63 A/R Turbine Housing	118
4	B16A	Greddy Civic Si at 5.5-psi Boost	120
5	B16A	Greddy Civic Si at 7.1-psi Boost	122
6	B18C	Greddy GSR at 8.5-psi Boost	124
7	B16A	Drag Civic Si at 8.9-psi Boost	126
8	B16A	T3 versus T3/T04B Hybrid on B16A Motor	128

Chapter 7 Nitrous, ECUs (Chips), and Underdrive Pulleys 130

Test	Engine	Comparison	
1	B20/VTEC	June ECU versus Mugen ECU	132
2	B16A	Stock ECU versus Hondata ECU	134
3	B16A	APEXi VTEC Controller versus Stock	136
4	B16A	Remove Power Steering Pump	138
5	B16A	Unorthodox Racing Underdrive Pulley	140
6	B16A	Stock ECU versus Mugen ECU	142
7	B18C5	Stock ECU versus Comptech ECU	144
8	D16Z	Horsepower from an Oil Change: Redline Synthetic Oil	146
9	D15B	Air Conditioning and Lights	148
10	B18A	ZEX Nitrous Oxide	150

Chapter 8 Engine Buildups 152

1	Supercharged D16Z	153
2	USTCC B16A 1.6L	156
3	Bonneville 2.0L LS/VTEC	159
4	1834cc LS/VTEC	162
5	Street Performance D16Z	165
6	JG Engine Dynamics 2.0L Drag Motor	167
7	JG Engine Dynamics B18C Turbo Race Motor	170
8	Killer Bee Racing Supercharged B18C Stroker Motor	172

Appendix Source Guide 175

ABOUT THE AUTHOR

Richard Holdener is a freelance journalist specializing in dyno test comparisons. Although perhaps best known for his work with Ford engines and cars, Holdener is a diehard Honda/Acura fanatic. "When I was approached about writing this book on Honda/Acura performance I was very excited. Like the Ford fuel injection market of 10 years ago, there is so much misinformation out there regarding Honda/Acura performance products. Only through real-world dyno testing can the true worth of performance parts—both factory and aftermarket—be demonstrated."

"Though I'm often labeled a Blue-Oval boy, the truth is that I have owned more Honda/Acura-powered vehicles than any other manufacturer." Holdener has owned everything from a 1972 Honda CL100 motorcycle to a 1991 Acura NSX. But he doesn't just own these cars—he wrenches on them and races them too. In addition to the NSX, Holdener's stable includes a 1990 Integra GS (with an LS/VTEC hybrid motor), a 1995 Civic Del Sol, and a 1999 Civic Si.

In addition to being used extensively for testing (more than 750 dyno runs!), the Del Sol was a three-time road race champion. The B16A-powered Del Sol won the Motorola Cup endurance championship twice before Holdener used it to win the inaugural United States Touring Car Championship in 2000. NASA's USTCC Pro-Racing format pitted cars with lightly modified engines and highly modified suspensions on road courses across the United States. As this book goes to press, Holdener and the Del Sol are at it again, closing in on the TCCRA 2.2L Cup road race championship. Holdener was also recently offered a ride in a 2000 Japan-Spec Integra Type R for the remainder of the 2002 USTCC season.

The B16A Del Sol is not Holdener's only serious Honda-powered machine. His daily-driven 1999 Civic Si can lay legitimate claim to the title of World's Fastest Honda Civic. Powered by a Vortech supercharged 2-liter B18C, the 500-horsepower big-bore GSR motor has pushed the Civic to nearly 200 miles per hour. "The car has run 191 miles per hour, but it will go 200 mph the next time out!" says Holdener.

Holdener was also responsible for a few top-speed records in Honda Civics; G/PRO and F/BALT records at Bonneville and a G/PRO record at El Mirage using motors built by Holdener.

Where does this love for Hondas come from? Well, Holdener's previous Honda/Acura machinery included a 1984 ITC Civic, a 500 Interceptor motorcycle, and Holdener's favorite of all his Hondas, a 1977 Accord hatchback nicknamed the *Silver Bullet*. Of that car, Holdener says, "The *Silver Bullet* has a long history. I got it for the cost of two tacos from the local taco stand. We were standing around wanting food, but no one wanted to go get it. My life-long friend Harold offered the *Silver Bullet* to me if I would pick up the food. I had to think it over for a while, the *Silver Bullet* was in pretty bad shape, but I did it and so began my adventures with the *Bullet*. The car got its name from a quickie silver paint job that was so shiny it was difficult to look at in direct sunlight. Lucky for us, the 'auto parts store special' spray paint quickly faded to a more livable gray."

"The *Silver Bullet* had 225,000 miles on the odometer, which had been busted for some time. The motor ran okay, but the tranny was missing fifth gear and the synchros were gone in third. The driving technique consisted of winding it up in second and skipping third. Not running fifth caused the motor to rev a little in fourth gear on the freeway, but it never complained. The car survived a bizarre Southern California flood that filled it with water nearly to window level. We simply opened the doors to let it all drain out, started the motor, and drove it around. We never so much as looked at the tranny or oil levels (or the water there in).

"I drove the *Bullet* for several years, though I was too embarrassed to pick up dates in broad daylight. Eventually, some idiot stole the stereo. He broke a $100 window in a car worth about $10 to steal a stereo that was already broken. I eventually traded the car for an intercooler from a Supra Turbo. My adventures with the Silver Bullet are why I decided to run the Del Sol in the USTCC and why I eventually bought the NSX. Honda really knows how to build cars!"

In addition to this book, Holdener has also written *5.0 Liter Ford Dyno Tests* and *Building Short-Track Ford Power* for S-A Design. He writes a monthly column on forced induction for *Muscle Mustangs & Fast Fords* along with contributing numerous tech articles to enthusiast magazines.

INTRODUCTION

DYNO TESTING

Currently (circa 2002), Honda and Acura owners have some of the most sophisticated power plants available to the general public. Think about it, how many companies build motors that not only reach the magical 100 horsepower-per-liter mark, but actually eclipse the number by a significant margin? To date, Honda (Acura) is credited with building a street engine with the highest specific power output. The two-liter motor powering the sporty S2000 convertible boasts an industry leading 120 horsepower per liter. Many dedicated race motors don't produce 120 horsepower per liter, let alone ultra low emission street motors back by a full factory warranty. To put this number into perspective, a typical 4.6L Mustang V8 would have to produce 552 horsepower to achieve the same specific output. Sure, elevated specific outputs become more difficult with increased displacement, but the fact that the Mustang boys only produce 20 more horsepower from 2.6 liters of additional displacement demonstrates the inefficiency of the relatively low-tech V8s.

Credit for the impressive efficiency has to go to the signature VTEC system employed by Honda on their performance motors. The trick dual-cam profile of the VTEC system produces an engine with nothing less than a Jekyll and Hyde personality. The use of two cam profiles allows the engine to run on the milder profile under most driving conditions. The milder cam profile provides improved low-speed torque, throttle response and reduced emissions, not to mention impressive fuel economy.

The key to the elevated specific outputs produced by the Honda/Acura motors is the secondary (VTEC) cam profile(s). At a pre-determined engine speed (and load), the engine switches over to the secondary, more aggressive cam profile. The increased lift and duration offered by the secondary cam(s) transform the little economy motor into an honest-to-goodness street terror. Other manufacturers are forced to build motors with a compromise between the cam profiles, as the secondary (VTEC) cams are too wild for idle, emissions and fuel economy, while the primary cams simply don't produce sufficient power. A few manufacturers have made attempts to duplicate the dual-cam operation of the patented VTEC system. Most attempts thus far have met with limited success. The vast majority of manufacturers have simply opted for the compromise that comes with a single cam profile.

Unfortunately for Honda/Acura enthusiasts, it is the impressive specific outputs that make performance improvements downright difficult. Unlike their big domestic counterparts, where power gains of 10, 15 and even 20

Progress Civic at El Mirage.

How to Build Honda Horsepower

Introduction

horsepower are available from simple bolt-ons, Honda engines are not quite so responsive to simple air intakes, throttle bodies and headers. The reason for the lack of responsiveness to the aftermarket components is that the factory components are already close to ideal in terms of power production. Think about it in terms of specific output. It is much easier to add power to a 4.6L motor that only produces a lackluster 56 horsepower per liter than it is to add power to a 1.6L motor that produces 100 horsepower per liter. Honda simply did not leave a great deal of power on the proverbial table when they offered VTEC motors producing 100 horsepower (or more) per liter. What this means is that you will likely be disappointed if you plan on adding 25 horsepower with your air intake, throttle body and header. Chances are the number will be much closer to 10 total horsepower between the three components.

Does the elevated specific output mean that it is impossible to increase the power output of a Honda/Acura motor? Not by a long shot, otherwise this would be a very short book. It is possible to increase the power output of a VTEC motor, it just takes the proper combination of components. Don't expect huge power gains from simple bolt-ons, but the elevated efficiency of the VTEC motors make them an ideal candidate for forced induction. Nothing will wake up a VTEC motor like a turbo or supercharger system. You would be money ahead if you saved up your bucks and popped for a small turbo or supercharger kit rather than spending it on an air intake, header and exhaust system. Sure, the turbo or supercharger kit will cost significantly more, but the power gains will be commensurate with the expense. For about what you would pay for an LS/VTEC hybrid, you could install a complete turbo kit. Where the LS/VTEC might get you an extra 40-50 horsepower over a typical B16A, the turbo kit should easily add 75-100 horsepower and a sizable increase in mid-range torque. The same goes for a supercharger from Jackson Racing or Vortech. Nothing makes power like combining VTEC efficiency with forced induction.

The B16A-powered Killer Bee Racing Civic Del Sol was used for extensive dyno testing.

The question now is which component is best for your motor? The answer of course depends a great deal on your exact combination, but chances are that you will find an answer to that question within these pages. The original idea for this Honda/Acura performance book came to me while running dyno test number 250 on my B16A-powered road race Del Sol. Like many enthusiasts, I was looking for more power from my VTEC motor. Unlike most enthusiasts, I was able to make literally thousands of dyno runs testing various components and combinations on the DynoJet to determine which one(s) worked. A big thanks goes to Steve at PowerTrain Dynamics in Huntington Beach, California, for use of their dyno facility. Without his help, this book would have never been written.

Within these pages are answers to some of the more common performance questions that Honda performance enthusiasts ask. Do long (AEM style) air intakes work better than short ones? Are big throttle bodies really worth the money? How much is head porting worth? Are the right cams really worth 10-12 horsepower? How much power is each pound of boost worth? Is it possible to build a turbo kit for less than $1000? The answer to these and many more, including—is it possible to build an honest-to-goodness 200 mph Street Civic?—are answered in *How to Build Honda Horsepower*.

Stuff any B-series VTEC motor in nearly any Civic and you have the makings of a serious street performer.

Chapter 1

The Long and Short of Air Intake Systems

One of the first performance components to be installed on any Honda/Acura motor is usually some kind of air intake system. How popular are these upgrades? Look through any enthusiast magazine and count the number of aftermarket companies currently offering intake systems for Hondas and/or Acuras. The sheer number of different offerings is staggering. The reason for the vast number of available intakes is in direct proportion to two related variables, the first of which is the number of Honda/Acuras on the road. The large number of cars sold indicates popularity, which provides a sizable market for aftermarket companies. Perhaps more important than sheer sales volume is the number of enthusiasts interested in modifying their motors to increase the performance. Add to this availability the fact that air intakes rank up near the top of the list in ease of installation and bang for the buck and you begin to understand the popularity of import intake systems.

Although a number of aftermarket companies currently offer intake systems for the Honda/Acura lineup, the offerings fall into one of three categories: drop-in replacement air filters; short-tube, open-element cone filters; and full-length air intake systems. The first category covers the replacement air filter. This rather simple upgrade consists of replacing the factory paper-element air filter with a unit designed to improve airflow through the system. K&N Engineering sells a number of replacement performance drop-in filters for Honda/Acura applications. The reasoning behind the drop-in filter is that more airflow equals more power, but don't expect sizable power gains from such a simple bolt-on upgrade. As you will see, the power gains usually go hand in hand with both the cost and complexity. Besides, the entire factory air intake

This RS Akimoto air intake made impressive power but would be best when combined with a dedicated cold air source.

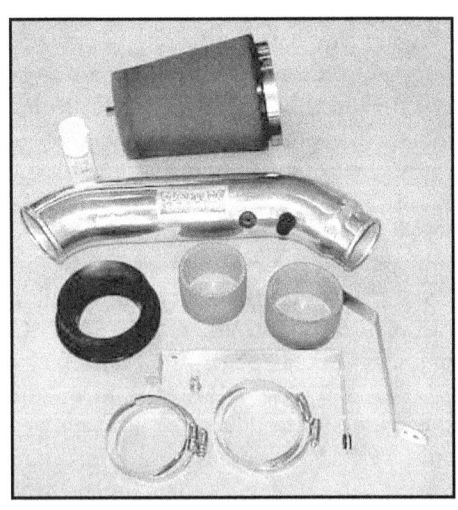

Comptech offers a number of high-quality air intake systems for Honda applications.

system is responsible for the airflow restriction, not just the filter.

Next up in terms of popularity is the short-tube, open-element cone filter. DC Sports, RS Akimoto, and Ingen Technology are but three of the multitude of companies currently offering shorty air intake systems for Honda and Acura applications. The shorty-style air intakes generally consist of a length of mandrel-bent steel or aluminum tubing used to connect the throttle body to the air filter assembly. Most shorty intakes use some sort of open-element cone filter to maximize airflow into the motor. These various kits from various manufacturers differ cosmetically in their tubing and filter size and the entries into the filter and throttle body. Although full-radiused entries are important to airflow, they may not actually add power over a non-radiused entry at stock and mildly modified power levels. If the 160-hp VTEC motor only requires 220 cfm, then a 3-inch tube that flows 700 cfm will have no trouble feeding the airflow needs of the motor (radiused entry or not). The one downside to this type of air intake system is that it places the open-element filter in the engine compartment where it is forced to ingest a diet of hot air (not good for power).

The final type of air intake system is the full-length design made famous by Advanced Engine Management (AEM). Recognizing the need for a constant source of cold air (and its effect on power), AEM designed a system to place the free-flowing cone filter in the fenderwell away from the engine heat. The full-length air intakes do an excellent job of providing an unrestricted cold air source for the engine, something that helps improve power (colder air has more oxygen molecules) and reduces the chance of detonation. Even though the full-length air intake is superior to the shorty air intake in terms of air inlet temperature, the shorty style can actually make more power due to the tuning effect of the tubing length. On Honda/Acura motors (especially VTEC-equipped units), the length of the intake tubing has the same effect that intake manifold runner length has on the power curve. While both the long and shorty-style air intakes offer a measurable improvement over the stock air cleaner system, they affect the power curve differently. As is the case with long-runner intake manifolds, the full-length air intakes offer significantly more power right up to the VTEC operation point. The shorty air intakes offer less power below VTEC, but more power (compared to the full-length) above the VTEC operation point.

If you look at the comparison between the full-length and shorty style air intakes included in this chapter, you will notice that the power gains offered by each are dramatically different. It should be noted that the power numbers generated during the testing were achieved on a DynoJet chassis dyno with the hood open. This is important, as the testing procedure artificially enhanced the power output of the shorty intake. How does the testing procedure affect the results you ask? Remember we mentioned earlier that both the full-length and shorty intakes differed in terms of tubing length and placement of the cone filter? The shorty air intake places the filter in the engine compartment, where the full-length system places the filter in the fenderwell. This placement is critical, as the full-length system provides a cold air source-something not available with the shorty air intake. By running our dyno testing with the hood open, we artificially provided the shorty intake with a source of cold air. The power gains offered by the shorty-style intakes are dramatically reduced in the real world with the hood closed. It is, however, possible to build an air box to enclose the filter on a shorty intake system to allow the system to only breathe cold air. This provides the top-end power of the shorty system with the cold air source of the full-length. The author employed such a system on his Championship-winning USTCC road race Civic Del Sol. Comptech now makes such a system for street Civics.

Using an air box to surround the cone filter on the shorty intake used on the USTCC race Del Sol allowed us to take advantage of the superior top-end breathing offered by the shorty intake. This system did not however, provide us

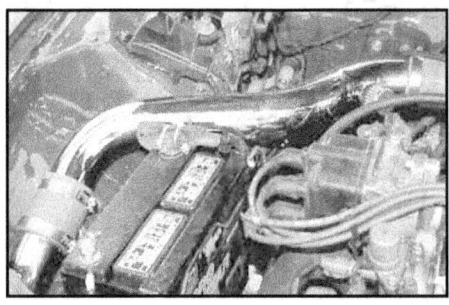

Early (pre-1994) Integras position the air intake behind the battery-somewhat away from the heated engine compartment.

the significant pre-VTEC torque gains offered by the full-length system. As our racecar never saw engine speeds below 5,000 rpm, this was not much of an issue, but the added torque of the full-length intake can definitely be taken advantage of on the street. To that end, the author designed a unique dual-runner air intake that provided the low-speed torque benefits of the full-length intake with the top-end power of the shorty. The answer was to employ both tubing lengths in one system with a vacuum-operated switching device (similar to the unit employed on the GSR intake manifold) to provide transition between the runner lengths. The full-length tubing is used until the operation of the VTEC at which point the short runner intake length comes into use. The result is a power curve that offers the maximum gains from each system.

This chapter offers a number of dyno comparisons between different air intake systems. The chapter includes horsepower and torque gains, as well as the effect on top speed and air inlet temperature. The chapter covers testing on drop-in filters, full-length and shorty intake systems on both normally aspirated and supercharged motors. In an effort to offer complete information, we tested the different air intake systems on a variety of (popular) different engine combinations. While it is impossible to test every conceivable combination of engine, air intake, and filter, the testing in this chapter should provide sufficient information to allow the reader to make an intelligent decision when purchasing an air intake for a Honda/Acura.

Test 1: AEM versus RS Akimoto

1992 Civic Si

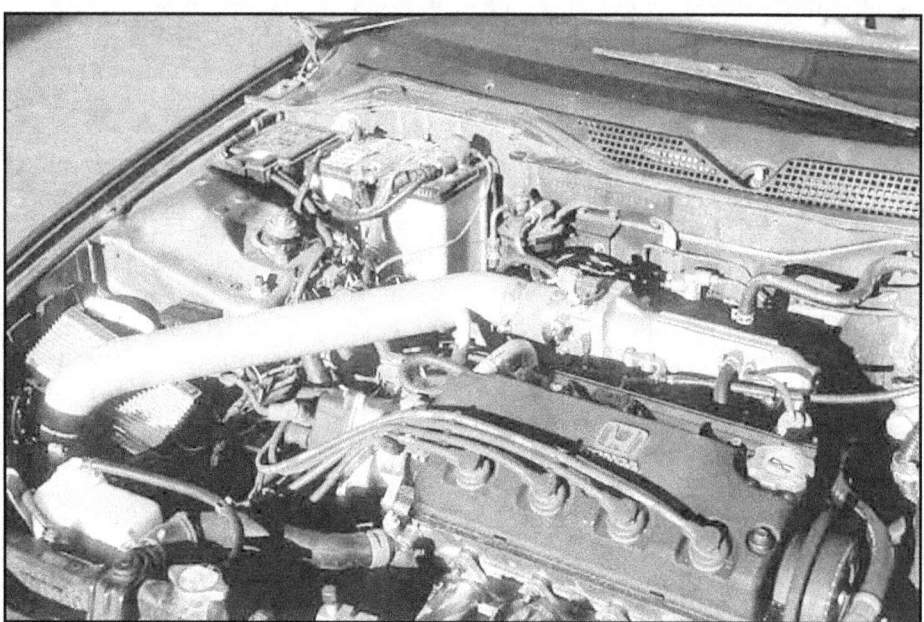

These power graphs clearly demonstrate the different power curves generated by the two different styles of air intake systems. The full-length AEM air intake places the air filter down in the passenger-side fenderwell, while the shorty-style RS Akimoto system places the filter in the engine compartment. The filter placement has a twofold effect on the overall power output. First, the length of tubing used on the system (and to some extent, the tubing diameter) dramatically affects the power curve. Note that the longer AEM system produced much more torque down below the VTEC operation point on this 1.6L Civic EX motor, while the shorter RS Akimoto produced better top-end power. This difference in power curve can be attributed to the difference in inlet tubing length.

It should also be pointed out that the filter placement plays anther important role in power output. In addition to system length, the placement of the filter also affects power by way of inlet charge temperature. The power output of a motor is affected greatly by temperature. As a general rule of thumb, power output is reduced by 1 percent for every 10-degree increase in air temperature. On a subsequent test, both of these air intake systems were tested for air temperature and maximum (top) speed against the stock air box. The full-length AEM air intake posted the fastest top speed of 121 mph with the RS Akimoto lagging back at 119 mph. The Civic could only manage 117 mph with the stock air intake. During the top-speed test, we took air inlet temperature measurements and noted that the inlet air temperature was some 25 degrees hotter when running the shorty-style (open element filter in the engine compartment) RS Akimoto system. Thus, the same shorty air intake system that produced more power on the DynoJet chassis dyno (with the hood open) lost power in the real world due to heat.

Of course, the answer to this dilemma is to build a box to enclose the air filter used on the shorty-style system to provide a cold air source. This

would allow it to have the power produced by the short inlet tubing length and the benefit of cold air. Check out the test on the Comptech intake system to see what we have in mind. Regardless of the addition of cold air, the shorty-style air intake will never match the low-speed power of the full-length air intake system. The full-length AEM air system offers power gains where they are most useful on the street. Although we all like to see big power numbers (and top speeds) generated on the dyno, the reality is that most of our time driving is spent with the motor below 5,000 rpm. The added grunt offered by a full-length system comes into play much more often than the top-end charge of the shorter intake. The ideal system would offer cold air, a long runner for low-end, and a short runner that switches over for big top-end power. Check out the dyno test on just such a system designed by the author elsewhere in the chapter.

The Long and Short of Air Intake Systems

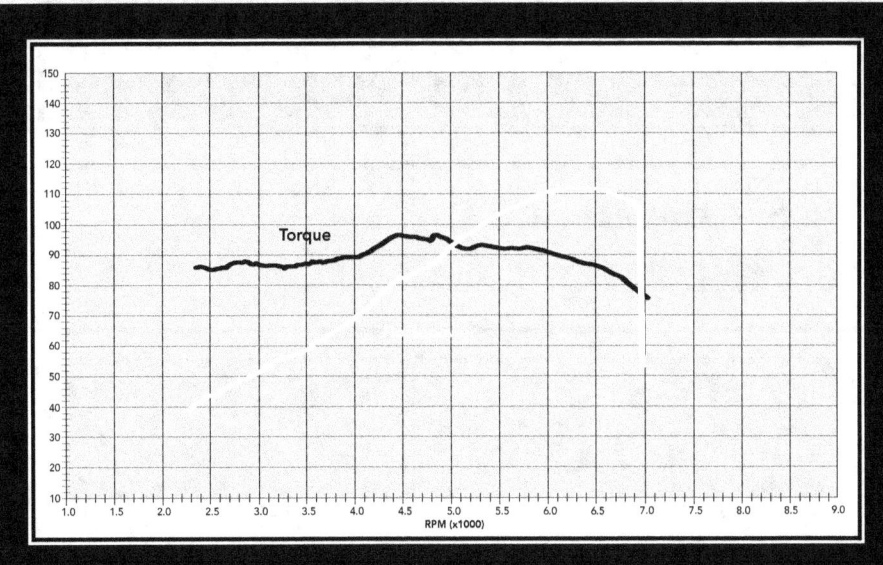

Baseline: D16Z with AEM

This air intake test showed the effect of tubing length, and the importance of a dedicated cold air source. In fact, the power gained by the short intake length was more than canceled out by the hotter air intake temperature.

Peak Horsepower – AEM	113.5 hp
Peak Torque – AEM	100.5 ft-lbs

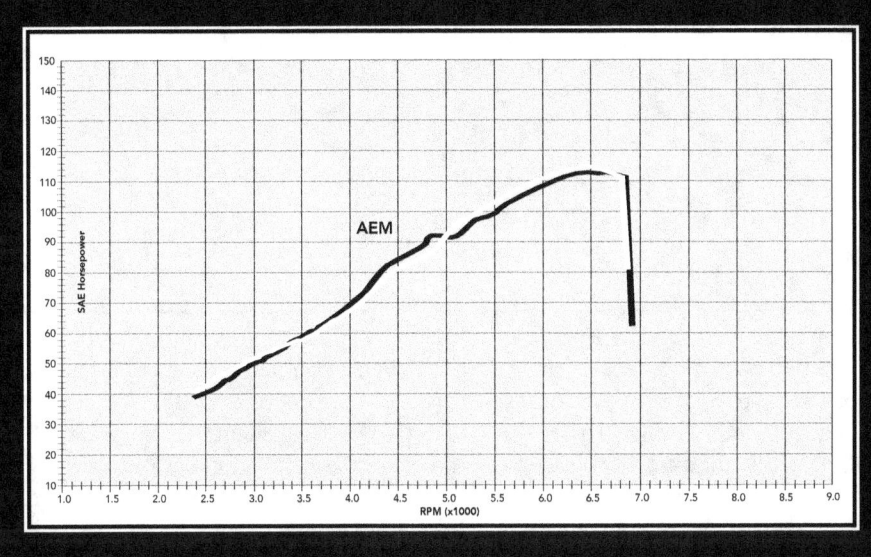

AEM versus RS Akimoto: Horsepower

Peak Horsepower – AEM	113.5 hp
Peak Horsepower – RS Akimoto	115.5 hp
Largest Horsepower Gain	3.5 hp

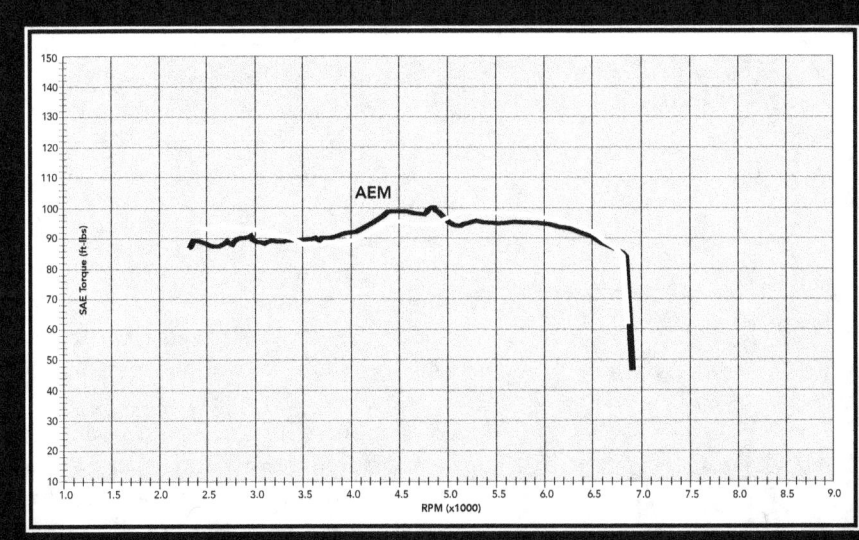

AEM versus RS Akimoto: Torque

Peak Torque – AEM	100.5 ft-lbs
Peak Torque – RS Akimoto	99.3 ft-lbs
Largest Torque Gain	5.1 ft-lbs

Chapter 1

Test 2: Iceman versus Modified Iceman

1998 Civic Si (converted EX)
B16A 1.6L VTEC

This air intake test is another perfect example of how the tubing length used on the air intake system affects power. The motor used for the testing was a modified B16A installed in a 1998 Civic EX (pseudo Si). This motor was used in an attempt to set a land speed record at El Mirage, but fell a little short due to a few tuning problems and lack of ultimate power. The car was run in an under-2-liter class, so the 1.6L motor was small compared to the competition. This motor was eventually removed and a 2-liter stroker motor was installed in its place, using the same cylinder head from this 1.6L combination. The 2.0L went on to set the record on its first attempt, showing that there really is no replacement for displacement. A complete rundown on the 2.0L record holder can be seen in the chapter on engine buildups.

Before replacing the 1.6L B16A, we attempted to tune the combination on the PowerTrain Dynamics DynoJet chassis dyno. We did eventually manage to coax more power from the combination, but not quite enough to set the record. One of the modifications recommended by the author during the testing was to remove part of the intake tubing length from the Iceman air intake. Like the AEM system, the Iceman used on this B16A motor was of the full-length variety. While excellent for street use and to ensure a good cold air source, the long inlet tubing also restricted top-end breathing. The change in power (evidence of the restriction) was more pronounced on this high-horsepower application (compared to the AEM/RS Akimoto comparison test run on the single cam EX motor). Producing nearly 170 hp at the wheels, the twin cam B16A motor required plenty of airflow to meet the top-end breathing needs. Shortening the inlet tubing length (and placing the filter back on) resulted in a sizeable power gain. Although a 4-hp gain peak-to-peak is nothing to sneeze at, even more impressive were the gains offered from the VTEC operation point up to the power peak. We made sure to get a cold air source for the air intake during the top-speed record runs, but in the end, the 1.6L was simply not powerful enough, even with the added power from the air intake change.

How to Build Honda Horsepower

The Long and Short of Air Intake Systems

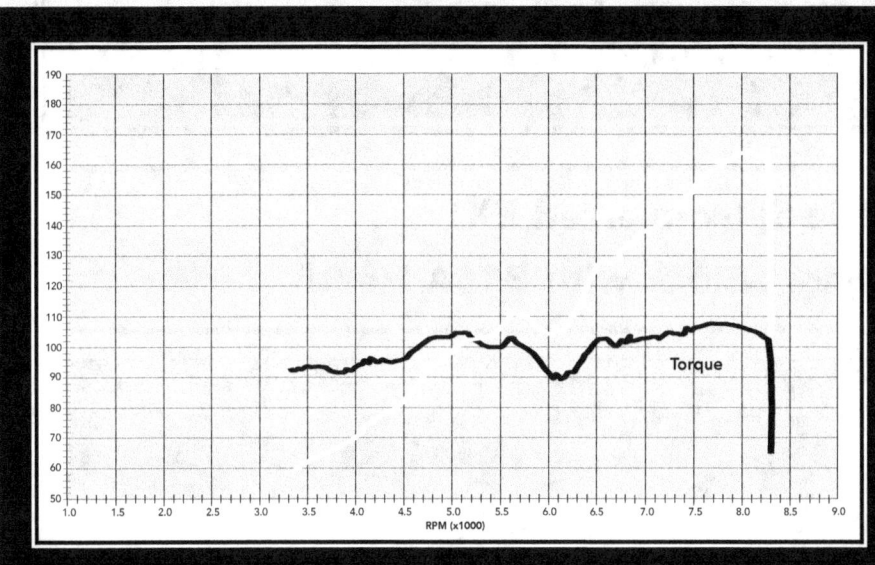

Baseline: B16A with Iceman

It's amazing what you find while running on the dyno. Simply removing a section of the full-length Iceman air intake improved the power output dramatically.

Peak Horsepower – Iceman   164.4 hp
Peak Torque – Iceman   107.8 ft-lbs

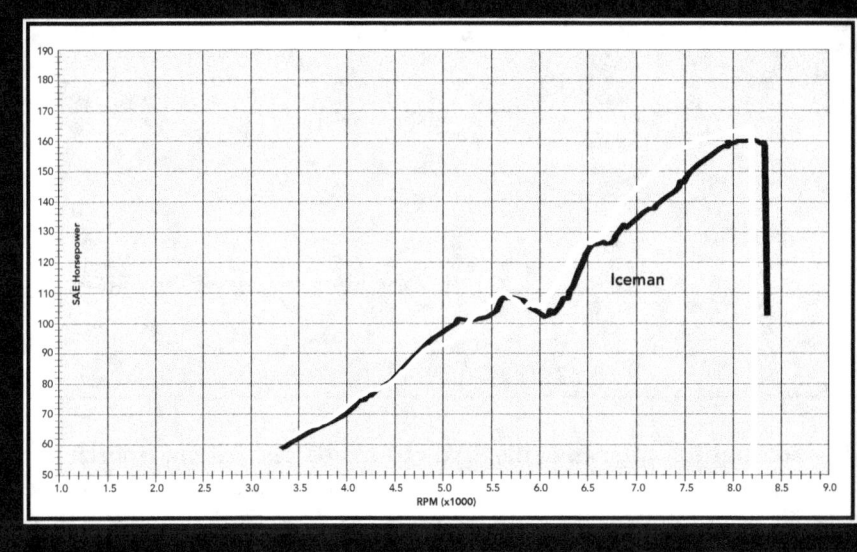

Iceman versus Modified Iceman: Horsepower

Peak Horsepower – Iceman   164.4 hp
Peak Horsepower – Mod Iceman   168.2 hp
Largest Horsepower Gain   13.9 hp

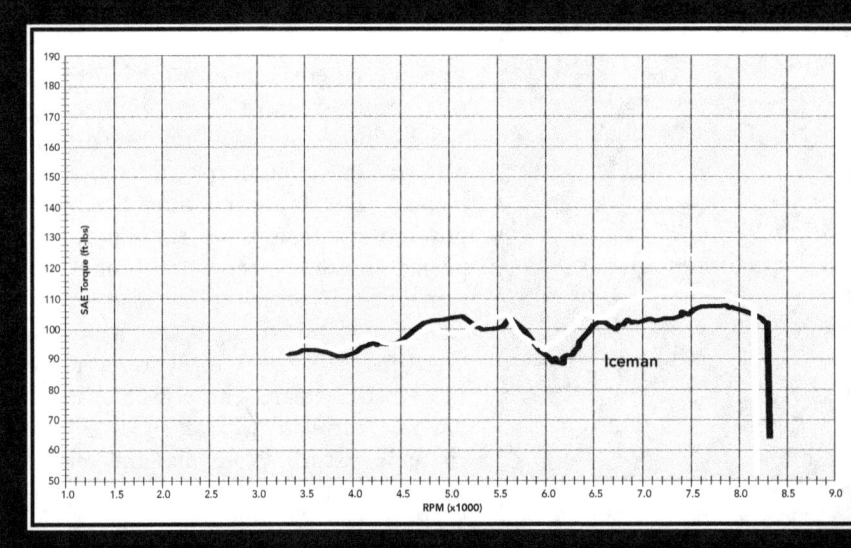

Iceman versus Modified Iceman: Torque

Peak Torque – Iceman   107.8 ft-lbs
Peak Torque – Mod Iceman   113.9 ft-lbs
Largest Torque Gain   9.3 ft-lbs

Chapter 1

Test 3: Modified Iceman versus Hosetech

1998 Civic Si (converted EX)
B20 2.0L CRV Short Block with B16A Head

This particular test was run at about 2 A.M. before rushing out the next morning to set a land speed record in the 2.0L-equipped Civic. The Civic was equipped with a modified CRV 2.0L equipped with a B16A VTEC cylinder head. You can check out the complete details on the 2.0L race motor buildup in the chapter on engine combinations. While we were tuning the motor for the run at El Mirage, we opted to run this comparison test to determine which intake system would be most beneficial to the already-impressive 2.0L. Given that the air intakes in question were originally designed for a 1.6L Civic Si making 160 hp, the fact that they worked so well on this motor making 75–80 hp more was impressive.

The Iceman used for the test was a shortened version of the original (see results of Modified Iceman test). A section of the Iceman was removed in an attempt to maximize top-end power.

The previous test comparing the two different lengths of the Iceman intake clearly demonstrated that the VTEC motor favored the shorter air intake length—at least as far as top-end power was concerned. Confident that the modified Iceman was plenty powerful and well suited to the 2.0L application, we wondered how the air intake system from Hosetech would fare. With a unique, tapered air entry, the Hosetech was impressive from an engineering standpoint. As it turned out, the design offered some benefits over the modified Iceman. The Hosetech offered similar power through most of the range, but posted an odd power hump near 6,000 rpm. The Hosetech piece also offers superior power from 7,000 rpm on up, averaging gains of 2 to 3 hp over the shortened Iceman. The power changes did not correlate with changes to the air/fuel mixture. Note that the motor leaned out a tad at the onset of the VTEC (around 500 rpm), but soon tapered off down below 13:1.

How to Build Honda Horsepower

The Long and Short of Air Intake Systems

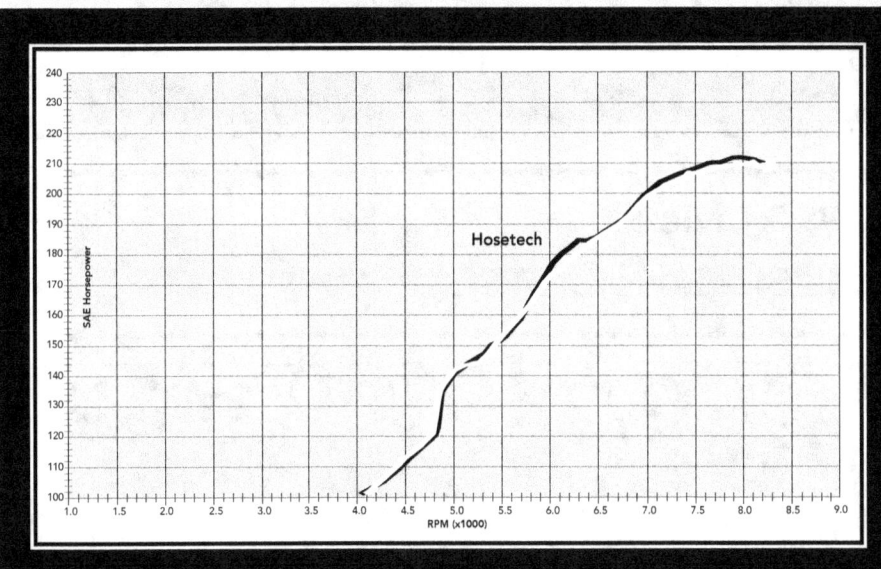

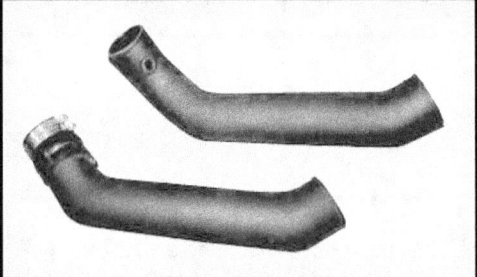

Iceman versus Hosetech: Horsepower

Peak Horsepower – Iceman	211.0 hp
Peak Horsepower – Hosetech	212.3 hp
Largest Horsepower Gain	4.8 hp

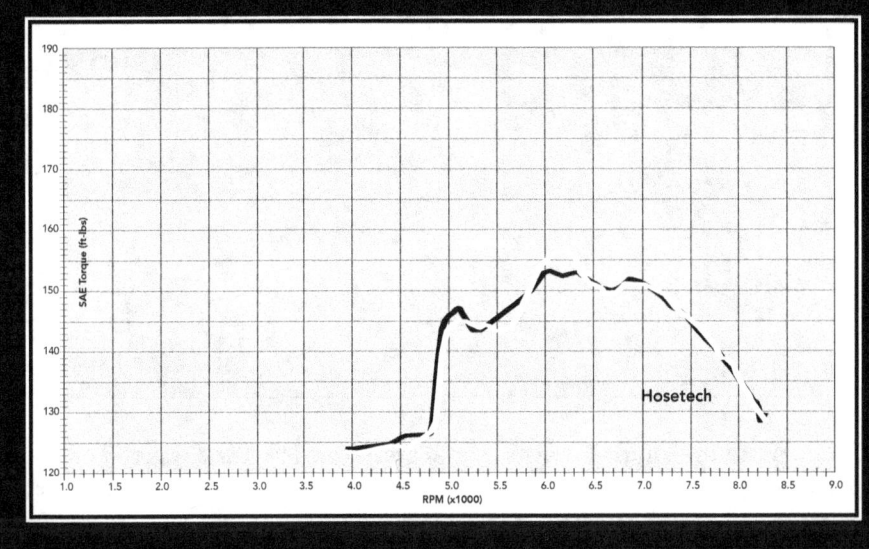

Iceman versus Hosetech: Torque

Peak Torque – Iceman	151.6 ft-lbs
Peak Torque – Hosetech	155.1 ft-lbs
Largest Torque Gain	4.1 ft-lbs

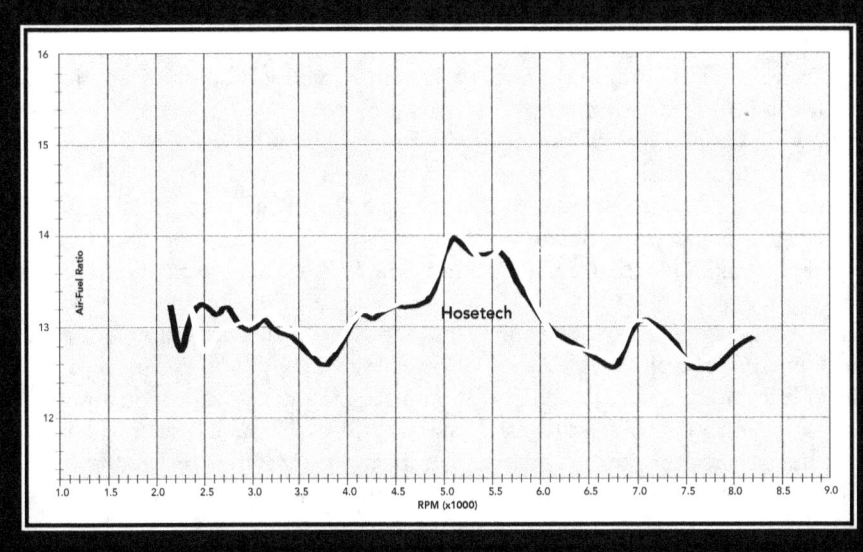

A Hosetech system did better than the modified Iceman air intake. Though similar in power through most of the curve, the Hosetech offered an interesting power bulge near 6,000 rpm.

How to Build Honda Horsepower

Chapter 1

Test 4: K&N Drop-In Filter versus K&N Air Intake

1998 Civic EX
D16Z 1.6L Single-Cam VTEC

The most popular performance component sold for Honda/Acura machinery has to be some type of air intake. It seems like every ad you run across in the popular import car magazines offers some sort of air intake system designed to improve power. In this particular test, we compared a pair of different air intake systems from the same company to determine which system had the most to offer in terms of power. This particular test actually happened by accident, as the test was originally designed to demonstrate the effectiveness of the K&N air intake system. Unfortunately, (or fortunately) for us, the owner of the 1998 Civic EX test vehicle had already installed a K&N drop-in filter long ago. The drop-in filter is quite popular, as it allows airflow improvements without removal of the entire factory air intake system. Simply plop in a better-flowing filter element and away you go. As this test demonstrated, while beneficial, the power gains offered by the drop-in filter don't quite match those offered by a complete air intake system.

That a drop-in K&N filter is no match for a complete system should not come as a big surprise. Although beneficial, the drop-in filter does nothing to remove the restriction inherent in the remainder of the factory air box. With the myriad twists, turns, and acoustical baffles, the stock air filter assembly clearly was designed to minimize noise and not maximize performance. Operating as a muffler for the intake tract, restrictions in the stock air box result in less inlet noise (especially important on VTEC motors). The tradeoff for the noise reduction is obviously airflow. Less noise equals less airflow, which in turn equals less power. This does not even take into account the tuning effect of the change in relative air intake system runner length (see long versus short air intake).

This air intake comparison was run on a 1998 Civic EX equipped with a single-cam VTEC motor. The camshaft-challenged single-can D16Z still has plenty to offer in terms of power potential even when compared to the B16A (and related B-series variants). In addition, it responds well to air intake system modifications. The Civic was run on the PowerTrain Dynamics 248E DynoJet chassis dyno with every effort made to keep the engine oil, coolant and air inlet temperatures consistent between runs. Keeping the variables consistent is paramount to repeatability. Given that we were (in some cases) looking for just a couple of horsepower, repeatability was the key to successful testing. The motor was run with the K&N drop-in filter and then again with the complete K&N air filter system (incorporating a free-flowing cone filter). The dyno curves tell the story that the air intake offers a good bit more power than the simple drop-in. Power was up by 4 to 5 hp, with the complete air intake system out-powering the drop in starting at 3,500 rpm. Significant gains were realized around 5,000 rpm, although a resonance effect of the inlet length offered a power boost at 2,000 rpm.

The Long and Short of Air Intake Systems

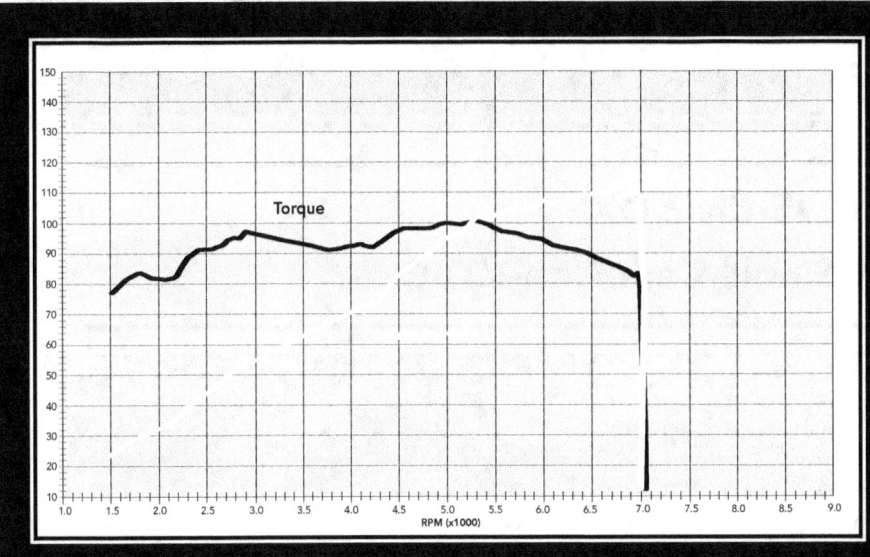

Baseline: D16Z with Filter

Rather than replace the whole air intake system, many enthusiasts opt for a drop-in filter change. Though easy, the power gains are usually not exceptional, as new paper element filters actually flow well.

Peak Horsepower – Filter	110.0 hp
Peak Torque – Filter	99.9 ft-lbs

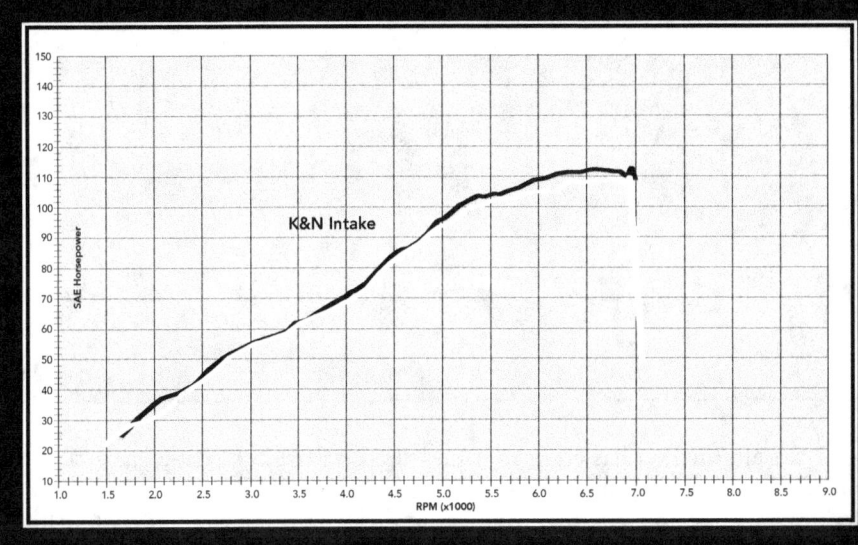

K&N filter versus K&N Intake: Horsepower

Peak Horsepower – Filter	110.0 hp
Peak Horsepower – Intake	113.3 hp
Largest Horsepower Gain	4.1 hp

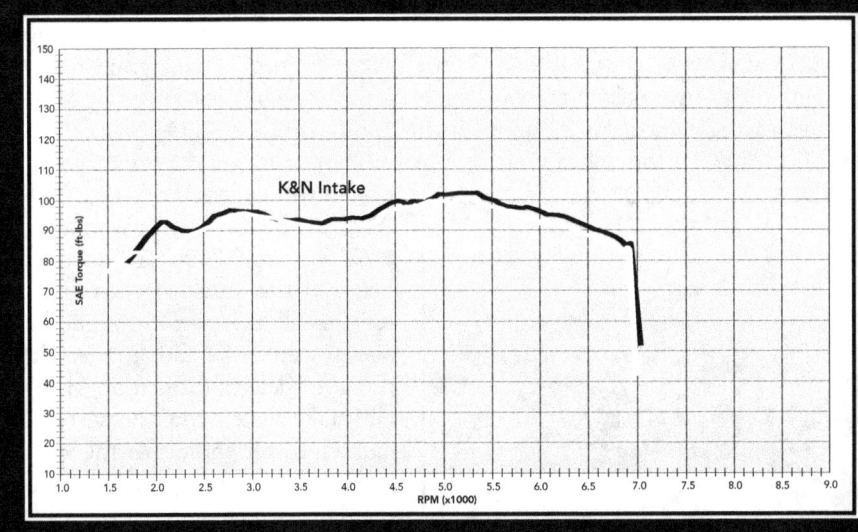

K&N filter versus K&N Intake: Torque

Peak Torque – Filter	99.9 ft-lbs
Peak Torque – Intake	102.3 ft-lbs
Largest Torque Gain	12.2 ft-lbs

How to Build Honda Horsepower

Chapter 1

Test 5: Stock Air Intake versus APC Toucan

1995 Civic DX
D15B 1.5L Single-Cam Non-VTEC

Sure, the vast majority of Honda/Acura owners and enthusiasts out there have VTEC on the brain, but you might be surprised to hear that Honda actually makes motors without their signature VTEC hardware. In fact, the vast majority of Honda products rolled off the production line sporting non-VTEC motors. The DX used for this test is one such example. Sporting both less displacement and but one cam profile, the DX motor has never shared the limelight with the B16As, B18Cs and H22s of the world. However, the VTEC-challenged DX motor does have something in common with its high-winding relatives. The DX motor will respond favorably to performance modifications. For this test, we installed an aftermarket air intake system from APC in place of the stock air box assembly.

Like most of the Honda models, including those adorned with a VTEC logo, the factory air filter assembly represents an airflow restriction. The reason for this restriction is not because Honda does not know how to build a high-flow air intake assembly, but rather the need to reduce the noise generated by the engine. It seems that some (not so performance oriented) individuals do not care for the noise generated by a free-flowing air intake. Honda went to great lengths to tune the resonance out of the factory air intake. The result was a convoluted air filter assembly that creates a torturous path for the inlet air. Reducing the noise also reduces the airflow—thus reducing the potential power. Lucky for us enthusiasts, the aftermarket has come to the rescue with improved air intake systems that offer superior airflow for added performance.

We applied one such system from APC on the 1995 Civic DX test mule. The motor was run in baseline trim using the factory air box assembly and paper-element filter. In stock trim, the DX motor produced almost 96 hp and 93 ft-lbs of torque at the wheels, as

measured on the DynoJet chassis dyno. The motor produced a dual torque peak, with torque readings exceeding 90 ft-lbs at 3,000 rpm and again from 4,300 rpm to 5,300 rpm. The torque curve suffered a significant dip between those peaks. Adding the APC air intake (consisting of a length of tubing and cone filter) greatly improved low-speed power from 1,700 rpm to 2,700 rpm. The improvement was very noticeable in part-throttle street driving. The APC air intake lost power from 2,700 rpm to 3,700 rpm and then bettered the stock air box by a few hp all the way through the power band. We did not test it, but a full-length (Stillen or AEM) air intake system might have been a much better choice for the low-rpm DX motor, especially given the daily driver status of this particular test vehicle.

The Long and Short of Air Intake Systems

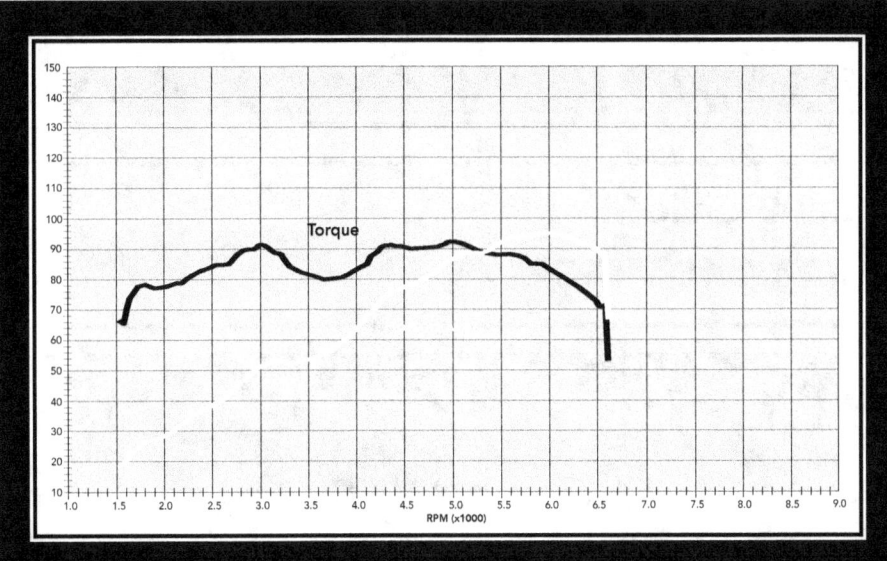

Baseline: D15B (Stock)

The APC air intake improved power on the Civic DX, but the gains weren't constant through the entire rpm range. A full-length air intake would be a better choice for the low-rpm (non-VTEC) DX motor.

Peak Horsepower – Stock	95.6 hp
Peak Torque – Stock	99.9 ft-lbs

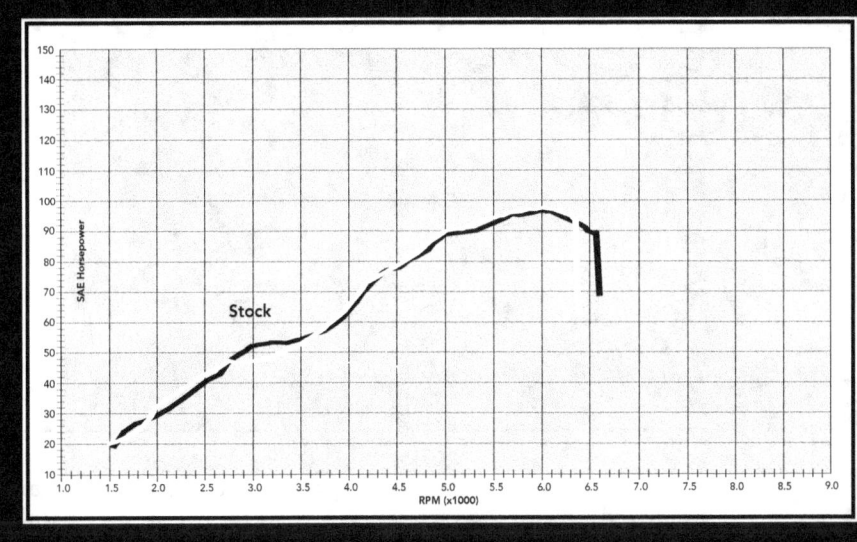

Stock versus APC: Horsepower

Peak Horsepower – Stock	95.6 hp
Peak Horsepower – APC Toucan	96.5 hp
Largest Horsepower Gain	3.7 hp

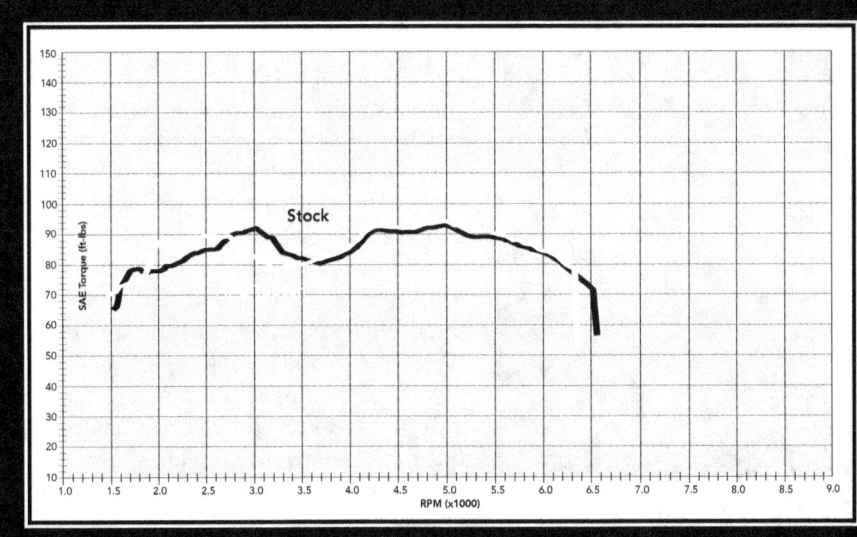

Stock versus APC: Torque

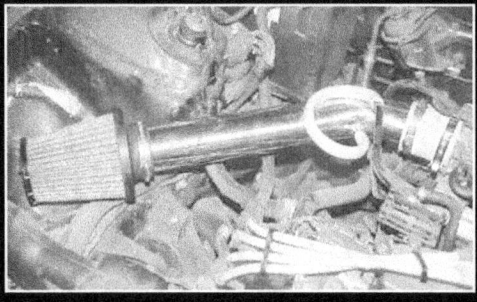

Peak Torque – Stock	99.9 ft-lbs
Peak Torque – APC Toucan	102.3 ft-lbs
Largest Torque Gain	9.1 ft-lbs

How to Build Honda Horsepower

Chapter 1

Test 6: Stock Air Intake versus Comptech

2000 Civic Si
B16A3 1.6L VTEC

The sharp reader may have noticed that there is a horsepower trend when it comes to air intake systems. The long air intake systems, such as those offered by AEM, produce good power up to the VTEC actuation point, but tend to fall off in power compared to the shorter (larger diameter) versions. The problem with the short, open element filter air intake system is that the open element draws hot inlet air from the engine compartment. Hot air is the enemy of horsepower, as cooler air contains more oxygen molecules per volume. More oxygen molecules mean more horsepower. Often the power gains offered by the tuning length of the air intake are negated by the heated inlet air. In a test conducted during some top speed runs, the short-runner air intake system actually produced a slower top speed due to the heated air even though the design showed superior horsepower on the chassis dyno (tested with the hood open).

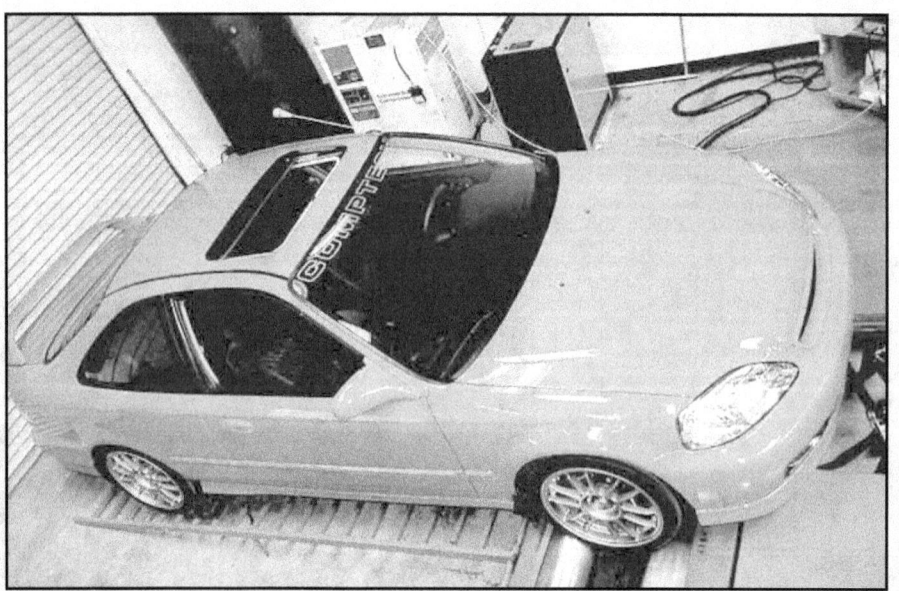

The 1999–2000 Civic Si system from Comptech combined the power tuning of the short intake length with the ambient air source of a long intake. This was accomplished by enclosing the typical open-element filter inside a cold air box sealed to the fenderwell opening. The air intake pipe is sized both in length and overall diameter to provide exceptional post-VTEC power while the "Ice-Box" enclosure ensures a steady supply of cool air. This dyno test only provides half of the real benefit of the Comptech system, as the real power gains will come when driving, especially when you are matched up against a like-motored Civic equipped with a simple open-element filter and intake pipe. When his motor is sucking hot air, your "Ice-Box" equipped Civic will just walk away—its motor will be breathing plenty of cool, powerful air. The Comptech air intake was worth 5 to 6 hp, but remember, racing takes place with the hood closed.

The Long and Short of Air Intake Systems

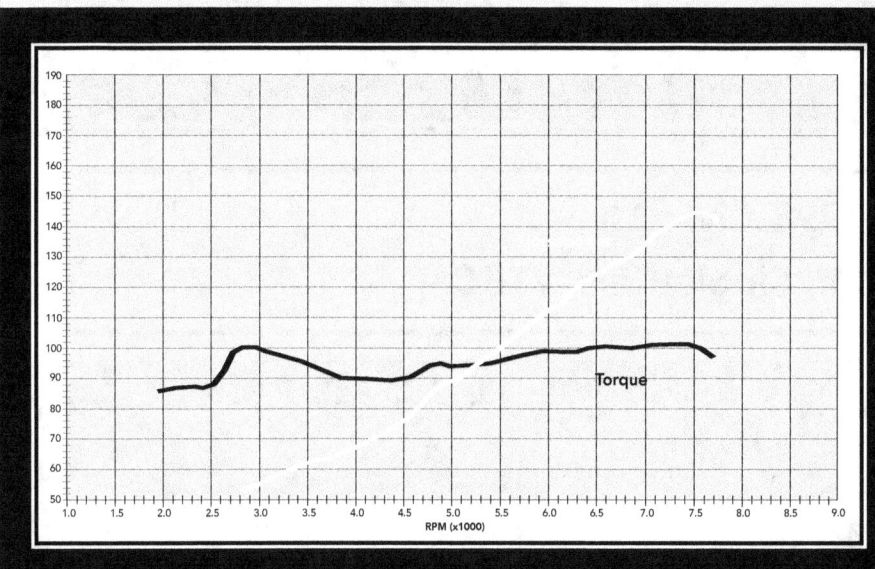

Baseline: B16A3 (Stock)

Comptech's Iceman system shows what happens when a company races what it sells. Comptech understands the importance of both a short-runner air intake for VTEC motors and the need for a true cold air source.

Peak Horsepower – Stock	144 hp
Peak Torque – Stock	101 ft-lbs

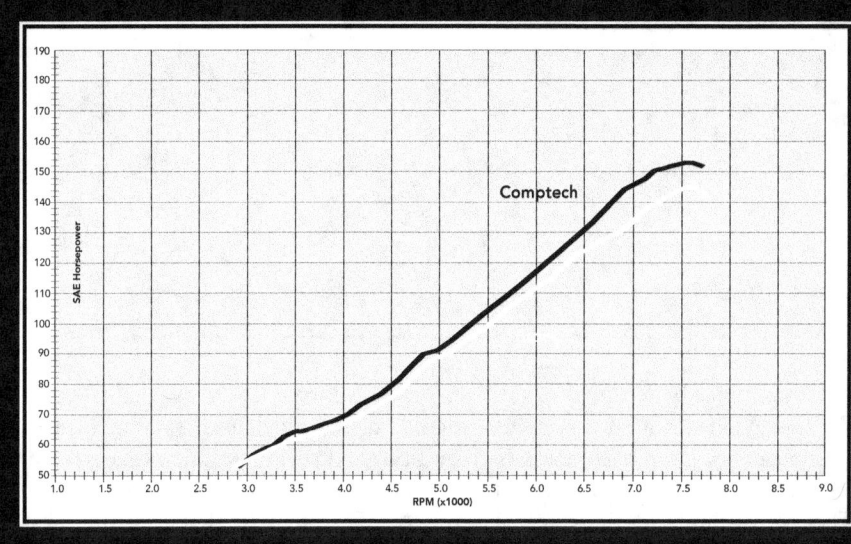

Stock versus Comptech: Horsepower

Peak Horsepower – Stock	144 hp
Peak Horsepower – Comptech	147 hp
Largest Horsepower Gain	6 hp

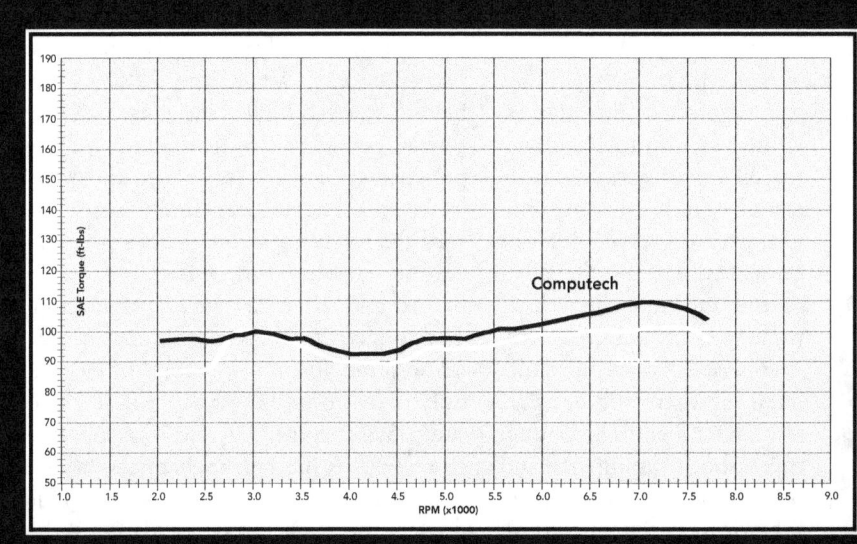

Stock versus Comptech: Torque

Peak Torque – Stock	101 ft-lbs
Peak Torque – Comptech	106 ft-lbs
Largest Torque Gain	5 ft-lbs

Chapter 1

Test 7: Stillen versus K&N versus APC

1998 Civic EX
D16Y 1.6L Single-Cam VTEC

This test was a textbook example of the classic battle between air intake styles. Like the full-length AEM versus shorty RS Akimoto test run on the 1993 Civic Si, this test clearly demonstrated the effect of different style air intakes. The Honda motors, and especially the VTEC variants, are very sensitive to changes in the size and length of an air intake system. The air intake has a tuning effect on the motor. Much like the tuning effect of intake manifold runner length, the longer the air intake the better the low-speed power production. A shorter air intake runner length generally produces better top-end power, but usually at the expense of low end. There is usually a tradeoff, as no one system can provide the power of the short runner intake with the torquey response of a full-length system. Thus, an intake system should be tuned to the individual motor and (more importantly) driving characteristics.

This test centered around three different intake systems. The three intakes were run on a 1998 Civic EX equipped with a 1.6L single-cam VTEC motor. The three players included systems from K&N, APC,

and Stillen. You might be tempted to put the K&N and APC air intake systems into the same category, but they actually performed quite differently on our test motor. They share similar designs in that they both offered a (relatively) short length of tubing and a free-flowing cone filter. Naturally, K&N opted for their own filter while the APC system incorporated an enclosed filter canister. This canister will allow the use of an additional hose section to transform the APC system into a dedicated cold air system. Unfortunately, we did not get a chance to test the effect of the additional length of tubing on the APC system. The two shorty systems differed in their tubing size, with K&N coming out on top in both tubing size and overall power production. Obviously, size mattered on this test motor.

The shorty K&N was also compared to the full-length system offered by Stillen. The Stillen air intake system for the 1998 EX was similar in design to the AEM system in that the filter was positioned in the fenderwell away from unwanted engine heat. The two systems shared identical tubing diameter, yet the two produced dramatically different power curves. Where the APC lagged behind the K&N for the length of the power curve, the Stillen intake traded punches with the K&N right up to the bitter end. The Stillen actually out-powered the K&N by a couple of horsepower, but the big difference came right before and after the VTEC operation. The longer Stillen intake offered a dramatic jump in power before 4,500 rpm only to lose out to the K&N for 700 rpm (until 5,200 rpm). The two were pretty close until 6,400 rpm, where the Stillen system offered a few extra ponies. This power curve once again illustrates the effect the air intake design has on power.

The Long and Short of Air Intake Systems

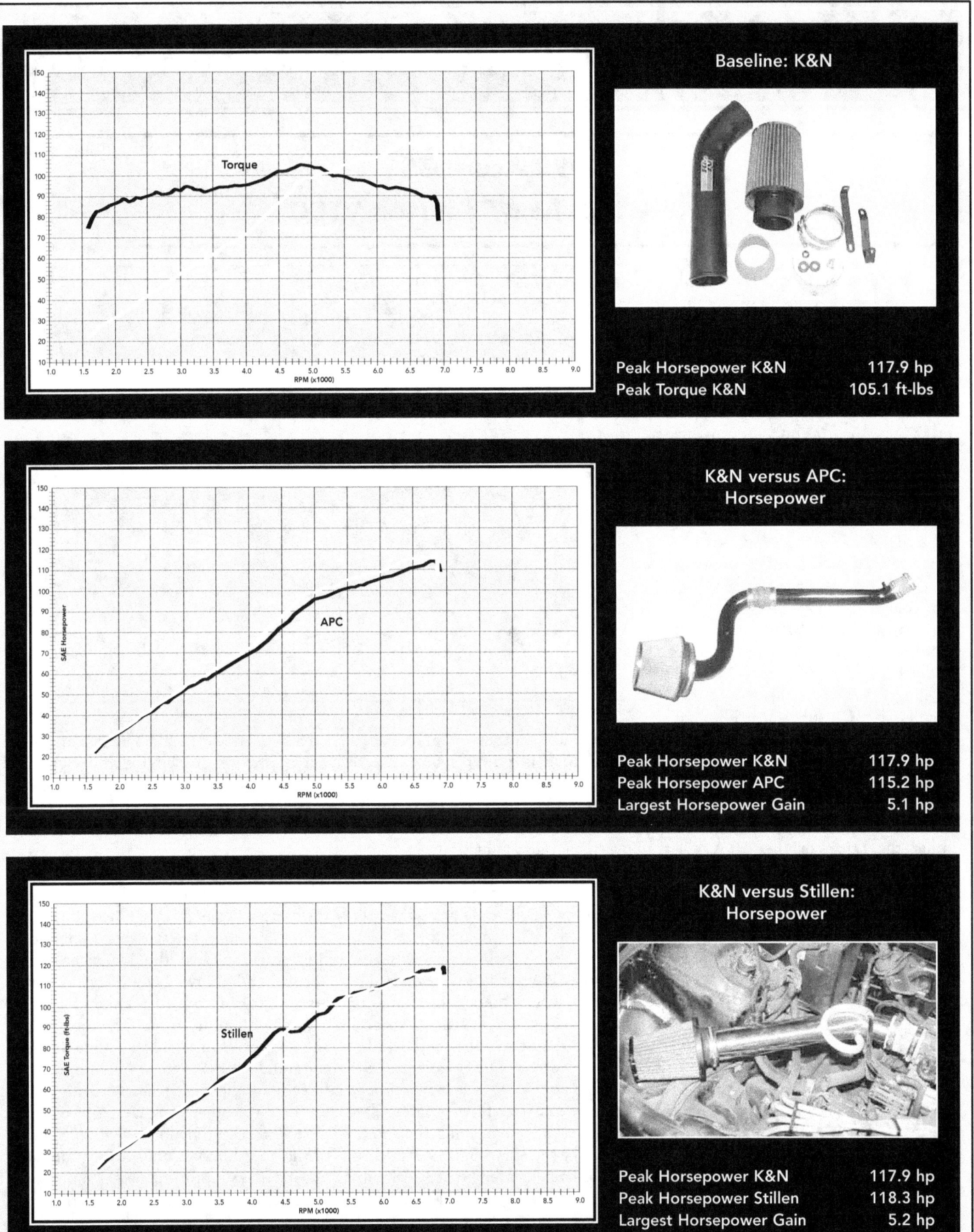

Baseline: K&N

Peak Horsepower K&N	117.9 hp
Peak Torque K&N	105.1 ft-lbs

K&N versus APC: Horsepower

Peak Horsepower K&N	117.9 hp
Peak Horsepower APC	115.2 hp
Largest Horsepower Gain	5.1 hp

K&N versus Stillen: Horsepower

Peak Horsepower K&N	117.9 hp
Peak Horsepower Stillen	118.3 hp
Largest Horsepower Gain	5.2 hp

Chapter 1

Test 8: Stock Air Intake versus RS Akimoto

1990 Acura GS
B18A 1.8L Twin-Cam Non-VTEC

Slotted between the D16Z 1.6L EX (or Si) single-cam VTEC motors and the B16A 1.6L twin-cam VTEC motors in terms of performance is the B18A 1.8L Integra. The 130 hp (140 for later B18B) rating puts it squarely between the 125 hp rating of the D16Z and the 160 hp rating of the B16A. While the power numbers might suggest that the performance of the 1.8L is similar to the D16Z, the reality is that the performance offered by a B18A or B motor is actually much closer to the high-winding, 160-hp B16A. The reason for this is two-fold. Part of the reason for the performance of the B18 A or B series motors is that the 1.8L motor actually displaces 1,834 ccs. Credit a slightly longer stroke (compared to the smaller B18C) for the additional cubic centimeters. Though the added displacement does nothing for the maximum power rating, the longer stroke really adds power in the meaty part of the rev range. Compared to either the D16Z or the B16A, the B18A or B motors offer a significant torque advantage to help accelerate a car. Running a B18A or B against a D16Z would be no contest in similar cars. In fact, it would take a good-running B16A to out-accelerate a B18A or B.

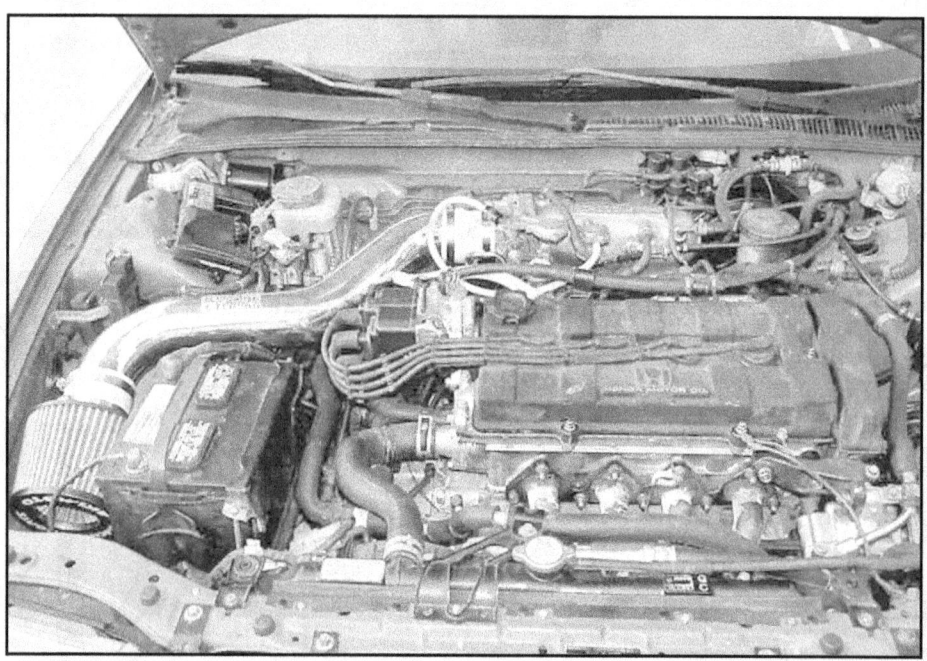

Like the other Honda/Acura motors, there is power hiding in the stock air intake of the B18A (B). Honda went to great length to tune the noise out of the intake systems. Unfortunately, in doing so, they also reduced the efficiency of the stock air filter assembly. The 1.8L Integra air filter assembly is actually significantly better in some areas than the system used in a comparable 1.6L, but worse in others. The stock air box and filter assembly leaves a little to be desired in absolute flow, but the air inlet tube (to the throttle body) is actually considerably larger than that used on the 1.6Ls, especially the non-VTEC variants. Like all stock systems, a nice mandrel-bent intake tube and free-flowing cone filter goes a long way to helping the motor breathe. The system from RS Akimoto is proof positive that a length of 3-inch tubing and free-flowing cone fitler can work wonders on a 1.8L GS motor.

The RS Akimoto system was tested on a high-mileage 1.8L. The motor had been previously upgraded with a Thermal exhaust and Chikara header and was literally begging for an air intake. Although an open-element filter in the heated engine compartment is less than ideal system, the system from RS Akimoto positioned the filter behind the battery (away from the heat source). The 1990 Integra test vehicle sported the battery behind the passenger-side headlight. Removing the stock filter assembly provided sufficient room for the RS Akimoto filter. The position allowed access to a cold air source (from the fenderwell) while shielding the filter from the engine heat. Such is not the case on other Honda/Acura models/engine combinations. The addition of the RS Akimoto intake to the modified 1.8L GS motor yielded as much as 4 hp and 5 ft-lbs. Oddly enough, the air intake lost a little power between 2,000 rpm and 3,300 rpm.

The Long and Short of Air Intake Systems

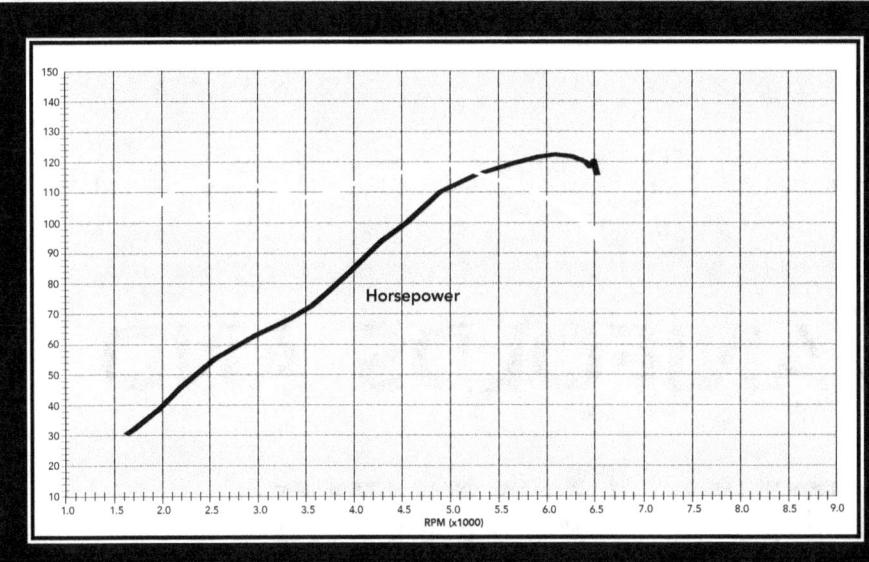

Baseline: B18A (Stock)

This system from RS Akimoto was actually a medium-length system, as the 1990 Integra's battery position required the air inlet tube to snake around to reach the filter, which is located behind the battery.

Peak Horsepower – Stock	122.2 hp
Peak Torque – Stock	119.1 ft-lbs

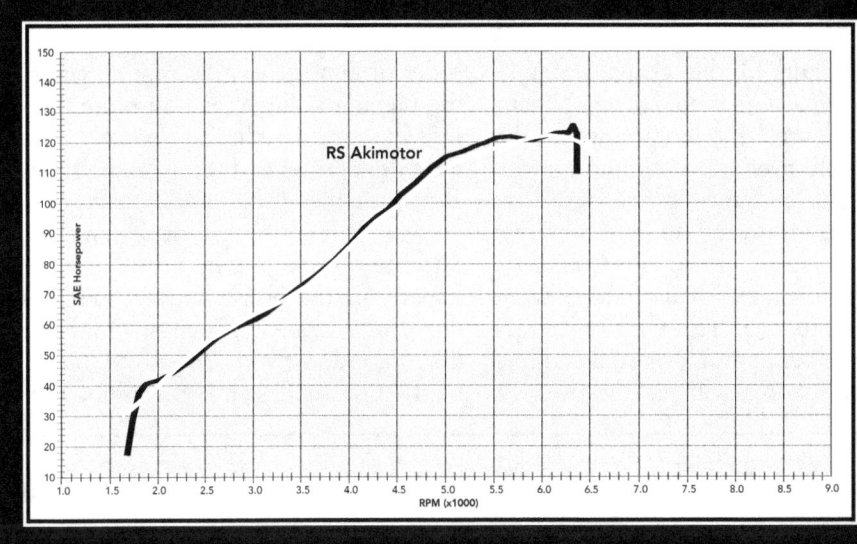

Stock versus RS Akimoto: Horsepower

Peak Horsepower – Stock	122.2 hp
Peak Horsepower – RS Akimoto	126.1 hp
Largest Horsepower Gain	4.2 hp

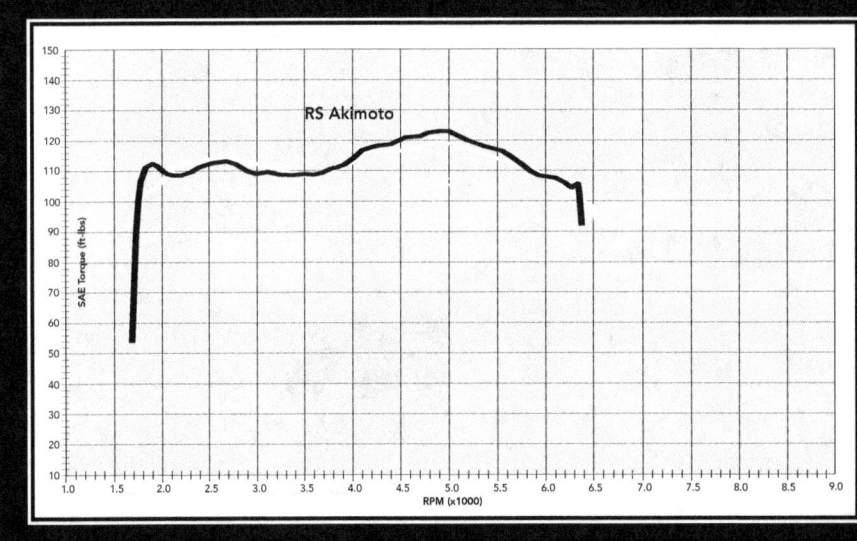

Stock versus RS Akimoto: Torque

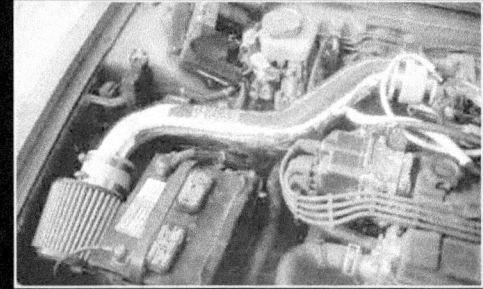

Peak Torque – Stock	119.1 ft-lbs
Peak Torque – RS Akimoto	123.1 ft-lbs
Largest Torque Gain	4.9 ft-lbs

How to Build Honda Horsepower

CHAPTER 2

INTAKE MANIFOLDS AND THROTTLE BODIES

The intake manifold is simple in function but quite complex in design. The obvious function of a manifold is to get air into the combustion chambers. The manifold's effectiveness at performing this feat is determined by many different design criteria. While a complete rundown on the theory and design of intake manifolds would easily fill an entire book, it is important to understand at least the basics to fully appreciate the results of this chapter. Simply put, the intake manifold helps (if not outright controls) determine where the motor will produce optimum power. Working in conjunction with the cam timing, head flow, and (to a lesser extent) exhaust system, the intake manifold shapes the entire power curve, from beginning to end. Three major factors (and a number of minor ones) determine where the motor will make power. In order of importance, the runner length, the plenum volume, and absolute flow rate all work together to not only produce peak power and torque figures, but also shape the overall power curve.

You will notice that the design characteristics were put in order of their impact on the power curve. This was done for a reason, as one of the major misconceptions with regard to (aftermarket) intake design is the importance

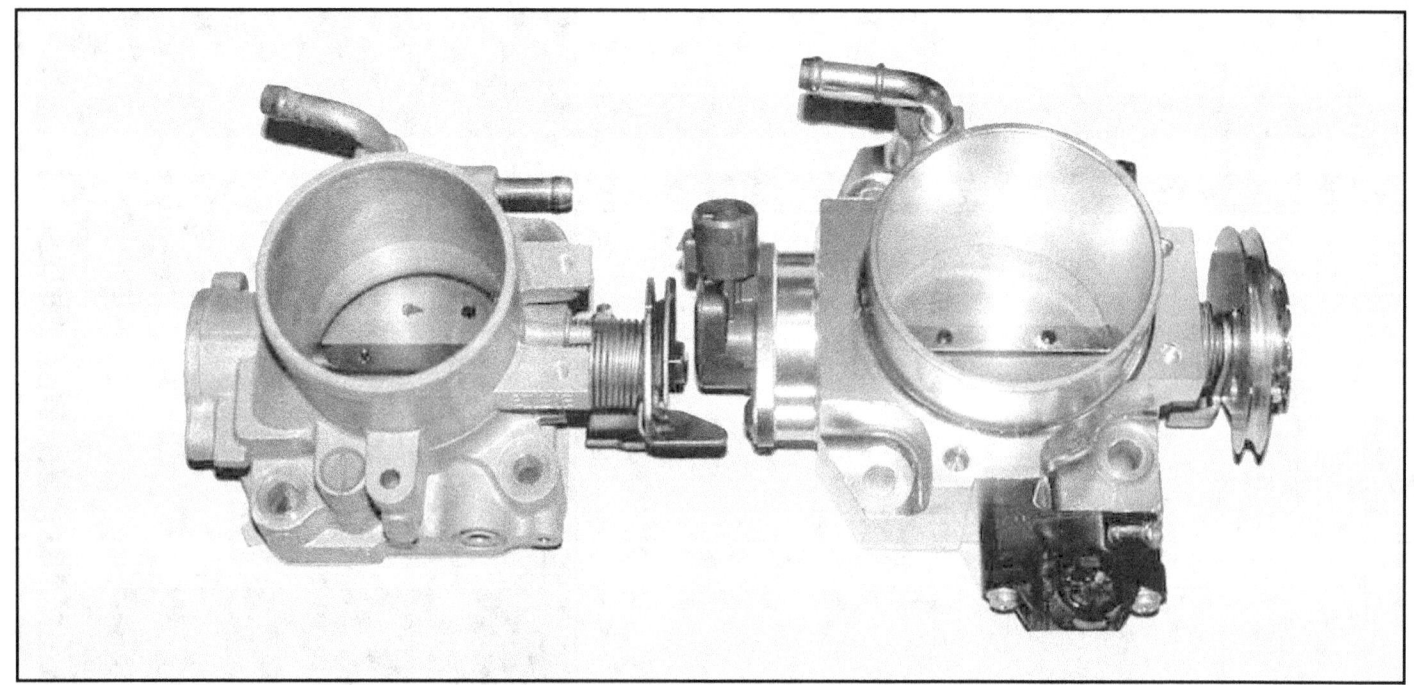

Big throttle bodies are a hot seller, but your stock VTEC motor might not really need more airflow.

Intake Manifolds and Throttle Bodies

of absolute airflow. This absolute airflow misconception has unfortunately carried over to cylinder heads as well. With respect to intake manifolds, the absolute airflow of an intake runner is important, as the motor will not be able to produce adequate power without sufficient airflow. Internal combustion engines are, after all, nothing more than glorified air pumps—the more air processed through them the more power they will produce. Unfortunately, runners that flow more air may not produce more power (the same holds true for throttle bodies). The reason is that a motor will only produce more power if it processes more air. The whole motor must move the air, not just one component.

Intake manifolds are even more complex than the rather simple throttle bodies. A bigger throttle opening (blade size) will allow more airflow. If the motor does not need any more airflow—the bigger throttle body will be of no benefit. The same holds true with intakes, but it is possible for two runners to flow the same (as measured on an airflow bench) and produce dramatically different power curves. A long runner and a short runner may produce identical flow numbers on an airflow bench yet they will most certainly yield different horsepower and torque curves. As a rule, long runners help bolster low-speed and mid-range cylinder filling, while short runners promote top-end power. Another curveball thrown in here is that the displacement of the motor is also a determining factor on the affects of intake runner length. There is an ideal runner length for making power at a given engine speed, but no street motor (or race motor for that matter) runs under full load at a constant engine speed. Therefore, we must select an intake runner length that supplies the best overall curve for our performance needs. As it turned out, the factory Honda/Acura manifolds yielded some of the best results for anything less than an all-out (meaning very high rpm) race motor. Even the much-hyped Integra Type R intake took a back seat to its little brother—the B16A intake. Hard to believe, but the results speak for themselves.

Before you dismiss the factory intakes, this big-bore B20 produced over 500 horsepower with nothing more than a B16A intake manifold.

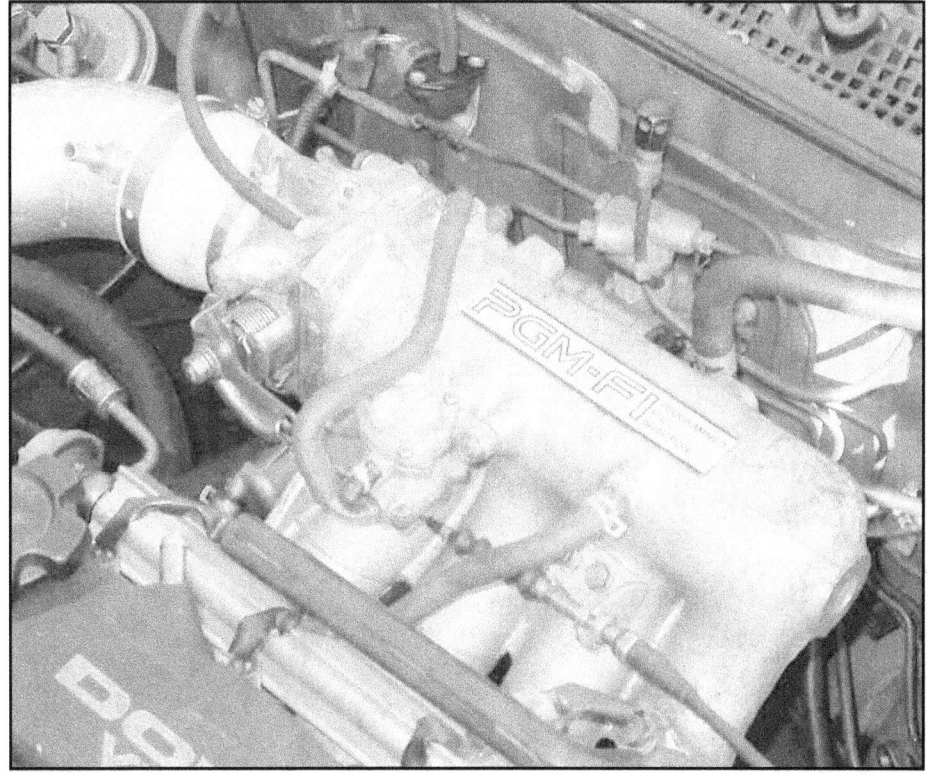

The B16A intake has a lot to offer, especially in modified form like this unit from Killer Bee Racing.

How to Build Honda Horsepower

Chapter 2

Test 1: Stock Throttle Body versus RC Engineering 64.5-mm Throttle Body

1998 Civic Si (Converted EX) B20 2.0L LS/VTEC Hybrid

This test was one of those where the results seemed to defy logic. In my testing of throttle body sizes, I have not come across very many four-cylinder Honda/Acura motors that benefit from larger throttle bodies. It is not that larger throttle bodies don't flow more air than smaller units—they obviously do. The problem lies in the fact that the motor never sees (or needs) any of that additional airflow. The stock throttle body from a B16A motor flows almost 600 cfm. To give you an idea how good the stock throttle body is, that amount of airflow will support right near 400 hp. Be honest, how many 400-hp four-cylinder Honda motors have you ever seen? While the math tells us that the stock throttle bodies will feed a great deal more power than the motors will ever produce, motors don't always listen to mathematical equations. Sometimes, bigger throttle bodies do add power, but the increase is generally small and the motor in question needs to be really healthy. Your stock D16Z, or even a high-winding B16A, will not likely benefit from the installation of a larger throttle body. How do I know? Dyno tests were run on both motors comparing stock and over-sized throttle bodies with no measurable change in power.

One of the problems associated with running dyno comparisons is selecting a suitable test candidate. While the throttle body testing performed on stock motors yielded no power gains, what would happen if one of the larger throttle bodies was installed on a much larger stroker motor? Obviously the larger (or more correctly put, more powerful) the test motor, the more likely it is to take advantage of the additional airflow offered by the larger throttle body. Where a stock throttle body might easily feed the airflow requirements of a 160-hp B16A, what happens when you increase the displacement of the test motor to 2.0Ls and the power output to well over 200 hp? Is the stock throttle body sufficient or will the larger LS/VTEC Hybrid motor require more airflow? The answer is that the installation of a larger 64.5-mm throttle body (bored stock B16A unit from RC Engineering) resulted in slightly more power in the midrange but no more peak power. The gain of 2 to 3 hp represented an increase of just 1 percent on this test motor and may well be considered insignificant. The bigger throttle body did not harm power in any way, but there certainly were no huge gains from the bigger throttle opening—even on a motor that produced over 200 hp at the wheels (on a conservative dyno yet).

Intake Manifolds and Throttle Bodies

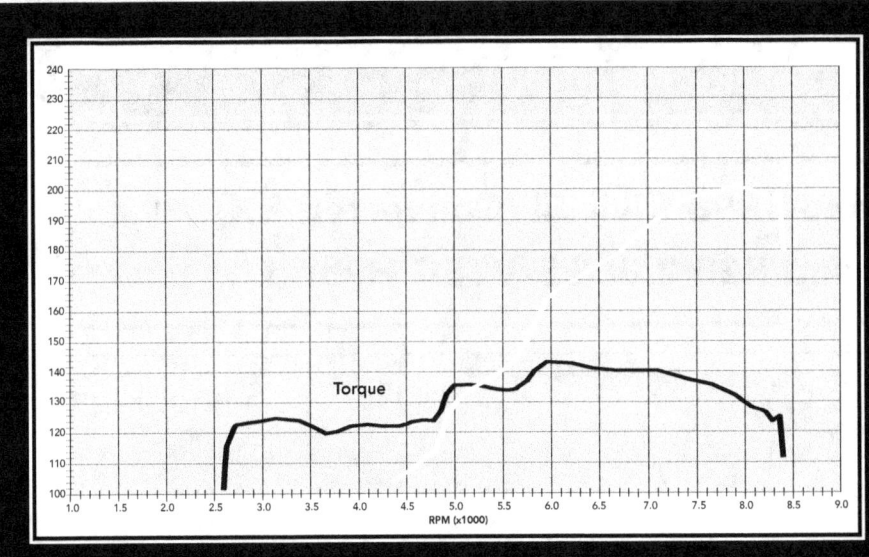

Baseline: Stock Throttle Body

Big throttle bodies are a popular performance upgrade, but it's important to have enough motor to go with one. This 2.0L stroker motor benefited from the RC Engineering big-bore throttle body, but most stock motors won't.

Peak Horsepower – Stock	200.1 hp
Peak Torque – Stock	143.5 ft-lbs

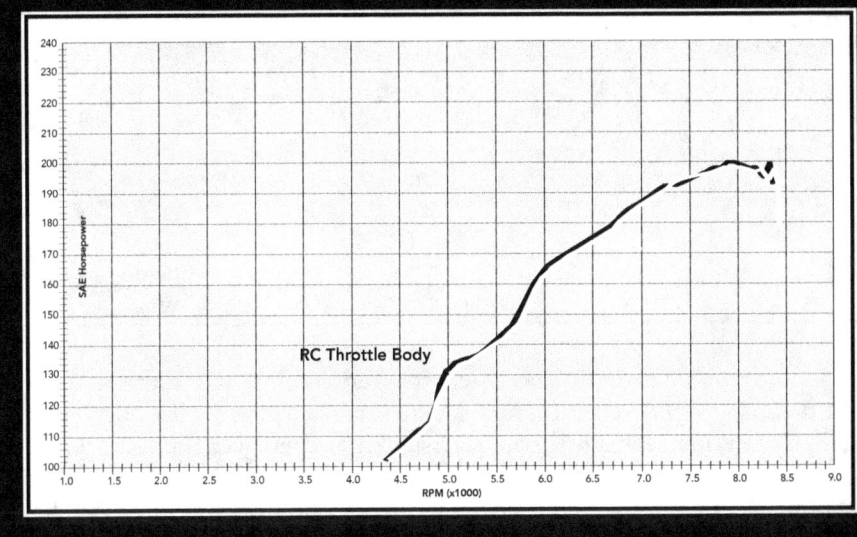

RC Throttle Body: Horsepower

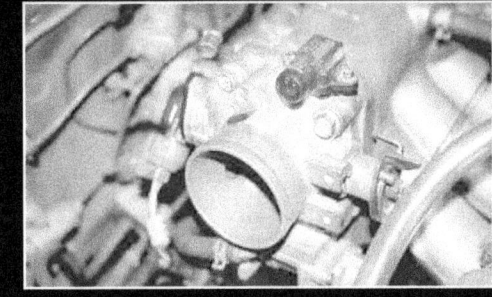

Peak HP Stock	200.1 hp
Peak HP RC Throttle Body	200.9 hp
Largest Horsepower Gain	2.8 hp

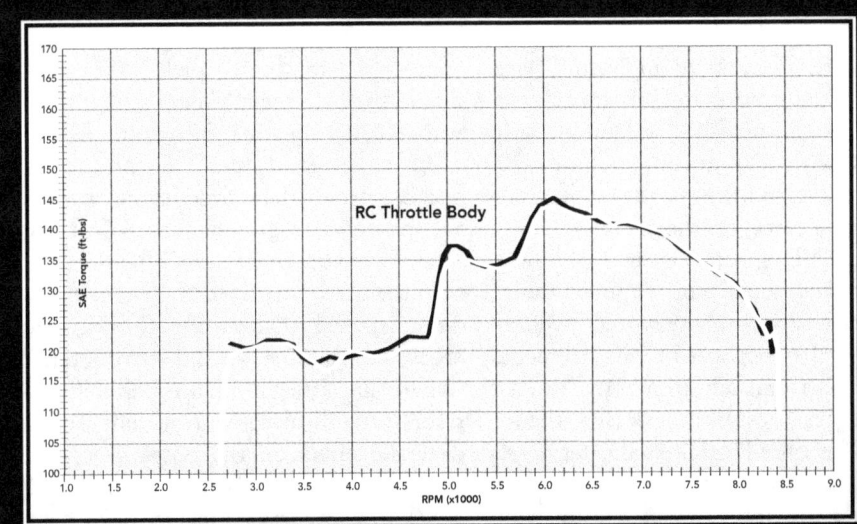

RC Throttle Body: Torque

Peak Torque Stock	143.5 ft-lbs
Peak Torque RC Throttle Body	144.7 ft-lbs
Largest Torque Gain	3.3 ft-lbs

How to Build Honda Horsepower

Chapter 2

Test 2: Del Sol Intake Manifold versus Type R Intake Manifold

1995 Civic Del Sol and 1998 Civic Si (Converted EX) B16A 1.6L VTEC and B20 2.0L LS/VTEC Hybrid

The comparison between the B16A and the Type R intakes actually came about when I went searching for more power for my USTCC race motor. Although we could not run the Type R intake in the USTCC series (rules required a stock B16A intake), I was curious about the power potential of the bigger, exotic Type R intake on the smaller B16A motor. My curiosity was further spurred by the fact that I intended to run the USTCC Del Sol in a few SCCA World Challenge events, whose rules did allow the Type R intake. As it turned out, the car never ran any of the World Challenge events and wouldn't have done well with the Type R intake anyway. As is often the case with testing Honda/Acura motors, I discovered how to lose power rather than gain power. The B16A intake proved to be far superior to the larger Type R all the way past 8,000 rpm. The two produced similar power to 4,500 rpm and again about 6,200 rpm, but the rest of the curve belonged to the B16A Del Sol intake. As always, we tuned each combination for maximum power using air/fuel ratio and ignition timing.

While the many tests run in this chapter have shown that the B16A is "THE" intake to beat, I couldn't help but wonder if the results might be different on a motor with greater displacement than the many B16A test motors. After all, the Type R intake was originally designed for use on a healthy 1.8L B18C5 motor and was probably never intended for the B16A. Surely, the Type R intake would fare better on a much larger motor, right? Test number 2 was run on an LS/VTEC hybrid that displaced 2 liters thanks to an 84-mm bore and an 89-mm stroke. This motor was used to set a number of land speed records with the author behind the wheel at both El Mirage and (by the time this goes to print) Bonneville.

The 2.0L sported over 12:1 compression and a pair of Type R cams. Surely, the Type R intake would respond better to the increase in displacement, compression, and cam timing.

The test results speak for themselves. The Type R intake did offer more power from 7,600 rpm to 8,500 rpm, but the little B16A intake was superior from 4,300 rpm all the way to 7,600 rpm. The motor made peak power with the B16A intake some 800 rpm sooner (7,300 rpm versus 8,100 rpm), yet the peak power numbers were within 3 hp. Even on the big stroker motor, the B16A Del Sol intake offered improvements of 10 hp and 9 ft-lbs. The Type R did offer more power than the B16A after 7,600 rpm, with a gain of 12 hp available at 8,000 rpm. It is tempting to pick the Type R due to the increase in power available up near 8,000 rpm, but the reality is that most street (and race) motors spend much more of their time in the area (of the power curve) where the Del Sol intake was superior to the Type R rather than the other way around. This test also demonstrated that, while shifting the crossover point between the two intakes (where the Type R finally bettered the B16A), the displacement did not have a dramatic effect on the outcome of the test. On both the B16A and the B20 (LS/VTEC hybrid), the Del Sol intake out-performed even the mighty Type R.

How to Build Honda Horsepower

Intake Manifolds and Throttle Bodies

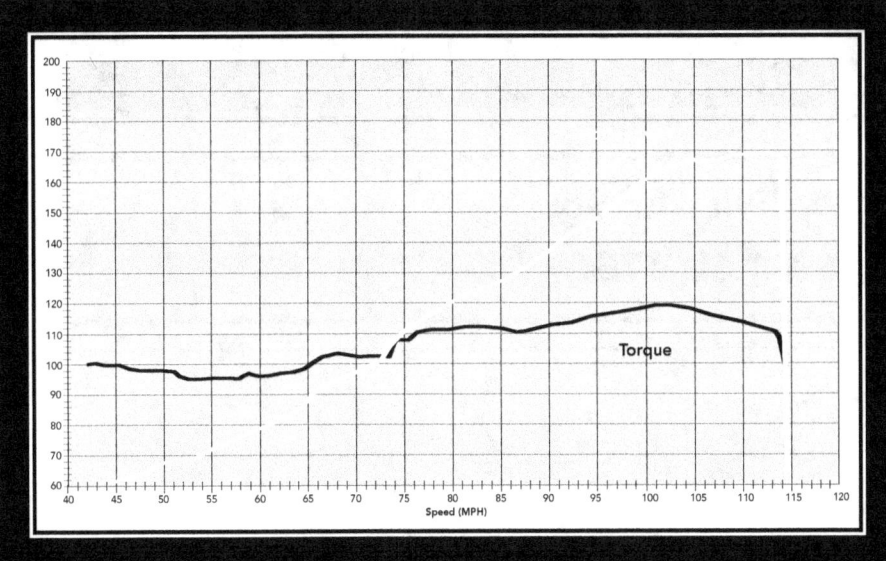

Baseline: B16A Del Sol

Honda/Acura owners are hot after anything that says Type R — for good reason. The 195-hp 1.8L motor is great, but don't count on its intake making more power on your B16A; the stock intake is actually slightly better.

Peak Horsepower – Del Sol	168.3 hp
Peak Torque – Del Sol	117.9 ft-lbs

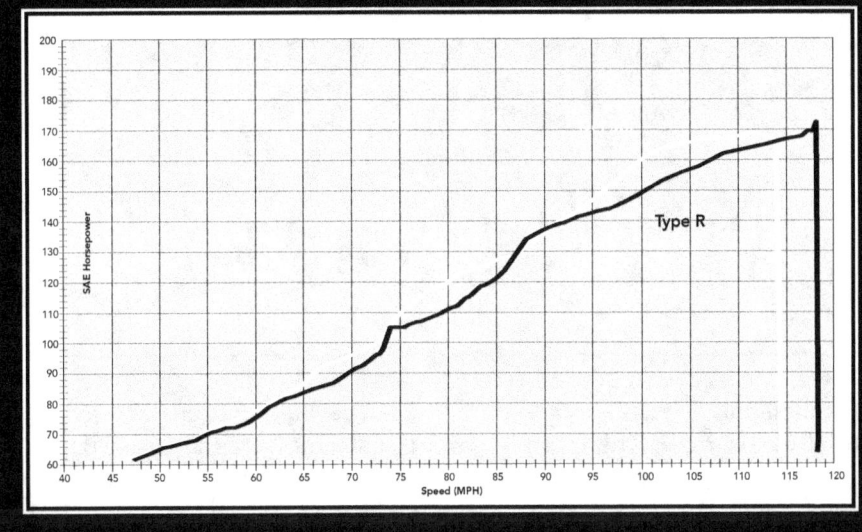

Del Sol versus Type R Intake on B16A: Horsepower

Peak Horsepower – Del Sol	168.3 hp
Peak Horsepower – Type R	170.1 hp
Largest Horsepower Gain	12.5 hp

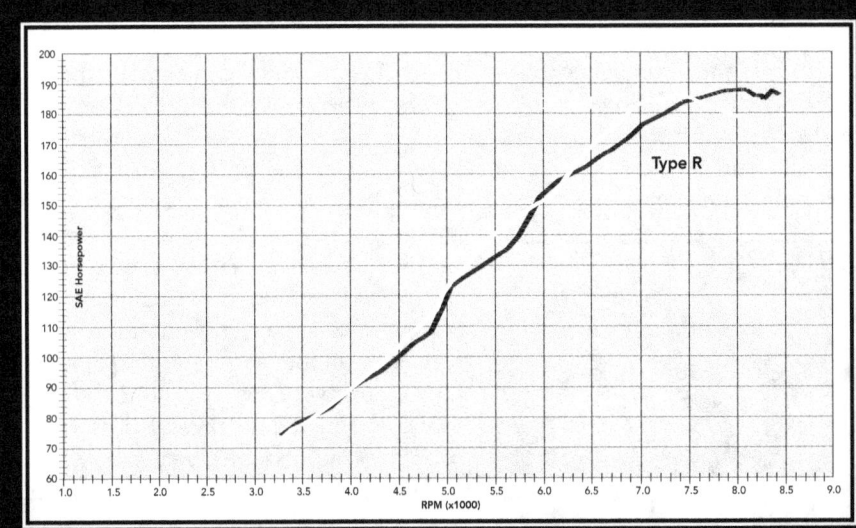

Del Sol versus Type R Intake on B20: Horsepower

Peak Horsepower – Del Sol	196.7 hp
Peak Horsepower – Type R	199.6 hp
Largest Horsepower Gain	11.1 hp

How to Build Honda Horsepower

Chapter 2

Test 3: Stock B16A Intake Manifold versus Extrude Hone–Ported Del Sol Intake Manifold

1995 Civic Del Sol
B16A 1.6L VTEC

The one thing you should take away from this chapter is that the stock B16A intake manifold (Del Sol/Civic Si) is pretty impressive. In fact, it worked so well on all of the testing that only one factory or aftermarket intake was able to better the power output in a usable rpm range. It seems that the comparatively long runner lengths combined with small cross sectional runners and small plenum volume makes for an ideal power combination. Compared to the larger Type R or any of the fabricated intakes, the B16A manifold offered superior power across the power band. Only when run on a wild 2.0L hybrid combination did the Type R intake offer any significant power advantage, and all of the added power came after 7,600 rpm. Below that figure, the B16A was the hands-down winner.

As good as the B16A intake works on most any B-series motors, there is a way to improve it. Porting is a tried and true method of improving airflow, as long as it is done correctly. One of the problems associated with porting fuel-injected intake manifolds is access to the entire runner length. While port matching the manifold to the cylinder head is quite simple, continuing that porting to further improve the flow rate of the manifold all the way through the runner is difficult if not impossible with conventional porting. Although some porters have actually gone to the trouble of cutting the manifold in half to allow access to the runners, porting them and then welding the sections back together, this is obviously difficult, time consuming and leaves a sizable welding scar across the intake. One way to eliminate all of the cutting and welding is to simply have the manifold Extrude Hone ported. The porting process involves forcing a putty (similar to Silly Putty) impregnated with silicon carbide or similar abrasive particles through the passages using hydraulic machinery. As the abrasive media is forced through (back and forth in some instances) the interior of the intake (taking the same path as the airflow), material is removed. The Extrude Hone porting essentially ports where the putty encounters flow restrictions.

Extrude Hone porting is used by some of the quickest and fastest import drag racers including Lisa Kubo. The porting is used not only on their intake manifold but also on the exhaust manifold, cylinder head, and even the turbo charger. For this test, I had Extrude Hone subject one of my late-model B16A (Del Sol) intake manifolds to their porting process. The manifold came back with a near-mirror surface finish, a byproduct of the porting process. The smooth texture looks impressive, but the airflow improvements come not from the smooth walls but rather the material removed elsewhere. One important area is the radius from the plenum into each runner. A smooth entry is critical to maximum airflow. Obviously, the Extrude Hone porting did the trick, as a back-to-back test against an identical (stock) intake resulted in a consistent gain in power across the curve, with plenty of additional power up near 7,000 rpm.

Intake Manifolds and Throttle Bodies

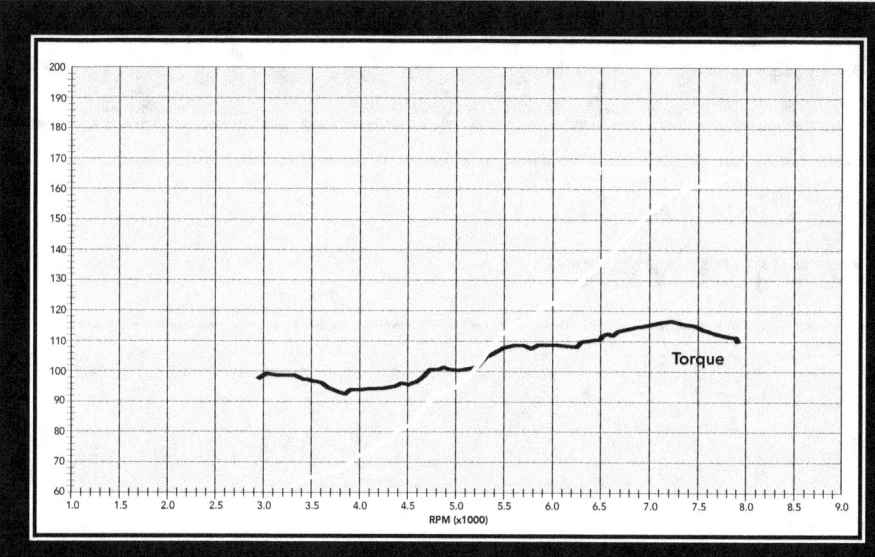

Baseline: B16A (Stock)

Long-runner fuel injected manifolds make porting difficult. Extrude Hone porting can dramatically improve flow rates and add some much needed power.

Peak Horsepower – Del Sol	163.3 hp
Peak Torque – Del Sol	116.1 ft-lbs

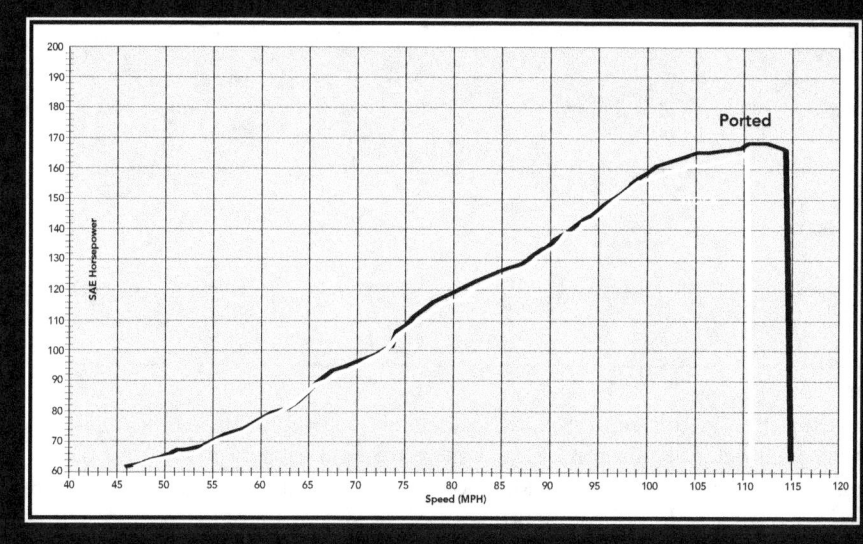

Stock versus Ported Del Sol: Horsepower

Peak Horsepower – Del Sol	163.3 hp
Peak Horsepower – Ported	168.2 hp
Largest Horsepower Gain	4.9 hp

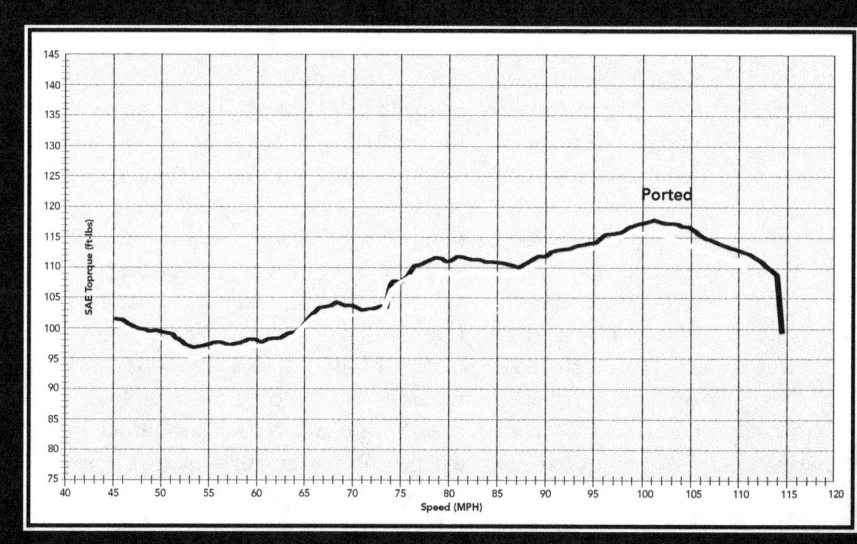

Stock versus Ported Del Sol: Torque

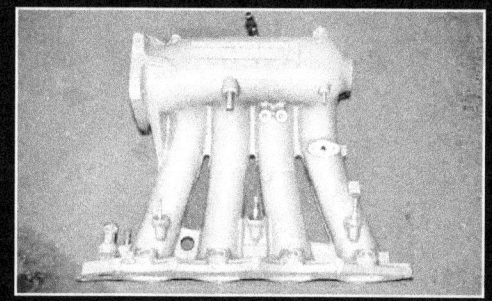

Peak Torque – Del Sol	116.1 ft-lbs
Peak Torque – Ported	118.2 ft-lbs
Largest Torque Gain	3.6 ft-lbs

Chapter 2

Test 4: Del Sol Intake Manifold versus Venom Intake Manifold

1995 Civic Del Sol
B16A 1.6L VTEC

This is one of the many comparisons run using the B16A (Del Sol) intake. Although many enthusiasts (and tuners) may be tempted to compare the aftermarket intake manifolds to the more exotic Type R, the testing in this chapter has shown that the B16A Del Sol intake offers a much better power curve on all but a full-on race motor. This test is an excellent example of choosing the wrong manifold for a given engine combination. While a reader might be tempted to dismiss the Venom (or other similar designs) based on the results of this test, the Venom intake does have its place. That place, however, is not on a street motor, at least one that never sees the high side of 8,000 rpm. The large, short runners and sizable plenum used on the Venom intake simply do not provide sufficient cylinder filling at the engine speeds run on most street cars.

As is evident by the power curve generated during the test on this modified B16A motor, the B16A intake offered significantly more power all the way up to 7,800 rpm. The Venom intake just started to show its worth beyond that, but given

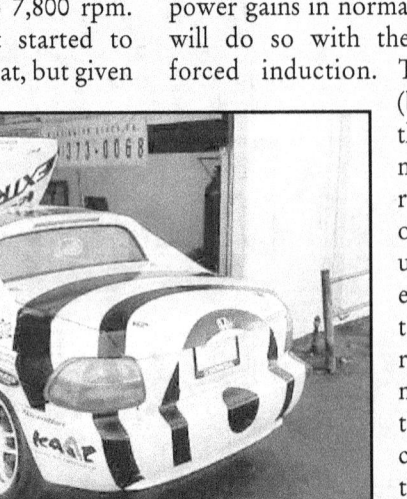

the mild cam timing, this motor made peak power well below 8,000 rpm. One of the misconceptions in the aftermarket industry is that this welded-box intake was designed for forced induction applications. The reality is (dyno proven) that an intake (like the B16A) that offers power gains in normally aspirated form will do so with the introduction of forced induction. The presence of (boost) pressure in the manifold does not change the runner size, length, or plenum volume—all the major elements that dictate the effective rpm range of the manifold. What all this technobabble comes down to is that intake manifolds are much less normally-aspirated/turbo specific than they are operating rpm specific. Check out the tests run on the similar STR intake to verify this fact.

The Venom intake test was a clear indication that it was the wrong manifold for this B16A application. What the Venom intake really needed to shine was a high-rpm motor (normally-aspirated or turbo/supercharged). The large, short runners combined with the relatively large plenum volume were all designed to run at a much higher engine speed than our 8,000-rpm test motor. Note that the Venom was just getting started as the B16A intake was signing off. Unfortunately for the Venom, the mild cam timing did not allow it to keep revving to demonstrate the high-rpm breathing characteristics inherent in the design. Whether turbocharged, supercharged, or normally aspirated, the B16A intake was clearly the better choice for a mild street motor.

34 *How to Build Honda Horsepower*

Intake Manifolds and Throttle Bodies

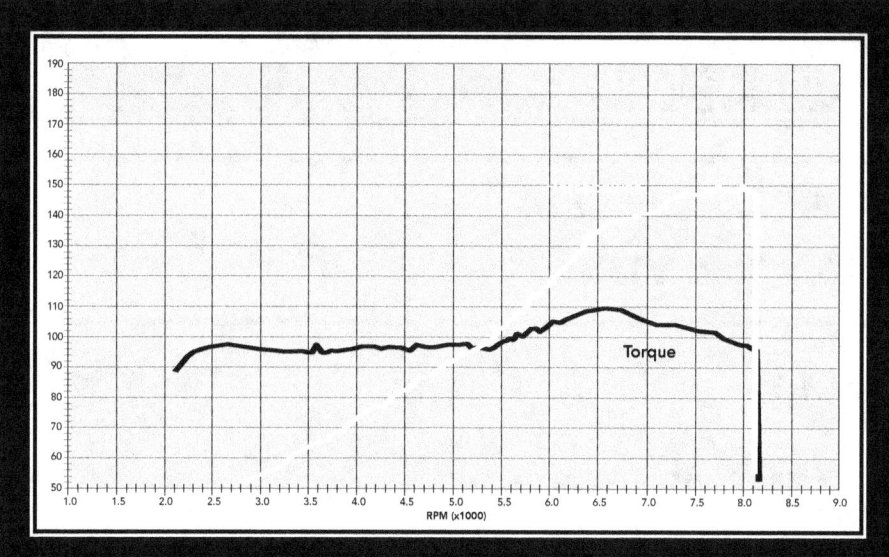

Baseline: B16A (Stock)

The fabricated short-runner intakes look plenty cool and flow like mad at high rpm, but they don't belong on your street motor, which will probably never see the high side of 8,000 rpm.

Peak Horsepower – Del Sol	153.4 hp
Peak Torque – Del Sol	115.4 ft-lbs

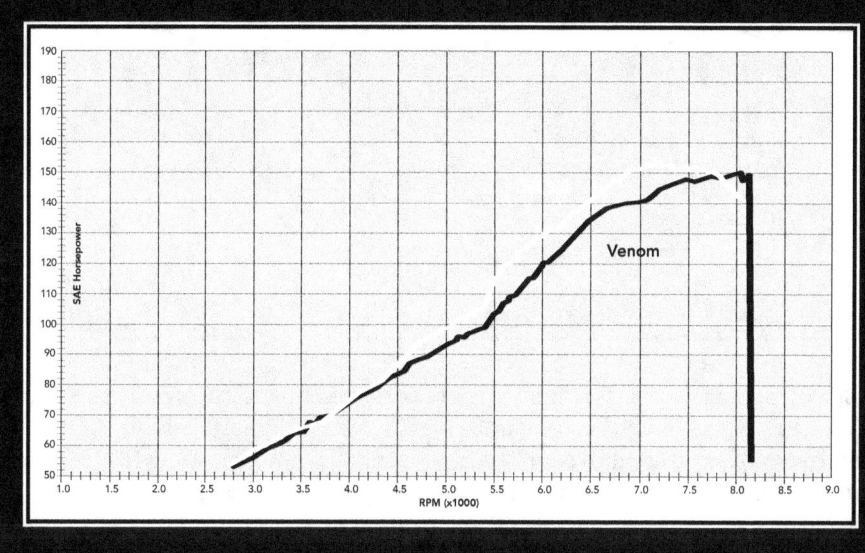

Del Sol versus Venom: Horsepower

Peak Horsepower – Del Sol	153.4 hp
Peak Horsepower – Venom	149.8 hp
Largest Horsepower Gain	11.1 hp

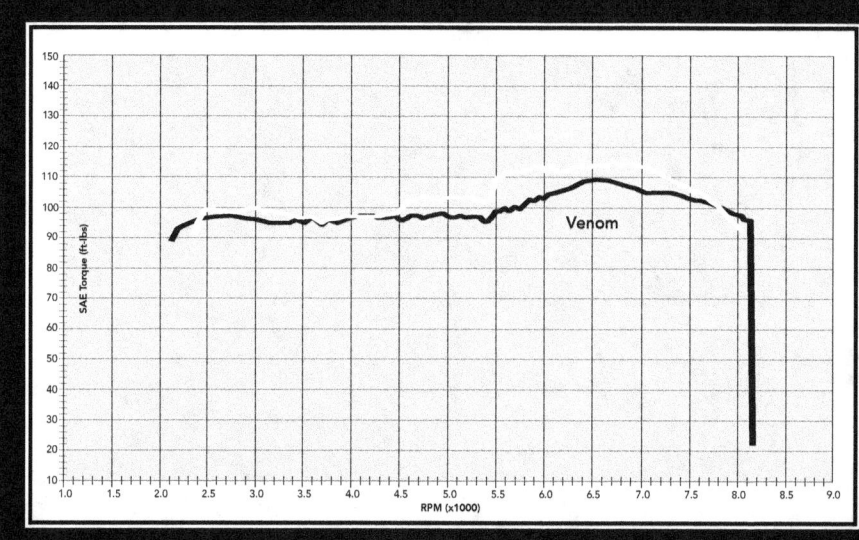

Del Sol versus Venom: Torque

Peak Torque – Del Sol	115.4 ft-lbs
Peak Torque – Venom	109.5 ft-lbs
Largest Torque Gain	11.2 ft-lbs

How to Build Honda Horsepower

Chapter 2

Test 5: Del Sol Intake Manifold versus Skunk Intake Manifold

1995 Civic Del Sol
B16A 1.6L VTEC

The Skunk 2 intake looked like an identical twin to the factory Type R and the performance indicated that the two were at least brothers. Actually, the Skunk 2 intake performed slightly better than the Type R in a comparison against the B16A Del Sol intake. Like the Type R, Venom, and STR, the Skunk 2 intake was designed with elevated engine speed in mind. The short runner, big-plenum design certainly favored high-rpm breathing, not quite to the extent of the Venom or STR intakes. One nice thing about the new Skunk 2 casting that bears mentioning is that they offer a mounting flange for use on the GS-R cylinder head. Until now, GS-R owners had to either swap on a B16A-based head or modify the flange on a Type R to work on the GS-R head. The Skunk 2 intake is a direct bolt on, making life much easier for GS-R owners looking for better top-end power over their dual-stage stock intake.

From the power curves generated on the modified B16A motor, it is obvious that the B16A intake once again out-performed the aftermarket (Skunk 2) intake all the way to 8,000 rpm. It is also evident that the B16A/Skunk curves were quite similar to those generated in the B16A/Type R test. Note that the two manifolds offered similar power up to 4,500 rpm at which point the longer, smaller runners on the B16A offered superior cylinder filling. From 4,500 rpm to 5,600 rpm, the B16A offered a sizable power gain, but Skunk 2 managed to equal and even slightly better the smaller intake from 5,600 rpm to 6,500 rpm. After 6,500 rpm, the B16A was clearly better until the tach needle

passed 8,000 rpm. Had this test motor been equipped with a wilder set of cams (we ran Crower 401s) that allowed it to rev up to 9,000 rpm, the Skunk 2 would

have offered superior power from 8,000 rpm to 9,000 rpm. As it is, this is yet another indication that the B16A intake is tough to beat up to 8,000 rpm.

Intake Manifolds and Throttle Bodies

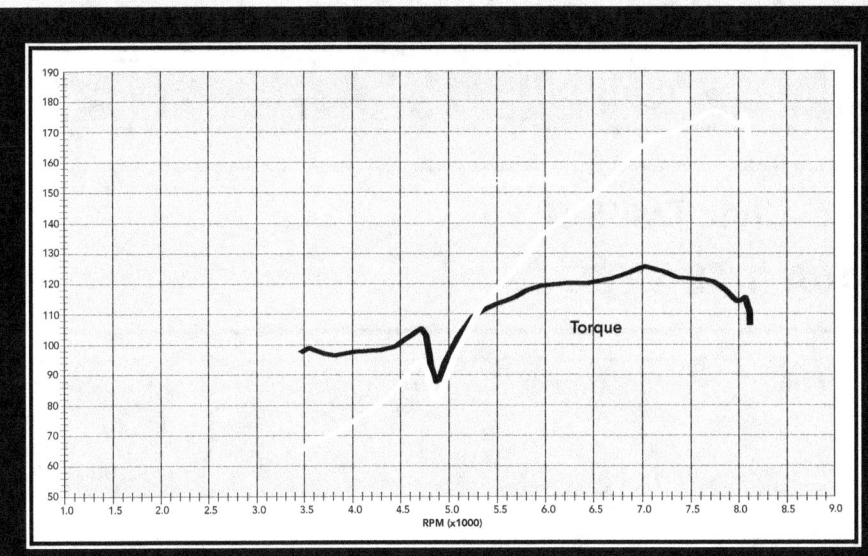

Baseline: Del Sol (Stock)

Peak Horsepower – Del Sol	173.9 hp
Peak Torque – Del Sol	118.6 ft-lbs

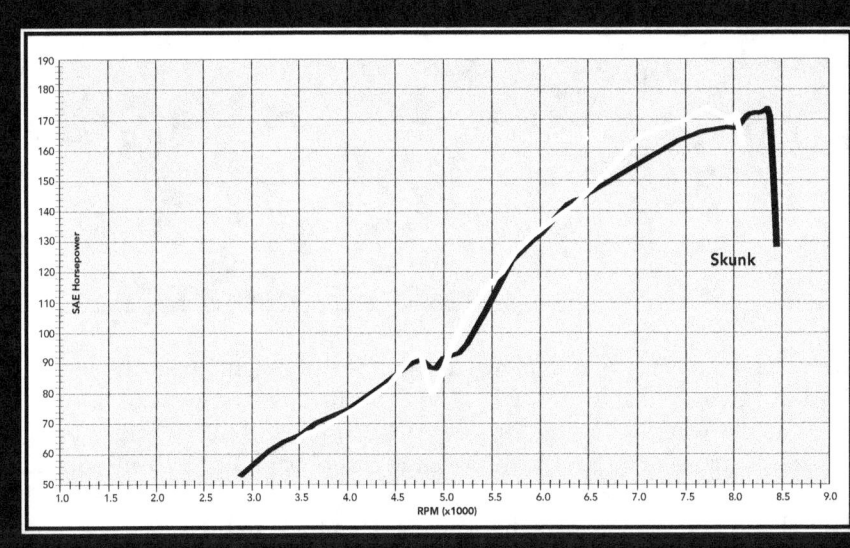

Del Sol versus Skunk: Horsepower

Peak Horsepower – Del Sol	173.9 hp
Peak Horsepower – Skunk	173.3 hp
Largest Horsepower Gain	12.1 hp

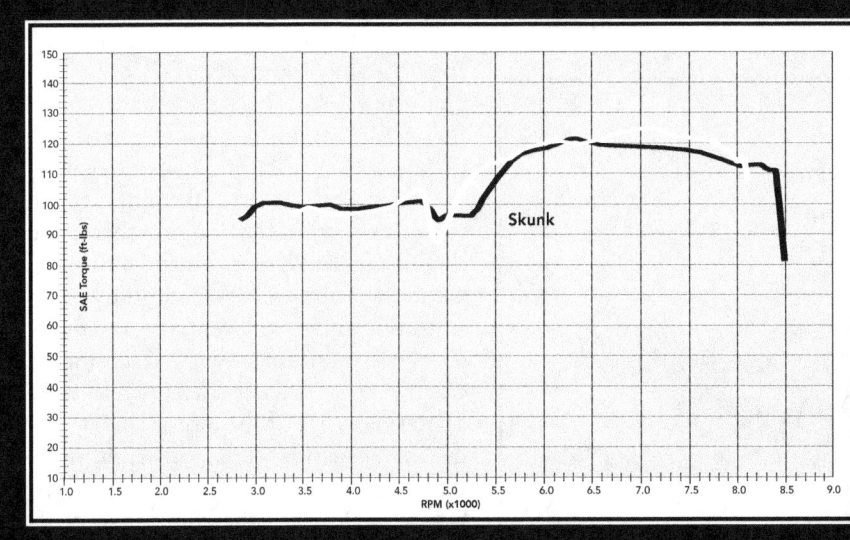

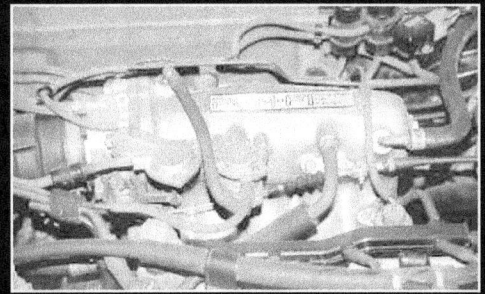

Del Sol versus Skunk: Torque

Peak Torque – Del Sol	125.1 ft-lbs
Peak Torque – Skunk	121.2 ft-lbs
Largest Torque Gain	12.3 ft-lbs

How to Build Honda Horsepower

Chapter 2

Test 6: Del Sol Intake Manifold versus STR Intake Manifold

1995 Civic Del Sol
B16A 1.6L VTEC

The two fabricated intake manifolds (STR and Venom) tested for this book were surprisingly similar in both looks and performance. If you take a look at the dyno results of the normally aspirated Venom fabricated intake test, you can see the results of the tests run on the STR, as both manifolds were tested on the same motor (on the same day). The power produced by the STR was a near mirror image of the curve produced by the Venom. This is not surprising since the two seemed like copies of each other, featuring near-identical runner lengths and volumes. The largest difference in power between the two was never more than 1 to 2 hp. As indicated in the test on the Venom intake, these fabricated manifolds are not ideal for street motors that spend most of their time below 8,000 rpm. The short runners maximize power at engine speeds above 8,000 rpm, especially on a 1.6-liter motor. The difference is less dramatic on a 2.0L stroker, but the B16A intake is still superior in terms of power and torque up to 8,000 rpm. This STR intake was run on a normally aspirated 2.0L LS/VTEC hybrid that produced over 200 hp at the wheels. The motor made best power up to 7,900 rpm with the B16A intake. Again, the short-runner STR intake is best suited to high-rpm power.

Since the STR and Venom intakes were marketed as turbo manifolds, this test was run to demonstrate the effectiveness of the design on a turbo motor. The B16A used for the previous normally aspirated test was turbocharged using a Drag turbo manifold, a T3 turbo, and Spearco intercooler. Running the B16A intake manifold and 10 psi, the turbocharged B16A produced 275 hp and 201 ft-lbs of torque at the wheels.

Installing the STR intake resulted in a drop in power all the way up to 7,900 rpm, at which point the STR out-powered the B16A. The STR peaked at 275 hp (at 8,000 rpm), but lost out in torque production. This test indicates that an intake manifold is less sensitive to forced induction than engine speed. An intake manifold that works well on a normally aspirated combination will do so on a turbo or centrifugal supercharged version as well. The intake design helps determine the effective operating range of the motor. Short runner intakes work best at high rpm, while the long-runner intakes operate best below 8,000 rpm (the rpm range of 99 percent of street motors).

Intake Manifolds and Throttle Bodies

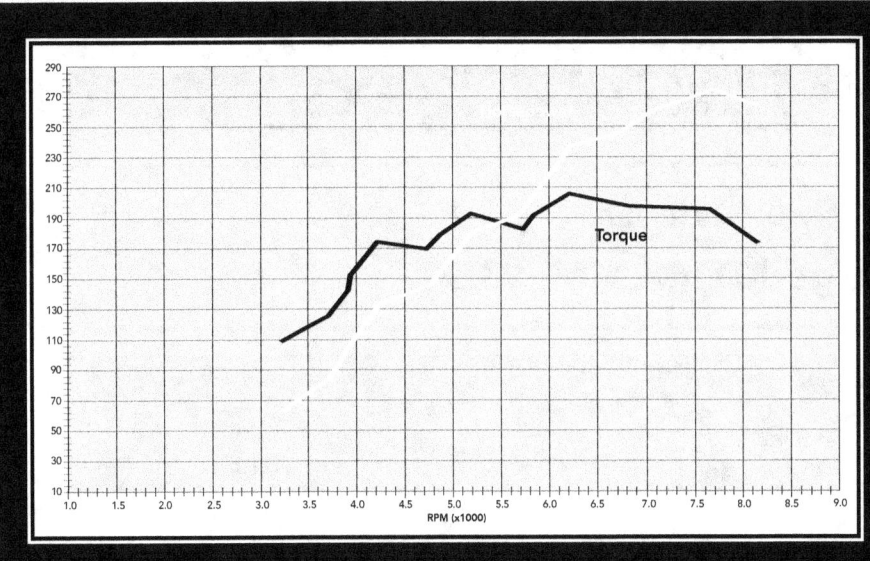

Baseline: Del Sol (Stock)

Like the Venom intake, the STR manifold belongs on a high-rpm motor. The short runners and big plenum enhance power at high rpm, whether the motor is turbocharged or normally aspirated.

Peak Horsepower – Del Sol	275 hp
Peak Torque – Del Sol	201 ft-lbs

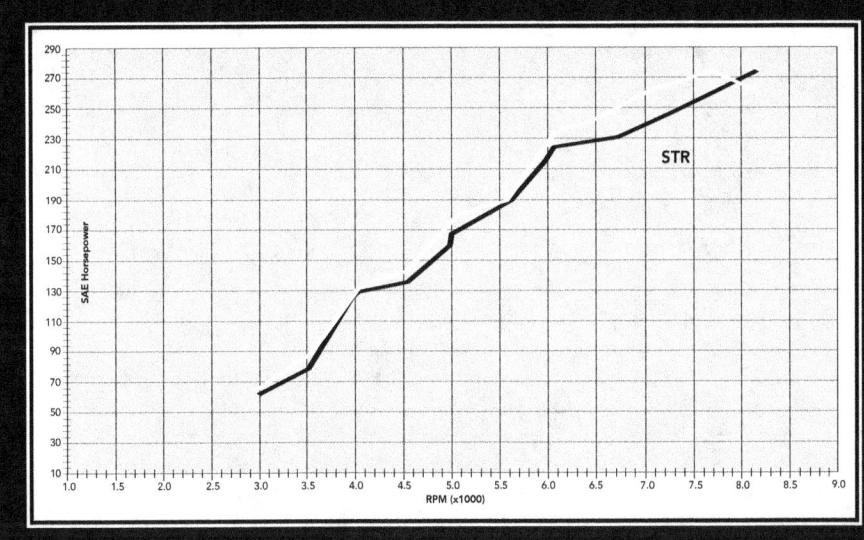

Del Sol versus STR: Horsepower

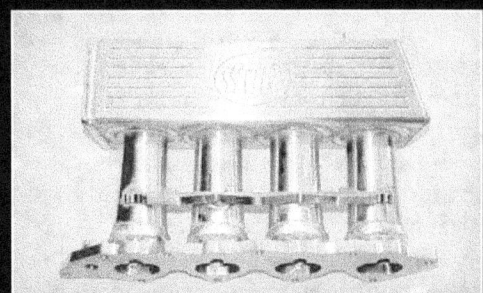

Peak Horsepower – Del Sol	275 hp
Peak Horsepower – STR	275 hp
Largest Horsepower Gain	15 hp

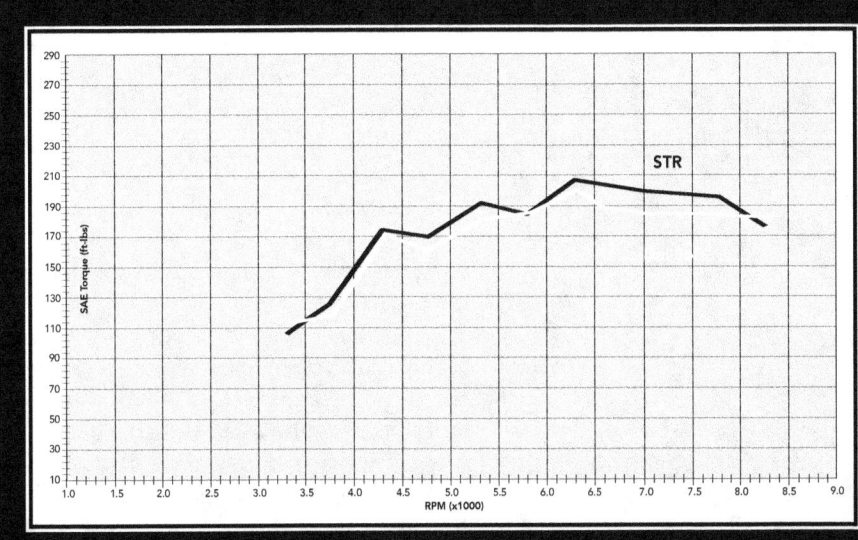

Del Sol versus STR: Torque

Peak Torque – Del Sol	201 ft-lbs
Peak Torque – STR	189 ft-lbs
Largest Torque Gain	13 ft-lbs

How to Build Honda Horsepower

Chapter 2

Test 7: Holley 62-mm Throttle Body versus Stock 55-mm (Supercharged)

1996 Civic EX
Supercharged D16Z 1.6L VTEC

This test illustrated the need for a larger throttle body on a supercharged motor. When you think about it logically, a Jackson Racing supercharged motor should require a larger throttle body before a turbocharged motor of similar power output. What is the difference you ask? The difference between a turbo D16Z and a Jackson Racing supercharged motor is that the turbo actually blows through the throttle body. The throttle body is downstream of the turbo but upstream of the supercharger. All of the airflow must be drawn through the throttle body by the supercharger, but the same air is being forced through on a turbo. An orifice will flow better under pressure, thus the throttle body will flow significantly better when pressurized by a turbo (or centrifugal supercharger). While larger throttle bodies have proven to provide minimal gains on most normally aspirated motors (stroker motors can be the exception), a positive displacement supercharged motor will usually benefit from a larger throttle body.

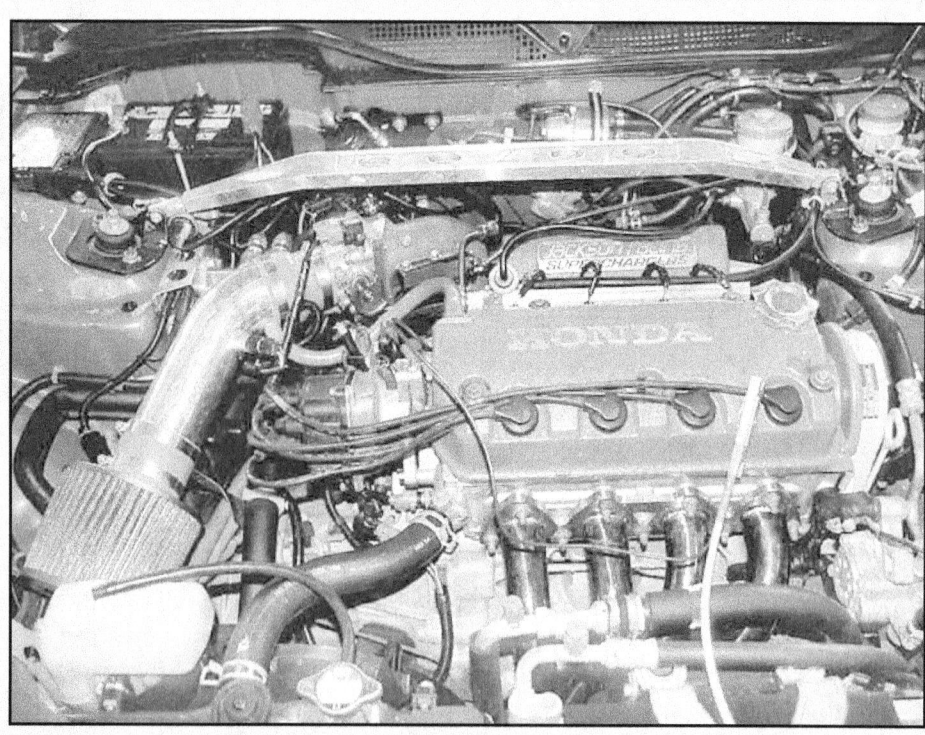

The 1.6L single-cam VTEC D16Z test motor sported the usual array of header and exhaust along with an open-element cone filter. So equipped, the supercharged 1.6L motor produced peak power readings of 153 hp and 122 ft-lbs of torque. Removing the stock 55-mm throttle body and installing the 62-mm Holley throttle body resulted in a power gain of 5–6 hp with a peak reading of 159 hp. The peak torque was up to 127 ft-lbs and the Holley throttle body showed a consistent (but not huge) gain across the rev range. As expected, the power gains increased with engine speed—something we've come to expect of changes in airflow restriction. The only downside to the larger throttle body was a slightly irregular idle. Though I did not get a chance to perform the test for this book, it might have been interesting to run a turbo and supercharger on the same motor and compare the outputs wit the stock and aftermarket throttle bodies. My testing has shown that the turbo motor would benefit very little if at all by the larger throttle body (at this power level).

Intake Manifolds and Throttle Bodies

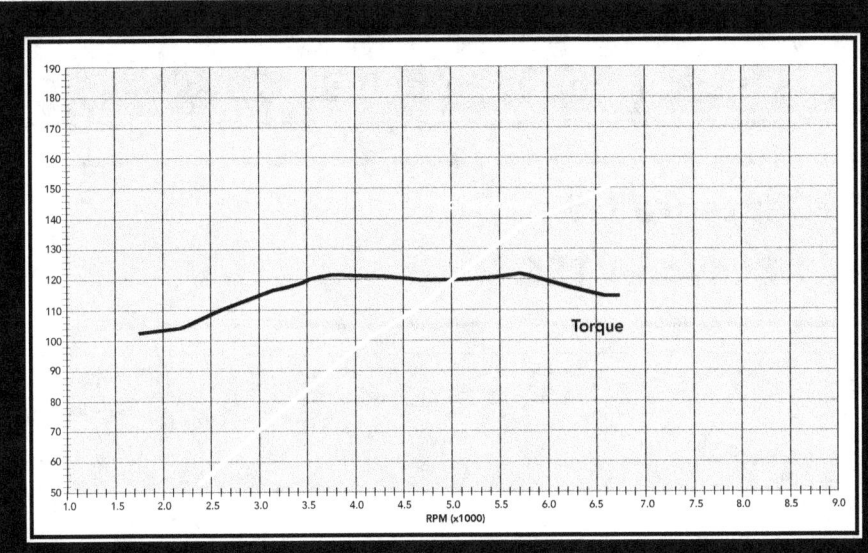

Baseline: Stock Throttle Body

The rules on throttle body size change slightly when running a positive displacement supercharger. Drawing through the throttle body means the airflow rate becomes more critical.

Peak Horsepower – Stock	153 hp
Peak Torque – Stock	122 ft-lbs

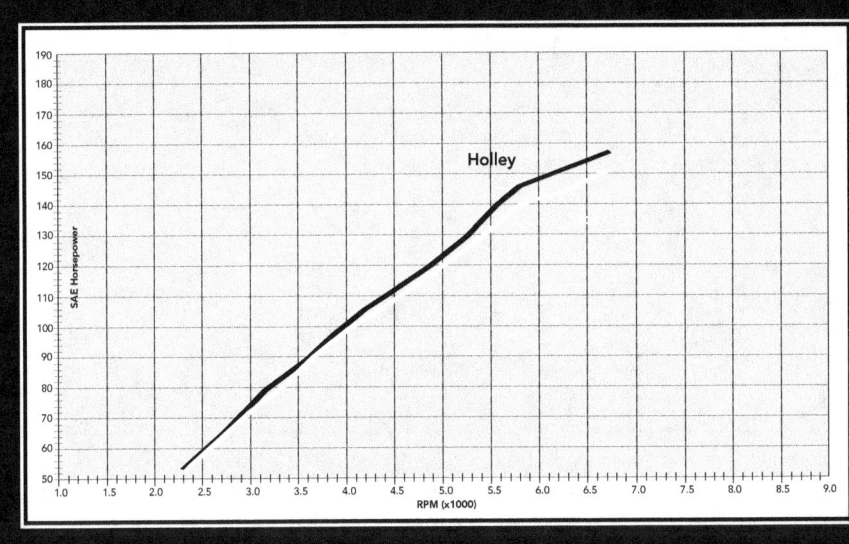

Stock versus Holley Throttle Body: Horsepower

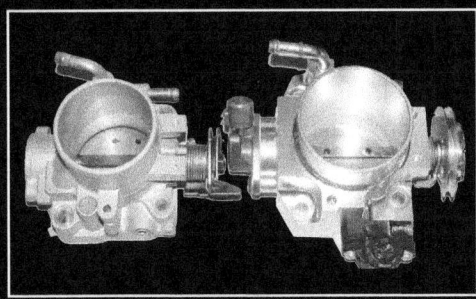

Peak HP – Stock	153 hp
Peak HP – Holley	159 hp
Largest Horsepower Gain	6.1 hp

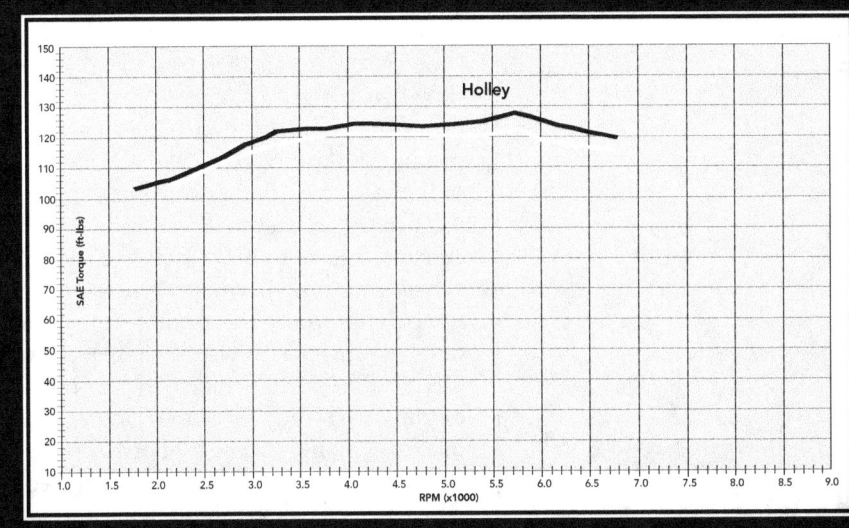

Stock versus Holley Throttle Body: Torque

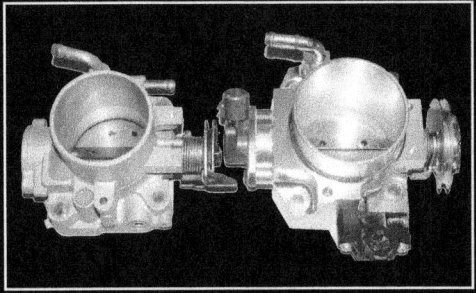

Peak Torque – Stock	122 ft-lbs
Peak Torque – Holley	127 ft-lbs
Largest Torque Gain	5.9 ft-lbs

Chapter 2

Test 8: Stock B18A Intake Manifold versus Extrude Hone–Ported B18A Intake Manifold

1990 Integra GS
B18A 1.8L Non-VTEC

Similar in concept to the porting performed to the B16A Del Sol intake, the Extrude Hone porting greatly improved the flow rate of the 1.8L B18A (non-VTEC) intake manifold. The non-VTEC intake on the 1.8L motor utilized relatively longer intake runners (compared to the B16A or Type R) to promote low-speed torque production. This is not surprising since the motor only revved to 6,600 rpm instead of the usual 8,000+ rpm seen by most VTEC motors. The longer runners on the stock B18A intake concentrated efficient power production in the low to middle portion of the rev range, though the motor made peak power at 6,400 rpm. Once treated to Extrude Hone porting, the added airflow increased the engine speed where the motor made peak power to 6,600 rpm. Unlike installing a completely different intake design, the ported stock intake simply enhanced the power output everywhere rather than shift the efficiency higher in the rev range. There was no tradeoff in low-speed power for the gains at 6,600 rpm.

One of the important aspects of porting any intake manifold is to maintain the flow balance between cylinders. Flow testing the individual runners in stock configuration revealed that the factory casting was pretty well balanced. The greatest flow difference between the runners was just 6 cfm (212 cfm versus 218 cfm). Credit Honda for a superior casting, as many intakes do not offer flow rates this close. To demonstrate the effectiveness of the Extrude Hone porting process, we tested the manifold on the flow bench once again after porting. The ported manifold was even better, with the maximum flow rate of the runners not only improved, but also slightly more balanced. The largest difference between runners was now only 4 cfm (251 cfm versus 255 cm). Extrude Hone porting not only improved the absolute flow rate but also the cylinder-to-cylinder flow balance. The porting improved the power output by 6 hp and 4 ft-lbs of torque. The manifold could have supported more power if the motor had been equipped with a ported cylinder head, wilder cams, and more compression.

Intake Manifolds and Throttle Bodies

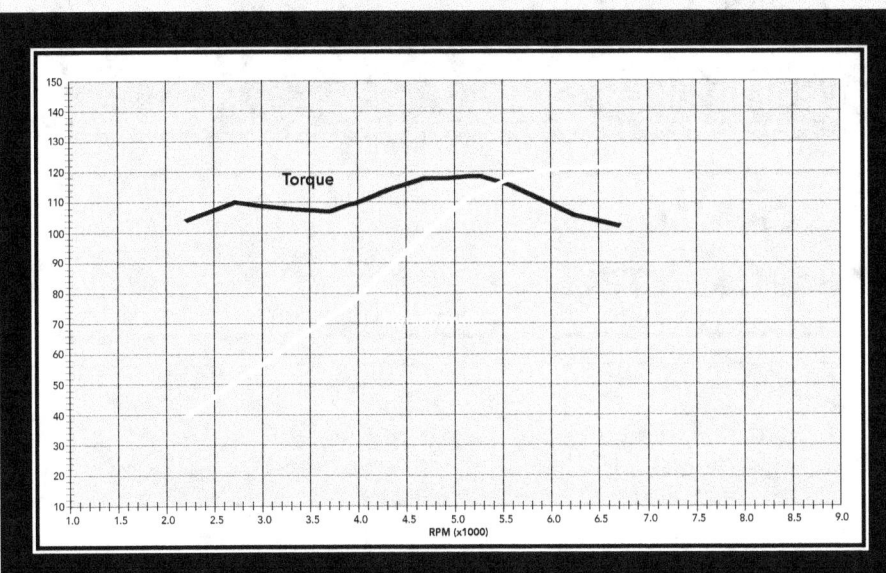

Baseline: B18A (Stock)

Peak Horsepower – Stock	125.2 hp
Peak Torque – Stock	120.0 ft-lbs

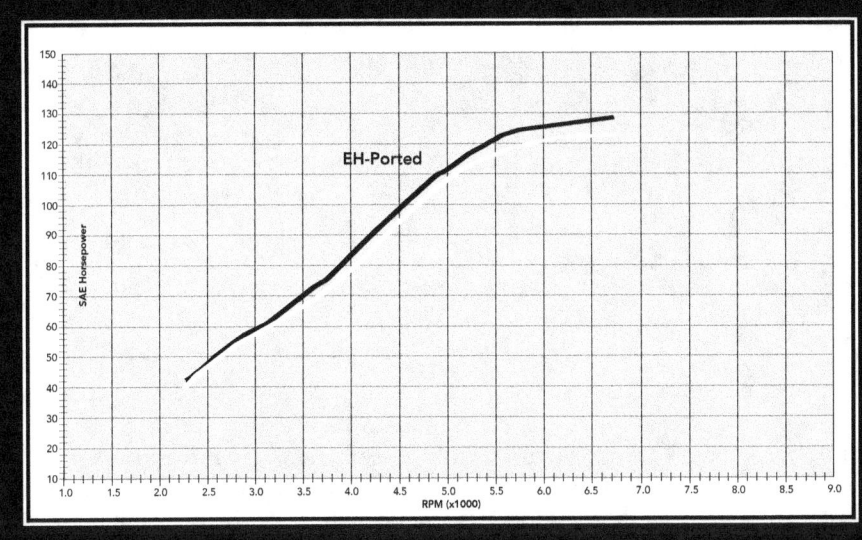

Stock versus EH-Ported B18A: Horsepower

Peak Horsepower – Stock	125.2 hp
Peak Horsepower – EH-Ported	131.3 hp
Largest Horsepower Gain	6.1 hp

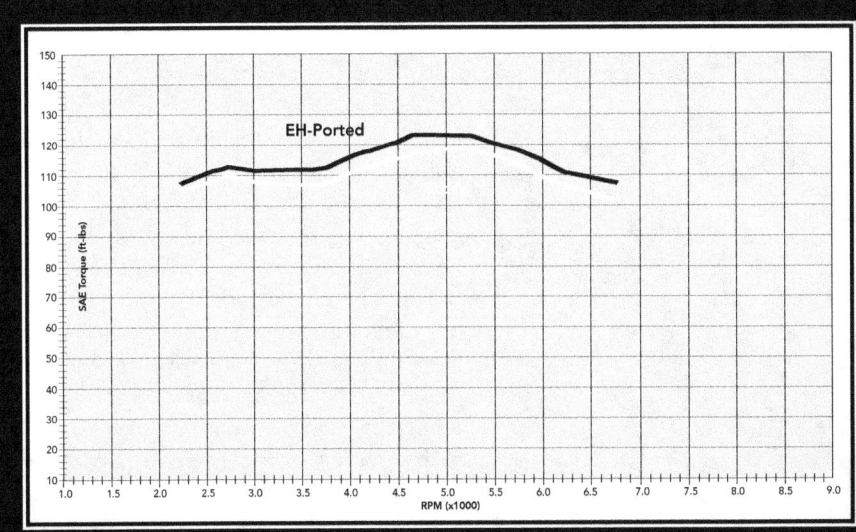

Stock versus EH-Ported: Torque

Peak Torque – Stock	120.0 ft-lbs
Peak Torque – EH-Ported	124.3 ft-lbs
Largest Torque Gain	5.1 ft-lbs

How to Build Honda Horsepower

Chapter 2

Test 9: Killer Bee Racing Intake Manifold versus Stock Del Sol Intake Manifold

1995 Civic Del Sol
B16A 1.6L VTEC

This particular intake was the result of hundreds of hours of dyno testing. It was obvious from the many dyno tests that the factory Honda intake manifolds were hard to beat, especially for the stock engines. The B16A was obviously better than the larger Type R, especially for the smaller B16A motors. The short-runner, larger plenum intakes offered in the aftermarket were not ideally suited for street use according to the dyno test results performed on any number of engine combinations. To find out how much power could be coaxed from the proper intake manifold, I decided to fabricate my own combination using the test results from this chapter as a guide. By the time this book goes to print, the Killer Bee Racing intake combination tested here will be available from a major manufacturer.

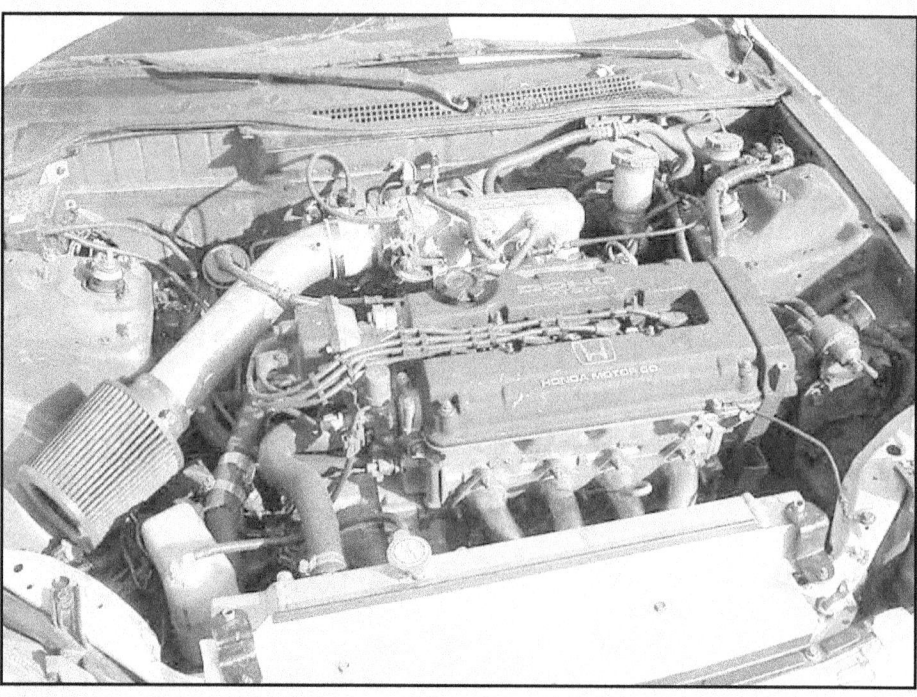

The intake started out as a late-model B16A, but the intake plenum was cut, modified, and a new plenum welded back together. The intake runners were ported (including the entry of each) to improve flow while the entry into the plenum was modified. As you might imagine, extensive modifications were made to the original manifold, but the internal modifications provided exceptional results, not only compared to the B16A, but also the Type R and other aftermarket variants. This test illustrated the results of a back-to-back test on a modified B16A. The test motor included a rebuilt B16A featuring a milled cylinder head, stock B16A cams (late Si), AEM sprockets, an RC Engineering throttle body, and APEXi header. In baseline trim with the stock B16A intake, the motor produced 168 hp and 121 ft-lbs at the wheels. After installing the Killer Bee Racing intake, the peak power increased to 174 hp while the peak torque increased to 124 ft-lbs. Note that most of the gains were experienced at the top of the rev range, something you would expect from an increase in airflow.

44 How to Build Honda Horsepower

Intake Manifolds and Throttle Bodies

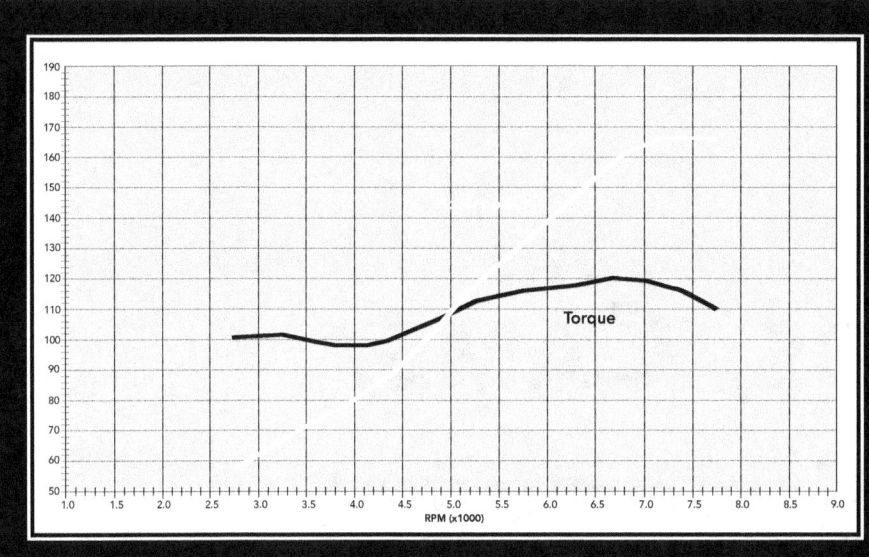

Baseline: B16A (Stock)

Using the results from earlier tests, the author designed a modified B16A intake that outperformed the already-good stock B16A intake manifold. A production version of this modified intake should be available soon.

Peak Horsepower – Stock	168 hp
Peak Torque – Stock	121 ft-lbs

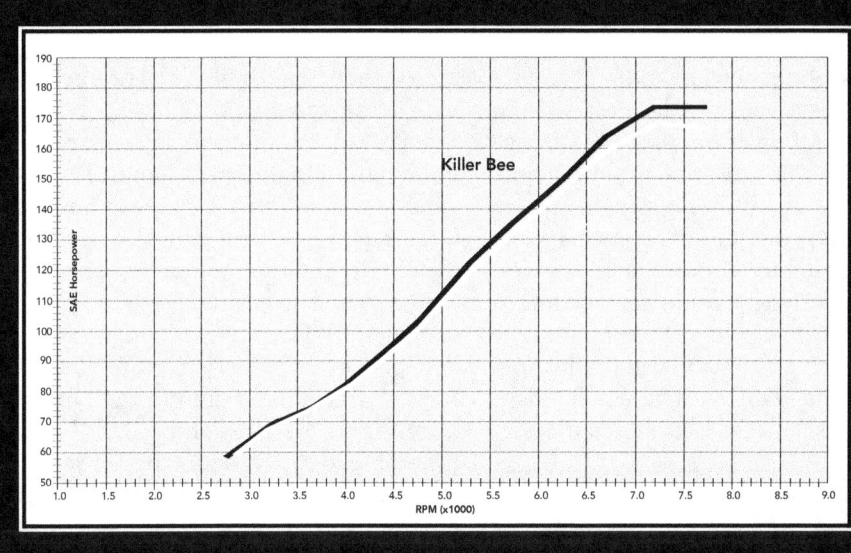

Killer Bee versus B16A: Horsepower

Peak Horsepower – B16A	168 hp
Peak Horsepower – Killer Bee	174 hp
Largest Horsepower Gain	7 hp

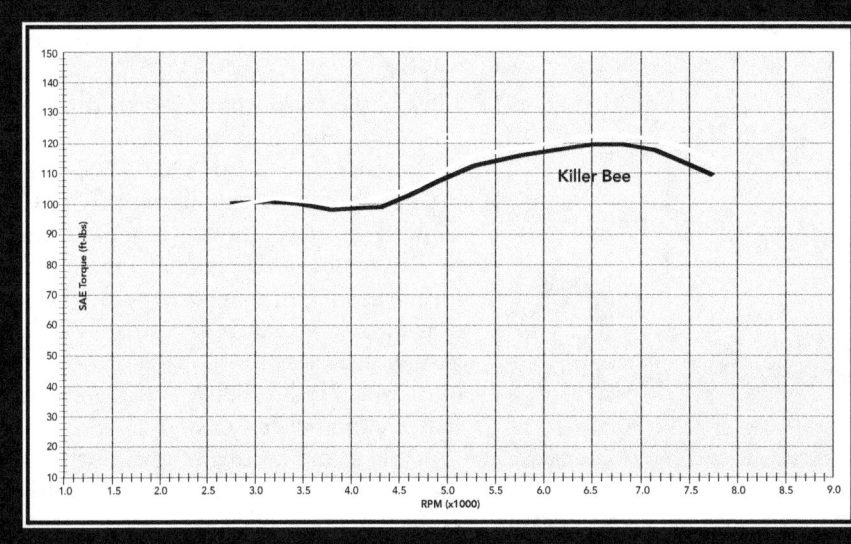

Killer Bee versus B16A: Torque

Peak Torque – B16A	121 ft-lbs
Peak Torque – Killer Bee	124 ft-lbs
Largest Torque Gain	4 ft-lbs

How to Build Honda Horsepower

CHAPTER 3

HEADS, CAMS, AND SPROCKETS

The key to optimum performance is a combination of components that work together to produce a desired power curve, and one of the keys to the elevated power outputs offered by Honda/Acura performance motors is the cam timing. Actually, the dual-cam timing made possible by the VTEC componentry is responsible for the near race-motor specific outputs. Short of forced induction, there is only one way for a small-displacement motor to produce big horsepower: engine speed. Given a specific displacement, the best way to produce big power from a small package is to tune the motor to produce peak torque at a relatively high engine speed. High-rpm power means running aggressive cam timing. Unfortunately, aggressive cam timing usually means limited low-speed power as the cam timing is tuned for high-rpm power production. Such is the tradeoff inherent in high-winding, small-displacement motors, a tradeoff inherent until Honda came out with a little thing called VTEC.

The advent of the VTEC (variable timing and electronic lift control) provided the motor with a split personality. Offering two distinct cam profiles and the ability to switch effectively between the two based on engine speed (and other variables), VTEC opened up a whole new performance world for Honda and Acura owners. First seen in the United States on the Ferrari-fighting 3.0L NSX, the technology was soon applied to the bread-and-butter Civic lineup. It is interesting to note that the NSX was offered in the United States in 1991, but the B16A was equipped with the dual-cam VTEC system back in 1989 (again, not available here in the United States). The dual-cam profile VTEC system allowed the motor to run at low rpm on mild cam timing, but come alive after the engine speed exceeded 5,200–5,500 rpm depending on the application. VTEC allowed the small-displacement motor to produce both acceptable low-speed torque and high-rpm power, not to mention ultra-low emissions status. Honda gave enthusiasts a mild-mannered economy car with the ability to charge right to 8,000 rpm when called upon.

When the testing began for this book, performance camshafts for Honda/Acura applications were in their infancy. Most performance cams were

When installing a wilder set of cams, don't forget a set of adjustable cam sprockets to fine-tune the new cam profile.

How to Build Honda Horsepower

regrinds using the factory cams. Before the book's completion, a number of companies began offering performance cam profiles for the Honda/Acura B and D series engines. Of course, the factory upgrades were always available. One example would be swapping in a set of B18C5 Integra Type R cams in place of the stock B16A cams. There were a number of different B16A cams used, but the Integra Type R (ITR) cams would be an improvement over the early, automatic, and current Si grinds. The next step up in terms of factory performance cams would be the Civic Type R grinds. Used in the 185-hp Civic Type R (not available in the United States), the Civic was equipped with a rather unique 1.6L combination. The Civic Type R sported a tall-deck B18C block equipped with a fully counterweighted B16A crank, long rods, and high-compression pistons. The ultra-high horsepower 1.6L also relied on wilder cam timing (compared to the standard B16A or ITR) to produce over 115 hp/liter. This bettered the specific output (108 hp/liter) of the more powerful 195-hp Integra Type R.

This chapter covers a number of different cam tests, including single and twin-cam motors, VTEC and non-VTEC applications. The twin-cam VTEC B-series motors get all the attention in the magazines, but the reality is that the vast majority of Civic and Integra owners sport single-cam D16Z or B18A (or B) non-VTEC motors. I have included cam tests for these owners as an option to an engine swap. It is possible to upgrade your existing D16Z or B18A motor with the right cam(s), compression, and exhaust rather than spend a small fortune on a B16A or LS/VTEC engine swap. Of course, the swap route will offer more power potential, but going the cam, compression, exhaust route will be considerably less expensive. In addition to the cam comparisons, I have included information on adjustable cam sprockets. The testing shows not only how to improve power by altering the cam timing, but what can happen when you adjust them incorrectly. It is much easier to lose power by adjusting the cam sprockets than achieve any type of gain. Sometimes, a gain at one rpm will be offset by a loss elsewhere. I have also demonstrated the importance of altering the ignition timing in conjunction with the cam timing, as the distributor is driven off the intake cam on B-series motors. Altering the intake cam timing also affects the static ignition timing. Finally, the chapter includes a few cylinder head tests, including the effects of milling a B16A head .035 and what happens when you treat a B16A head to Extrude Hone porting.

Replacing a pair of Honda B-series cams is an easy way to add 10-15 extra horsepower.

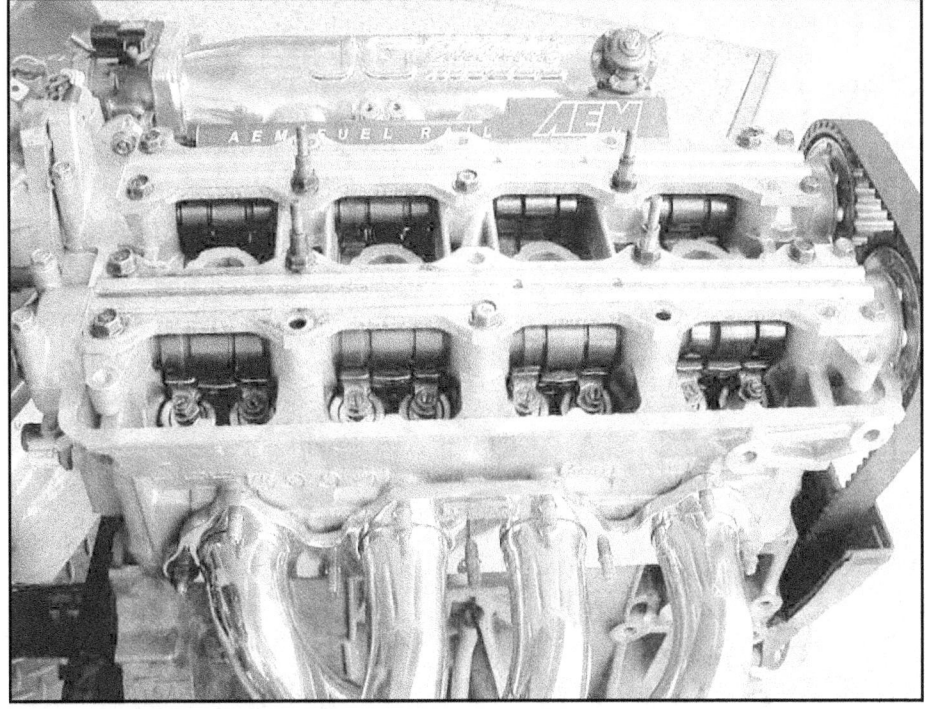

These Crower cams increased the power output of this B16A by 12 horsepower.

Chapter 3

Test 1: Type R Cams versus June Stage 3 Cams

1995 Civic (Engine Swap)
B18C 1.8L VTEC

While B16A-powered Civics are a dime a dozen, serious racers know that cubic inches rule the street. While the expense of the B18C motors make swaps considerably harder on the wallet, a B16A will never match the overall power curve of a larger B18C. While enthusiasts and tuners will argue that a B16A can make as much peak power as a B18C motor, I have never seen a B16A combination that wouldn't benefit from the infusion of the additional displacement (rod ratio notwithstanding). In every test I have ever run, the gains offered by the displacement always outweigh any inefficiency produced by a slight change in rod ratio. This certainly holds true for any type of street motor. In fact, the B18A/B crank and shorter rod (and attending lower rod ratio) will offer that much more power by increasing the displacement even further. It is simple mathematics. If you have a motor that produces 100 hp/liter (measured either at the flywheel or at the wheels) and you increase the displacement by .2 liters, you will increase the power by 20 hp. It has been my experience that it would take a near-impossible change in rod ratio to lower the efficiency to negate the 20 hp gained through displacement.

Enough about the common misconceptions associated with rod ratios and on to the cam test. This test was run on a modified B18C GSR motor. The test motor was equipped with a milled GSR head, Type R intake, and Integra Type R cams. Adjustable cam sprockets were used to dial in the Integra Type R cams. The motor was also equipped with a homemade 3-inch intake system (with open element filter), a JDM Type R header, and open exhaust. So equipped, the modified GSR motor produced 207 hp and 147 ft-lbs of torque at the wheels. The June Stage 3 cams were significantly larger than the factory Integra Type R cams (no specs were available directly from June). The added duration made itself known (again after adjusting the sprockets) after 7,000 rpm. The June Stage 3 cams increased the peak power to an impressive 218 hp at the wheels. (Pay no attention to the peak numbers listed, as they represent a spike at the end of the run). The June cams were worth a solid 10 hp peak-to-peak and as much as 15 hp elsewhere in the rev range. It is important to note that there was no loss in low-speed power with the larger June cams.

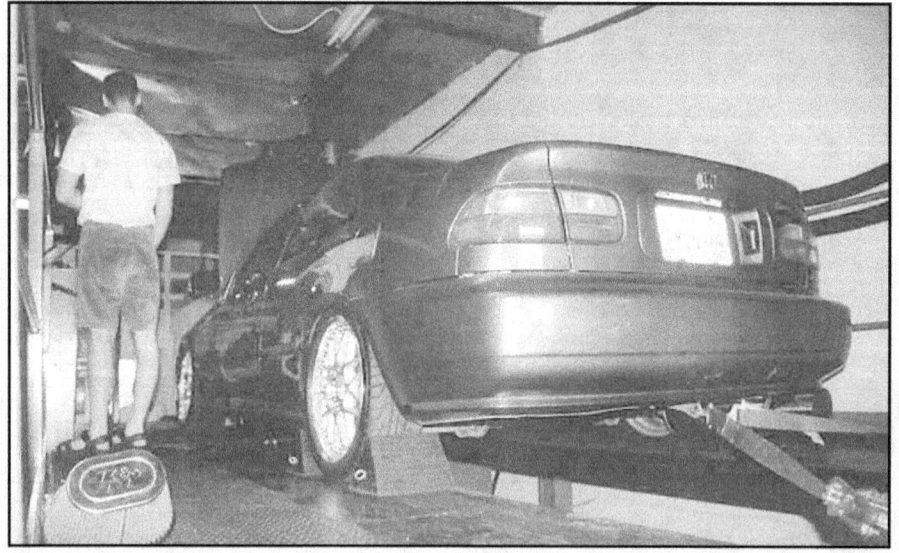

Heads, Cams, and Sprockets

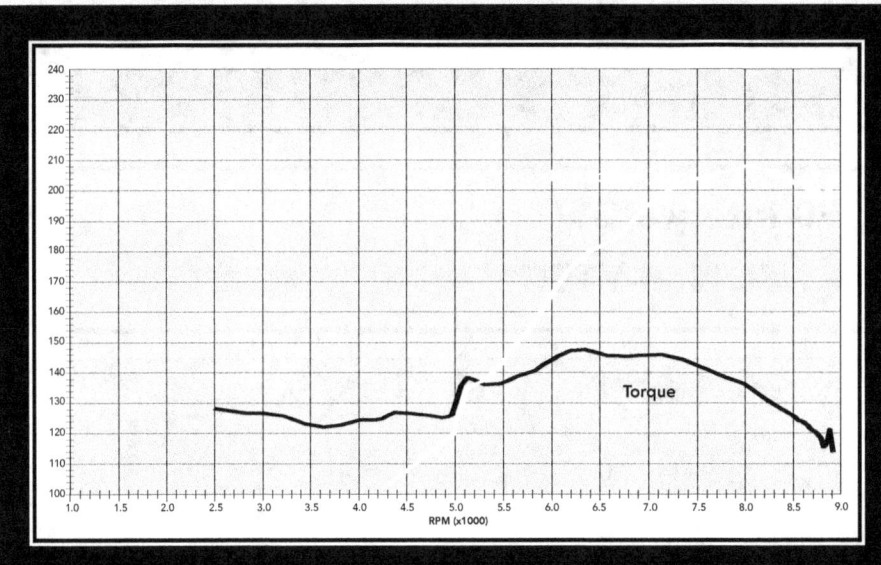

Baseline: B18C Type R Cams

For quite some time, the hot cams for your B-series VTEC motor were the factory Integra Type R cams. They offered a sizable power gain over the B16A cams, but now companies like June make cams that outperform the factory stuff.

Peak Horsepower – Type R	207 hp
Peak Torque – Type R	147 ft-lbs

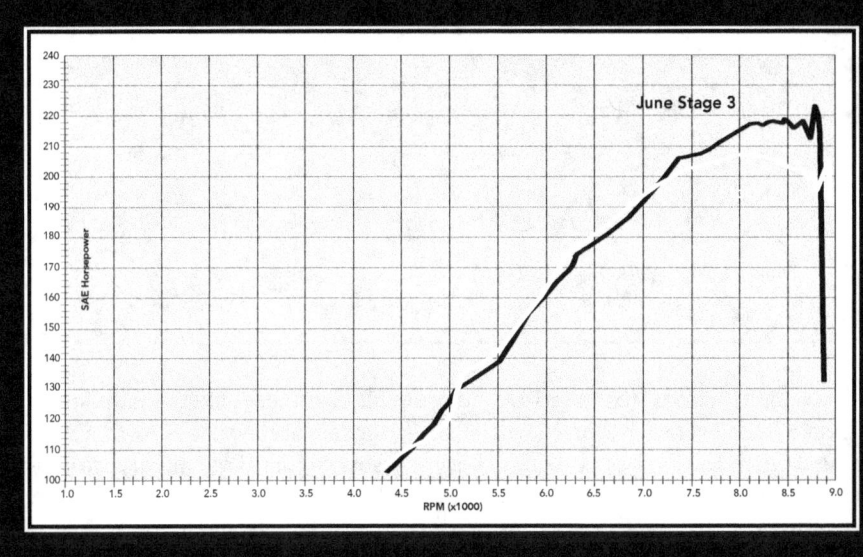

Integra Type R versus June Stage 3: Horsepower

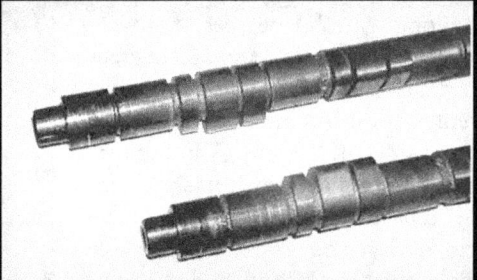

Peak Horsepower – Type R	207 hp
Peak Horsepower – June Stage 3	223 hp

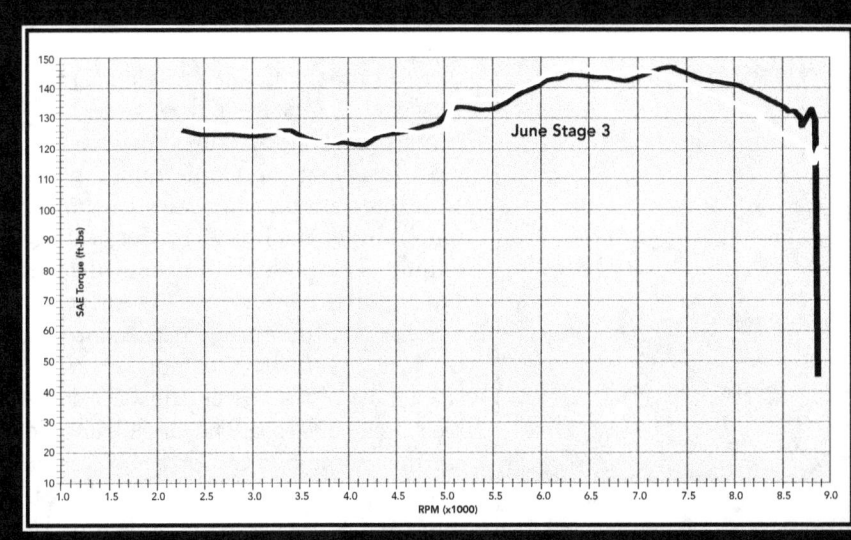

Integra Type R versus June Stage 3: Torque

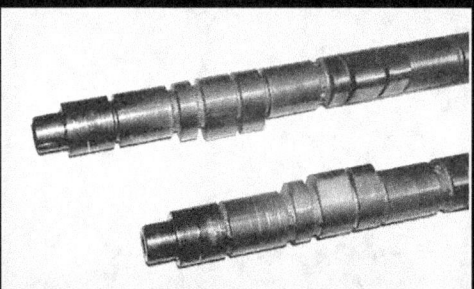

Peak Torque – Type R	147 ft-lbs
Peak Torque – June Stage 3	147 ft-lbs

How to Build Honda Horsepower

Chapter 3

Test 2: Stock Cams versus Crane Cams

1990 Integra GS
B18A 1.8L Non-VTEC

This test was performed on the author's own 1990 Integra GS prior to swapping in a B16A VTEC motor in place of the original B18A non-VTEC 1.8L. At the time of this writing, Crane offered no less than five different cam grinds for the 1.8L (1,834cc) Integra motor. Since the test vehicle was really a daily driver, we selected the middle of the five offerings from Crane (grind #s ACU-261-2S-9). This pair offered 10.15 mm intake lift, 9.85 mm exhaust lift, along with 261 degrees of (advertised) intake duration and 267 degrees of exhaust duration. The number represented healthy increases over the wimpy stock 1.8L cams. Another reason for choosing these grinds was that they did not require stronger valve springs. Crane does offer a set of valve springs (that are recommended), especially if your stock springs have a ton of miles on them, but the cams were installed using the stock valve springs with excellent results. Shortly after the cam test, the non-VTEC motor was

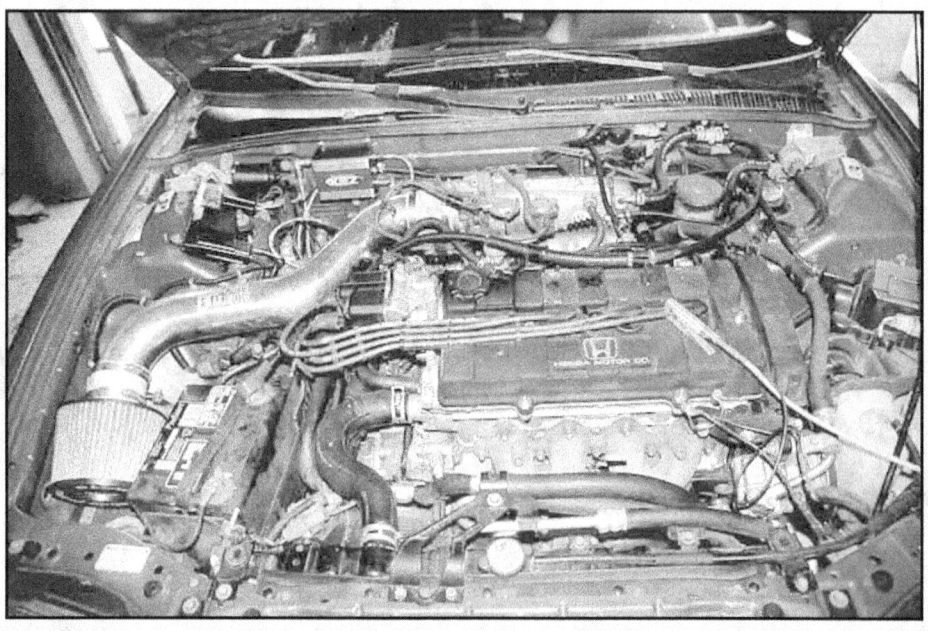

removed to make room for a B16A VTEC motor that eventually provided superior performance.

Swapping the cams was quite easy. It is important to note that the Crane Cams were installed using the factory non-

adjustable cam sprockets. Adjustable cam sprockets are available from a variety of sources and are highly recommended when swapping cams. The adjustable sprockets allow you to dial in the cam timing for optimum performance. The sprockets are critical if the cylinder head has been milled, as milling actually alters the cam timing. As it turned out, the Crane cams performed very well considering they were hampered by the stock non-adjustable cam gear. Installing the Crane cams on the 1.8L Integra motor increased the power output by as much as 20 hp out near the redline. The peak power jumped from 123 hp at the wheels to 137 hp at the wheels. That the torque peak improved by just 3–4 ft-lbs was not surprising since most of the power gains were realized after 4,500 rpm. The Crane cams did sacrifice some power below 4,000 rpm, but the overall acceleration of the car improved considerably with the installation of the cams.

Heads, Cams, and Sprockets

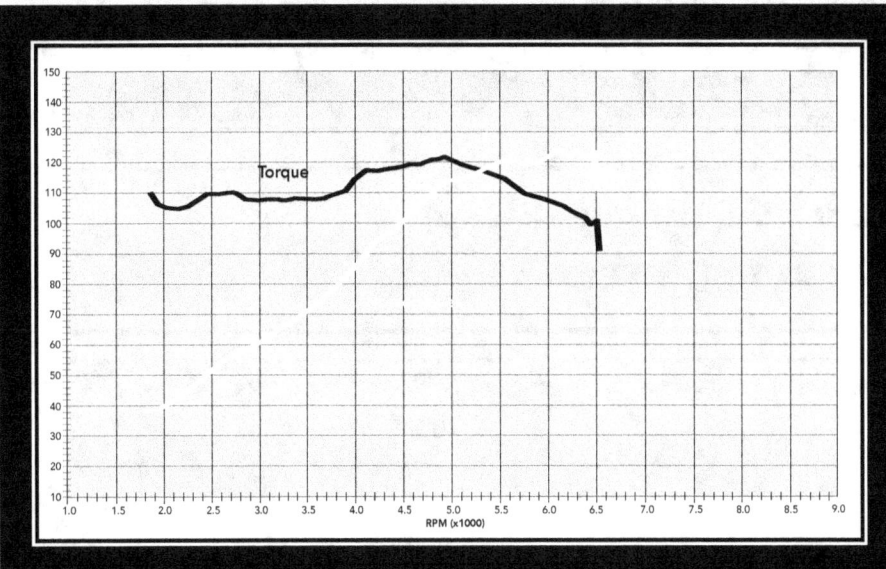

Baseline: B18A (Stock)

Though the VTEC motors grab all the glory, several companies offer cam grinds for the lesser non-VTEC Integra motors as well. These Crane 1.8L B18A/B cams offered a sizable chunk of power.

Peak Horsepower – Stock	123 hp
Peak Torque – Stock	122 ft-lbs

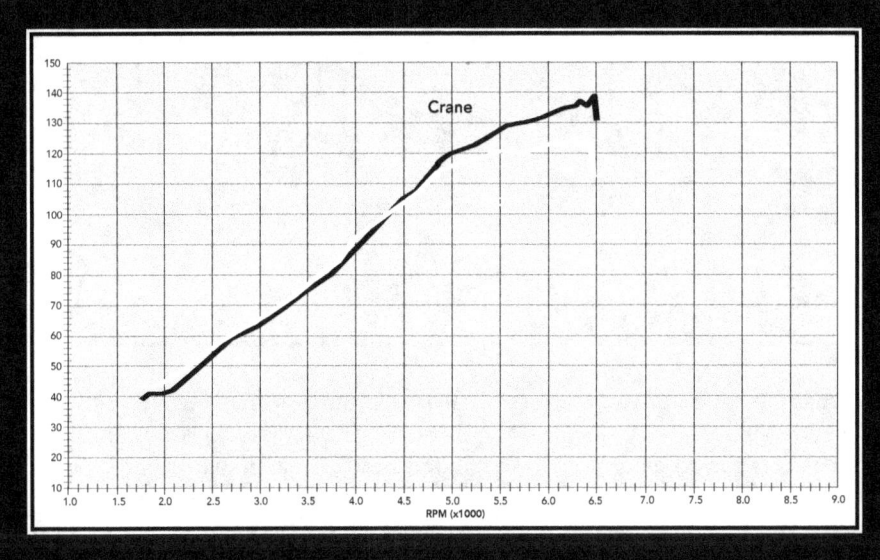

Stock versus Crane: Horsepower

Peak Horsepower – Stock	123 hp
Peak Horsepower – Crane	138 hp

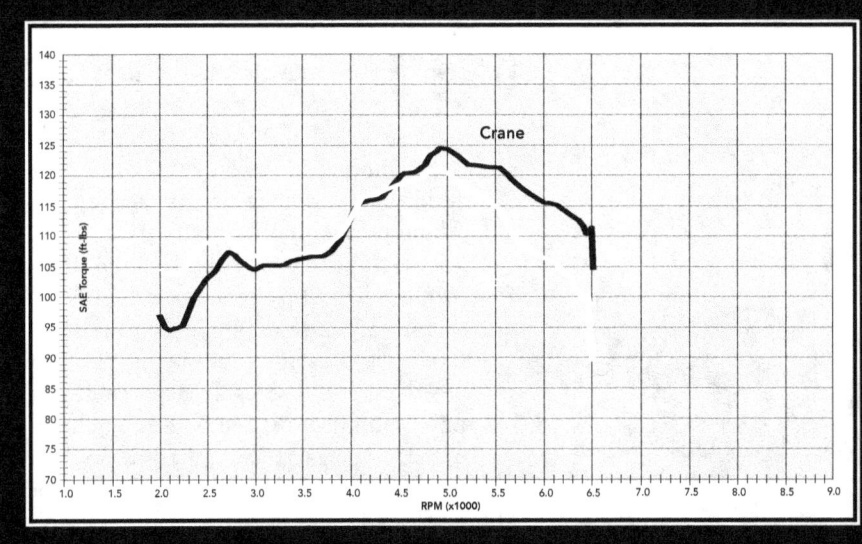

Stock versus Crane: Torque

Peak Torque – Stock	122 ft-lbs
Peak Torque – Crane	126 ft-lbs

How to Build Honda Horsepower

Chapter 3

Test 3: B16A Cams versus Crower 63401 Cams

1990 Integra GS (Engine Swap)
B16A 1.6L VTEC

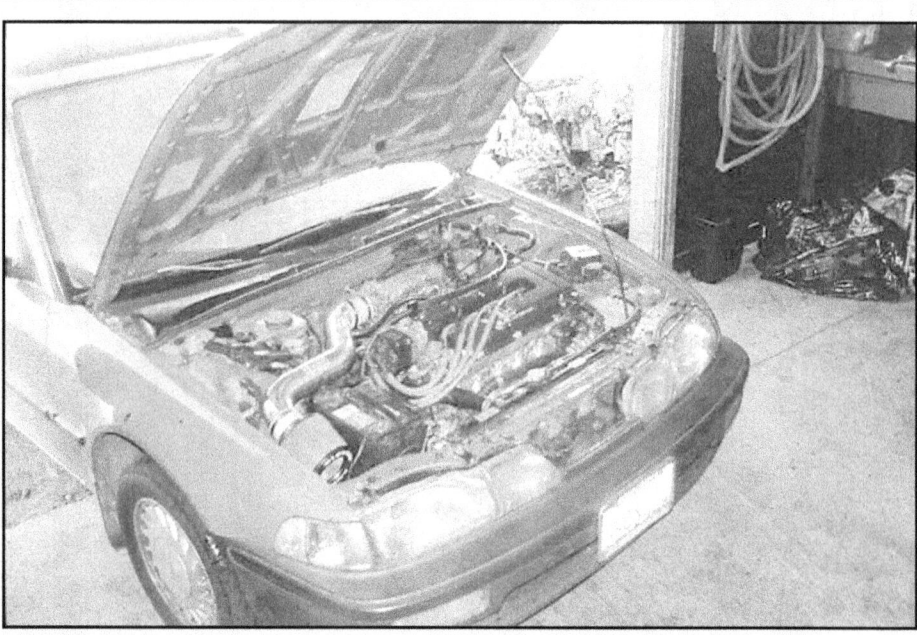

One of the early entrants in the import arena, Crower Cams now offers a number of cam profiles for not only the B-series Honda/Acura line-up, but also a number of other engine families. In addition to four off-the-shelf and numerous custom offerings for the B-series VTEC motors, Crower also offers performance cams for the non-VTEC B-series H22, and even the lowly D-series single-cam motors. Crower also has a number of non-Honda import applications as well. This particular test was run on the part number 63401 (Civic Type R+) profile. Advertised to offer 15–18 hp over a stock B16A cam, the CTR+ profile sported 11.37-mm (.446) intake lift, 10.69-mm (.413) exhaust lift. This compares to the stock B16A cams at .412-inch intake lift and .379-inch exhaust lift. The duration was likewise skewed in favor of the Crower sticks, as the Stage 1 cams increased the intake duration from a 265/267-degree split (intake/exhaust) to a much healthier 282/277-degree split.

This test was run to determine how effective the Crower cams were on a (near) stock B16A motor. Modified or stroker motors will likely benefit even more from larger (wilder) cams, but how much power is available (if any) on an internally stock B16A? This test was run to answer just that question. The Crower cams were tested on the very same 1990 Integra GS shortly after we swapped in the B16A in place of the Crane-cammed B18A (non-VTEC). After running the cam test on the B18A, the tired non-VTEC motor was replaced with a K-Wat special. The B16A was left completely stock internally. The only mods were the addition of a DC Sports header, RS Akimoto air intake, and Thermal stainless steel exhaust. So equipped, the B16A produced 135 hp at the wheels with full accessories including air conditioning. After the installation of the Crower 63401 cams and adjustable sprockets, the B16A pumped out 146 hp at the wheels, with power gains as high as 12 hp. The minimal pre-VTEC power gains can be attributed to the near-stock primary (pre-VTEC) cam timing.

How to Build Honda Horsepower

Heads, Cams, and Sprockets

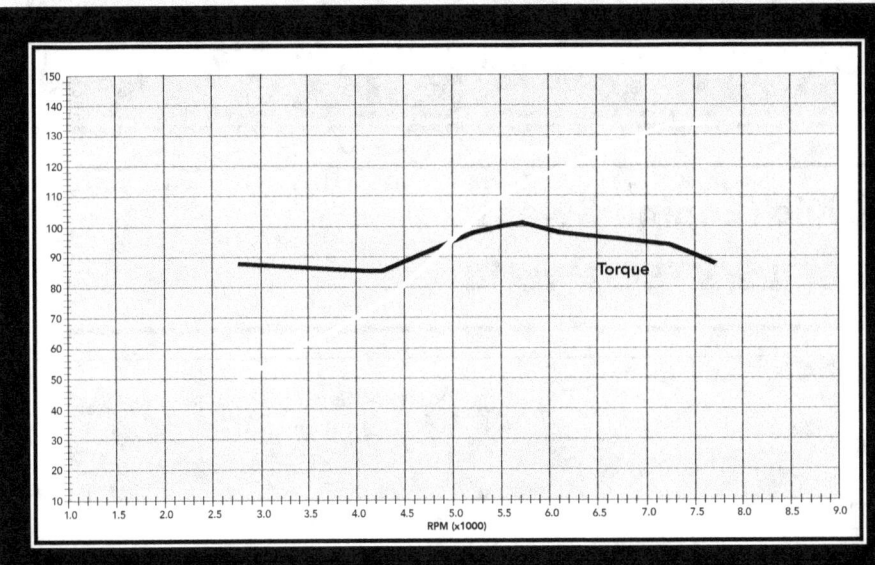

Baseline: B16A (Stock)

If you're looking for something just a bit hotter than a factory Integra or even Civic Type R cam combo, look no further than the Crower 63401 sticks.

Peak Horsepower – Stock	135 hp
Peak Torque – Stock	102 ft-lbs

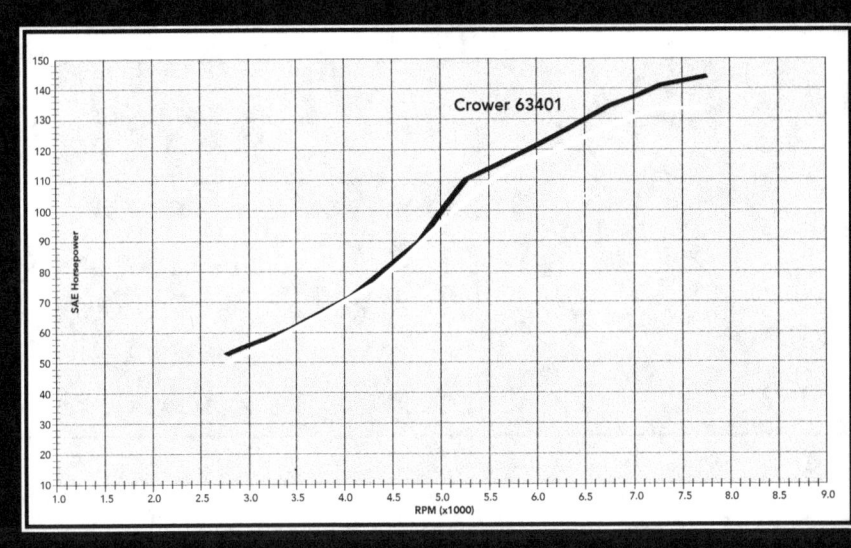

B16A versus Crower 63401: Horsepower

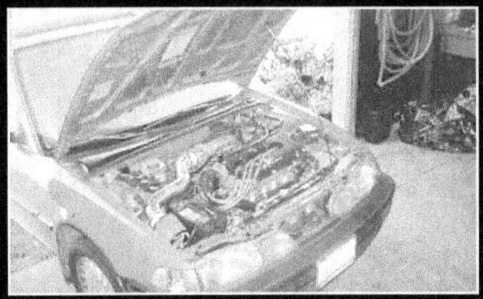

Peak Horsepower – Stock	135 hp
Peak Horsepower – Crower 63401	146 hp

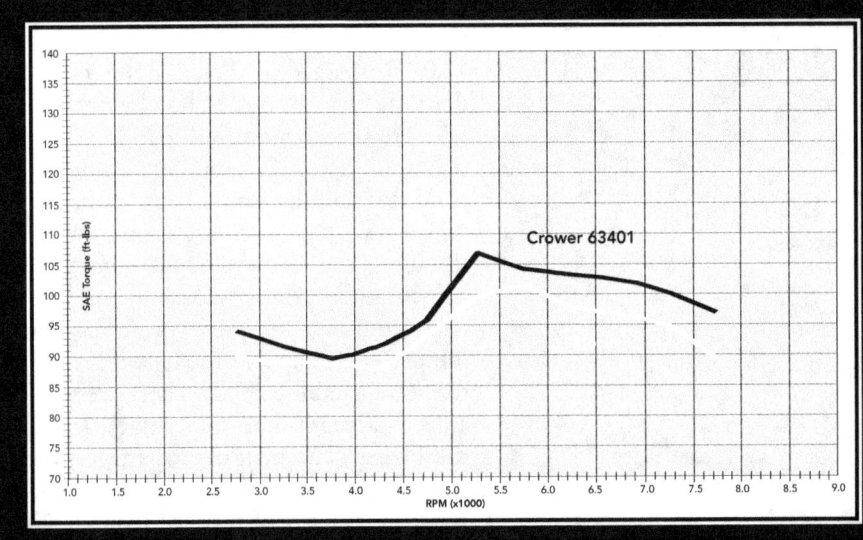

B16A versus Crower 63401: Torque

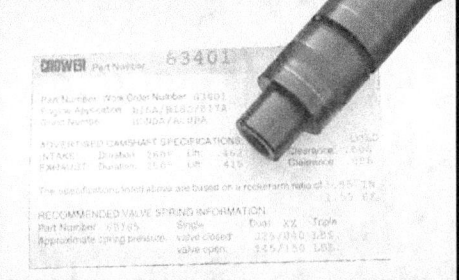

Peak Torque – Stock	102 ft-lbs
Peak Torque – Crower 63401	109 ft-lbs

How to Build Honda Horsepower

Chapter 3

Test 4: B16A Cams versus Crower 63402 Cams

1997 Civic (Engine Swap) B18B 1.8L LS/VTEC Hybrid

In addition to being rpm specific, cam timing is also displacement specific. What does this mean? Changes in cam timing will result in changes to the overall power curve of the motor. Wilder cam timing (usually defined as increased lift but especially duration) will tend to shift the power production higher in the rev range. Sometimes it is possible to achieve power gains across the board, but more often than not, gains in high-rpm power are usually traded for losses in low-end torque. We witnessed this when installing the Crane cams in the 1.8L non-VTEC Integra motor. The second part of the statement involving displacement simply means that larger motors will tolerate (and benefit from) wilder cam timing. A cam that might be considered wild for a street 1.6L might work great on a 2.0L stroker motor.

This test was run on a somewhat bizarre combination. Unlike the usual B18C Integra GSR, Type R configurations or the not quite as common 1,834-cc LS/VTEC hybrid, this test motor combined the two with good success. The test motor was built around an LS/VTEC hybrid using an 87.2-mm 1.8L GSR crank in place of the more common 1,834-cc (89-mm) crank from the LS motor. The motor was built with 12.0:1 JE forged pistons, a B16A cylinder head treated to mild bowl work and a ported and modified B16A intake manifold. The high-compression motor produced 208 hp and 147 ft-lbs at the wheels with the B16A cams. After installing the Crower 63402 cams and adjusting the cam sprockets to produce optimum results, the peak power jumped to 219 hp and 160 ft-lbs. Thanks to the adjustable cam sprockets, we were able to actually improve power across the board. The majority of the power gains were post-VTEC, but as much as 10 extra ft-lbs were realized from 4,000 rpm to 5,000 rpm.

Heads, Cams, and Sprockets

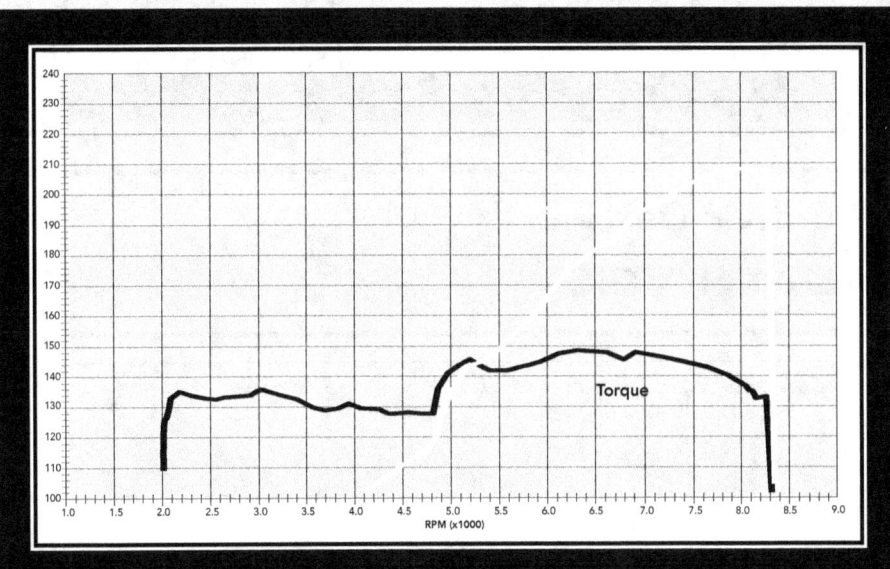

Baseline: B18B (Stock)

No matter how much power you have, you always want more. More is exactly what the Crower 63402 cams offer.

Peak Horsepower – Stock	208 hp
Peak Torque – Stock	147 ft-lbs

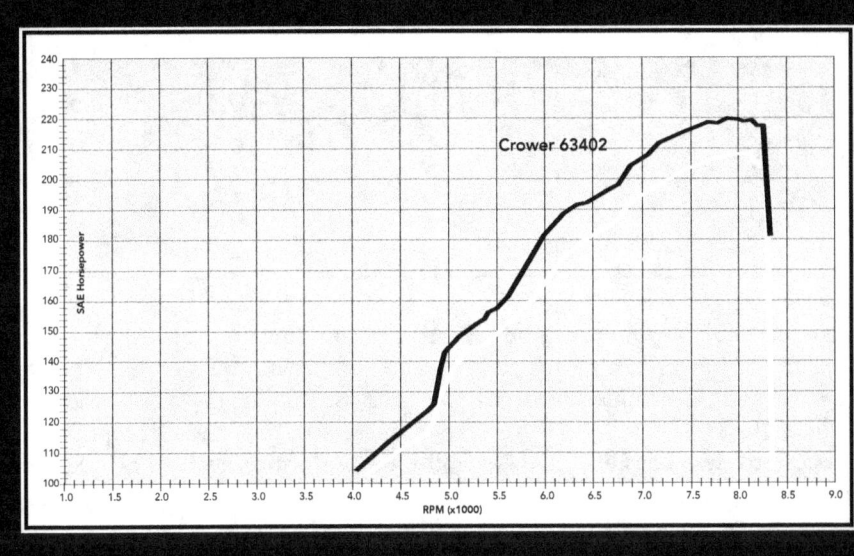

B16A versus Crower 63402: Horsepower

Peak Horsepower – Stock	208 hp
Peak Horsepower – Crower 63402	219 hp

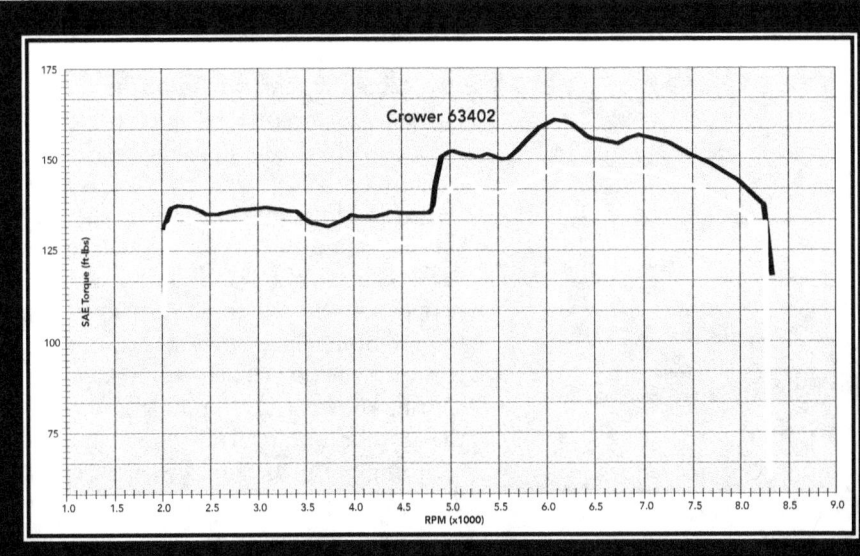

B16A versus Crower 63402: Torque

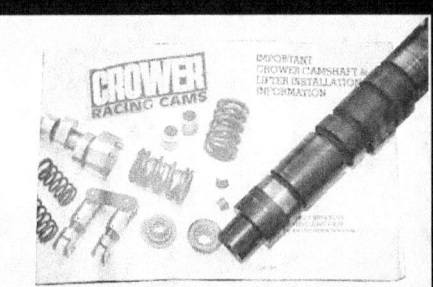

Peak Torque – Stock	147 ft-lbs
Peak Torque – Crower 63402	160 ft-lbs

How to Build Honda Horsepower

Chapter 3

Test 5: Adjustable Cam Sprockets, Take I

1995 Civic Del Sol
B16A 1.6L VTEC

This series of tests was run to demonstrate the effectiveness of adjustable cam sprockets. Although we used AEM adjustable cam sprockets on this B16A test motor, there are a number of other sprockets available for the B-series motors. In previous tests in this chapter, we have mentioned that the respective motors have run best with the cam timing optimized with the use of adjustable cam sprockets. These tests were run to demonstrate just how much power could be gained or lost by adjusting the sprockets. The power differences noted in these tests would likely be much higher had we run this motor with aftermarket cams. It has been my experience that the aftermarket cams require greater changes in cam timing via the sprockets than factory profiles (B16A, ITR or CTR etc.). These tests were run not so much to illustrate how to adjust cam sprockets for your particular application, but rather how much power can be lost if they are adjusted improperly for a given application.

The test motor was a modified B16A equipped with a milled B16A cylinder head. The motor was used to test a number of components and eventually installed in the author's 1990 Integra GS for street use. Milling the B16A head not only increased the static compression ratio, but unfortunately also altered the cam timing by bringing the cam sprockets closer to the crank. When milling the head, it is necessary to adjust the cams accordingly to bring the timing back to factory specs (milling the head retards the cam timing). You might think that advancing the cams would be the way to go, but our motor responded best to 2 degrees of retard on both the intake and exhaust cams. The first graph illustrates the power difference offered by retarding the intake and exhaust cams by 2 degrees each. The second graph illustrates what happens when you combined advancing the ignition timing in conjunction with retarding the cams 2 degrees. Remember, altering the intake cam timing also alters the ignition timing. The combination of retarding the intake and exhaust cams 2 degrees along with 4 degrees of additional ignition advance (with 100-octane race fuel) resulted in a power gain of 5–6 hp.

Heads, Cams, and Sprockets

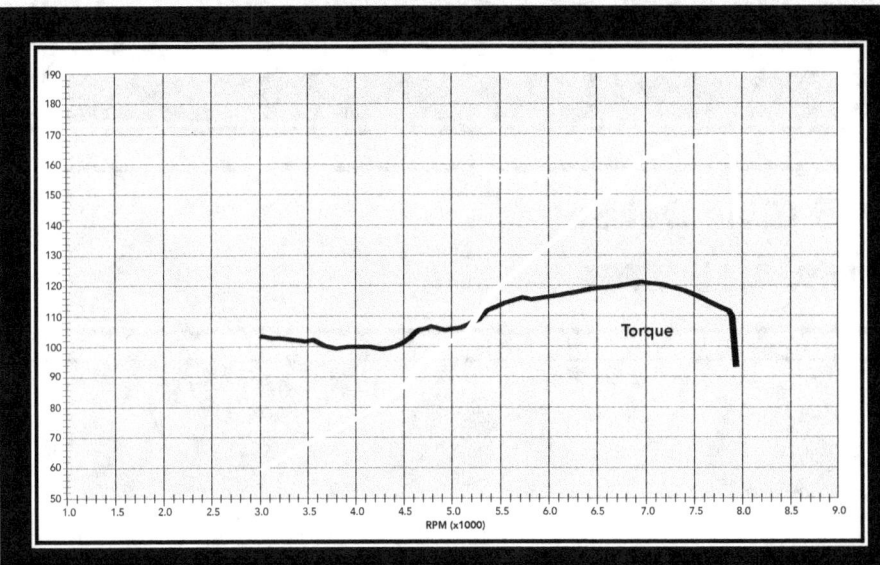

Baseline: 0-Intake, 0-Exhaust

Adjustable cam sprockets are necessary with milled heads. This test on a B16A motor with adjustable cam sprockets shows just how much power you can gain by adjusting the cam timing on a motor.

Peak Horsepower – 0I, 0E   162 hp

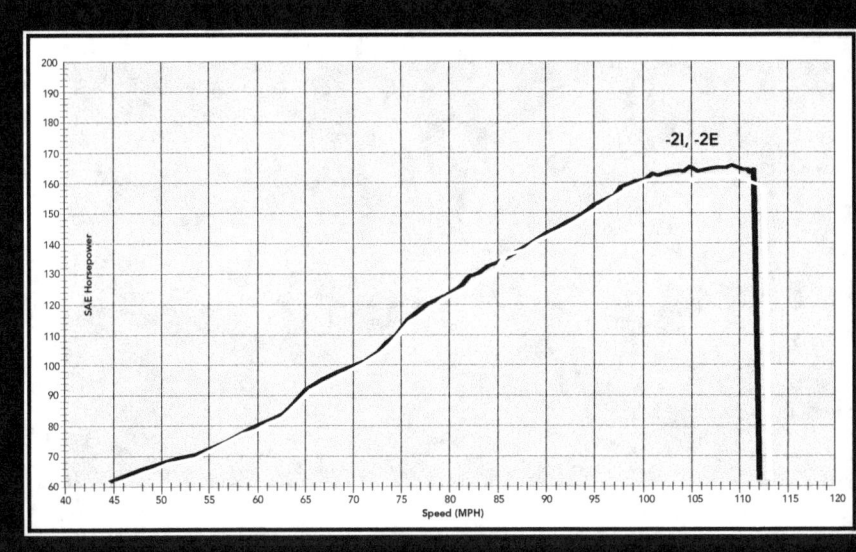

-2I and -2E: Horsepower

Peak Horsepower – 0I, 0E   162 hp
Peak Horsepower – -2I, -2E   167 hp

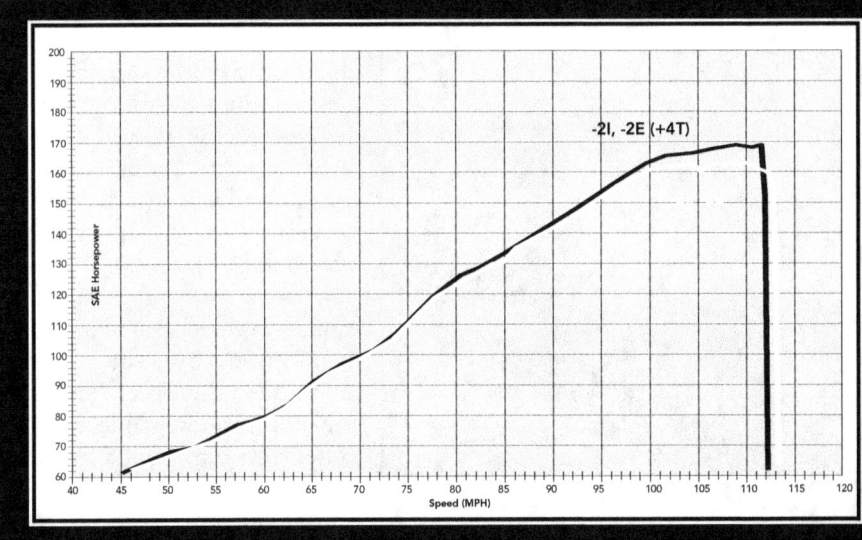

-2I, -2E, +4 degree Ignition Timing: Horsepower

Peak Horsepower – -2I, -2E   167 hp
Peak Horsepower – -2I, -2E, +4T   172 hp

How to Build Honda Horsepower

Chapter 3

Test 6: Adjustable Cam Sprockets, Take II

1995 Civic Del Sol
B16A 1.6L VTEC

The next series of tests were run to demonstrate what happens when the cam sprockets are adjusted improperly. The ideal combination for the modified B16A seemed to be 2 degrees retard on both the intake and exhaust cams combined with 4 degrees of ignition advance. A number of other ignition/cam timing combinations were tried before we realized that the -2I, -2E (+4) produced the best overall power curve. Since we gained power by retarding the stock B16A cams 2 degrees, why not try retarding them even more? We tried retarding both cams 4 degrees. The result was a loss in power across the board, but especially in the mid range. The next attempt was to keep the exhaust cam retarded 2 degrees and advance the intake cam 2 degrees. This resulted in a slight gain in power up to 6,500 rpm, but then a significant loss thereafter. The slight gains experienced below 6,500

rpm did not outweigh the large drop in top-end power. The final test was run to demonstrate the effectiveness of adding ignition timing. Note the power gains offered with 2 degrees of ignition advance (both tests were run with the cams retarded 3 degrees). Note that advancing the ignition timing offered gains up to 6,500 rpm, but the gains diminished thereafter. This is when a programmable computer (like our Hondata) can become useful, as ignition timing can be tailored to achieve gains at every rpm.

Heads, Cams, and Sprockets

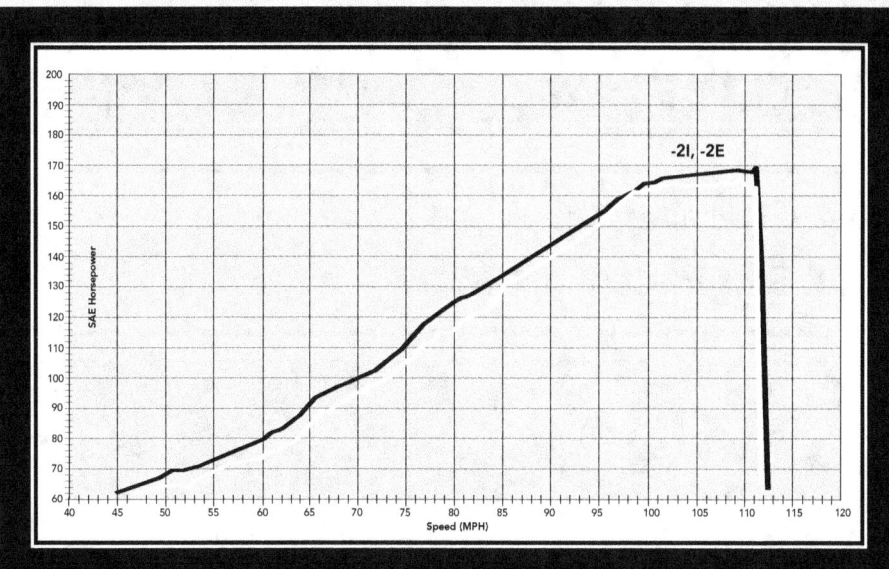

-2 degrees versus -4 degrees

The previous test showed the advantages of working with cam timing on the B16 – this test shows what happens when you go too far with cam timing adjustments.

Peak Horsepower B16A -2I, -2E   167 hp
Peak Horsepower B16A -4I, -4E   164 hp

+2I and -2E: Horsepower

Peak Horsepower -2I, -2E   167 hp
Peak Horsepower +2I, -2E   159 hp

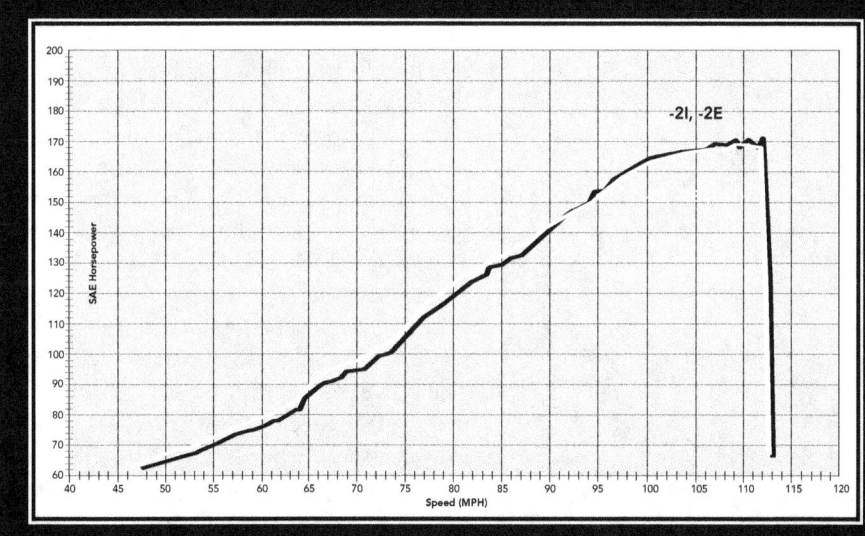

-2I, -2E, +4 degree Ignition Timing: Horsepower

Peak Horsepower -2I, -2E   167 hp
Peak Horsepower -2I, -2E (+4T)   167 hp

How to Build Honda Horsepower

Chapter 3

Test 7: Stock D16Z versus Competition Cams 59300

1994 Civic Del Sol
D16Z 1.6L Single-Cam VTEC

As promised, here is one of the tests for the non B-series motors. Although overshadowed by the twin-cam VTEC motors, the single-cam D16Z can be made to produce exceptional power in normally aspirated form. I have seen single-cam D-series street motors pump out over 140 hp at the wheels without resorting to excessive static compression that would be incompatible with premium-unleaded pump gas. One of the keys to increasing the power output of the D series motor is to install a more aggressive camshaft. When combined with a ported and milled cylinder head, the right header, and cold-air intake, a D16Z can be made to surprise even a B16A-powered Civic Si. By the time this book goes to print, Killer Bee Racing will have a dedicated D16Z intake manifold that should improve the power potential even further.

For this test, we selected a 1994 Del Sol Si equipped with a modified

D16Z single-cam VTEC motor. Unlike the B16A, the D16Z only offers the dual-cam VTEC system on the intake cam. Thus, the exhaust cam timing is fixed.

The test motor featured a milled (but not ported) cylinder head, on a stock short block. The head had been milled .030 to increase the compression without resorting to a piston change. The motor was also equipped with a DC Sports header, no cat, and custom 2.5-inch stainless steel cat-back exhaust. The intake manifold was fitted with an RC Engineering throttle body and RS Akimoto air intake system. The motor was further tuned with an adjustable cam sprocket—important with the milled head. The power output was impressive, as the D16Z produced 118 hp at the wheels with the stock cam. After installing the Comp 59300 cam (214/210 at .050, .440/.400 lift), the peak power increased to 131 hp at the wheels. The power gains required a slight adjustment of the cam sprocket. The peak torque also increased, from 104 ft-lbs to 109 ft-lbs. Except for a slight loss at 3,500 rpm, the Comp Cam improved power across the board.

Heads, Cams, and Sprockets

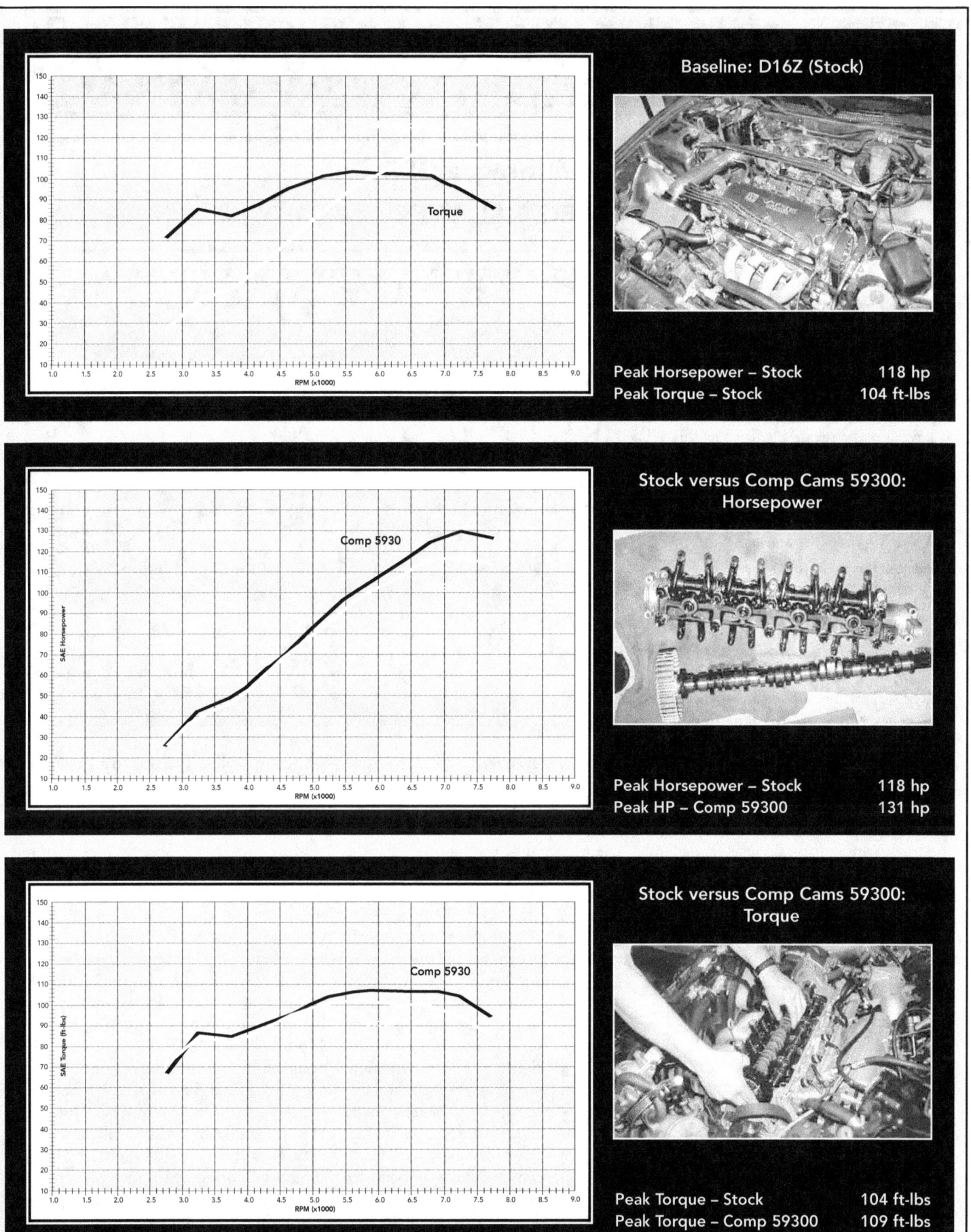

Baseline: D16Z (Stock)

Peak Horsepower – Stock	118 hp
Peak Torque – Stock	104 ft-lbs

Stock versus Comp Cams 59300: Horsepower

Peak Horsepower – Stock	118 hp
Peak HP – Comp 59300	131 hp

Stock versus Comp Cams 59300: Torque

Peak Torque – Stock	104 ft-lbs
Peak Torque – Comp 59300	109 ft-lbs

How to Build Honda Horsepower

Chapter 3

Test 8: Stock B18C (GSR) versus Competition Cams 57200

1996 Integra GSR
B18C 1.8L VTEC

This particular test was performed by Comp Cams and not by the author. The manufacturer provided the dyno results for this book. The power gains demonstrated by the Comp Cams 57200 B-Series combination are impressive to say the least. I have not witnessed gains of this magnitude in my testing, though the B18C GSR motor has never been impressive in stock form. The specs indicate that the GSR cams are slightly better than a B16A (Si); the GSR motors never seem to make the power they should. Some of the problem can be traced to the dual-runner intake. Swapping on the right intake can increase the peak power significantly, but there is usually a tradeoff in power somewhere in the mid range. It is important to note that the Comp grinds offered power gains across the board, not unlike the gains I tested on the D-series, single-cam motor. Credit altering the primary lobe profiles as well as the VTEC cams. It was not uncommon for cam grinders to restrict their efforts to the VTEC lobes, leaving the primary lobes alone. There are good power gains to be had from altering the mild primary cam timing. Of course, a dramatic change can negatively affect the drivability and/or idle quality, but the changes made by Comp cams do not fall into this category.

As expected of changes to duration (more so than lift), the power improvements were most impressive out beyond 7,000 rpm. The testing by Comp indicated that their 57200 cams were worth nearly 20 hp over the stock GSR cams at 7,800 rpm. One important point is worth mentioning here. When swapping in a set of cams, make sure to check the VTEC actuation point, as the new combination may benefit from altering the factory VTEC point. The new secondary cam profiles may want to be activated later in accordance with their longer duration specs. This may work out well if the primary cams are modified as well, as longer duration primary cams will most likely want a later VTEC actuation, as they will be able to provide power to a slightly higher rpm relative to the stock cams. Check out the results of changes to the VTEC activation rpm in the chapter on ECUs. Changes to the VTEC activation point are definitely necessary on cams where only the secondary profiles are changed. Comp Cams also offers several other B-series cam profiles, including their 57100 and 57300. The 57100 cam set is designed as a direct replacement for the B16A, B18C, and even B18C5. The cam is listed as an improved version of the ITR cam, offering additional performance over the Type R cam. The 57300 should be considered a race-only piece and should be combined with head porting, additional compression ratio, and a dedicated high-rpm intake manifold.

Heads, Cams, and Sprockets

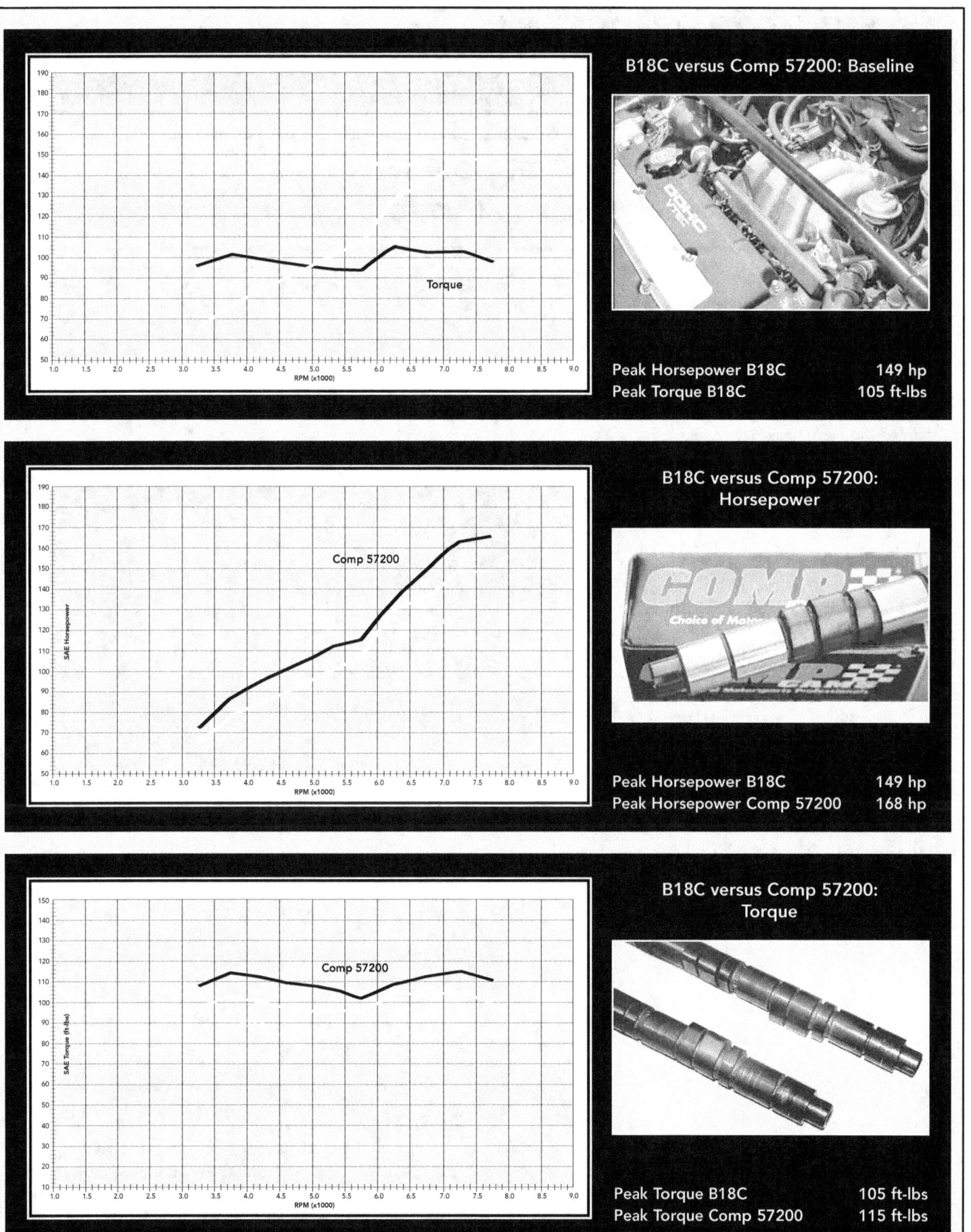

B18C versus Comp 57200: Baseline

Peak Horsepower B18C	149 hp
Peak Torque B18C	105 ft-lbs

B18C versus Comp 57200: Horsepower

Peak Horsepower B18C	149 hp
Peak Horsepower Comp 57200	168 hp

B18C versus Comp 57200: Torque

Peak Torque B18C	105 ft-lbs
Peak Torque Comp 57200	115 ft-lbs

How to Build Honda Horsepower 63

Chapter 3

Test 9: Stock B16A Head versus Extrude-Hone Ported B16A Head

1995 Civic Del Sol
B16A 1.6L VTEC

My original intent was to provide a dedicated chapter for cylinder head modifications, but time and space limited me to just a pair of cylinder head tests. This initial test involved running a modified B16A equipped with an APEXi header originally intended for a Japan-spec Integra Type R, an RS Akimoto air intake, a milled B16A cylinder head, a Killer Bee Racing intake manifold, Holley 68-mm throttle body and stock B16A camshafts. The engine was also equipped with a set of AEM adjustable cam sprockets, a Hondata programmable ECU, and 2.75-inch open exhaust. With some careful tuning via the Hondata, the B16A was able to produce 168 hp at the wheels and 122 ft-lbs of torque. Remember that this reading was taken at the wheels on a DynoJet and not at the flywheel. It is easy to confuse the issue as a B16A is rated at 160 (flywheel) hp. This modified motor was some 30 hp stronger than a stock B16A. Though 168 hp was impressive for the little B16A, the real kicker was exceeding 120 ft-lbs of torque at the wheels.

After running the motor on the chassis dyno, the B16A head was removed and sent to Extrude Hone for porting. The unique porting process utilized hydraulic rams to force abrasive-impregnated media through the intake and exhaust passages to further improve the airflow potential. It is important to note that a B16A head is good right from the factory. I have seen as many ruined heads as I have improved versions when it comes to porting. The Extrude Hone process removes material only where it is needed, maximizing flow with a minimal of material removal. The best head is the one that flows well through the smallest port. This is even more important when installing the ported head on the smaller B16A. After porting, the head was treated to a factory-style valve job and reinstalled on the short block. Some minor fuel tuning was necessary, especially after the onset of the VTEC cams. The power dropped slightly (1–3 hp) from 3,000 rpm to 4,000 rpm, but there were nothing but gains from there on out. The porting improved the power output by as much as 11 hp at 7,500 rpm. The relative gain remained through 8,000 rpm.

Heads, Cams, and Sprockets

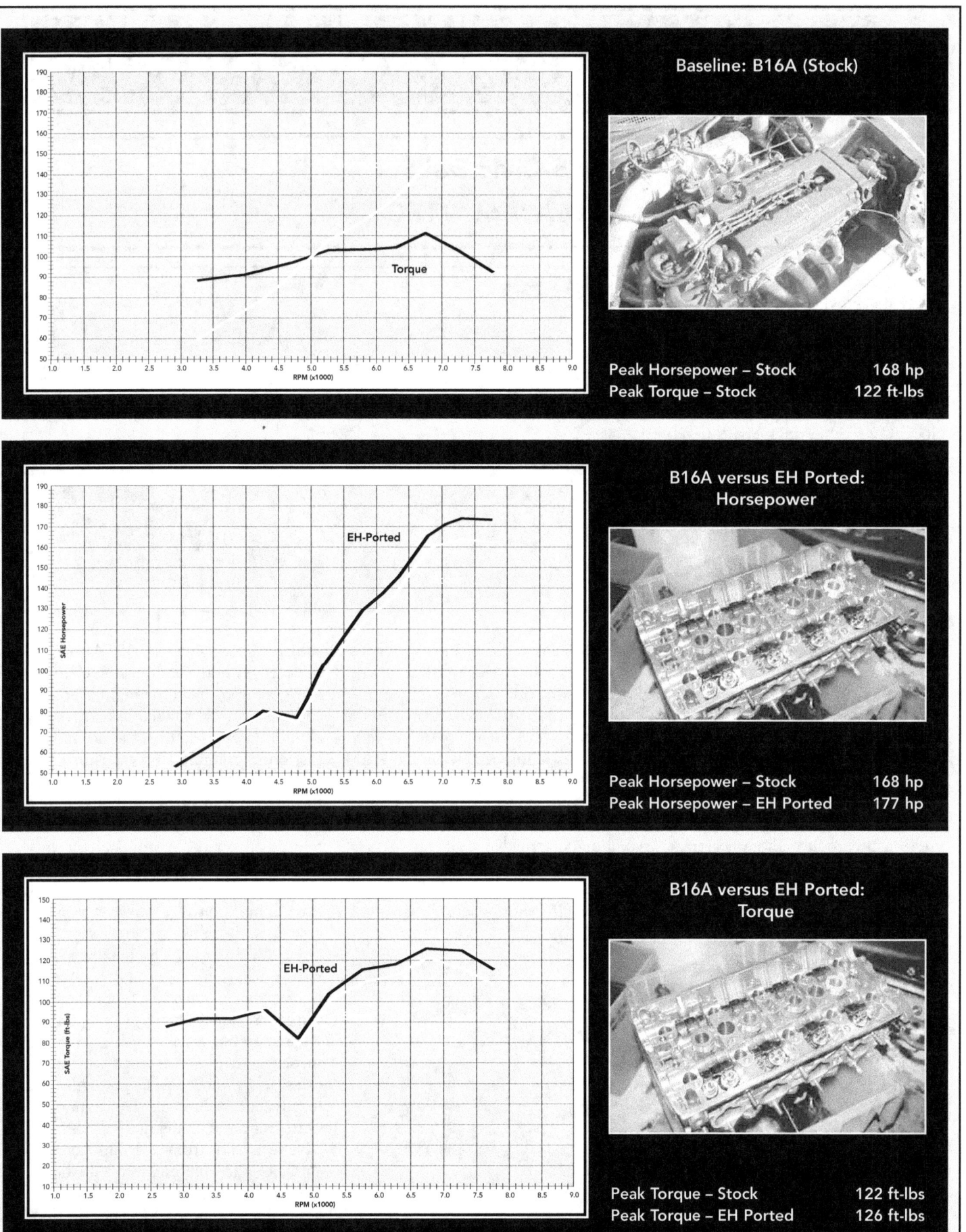

Chapter 3

Test 10: Stock B16A Head versus Milled B16A Head

1995 Civic Del Sol
B16A 1.6L VTEC

The final test for this chapter involved removing the cylinder head for milling. Milling the cylinder head is done for two reasons. The first reason for milling the head is to straighten the deck surface to provide a leak-free seal between the head, head gasket, and block. Only by having parallel (level) surfaces can there be true sealing. The next reason for milling the cylinder head is to increase the static compression ratio. Milling the cylinder head removes material, thus reducing the size of the combustion chamber. The size of the combustion camber is one of the determining factors that dictate static compression ratio. Smaller combustion chambers equal higher compression and higher compression equals more power. The good thing about a change in static compression ratio is that an increase will generally improve power across the board, as the effect is felt throughout the power band. Unlike other changes (cams, intake, and exhaust), a change in compression can produce a healthy average power gain, as opposed to a peak-to-peak gain. What I mean is that it is always better to gain 6 hp from 3,000 rpm to 8,000 rpm, than gain 8 hp at some high-rpm point. Average power is what accelerates the car.

The mild B16A was run on the DynoJet to establish a baseline. The motor was equipped with an AEM shorty intake system, a stock throttle body, intake, and cylinder head and a DC Sports tri-Y header. This mild combination yielded peak numbers of 146 hp and 110 ft-lbs of torque. The head was then removed and sent to a local machine shop where the deck was subjected to a cut of .035. All of the sharp edges in the combustion chamber were removed from the milling process and great care was taken to remove any aluminum chips left by the machining. Just one aluminum chip can ruin a perfectly good motor; take care to clean the motor thoroughly if you plan to have your head milled. The head was reinstalled on the motor and the new combination responded with 152 hp and 113 ft-lbs of torque. As expected, the milling improved power across the board, with gains of 9 ft-lbs present down at 3,500 rpm. Though tested on a B16A, head milling can be done to nearly any Honda/Acura motor with similar results. Our power numbers were achieved after adjusting the cam sprockets. Milling the head retards the cams, so (in most cases), you will need to advance both cams a like amount. Ours required 2 degrees, though we have seen gains from retarding the cams as well. The combination will dictate the ideal cam timing, but milling the head is definitely worth some additional power.

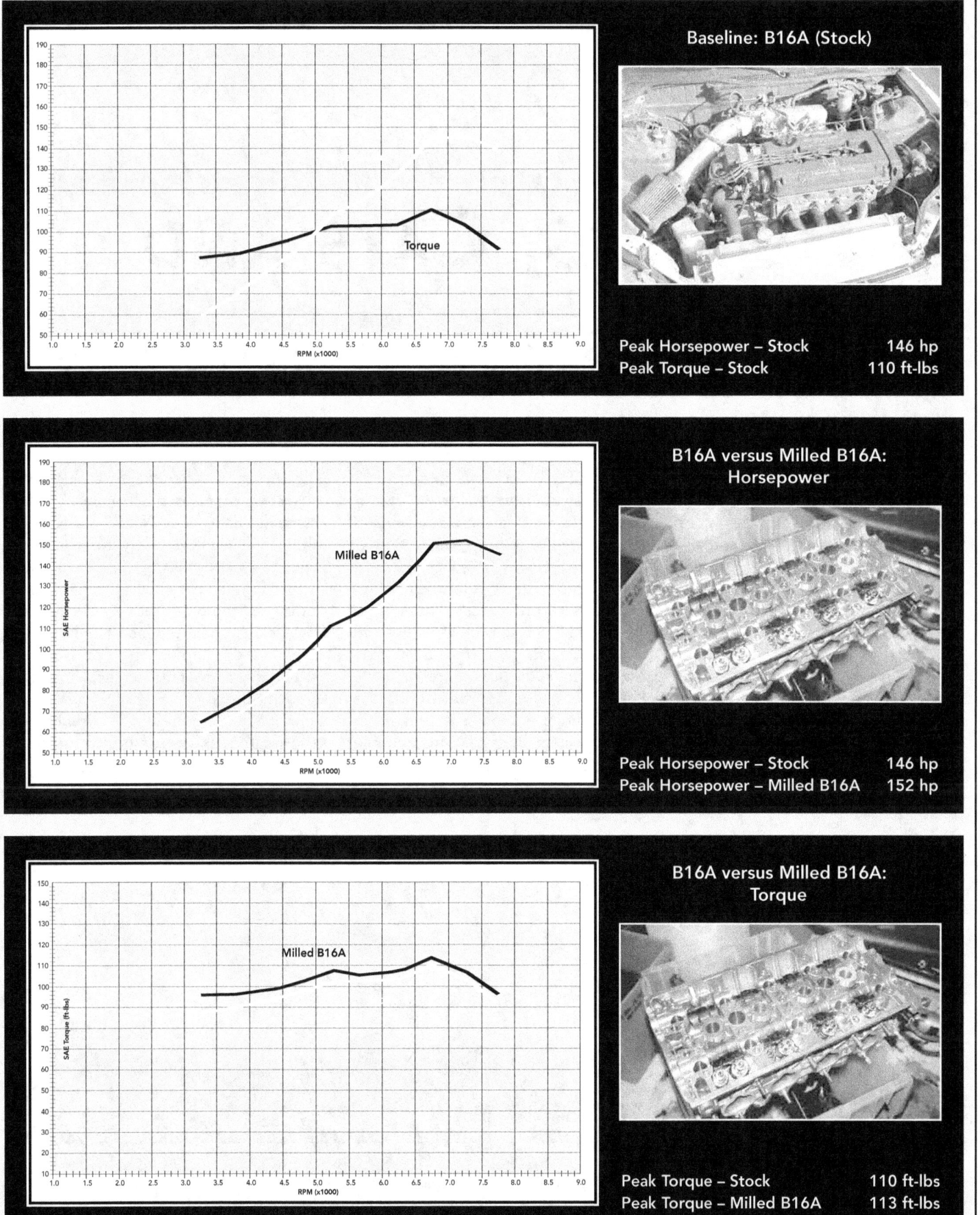

CHAPTER 4

HEADERS, CATS AND PERFORMANCE EXHAUSTS

Since the power output of a motor is determined by the airflow into and out of a motor, it seems only natural to make every effort to improve exhaust flow. While more airflow is good, mistakes are often made in the name of maximizing airflow. The problem with "maximum" air (exhaust) flow is that both our theory (more air in-more power out) and measuring device (airflow bench) are based on static flow rates. Take a stock exhaust for instance. If we install and test an exhaust system on an airflow bench, we find that the exhaust system will flow a certain amount of air at a given pressure drop. If we wanted to improve the airflow of the exhaust, we could simply make the tubing larger. Larger tubing will allow air to pass through easier. Though the larger tubing will improve the flow rate of the exhaust, will the added flow result in any additional power?

Here is where the problems generally come in. If a Honda is running an exhaust system built of 2-inch tubing, will the motor benefit from a new exhaust that measures 2.25-inches? The answer is: it depends. While the larger tubing will most certainly flow better than the smaller tubing, the additional airflow is only potential airflow when run on the motor. If the stock exhaust flows 300 cfm and the motor only produces enough power to require an exhaust that flows 275 cfm, then chances are that the larger (2.25-inch) exhaust will not add any additional power. Even this situation is oversimplified, as we

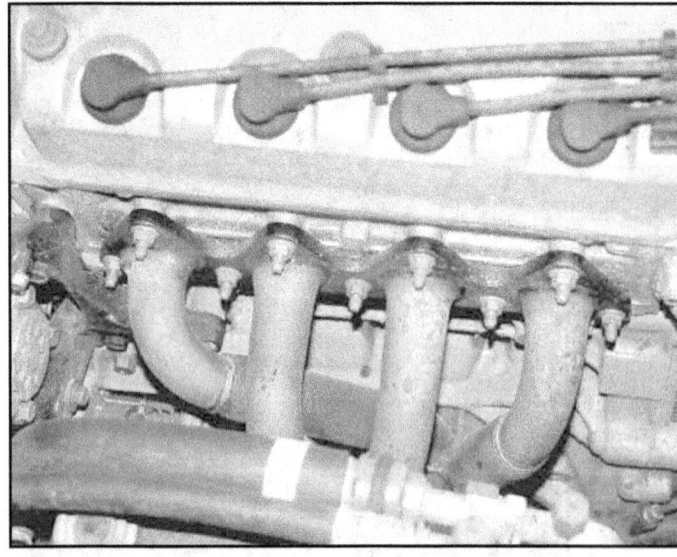

When choosing a header for your Honda/Acura engine, take my advice and go with stainless or at least something coated. Painted headers are nothing but trouble.

This header from Comptech featured stainless steel construction and machine-quality, precision welds.

Headers, Cats, and Performance Exhausts

have resorted to simple (static) airflow numbers. For a performance product to improve the power output of a motor it must not simply offer superior airflow characteristics to the component it is replacing, it must also improve the airflow through the motor. Simply because one exhaust flows more air (when measured on an airflow bench) means nothing if that exhaust will not improve the airflow through the motor. Every motor has an ideal size exhaust for a given application and/or rpm range. Finding the right one can be a matter of testing (or reading the right book on dyno testing!). Even then, the "right" aftermarket exhaust may still be a compromise and offer less power at some engine speeds and more power at others.

The point made about improving airflow through the motor is an important one to remember. Though important when discussing exhaust systems, it is downright critical when covering headers. While a traditional header may indeed offer greater total airflow compared to a stock (cast iron) exhaust manifold, the real trick to improved performance goes way beyond simply flow numbers. A header is much more than a series of interconnected tubes designed to allow the exhaust to escape from the combustion chambers. The tubing diameter, primary and secondary length, and even collector design all play an important role in exhaust flow. Unlike a simple tube, the header pipes act like suction devices to help improve the flow rates of adjoining pipes. As the air speeds through one primary tube, it creates a vacuum in an adjoining tube. This vacuum improves the breathing of the adjoining tube by scavenging (sucking) the exhaust flow.

This scavenging effect will happen at a given rpm range dictated by the engine components (intake length, cam timing, and head flow) as well as by the header design. A well-designed header can have a dramatic effect on the power curve of a motor. Honda recognizes this and their exhaust manifolds (unlike their domestic counterparts) are good right from the factory. It takes a good header to improve upon a factory Honda exhaust manifold.

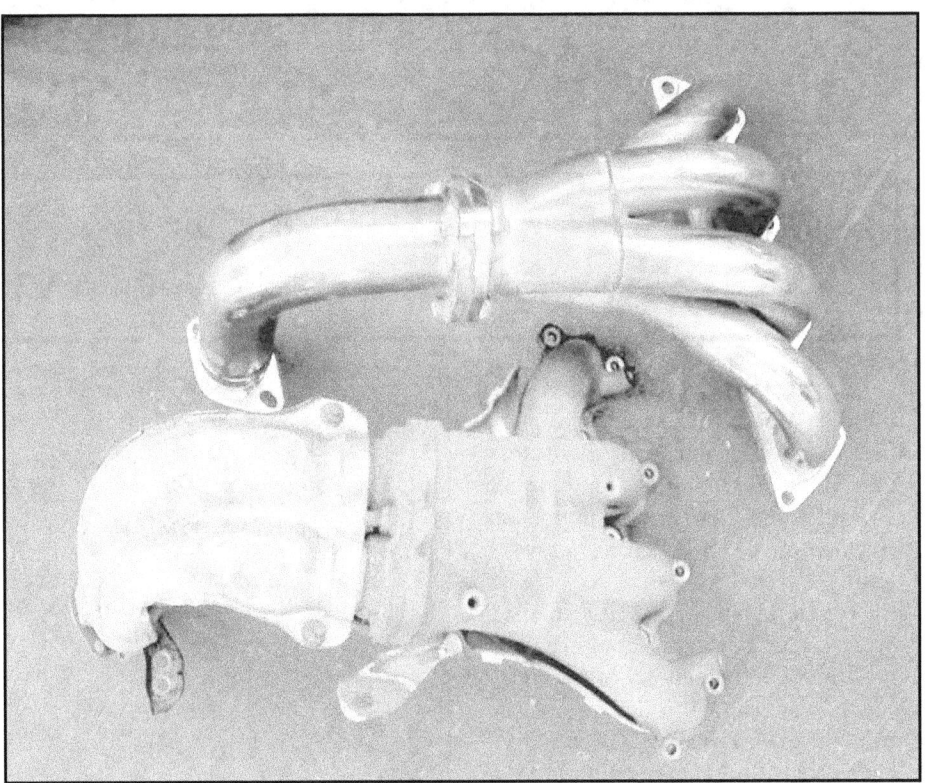

Though the stock B16A exhaust manifold is quite good compared to a typical American V8, there is power to be had with the right header.

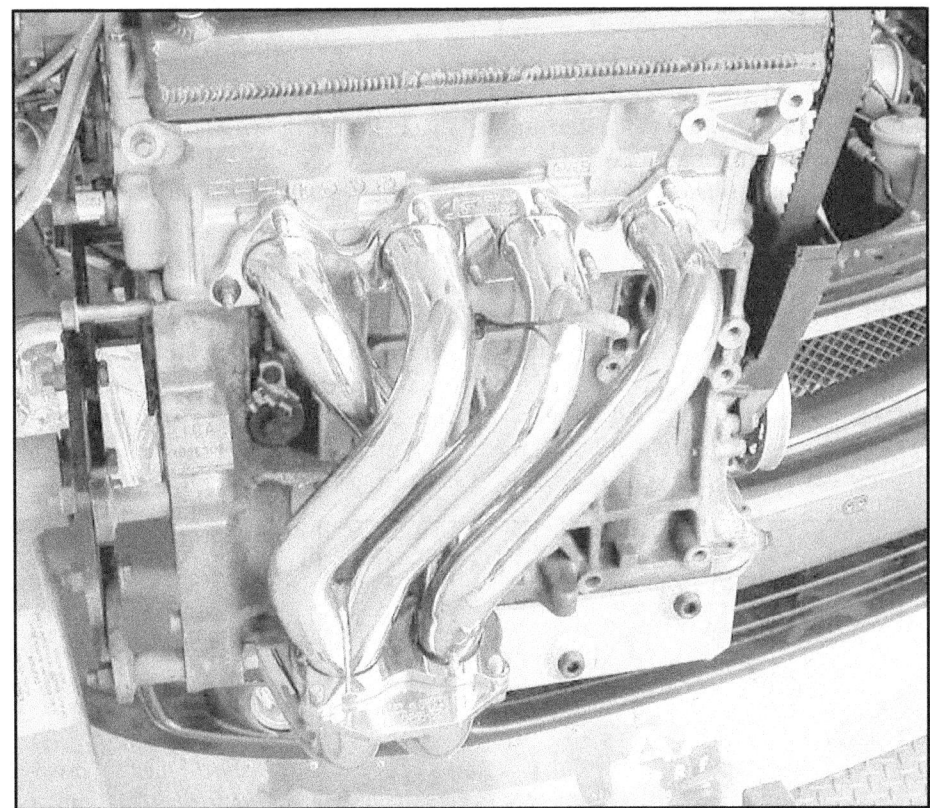

Though entering late in the game, Edelbrock stepped up with one of the best headers available for the B-series Honda. They even offer a racing B-pipe.

How to Build Honda Horsepower

Chapter 4

Test 1: MagnaFlow Cat-Back Exhaust and Chikara Header

1998 Civic EX
D16Z 1.6L Single-Cam VTEC

In previous chapters, we have run dyno comparisons between a single performance product and the factory unit as well as comparisons between two different aftermarket components (Iceman versus Hosetech air intake for example). This was done to simplify the results and make them easy to read. Space limitations in this book have significantly cut the number of tests originally planned. In order to include some of the additional dyno testing, I have decided to include multiple components in a single test where applicable. The exhaust chapter provides the opportunity to include two different systems in a single test (individual results are given for reach component). As the exhaust chapter covers the header, catalytic converter, and cat-back exhaust, we can squeeze one, two, or three of them into the pages designed for a single component test. In doing so, the reader benefits from the additional information.

This pair of tests was run on a 1.6L Civic EX equipped with a single-cam 1.6L VTEC motor. In stock trim, the D16Z motor is rated at 127 hp (varies slightly by year) and will usually generate between 105–110 hp at the wheels as measured on a DynoJet. This

particular test motor posted an impressive 111 hp at the wheels when equipped with a K&N drop-in filter and that power level was upped by the installation of a K&N air intake system. Equipped with the air intake system, the EX motor posted peak power numbers of 116 hp. The first exhaust performance upgrade was the MagnaFlow cat-back exhaust system. The system consisted of 2.25-inch mandrel-bent, stainless steel tubing and a 4-inch stainless muffler. The exhaust managed to improve peak power number by a couple, but only at the very top of the rev range. The results are a strong indication that the factory Civic EX exhaust was simply not overly restrictive at this power level.

The next power upgrade was the Chikara header from Hedman. Designed as a bolt-on replacement for the factory exhaust manifold and down pipe, the Chikara header offered larger-diameter tubing to maximize exhaust flow. This trick header also featured stepped (expanding size) tubing to further improve flow. The stepped tubing works kind of like an expansion tube on a 2-stroke motor. The small diameter tubing is used to keep velocity up, while the larger tube allows the gas to expand, further increasing velocity. Obviously, all of this trick expansion happens at a certain engine speed and the placement and sizing of the tubing is critical to exhaust tuning. The Chikara header offered more power improvements than the cat-back exhaust, with gains available from 5,500 rpm up to 7,000 rpm. Neither component lost power compared to the stock system, which was a plus. Often a performance upgrade will result in a trade-off, where a loss of power down low is traded for additional power up top. The mild power gains offered by the MagnaFlow and Chikara cost nothing elsewhere in the power band.

Headers, Cats, and Performance Exhausts

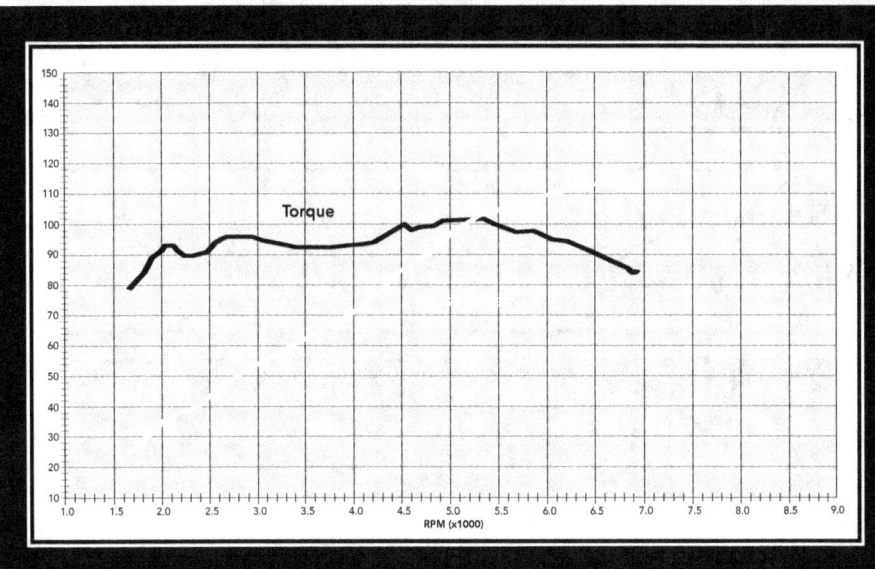

Baseline: D16Z (Stock with K&N Filter)

Peak Horsepower – Stock	113.2 hp
Peak Torque – Stock	102.3 ft-lbs

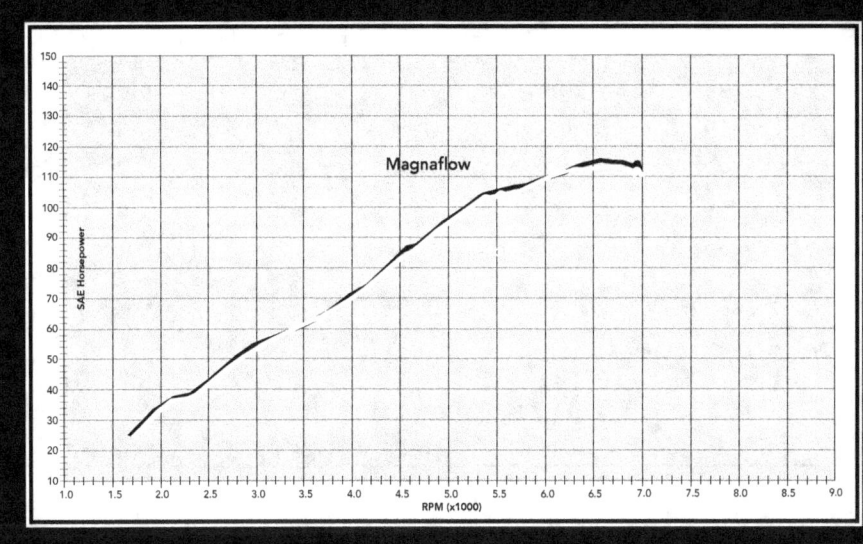

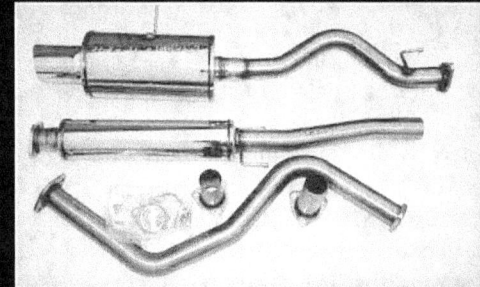

MagnaFlow Cat-Back Exhaust: Horsepower

Peak Horsepower – Stock	113.2 hp
Peak Horsepower – MagnaFlow	115.7 hp
Largest Horsepower Gain	2.6 hp

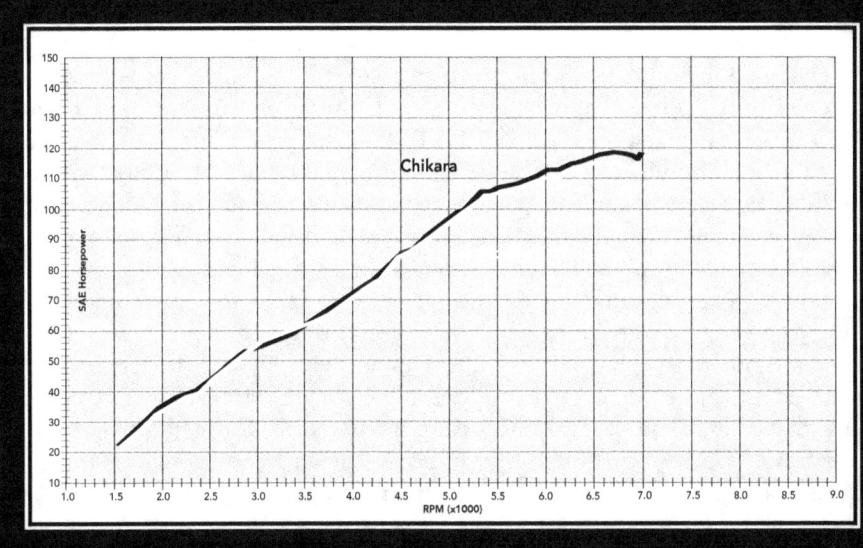

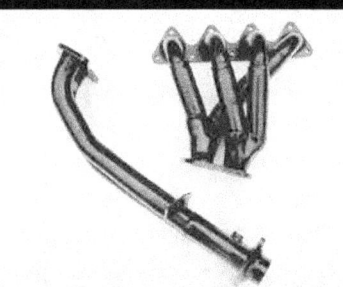

Chikara Header: Horsepower

Peak Horsepower – Stock	115.7 hp
Peak Horsepower – Chikara	118.1 hp
Largest Horsepower Gain	2.7 hp

How to Build Honda Horsepower

Chapter 4

Test 2: Stock Exhaust Manifold versus APEXi Civic and Integra Type R Headers

1995 Civic Del Sol
B16A 1.6L VTEC

Although the Civic Si grabs all the B16A attention, old-schoolers will remember that the B16A was offered in the Civic Del Sol way back in 1995. The factory offerings don't even take into account the number of Honda and Acuras out there running around with B16A swaps. With the prevalence of twin cam-powered Hondas out there, it is only natural that there be a whole slew of headers offered for the little wonder motor. Combine the B16A (Civic Si and Del Sol) offerings with those for the Acura B18-series motors (which also fit the smaller B16A) and you have a wide variety of headers to choose from. This test centered on a comparison between the stock exhaust manifold and down pipe and a B16A header from APEXi. We specify that the header tested here be for a B16A as we ran another test on this same motor equipped with a header designed for a Japanese-spec Integra Type R.

Given that the factory twin-cam exhaust manifolds flow very well and are nicely matched (tuned) for the power characteristics of the stock B16A motor, we were surprised by the power gains offered by the APEXi header. This particular header was originally designed to fit the Japanese-spec 185-hp Civic Type R

application. Given the high-rpm nature of the Civic Type R application, we were also surprised to see the significant power gains offered down low. Power gains were expected above the VTEC operation point, and we did not expect the additional power below the onset of VTEC. Obviously, the APEXi gang really did their homework on this particular header design, as it worked exceptionally well on an application it was originally intended for. Credit tube diameter, merge position and collector length for the big power gains. It should also be noted that the APEXi header offered first-rate build quality, something that cannot be said of the bargain brands.

Next up was a larger header offered by APEXi for the Japanese-spec 1.8L Integra Type R. The Integra header featured larger primary tubing, larger and longer secondary tubing, and a larger collector. We suspected that the larger header might be too big for the small 1.6L motor; the application might benefit from the additional exhaust flow. As this motor was currently residing in the USTCC road race Civic Del Sol, the high-rpm nature of the motor meant that we were essentially unconcerned about pre-VTEC power. We were more than willing to trade top-end power for a loss in low speed torque—something that should not be done on a streetcar! As it turned out, the larger header designed for the Integra offered the same power throughout the curve but bolstered the top-end enough to justify swapping the headers. The APEXi header was used to help the author win the USTCC championship in 2000.

How to Build Honda Horsepower

Headers, Cats, and Performance Exhausts

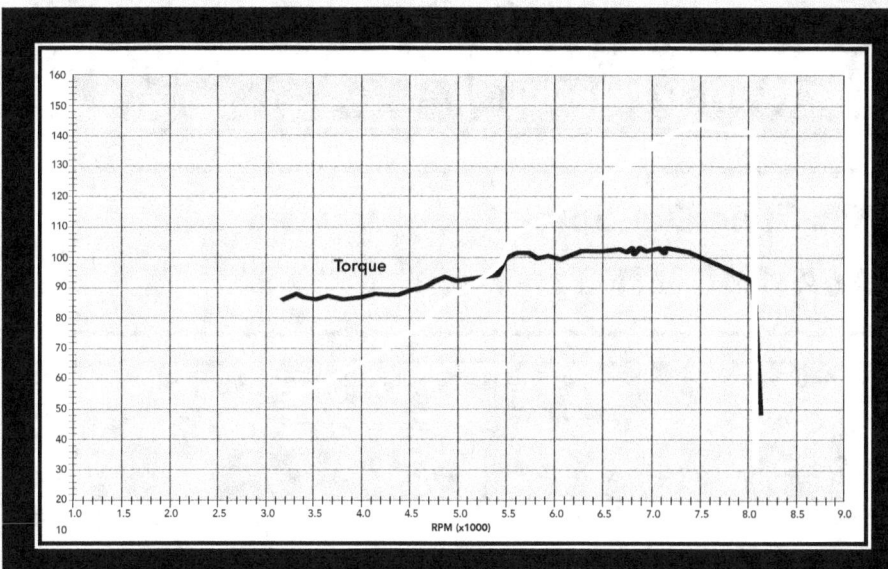

Baseline: B16A (Stock)

Honda did a pretty good job on the B-series VTEC exhaust manifolds. They look for all the world like a cast-iron tri-Y header, but power gains are available by replacing it with the right tubular header.

Peak Horsepower – Stock	144.6 hp
Peak Torque – Stock	104.3 ft-lbs

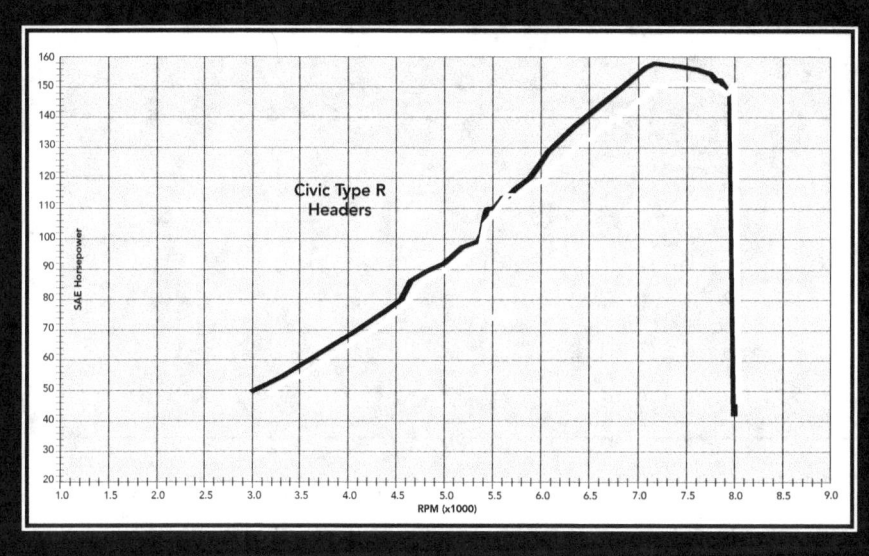

APEXi Civic Type R Header: Horsepower

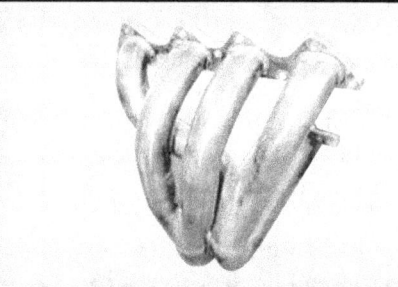

Peak HP – Stock	144.6 hp
Peak HP – Civic Type R header	150.1 hp
Largest Horsepower Gain	9.0 hp

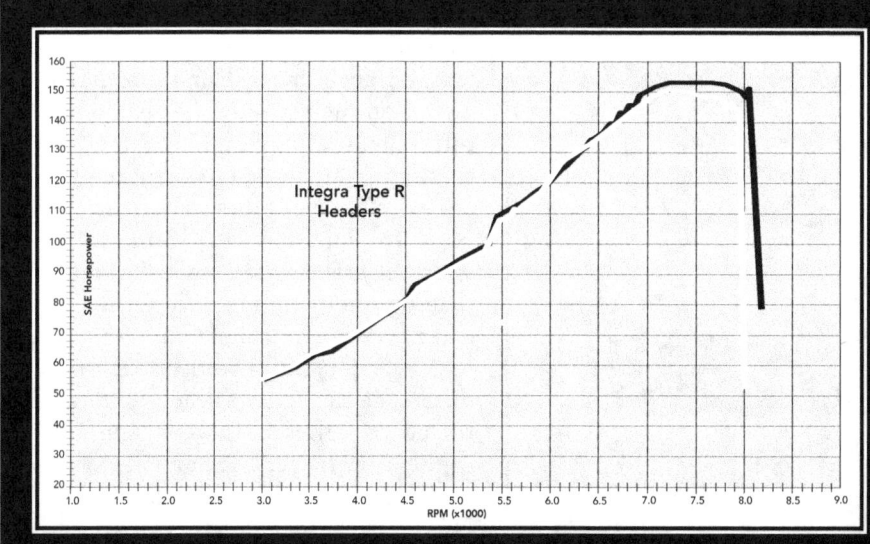

APEXi JDM Integra Type R Headers: Horsepower

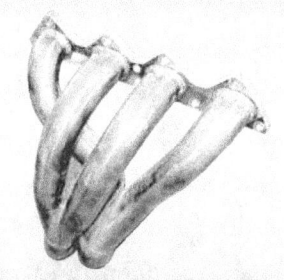

Peak HP – Stock	150.1 hp
Peak HP – Integra Type R Header	152.9 hp
Largest Horsepower Gain	7.4 hp

How to Build Honda Horsepower

Chapter 4

Test 3: DC Sports 4-1 Header versus DC Sports Tri-Y Header

1995 Civic Del Sol
B16A 1.6L VTEC

DC Sports has been in the sport compact car business for some time now and they have made a name for themselves with their line of quality performance products. Their headers are one such product. While we did not test either the 4-1 or Tri-Y header design versus the stock exhaust manifold system on the B16A, rest assured that either system offers plenty of power over the stock stuff. Instead of comparing the DC Sport headers to the stock stuff, we decided to compare the two header styles on the same motor. This was done to squash the rumor that the header styles offer power at different engine speeds. The current (street) theory is that the Tri-Y header design offers better low-end torque while the 4-1 promotes top-end horsepower. What better way to demonstrate the various merits of the two header designs than to test them on the same motor on the same day?

As expected, both DC headers offered good power, but the surprising thing was that neither demonstrated a significant advantage over the other. As indicated by the two power curves, the B16A used for testing seemed to favor the 4-1 header. The 4-1 offered superior low-speed power, much better midrange and a hair more horsepower on the big end. The peak power differences are minimal, something that can be attributed to slight temperature differences (every effort was made to make the runs identical, but small differences may still exist) rather than design or tuning differences. The extra power available from 4,500 rpm to 5,500 rpm can be attributed to the difference in the two header styles, as the power differences were significant in this rpm range. Given a street driven B16A (Civic Si or Del Sol), either DC Sport header design would serve you well.

Headers, Cats, and Performance Exhausts

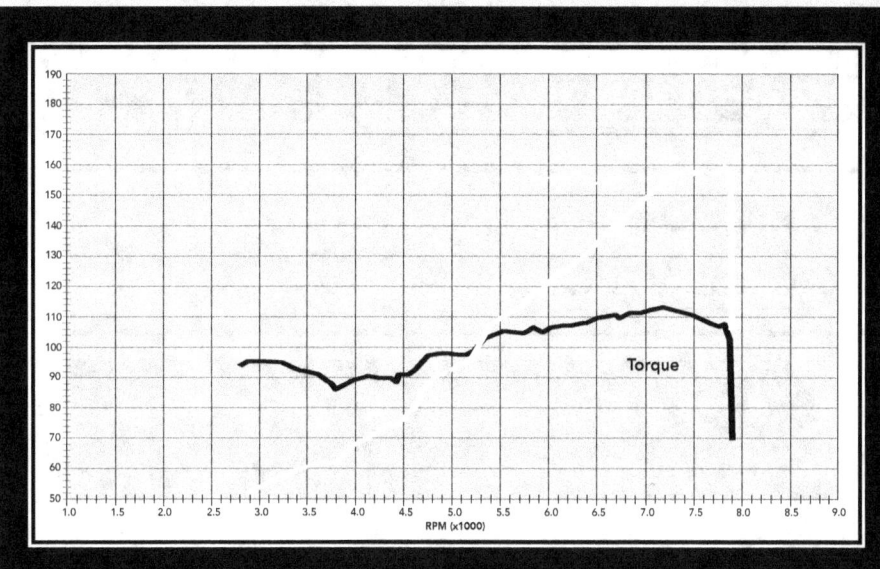

Baseline: DC Sports 4-1 Header

This test demonstrated that there really wasn't a significant difference in power between the DC Sport Tri-Y and 4-into-1 header designs. Either would make a welcome addition to your B16A.

Peak Horsepower – 4-1   157.6 hp
Peak Torque – 4-1   112.1 ft-lbs

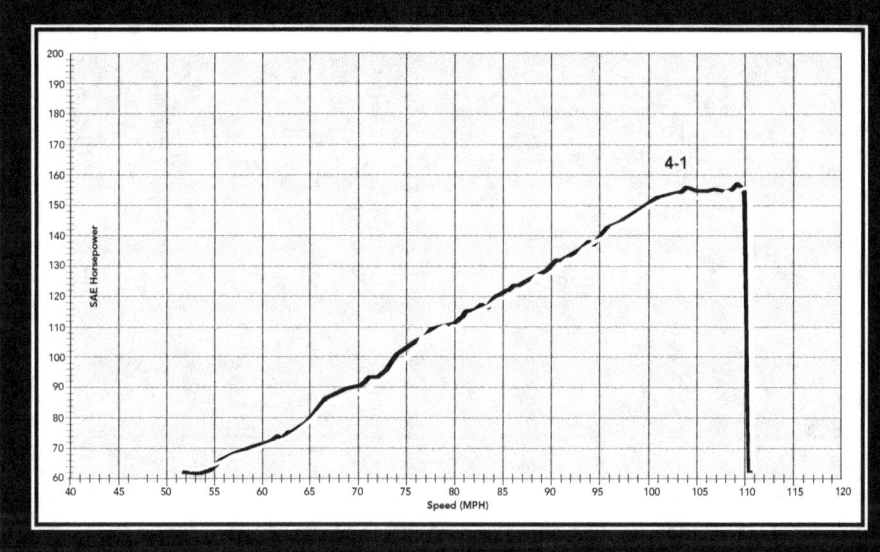

4-1 versus Tri-Y Header: Horsepower

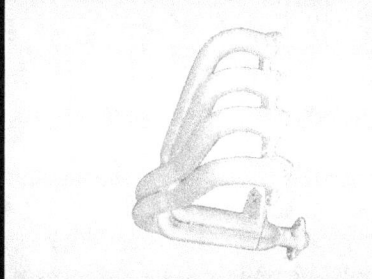

Peak Horsepower – 4-1   157.6 hp
Peak Horsepower – Tri-Y   156.0 hp
Largest Horsepower Difference   2.9 hp

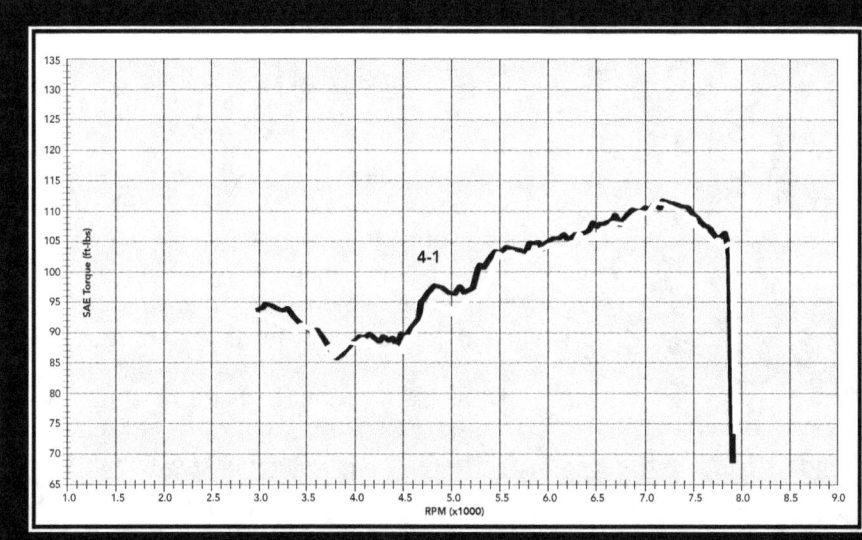

4-1 versus Tri-Y Header: Torque

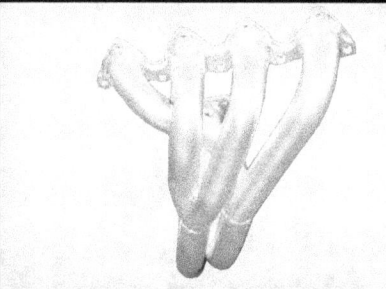

Peak Torque – 4-1   112.1 ft-lbs
Peak Torque – Tri-Y   111.6 ft-lbs
Largest Torque Difference   4.3 ft-lbs

How to Build Honda Horsepower

Chapter 4

Test 4: DC Sports 4-1 Header versus Kamakazi 4-1 Header

1995 Civic Del Sol
B16A 1.6L VTEC

After running the comparison between the two DC Sports header styles, we ran yet another header comparison. This time, we compared two different 4-1 headers. The DC Sports 4-1 header was compared to the Kamakazi 4-1 header. Although the two headers were both 4-1 designs, the net result of the finished headers was quite different. The DC Sports 4-1 header offered much longer primary runners before the tubes merged into the single collector. Unlike the DC Sport header, the unit from Kamakazi offered primary tubing that was both larger in diameter and much shorter before the merge. Having had excellent luck with this style header on a supercharged 1.6L single-cam VTEC motor, I was anxious to see how the design would fair on the twin-cam B16A motor.

Given the large difference in the header designs, we expected to see a significant difference in power production. We were not disappointed, as the two headers offered significantly different power curves. With the large, short primaries of the Kamakazi, we expected to see a loss in low-speed power but possibly offset by a sizeable power gain near the top of the rpm range. This was the case on the supercharged single-cam EX motor, but not so on this B16A. The VTEC motor did not like the Kamakazi header one bit and power suffered nearly everywhere. The power dropped off significantly after the operation of the VTEC and never managed to catch back up. Concerned by the dramatic drop in power (suspecting something was amiss) we elected to run a number of backup runs with identical results. We even went so far as to reinstall the DC header and were rewarded with our lost power. The B16A obviously did not like the short, large diameter runners in the Kamakazi header.

Headers, Cats, and Performance Exhausts

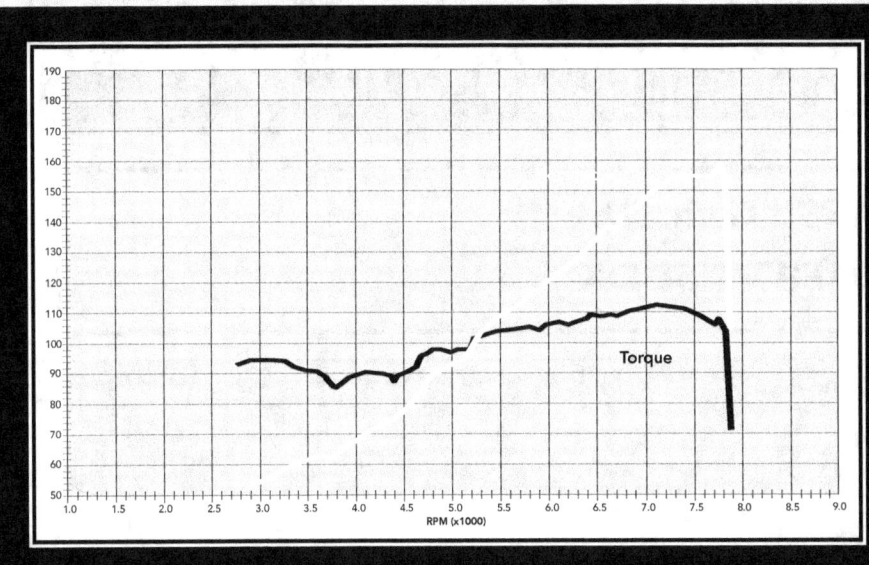

Baseline: DC Sports 4-1 Header

We have seen the Kamakazi short-primary header work well on a supercharged motor, but this B16A responded best to the longer primaries in the DC Sports header.

Peak Horsepower – DC 4-1   157.6 hp
Peak Torque – DC 4-1   112.1 ft-lbs

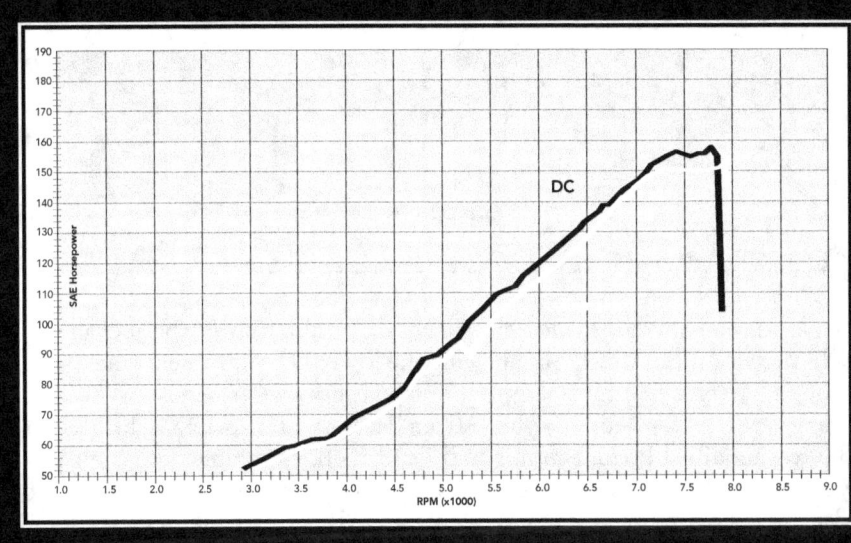

DC versus Kamakazi 4-1 Header: Horsepower

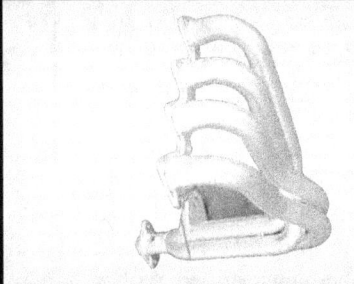

Peak Horsepower – DC   157.6 hp
Peak Horsepower – Kamakazi   152.2 hp
Largest Horsepower Gain   11.6 hp

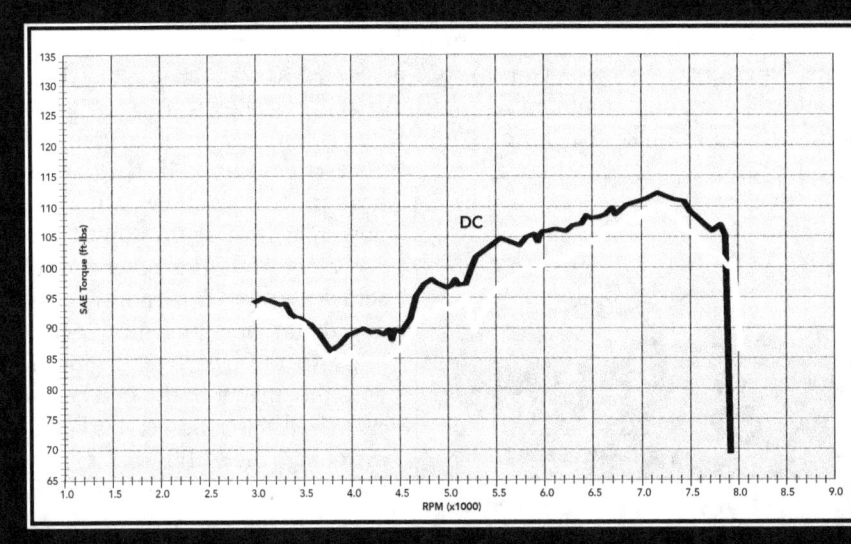

DC versus Kamakazi 4-1 Header: Torque

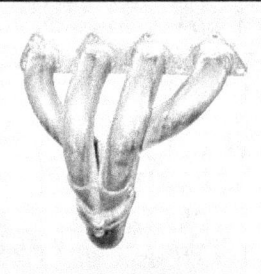

Peak Torque – DC   112.1 ft-lbs
Peak Torque – Kamakazi   110.0 ft-lbs
Largest Torque Gain   11.5 ft-lbs

How to Build Honda Horsepower

Chapter 4

Test 5: Stock versus Greddy Cat-Back Exhaust and Pacesetter Header

1995 Civic DX
D15B7 1.5L DX

Though the pages of this book are filled with dyno comparisons of the more exotic B16A, B18C, and H22 twin-cam motors, we have also included a number of tests on the more mundane single-cam (non VTEC) DX motors. The reason to include these more pedestrian brothers is that they are very prevalent on the streets. The DX Civics of the world deserve every bit as much coverage as the B-series monsters, as they easily out-number the Sis and related swap cars. Besides, regardless of what we have, we always want to make it faster, right?

This particular test was run on a 1995 Civic DX equipped with a 1.5L, single-cam, non VTEC mill that offered a whopping 94 hp at the wheels after being equipped with a Toucan air intake (see air intake chapter for test results). The test piece was a cat-back exhaust system provided by the folks at Greddy. The Greddy cat-back exhaust offered an increase in tubing diameter from less than 2 inches to nearly 2.25 inches, with additional exhaust flow to match. Given the rather mild power level of the DX motor, we did not expect much power from the cat-back. We were pleasantly surprised (why we do the testing in the first place) to see gains of as much as 6 hp. Even more impressive was the fact that the new Greddy exhaust offered power gains way down at 1,500 rpm and in fact, offered additional power throughout the power band.

The dyno indicated the exhaust to be worth a size-

able power gain, and the added power could really be felt on the street. Six hp may not sound like much, but it is a significant gain on a DX motor. If you added 6 hp to a modified Prelude motor that already pumped out 200 hp at the wheels, you might be hard pressed to feel it. Adding 6 hp to a 94-hp motor (at the wheels) makes for a noticeable difference. In addition to the power, the Greddy exhaust offered a pleasing exhaust note. Not too raspy or arrest-me loud, just more throaty and confidence inspiring. Something to make that Ford Focus driver think twice about challenging the lowly DX in the next lane!

Next up was a series of headers from Pacesetter for the DX. The headers differed in their tubing size, both primary and secondary. The headers also differed in the fact that the smaller of the two was thermal barrier coated while the larger header was simply painted. During our testing, the paint quickly turned into a cloud of smoke after start up. The coated header seemed to retain its finish and has shown no wear after numerous street miles. The gang at Pacesetter expected the larger header to produce superior power, at least at the top of the rev range, but the reverse was actually true. The motor produced not only the most peak, but also the best overall power with the smaller of the two headers. Credit the power curve to matching the tubing size and length with the flow requirements of the motor. Sometimes bigger simply isn't better.

Headers, Cats, and Performance Exhausts

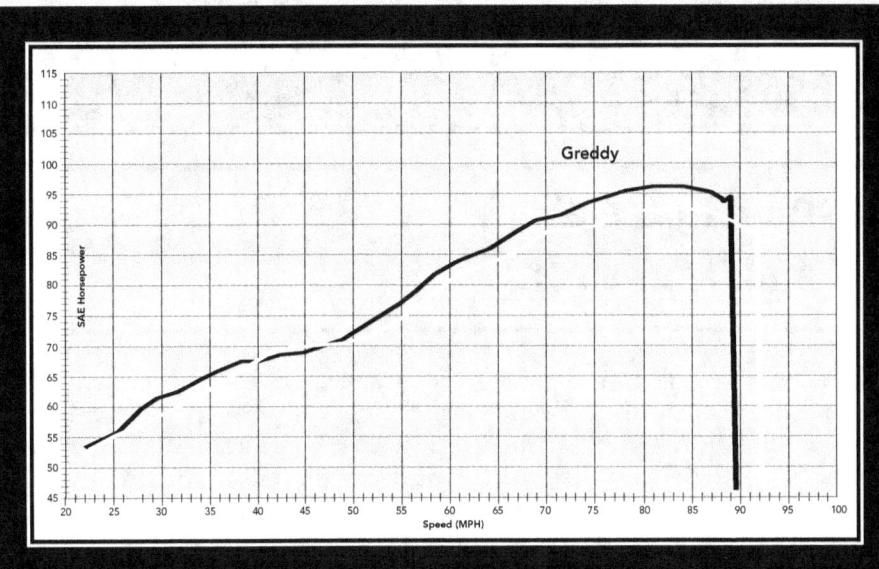

Greddy Cat-Back Exhaust: Horsepower

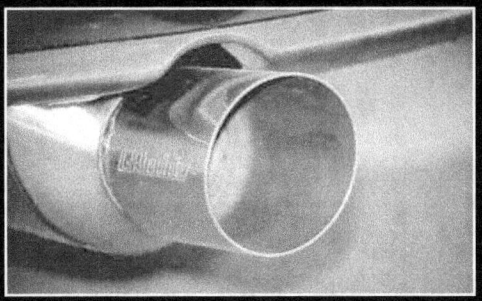

Peak Horsepower – Stock	96.5 hp
Peak Horsepower – Greddy	102.0 hp
Largest Horsepower Gain	6.7 hp

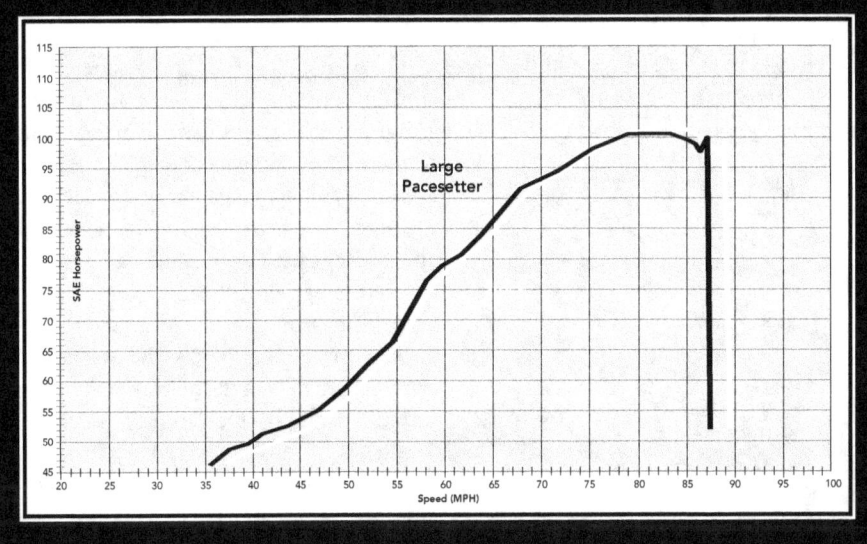

Pacesetter (Large) Header: Horsepower

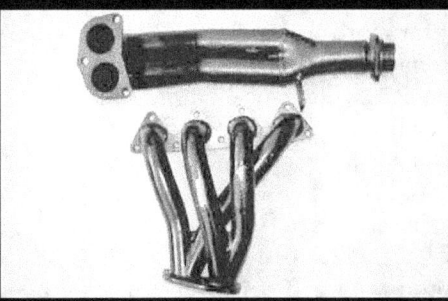

Peak HP – Stock	102.0 hp
Peak HP – Large Pacesetter	100.9 hp
Largest Horsepower Gain	2.3 hp

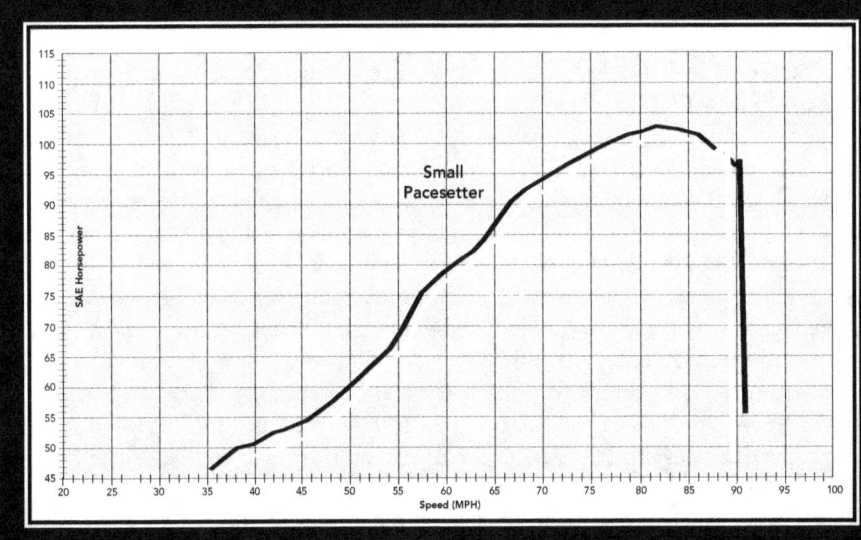

Pacesetter (Small) Header: Horsepower

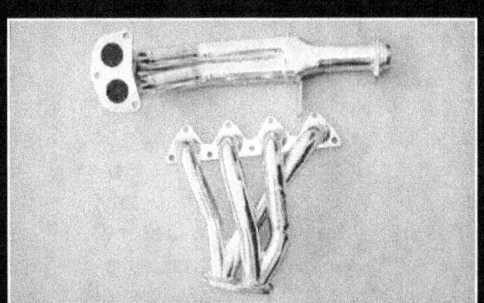

Peak HP – Stock	102.0 hp
Peak HP – Small Pacesetter	103.5 hp
Largest Horsepower Gain	3.8 hp

How to Build Honda Horsepower

Chapter 4

Test 6: Thermal Cat-Back Exhaust, Chikara Header, and Removed Cat

1990 Integra GS
B18A 1.8L Non-VTEC

With the popularity of the Acura Integra 1.8L "LS" motors for Civic engine swaps, it seems odd to find a dyno test that actually finds the engine at home in the bay of an older Integra. One of the author's many personal Honda/Acura machines, the 1990 Integra was originally purchased as a shop vehicle to fetch parts. Given the 1.8L motor, it was only a matter of time before the itch overcame me and I started to modify the motor in a quest for more power. After all, what self-respecting shop car could roll up to a light with a stock motor? As it turned out, the Integra GS was used for a great many dyno tests for this book, as well as numerous magazine articles.

The 1990 Integra came equipped with a B18A 1.8L twin-cam (non VTEC) motor. The venerable LS motor (a name used to describe the motor; all model Integras came with the same 1.8L) offered twin-cam performance but lacked the top-end charge of the VTEC boys. Due to its availability, affordability, and impressive torque curve (especially compared to the smaller 1.6L Civic motors where it usually found a swap home), the 1.8L motor became very popular. Civics that did not receive a B16A (B18C or H22 or 23 variant) usually received the B18A LS motor between the fenderwells. Compared to the 1.6L family, the B18A offered superior torque, especially down low. The added displacement of the 1,834 cc motor upped the power output of all the 1.6L motors with the exception of the twin cam B16A. Even still, it took a good running B16A to keep up with the torquey B18A.

This test was designed to test the effectiveness of an aftermarket exhaust system on a 1.8L B18A. We chose the Thermal stainless steel system designed for the 1990 Integra. The early Integra exhaust utilized the muffler as a cross over point. The exhaust ran down the passenger side then wound up exiting the tip located on the driver's side. The muffler on the Thermal (and stock) exhaust was oriented side to side. The all-stainless Thermal exhaust featured 2.25-inch mandrel-bent tubing, a 4-inch resonator, and

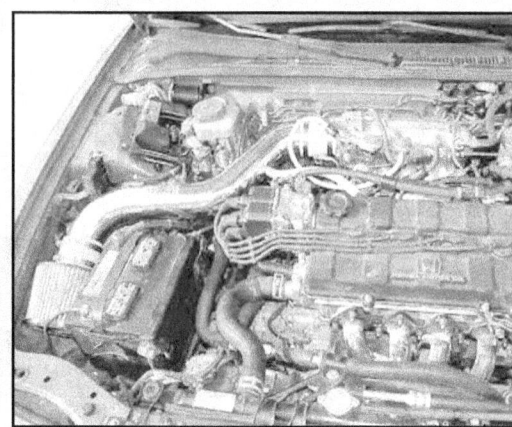

6-inch (oval) muffler. The exhaust also came with the requisite 4-inch tip letting the entire world know that your ride was sporting the Thermal performance piece. If they got close enough, they could easily read the Thermal name stamped on the stainless steel tip.

The factory 1.8L exhaust was obviously somewhat restrictive, as the Thermal exhaust increased the power output across the board. The peak gain was 4–5 hp with a like amount of torque occurring down near 2,500 rpm. The Thermal exhaust offered gains from 2,000 rpm to 3,500 rpm, at which point the stock exhaust matched the power output of the Thermal. Around 3,750 rpm, the Thermal once again demonstrated its superiority by improving the power output all the way to redline. The power gains from the exhaust upgrade were noticeable from behind the wheel, to say nothing of the cool exhaust note.

Since we had such good luck with the Thermal exhaust on the 1.8L Integra, we decided to continue the exhaust modifications. After the Thermal exhaust, we elected to install a Chikara header and then follow up the header installation by removing the catalytic converter. The Chikara header was a 2-piece Tri-Y design, which made it much easier to install in the tight engine confines of the Integra. The Chikara header offered stepped tubing to maximize flow. The one complaint we have about the Chikara was the use of a painted finish (the headers are available coated—which we highly recommend). Upon start up, the Chikara header filled our dyno bay with smoke—requiring us to back the car out of the shop until things cleared up. The header turned out to offer worthwhile power gains, but not where expected. The most significant power gains came below 2,500 rpm. We expected the additional exhaust flow to make itself known above 5,000 rpm, but no gains were present during this test. The final test on the 1.8L was to remove the catalytic converter and replace it with a "test" pipe. Obviously, this is for off-road use (track) only, but the cat did represent a significant restriction and the replacement resulted in a dramatic power increase. For running at the strip, building straight pipe is quite easy and the remove and replace procedure is very simple. The cat can simply be installed for street use and the replacement pipe installed for trips to the strip.

Headers, Cats, and Performance Exhausts

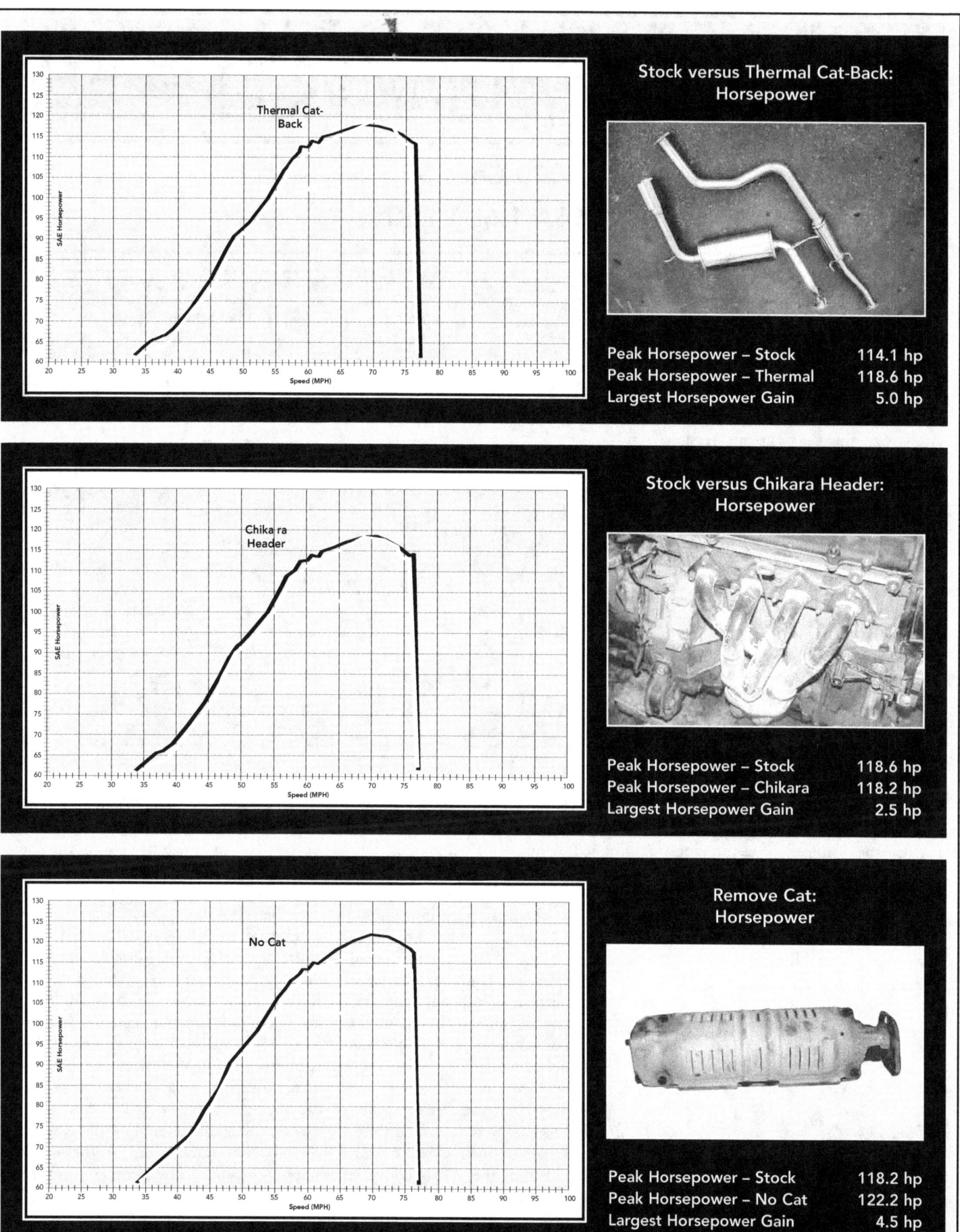

Chapter 4

Test 7: Stock versus Comptech Cat-Back Exhaust and Header

2000 Civic Si
B16A 1.6L VTEC

After the demise of the Del Sol, we here in the United States mourned the loss of the wonderful B16A from the Civic lineup. Sure, the D16Z single-cam VTEC offered acceptable performance with its 125 hp, but it just didn't compare to that feeling you got zinging the twin-cam version up to 8,000 rpm before shifting. Where the single-cam motor stepped lively once the secondary (intake only) cam profile engaged, the B16A flat out motored. While the B16A now seems tame compared to the Integra Type R, it was to the single cam what the Type R is the B16A. It was a long wait from the demise of the Del Sol to the born-again B16A of the Civic Si, but it was well worth the wait. Although not available in the smaller (and lighter) hatchback body style, the 1999 Civic Si offered plenty of performance in stock trim with literally an endless supply of performance available from the aftermarket.

One company to jump right into performance offerings for the zingy little twin cam was Comptech. No stranger to Honda/Acura performance, Comptech is the company responsible for supplying the winning engine to Juan Montoya (now in

Formula 1) when he crossed over from the CART ranks to contest the most famous of all motorsport events, the Indy 500. Along with winning achievements in CART and the Indy Racing League (IRL), the Comptech name can be seen on the championship-winning Real Time Integra Type Rs. The World Challenge Touring cars can be considered the ultimate expression of performance production cars, and Comptech products helped produce not only winners, but also champions.

To find out just how much performance Comptech had to offer, we elected to test a pair of their exhaust products for the B16A-equipped Civic Si. Unlike many of the other tuners in the industry, Comptech understands that power requirements differ between streetcars and racecars. Where it might be desirable to maximize top-end power for an all-out race motor, a streetcar will benefit most from a broad, usable power band. This means focusing the efforts on mid-range power gains that can be enjoyed with every shift rather than the occasional benefit derived from gains experienced at the top of the rev range. To that end, both their cat-back and stainless steel header were designed to offer big gains in the rpm range most often used by enthusiasts. Power gains can be seen from the cat-back from as low as 200 rpm with measurable gains offered all the way to redline. The same goes for the 4-2-1 stepped header. The Comptech header (a real work of art) offered a sizable post-VTEC power gain, with the header alone responsible for 7 hp.

Headers, Cats, and Performance Exhausts

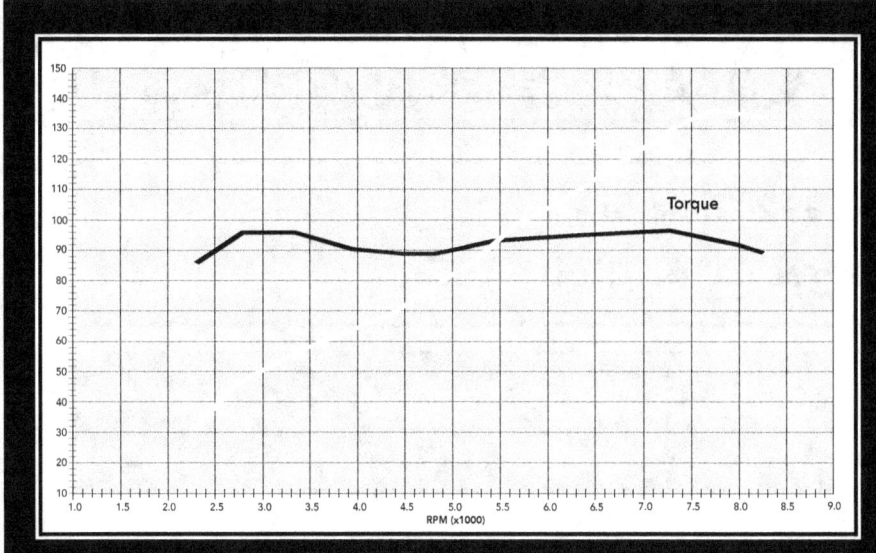

Baseline: Stock

Comptech components are first-rate in terms of quality craftsmanship. This test shows that their header and cat-back exhaust for the Civic Si are no exception.

Peak Horsepower – Stock	137.0 hp
Peak Torque – Stock	99.9 ft-lbs

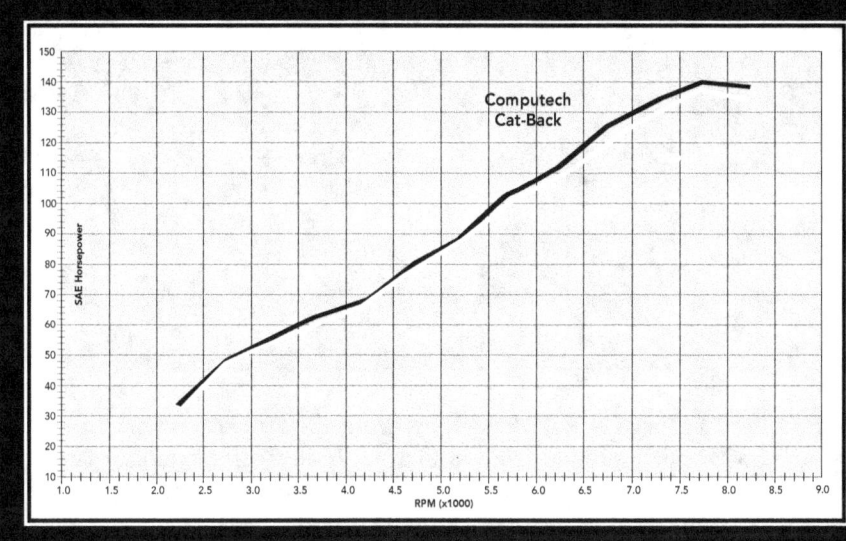

Comptech Cat-Back: Horsepower

Peak HP – Stock	137.0 hp
Peak HP – Comptech Cat-Back	140.0 hp
Largest Horsepower Gain	3.0 hp

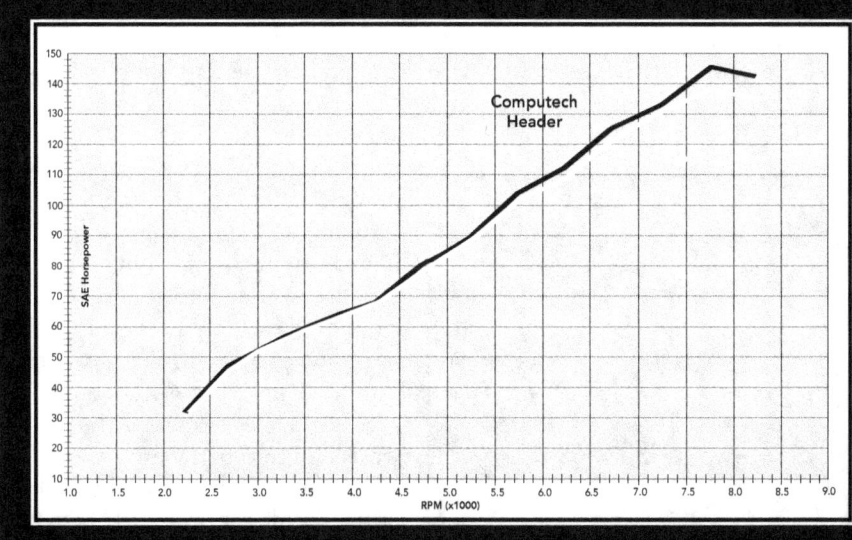

Comptech Header: Horsepower

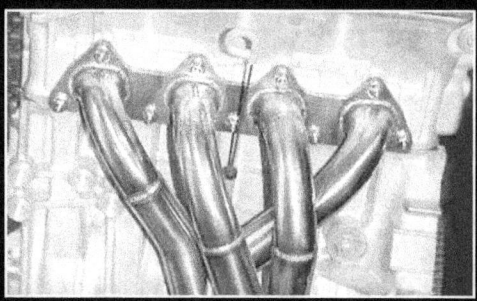

Peak Horsepower – Stock	137.0 hp
Peak Horsepower – Comptech	144.0 hp
Largest Horsepower Gain	7.0 hp

How to Build Honda Horsepower

Chapter 4

Test 8: Stock versus Stillen Header and No Cat versus Kamakazi Header

1992 Civic Si
Supercharged D16Z 1.6L VTEC

This series of tests was run several years ago when the author built up a 1992 Civic Si (hatchback) in the hopes of getting the hot hatch to reach 150 mph. Although we were unsuccessful in reaching our goal (we did manage to see 143 mph), we learned a great deal from the experience. A complete run down on the 1.6L supercharged motor is available in the chapter on engine buildups. The D16Z in the Civic Si was treated to a number of performance modifications, including a Jackson Racing supercharger kit. With plenty of airflow getting forced into the motor, exhaust flow became critical. Naturally, the stock exhaust manifold, down pipe and catalytic converter had to go. All the supercharging in the world cannot make up for a poor flowing exhaust system.

The supercharged motor was run with an AEM air intake, RSR cat-back exhaust, and 8 psi of boost pressure from the Jackson Racing supercharger. In this boosted configuration, the D16Z motor posted an impressive peak power reading of 153.7 hp at 7,200 rpm. The boosted motor simply kept making power as the engine speed increased. Off came the stock exhaust manifold, down pipe, and catalytic converter and on went a 4-1 header from Stillen along with a replacement pipe for the converter. It was obviously not emissions legal, but we wanted to extract every ounce of power out of our supercharged single cam motor. The installation of the Stillen Header and removal of the converter had a profound affect on the power curve. The

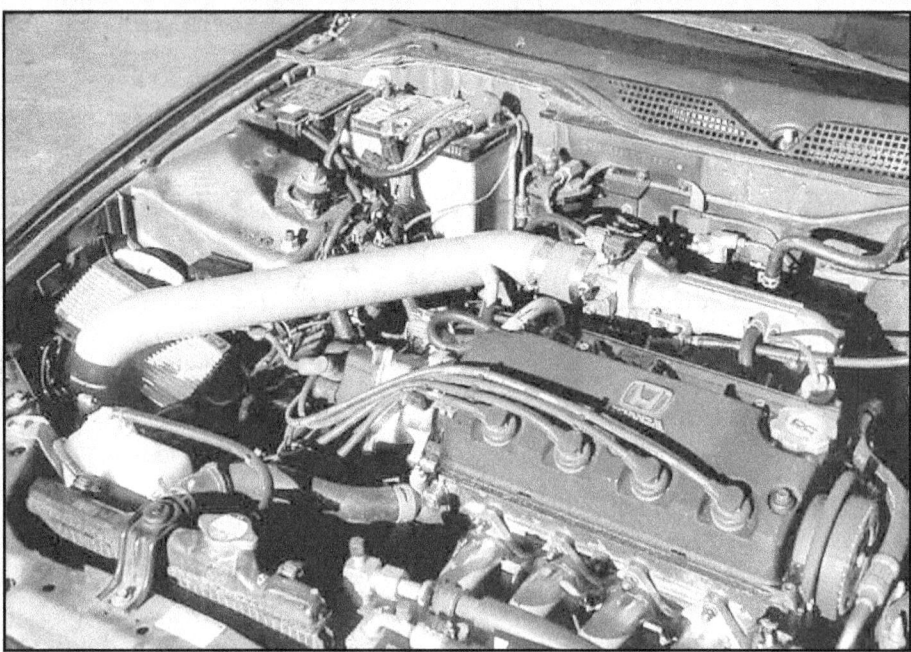

two changes netted a gain of over 11 hp at the wheels, with most of the gain coming near the top of the rev range. Though we were happy with the power gains offered by the header and straight pipe, we needed even more power if we were to see 150 mph.

In an effort to squeeze more power from the single-cam VTEC motor, we tried yet another header, this one from Kamakazi. The Kamakazi header dif-

fered from the Stillen piece in that the Stillen 4-1 header offered long, relatively small-diameter primary tubes. The Kamakazi header was technically a 4-1 like the Stillen unit, but the design of the Kamakazi differed greatly from the Stillen. The Kamakazi header featured primaries that were both larger in diameter and considerably shorter than those used on the Stillen header. The Kamakazi header was similar in design to the so-called shorty-style headers often seen on domestic (Ford) V8s. The design offered improved breathing, but at the expense of part-throttle drivability. The Kamakazi header upped peak power only slightly, but did offer 2–3 hp from 6,000 rpm to 7,200 rpm. The Kamakazi header was definitely better in terms of peak power production, but the Stillen header was a much better choice for daily driving.

Headers, Cats, and Performance Exhausts

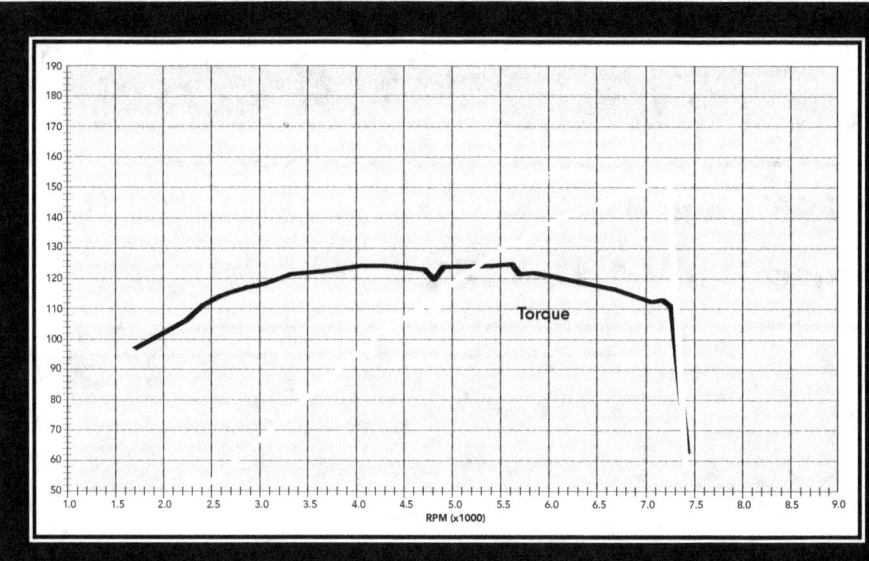

Baseline: Supercharged D16Z

In this test, a Kamakazi short-primary header out-paced the longer-primary Stillen header. The supercharged motor was less sensitive to the scavenging effect of the longer primary tubes.

Peak Horsepower – Stock	153.7 hp
Peak Torque – Stock	127.8 ft-lbs

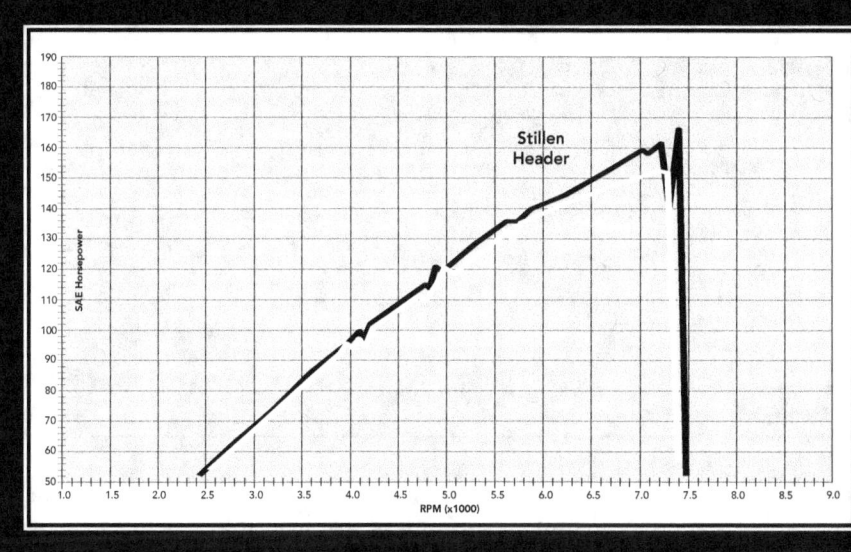

Stillen Header and No Cat: Horsepower

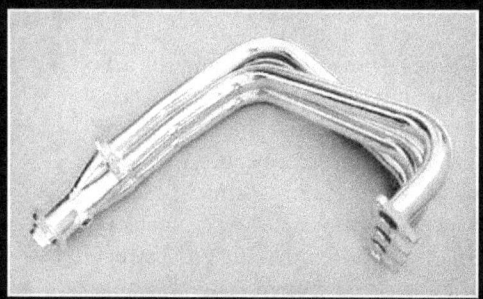

Peak HP – Stock	153.7 hp
Peak HP – Stillen Header	164.2 hp
Largest Horsepower Gain	11.7 hp

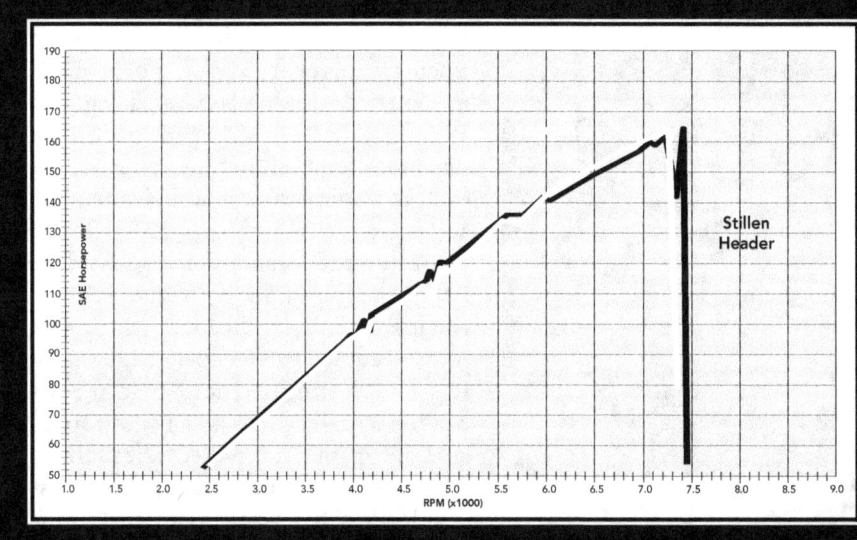

Stillen versus Kamakazi Header: Horsepower

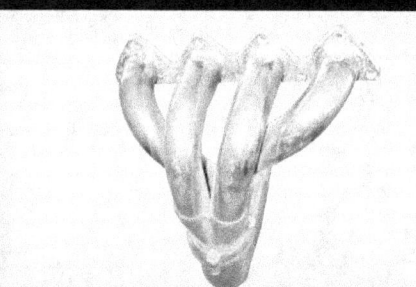

Peak Horsepower – Stillen	164.2 hp
Peak Horsepower – Kamakazi	164.4 hp
Largest Horsepower Gain	2.1 hp

How to Build Honda Horsepower

Test 9: Stock versus Jackson Racing Header

1996 Civic EX
Supercharged D16Y 1.6L VTEC

This test was run on a 1996 Civic EX equipped with the 1.6L single-cam VTEC motor. The test motor was also equipped with a Jackson Racing air intake, cat-back exhaust, and (of course) the Jackson Racing supercharger kit. This supercharged single cam motor was much more representative of a typical street motor than the test run on the author's personal Civic Si. Running a more conservative 8 psi, the 1996 EX motor was closer to what most street enthusiasts are likely to run. The test involved running the single cam motor with the factory cast-iron exhaust manifold and down-pipe and then again with a prototype of the new Jackson Racing 4-into-1 street header. Designed with optimum performance for supercharged street applications, Jackson Racing was able to utilize slightly larger primary tubing that might be the case on an equivalent normally aspirated single-cam motor. After all, not many single-cam VTEC motors produce 163 hp at the wheels.

The motor was run with the stock exhaust manifolds and then again, once the gang at Jackson Racing swapped out the header. No (tuning) changes we made between runs and Oscar himself made sure that the coolant temp was right at 190 degrees

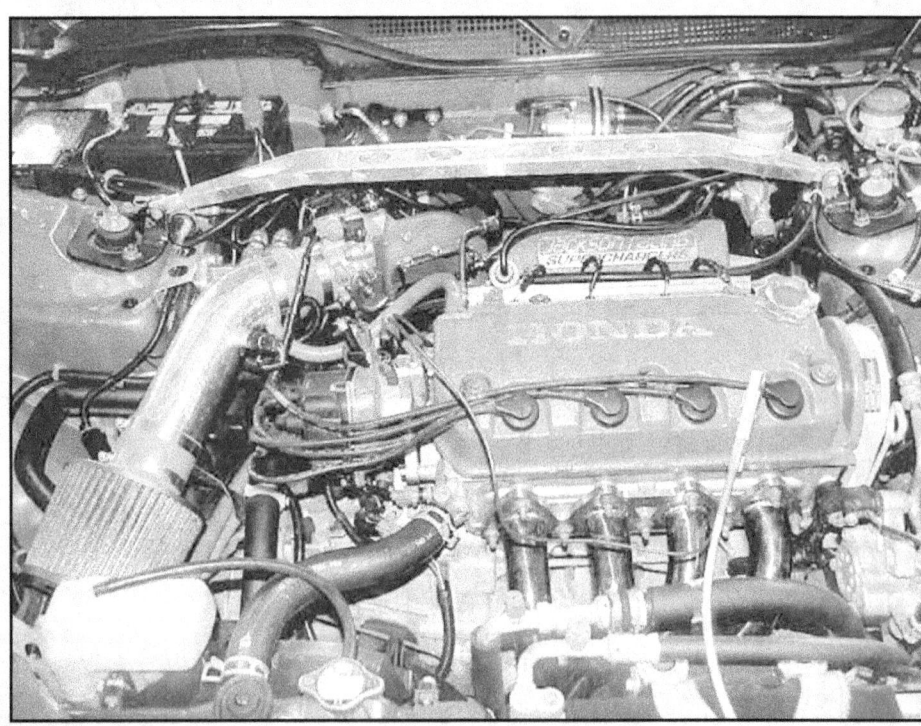

for each run. Temperature differentials can lead to inaccurate data, so care must be taken when dyno testing, especially given that we are looking for such modest power gains in most instances. Runs with the Jackson Racing supercharged EX motor made me long for the days when I had my 1992 Si. That car stomped more than one modified GSR before going out for each top speed run. The EX mustered 158 hp at the wheels and 123 ft-lbs of torque on the Jackson Racing DynoJet. After the installation of the Jackson Racing 4-into-1 header, the peak power jumped to 163 hp and 125 ft-lbs. It is interesting to note that the JR header actually lost a wee bit of torque at 3,500 rpm, but pulled ahead from 4,700 rpm, and demonstrated a measurable gain from there out to redline (7,700 rpm).

Headers, Cats, and Performance Exhausts

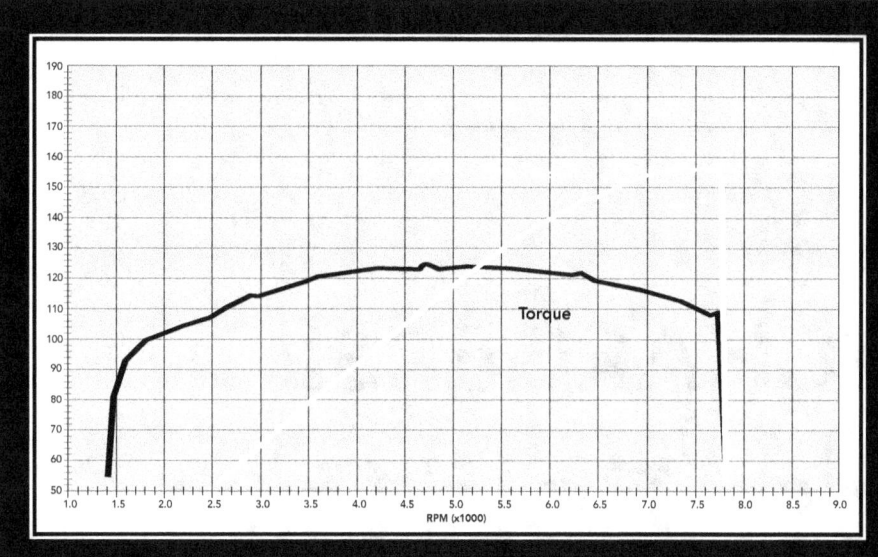

Baseline: Supercharged D16Y

Jackson Racing has years of experience with blown VTEC motors – and this test of their header on a supercharged Civic proves that they know what they're doing.

Peak Horsepower – Stock	158.3 hp
Peak Torque – Stock	123.9 ft-lbs

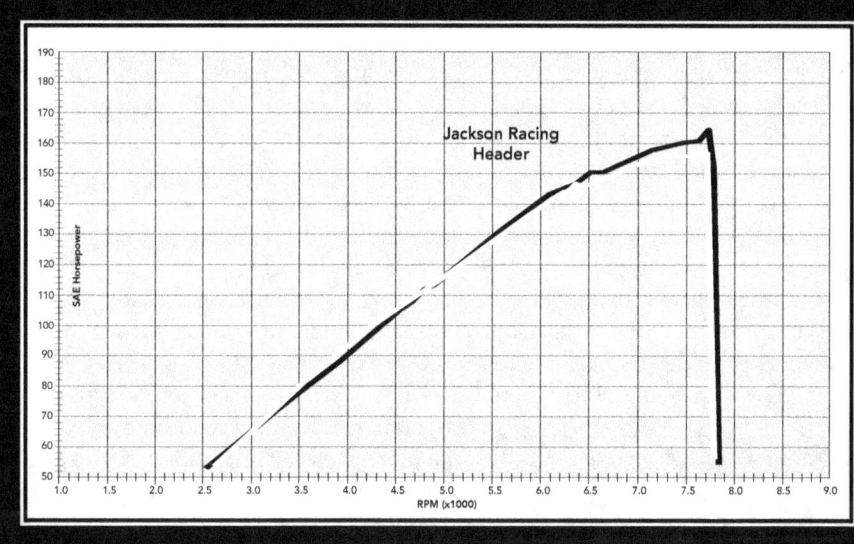

Jackson Racing Header: Horsepower

Peak HP – Stock	158.3 hp
Peak HP – Jackson Racing	163.7 hp
Largest Horsepower Gain	5.4 hp

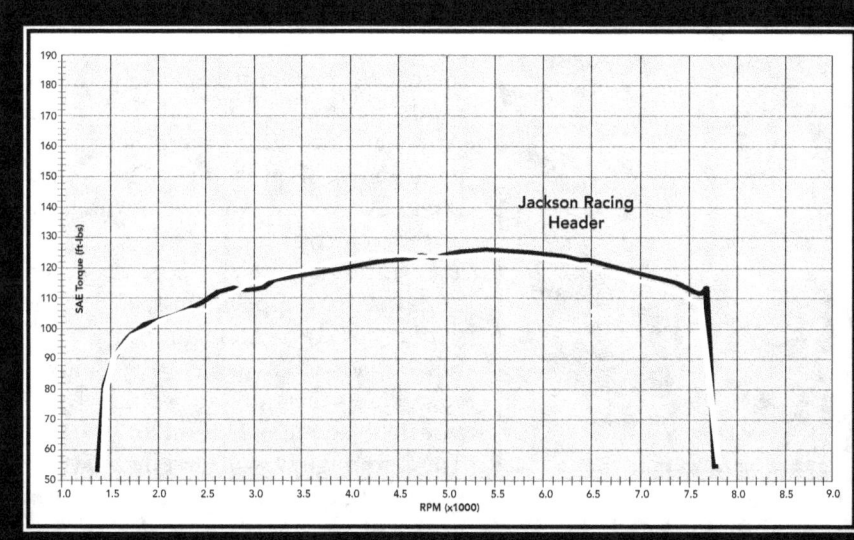

Jackson Racing Header: Torque

Peak Torque – Stock	123.9 ft-lbs
Peak Torque – Jackson Racing	125.0 ft-lbs
Largest Torque Gain	3.2 ft-lbs

How to Build Honda Horsepower

CHAPTER 5

SUPERCHARGERS: BIG BOOST BOLT-ONS

While the turbochargers dominate the strip, the street belongs to the superchargers. The reason for the popularity (and prevalence) of emissions legal supercharger kits has less to do with their efficiency compared to turbocharging than their effect on the exhaust energy. Any form of forced induction, whether it is a mechanically driven supercharger or an exhaust driven supercharger, provides additional air to the motor that it could not otherwise draw in of its own accord. Superchargers, whether positive displacement or centrifugal (the two types currently being used on Honda/Acura kits) are driven off the crankshaft via a drive belt. A turbocharger utilizes the exhaust energy to spin a turbine wheel that is connected via a shaft to a compressor. This compressor (impeller) wheel provides the airflow to the motor. The problem with turbocharging (with respect to emissions) is that they are installed between the exhaust valve or port and the catalytic converter. This limits the direct exhaust energy to the converter, causing a lag in converter light off. The result is that it is more difficult to get a turbo kit certified for street use than a comparable supercharger, which offers no such exhaust flow restrictions.

The two most common types of superchargers, and those employed on the kits tested for this book, are the positive displacement and centrifugal superchargers. It is beyond the scope of this book to cover the two forms of supercharging in detail, but such a scientific understanding is not necessary to appreciate their respective benefits. It is important to note that there is no one ideal method of forced induction. Anyone who tells you otherwise is uninformed or probably selling something. All of the various methods of forced induction have positive and negative attributes, which (more than anything else) are application specific. The world, not to mention the Internet, is full of individuals (some very knowledgeable—others not so) who feel passionately about one form or another. The turbo guys will scream that the supercharger drive systems cost power, usually neglecting to mention the backpressure inherent in any street system.

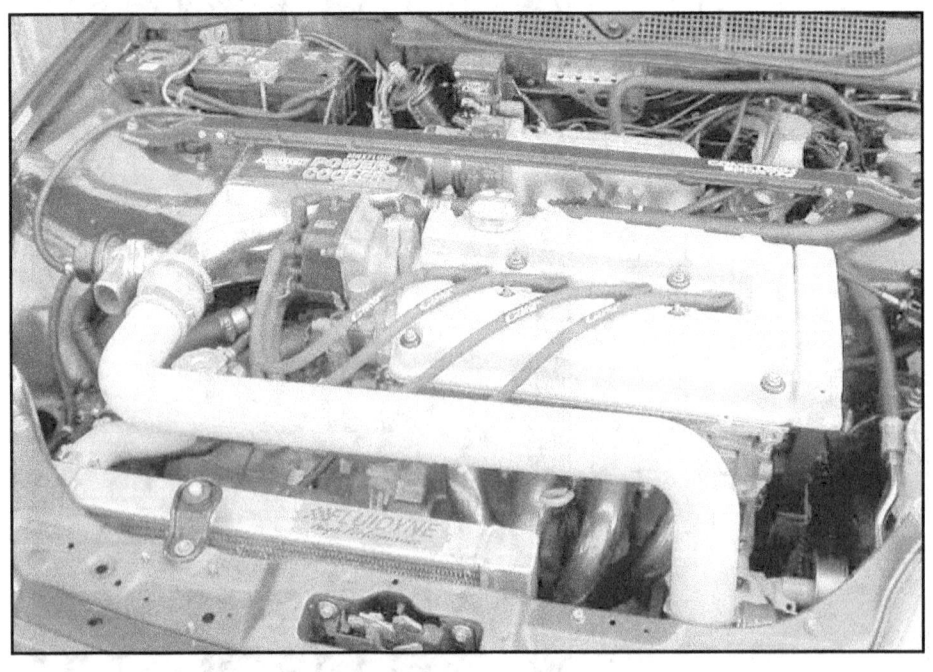

Not your typical Vortech blower set up, this supercharged 2.0L produced over 500 horsepower to propel the world's fastest Honda Civic to over 200 mph.

The positive displacement camp will counter with the immediate boost response versus turbo lag and the centrifugal guys will chime in with an efficiency comparison between their design and the positive displacement superchargers. The bottom line is that there is no one type of forced induction ideal for all applications. If there were one system that outshined all others, the market would ensure that the others would cease to exist.

The benefits of turbocharging are discussed in a dedicated chapter, but a few of the differences between the positive displacement and centrifugal superchargers are worth mentioning to better appreciate the dyno test results. The positive displacement supercharger is nothing more than an air pump, not unlike the internal combustion engine itself. As the name implies, the positive displacement superchargers moves a given amount of air from one side of the blower to the other. The blower grabs air from the throttle body opening and forces it into (usually) a lower intake manifold. The amount of air that travels from one side of the blower to the other depends on the size (displacement) of the blower and speed relative to the engine. When an engine is running, it requires a certain amount of air. If the size and speed of the blower are varied to push in more air than the motor can use, we get boost pressure between the blower and the intake valve (usually in the lower intake manifold between the blower and the cylinder head(s). Every time the intake valve opens, the positive pressure (boost) forces more air in than the motor could normally draw in. The result is extra power.

A centrifugal supercharger works the same way, but given the relatively compact design of the impeller (and the fact that a centrifugal supercharger is a true compressor), it must spin much faster to provide a similar amount of airflow. While a roots blower may run efficiently from 3,000–10,000 rpm (even slightly higher), most centrifugal superchargers require impeller speeds to reach 30,000 rpm before significant airflow is present. This design parameter produces a somewhat linear boost curve with

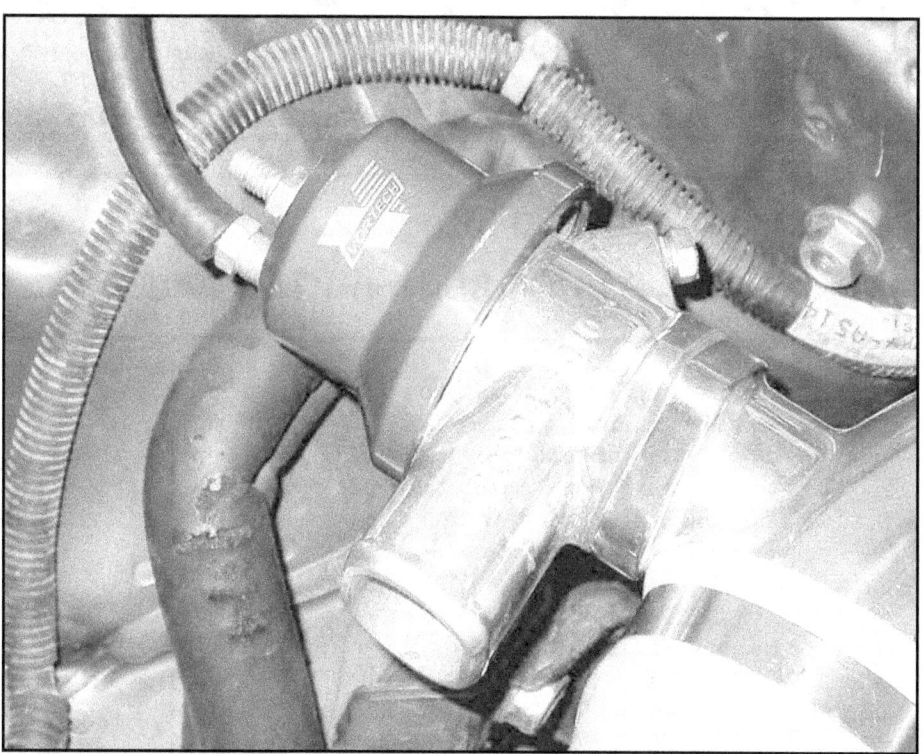

Like any good turbo system, a blower motor, especially a street version, will greatly benefit from a compressor bypass valve.

respect to engine speed. Where a roots blower (like the Eaton unit used in the Jackson Racing kits) may produce 6 psi at just 2,000 rpm and carry that boost level to redline (with a slight drop off at the VTEC operation), a centrifugal supercharger will gain boost pressure (and more importantly airflow) as the engine speed increases. The net result of this is that a roots blower will produce more boost (or airflow) at low engine speeds, offering better throttle response and significant torque gain in the low and mid range. At low boost levels (where the positive displacement supercharger offers acceptable efficiency), the positive displacement supercharger will offer sizeable horsepower gains as well. Witness the power gains offered by the Jackson Racing superchargers on the CRV, Prelude, and GSR.

At low boost levels (6–8 psi), the gains offered by the positive displacement supercharger will exceed those offered by the centrifugal. While the peak power numbers produced will be similar (compare the numbers of the Vortech and JR GSR kits), the positive displacement supercharger will simply offer better average power gains thanks to the better boost response at lower engine speeds. The positive displacement superchargers cannot (by design) continue this advantage once additional airflow and power levels are required. Stepping up to 10 psi, the centrifugal starts to walk away from the positive displacement, thanks to superior thermal efficiency. It is important not to confuse boost pressure with airflow or power. Just because a centrifugal and positive displacement supercharger both produce 10 psi doesn't mean that they will produce the same power. They will in fact not produce the same power, as boost pressure is not a measurement of mass flow—it is simply a measurement of pressure. To put this into perspective, the Vortech kit installed on a Civic Si (at 10 psi) will produce about 40 hp more than the Jackson Racing kit at the same pressure. The positive displacement superchargers work best at lower airflow and boost levels, while the centrifugals excel at higher boost and engine speeds. The choice does not come down to which type of supercharger is better, but rather the intended application.

Chapter 5

Test 1: PowerTrain Dynamics
LS and GSR (PowerDyne)

1990 Integra LS and 1993 Integra GSR
B18A 1.8L Non-VTEC and B17C 1.7L VTEC

Like their domestic counterparts, superchargers have invaded the import market (about the time this book was written). First on the scene was Jackson Racing with their kit for the single-cam VTEC motors. Soon thereafter, kits became available for the twin-cam B16A Del Sol, GSR, and Type Rs along with most of the other Honda/Acura line up. Vortech jumped into the mix, as did Paxton, in the form of an S2000 kit from Comptech. Long before any of the centrifugal superchargers showed up on the import scene, PowerTrain Dynamics built a couple of supercharger kits using a PowerDyne centrifugal supercharger. Unlike the Vortech and Paxton, the PowerDyne supercharger relied on an internal belt drive for the step up ratio (to increase the impeller speed relative to the crank speed). This unique feature all but eliminated the gear-to-gear noise associated with gear-driven superchargers (all Vortech and the latest Paxton models). Since the PowerDyne was originally sized to feed a healthy V8, the compact unit had no problem supplying the necessary airflow to dramatically increase the power output of the pair of Acura motors PowerTrain applied them to.

The bolt-on "kit" produced by PowerTrain mounted the PowerDyne supercharger near and facing the power steering pump. This was done in an effort to maintain both the power steering and air conditioning. The first application was installed on a 1990 Integra LS equipped with a non-VTEC 1.8L (the engines actually measure 1,834cc). Although engine management as such was at its infancy, the non-intercooled kit relied on a simple FMU for added fuel supply. The rising rate regulator (common in turbo and supercharger kits originally equipped with a return fuel system) increased the fuel pressure in relation to boost. It should be noted that these two kits are no longer available and the PowerDyne blower was actually sized incorrectly for the small-displacement applications, but the power gains were impressive nonetheless. The 1.8L LS motor gained nearly 60 hp and 40 ft-lbs of torque with just 6–7 psi of boost. This motor could have greatly benefited from aftermarket cams (Crane makes an excellent set of street cams for the LS motor) along with some fine-tuning of the air/fuel ratio, as the blower had plenty of power left to offer.

The next test involved the installation of the same PowerDyne blower on a 1993 Integra GSR. The early GSR was powered by a 1.7L version of the now-famous 1.8L B18C motor. This early GSR relied on a slightly smaller stroke to produce the smaller displacement level. The smaller engine still pumped out some impressive power numbers, especially after the installation of the supercharger by PowerTrain Dynamics. According to the graph, it is obvious that the horsepower curve was still climbing during this test. Fuel supply was the only thing that stopped this motor from easily exceeding 250 hp at the wheels (at 8,000 rpm). Given the nature of centrifugal superchargers, it is likely that additional power was available by removing the factory rev limiter and allowing the GSR motor to rev to 8,500 rpm (a safe number for the stock motor). Note that the VTEC motor made best power after the activation of the secondary cam. The PowerDyne was equipped with a pulley ratio to produce about 8 psi at 8,000 rpm. The author drove this particular GSR car and can testify that it was indeed impressive. Just ask the 5.0L Mustang that we stormed past during the test drive.

Superchargers: Big Boost Bolt-Ons

No Baseline Data Available

Long before Vortech ever offered a centrifugal supercharger for the Civic Si, PowerTrain Dynamics built a kit using a belt-drive PowerDyne blower. The test results were impressive, though no kit was ever mass produced.

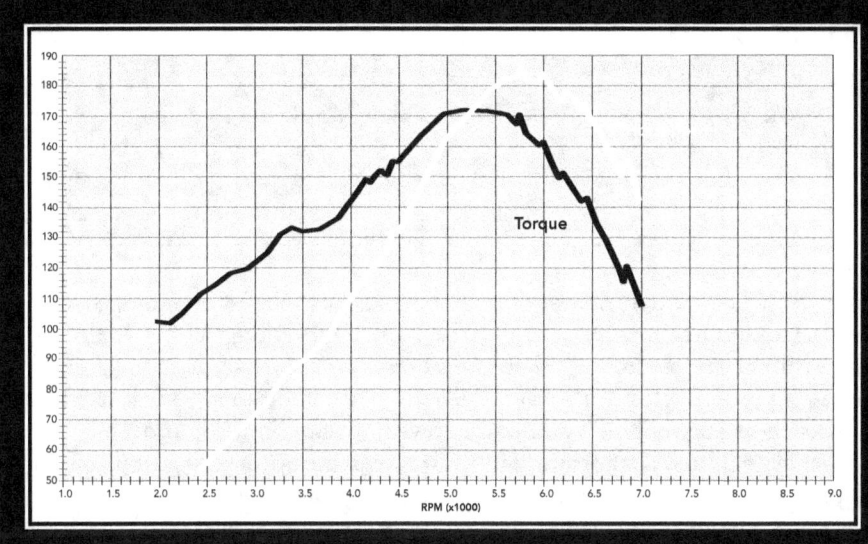

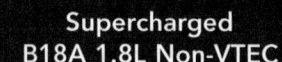

Supercharged B18A 1.8L Non-VTEC

Peak Horsepower – B18A	186.0 hp
Peak Torque – B18A	172.4 ft-lbs

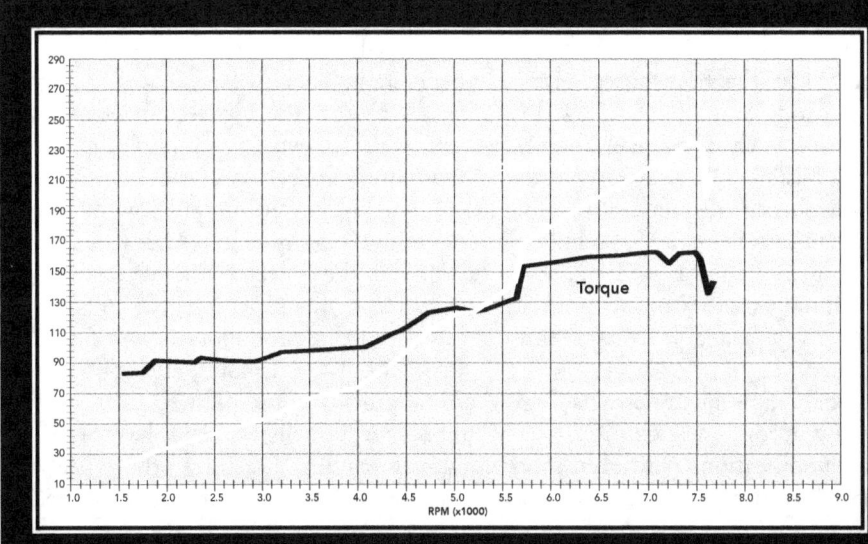

Supercharged B17C 1.7L VTEC

Peak Horsepower – B17C	237.3 hp
Peak Torque – B17C	166.7 ft-lbs

Chapter 5

Test 2: Jackson Racing Supercharger (Effect of Boost)

1992 Civic Si
D16Z 1.6L Single-Cam VTEC

The buildup of my first supercharged Honda motor resulted in a great deal of first-hand experience. The idea behind the buildup was to coax a 1992 Civic Si (3-door Hatchback) into running 150 mph. While the effort missed the mark somewhat, the same effort now would no doubt succeed for no other reason than a great deal of knowledge has been accrued since the completion of the project. The 1.6L single-cam VTEC motor was treated to the usual array of aftermarket performance components including an air intake, header, and exhaust system. So equipped, the little single cammer produced a whopping 112 hp and 98 ft-lbs at the wheels. The big power gains came from the installation of the Jackson Racing supercharger system. Boost is a great thing; in fact, the only thing better than boost is more boost. The first of the three power graphs illustrate what happened when we added the standard Jackson Racing supercharger kit making 6 psi to the slightly modified D16Z single-cam VTEC motor in the Si. The peak power jumped from 112 hp to 139.5 hp and peak torque took a 20 ft-lbs jump along with it.

Remember we mentioned that more boost is a good thing (with the correct amount of fuel of course)? The second graph is a clear indication of what happens when you turn up the boost on the Jackson Racing supercharger kit. Increasing the boost from 6 psi up to 8 psi had a positive effect on power. The kit is listed as supplying 8 psi, but the boost gauge indicated a maximum of only 7.5 psi during testing. The installation of a larger crank pulley provided the necessary boost increase. The fuel supply was also addressed in the form of an upgraded (high-flow) in-the-tank fuel pump and 240-cc injectors. Although not indicated by this horsepower graph, the peak torque was up to 124 ft-lbs, with gains across the rev range. The best part about this supercharger kit was the tremendous throttle response. It was like someone had installed a 2.3L Prelude or 2.5L V6 in place of the 1.6L. Even part-throttle running was much more fun as boost was always available from the little supercharger.

The final graph illustrates what happens when you combined additional performance modifications with even more boost. The lowest of the three lines was the run made with just 6 psi, the RSR exhaust, and AEM air intake. The middle line represents the motor equipped with the 8-psi pulley along with a Kamakazi header and no catalytic converter in place. The additional exhaust flow allowed a substantial improvement in power over the factory exhaust manifold. Naturally, the removal of the cat increased exhaust flow as well. A free-flowing exhaust system is critical on a supercharged motor as the supercharger is there to ensure plenty of intake flow. Power will be lost (or not gained) if all that extra intake flow has no way of exiting the motor. The highest power numbers were achieved by cranking up the boost even further to 10 psi. The little 1.6L single-cam motor was now pumping out 176.5 hp and 141.3 ft-lbs of torque at the wheels. To put that into perspective, this supercharged 1.6L was now producing more horsepower than a stock 1.8L Type R motor, and considerably more torque. The power was impressive, but we were still short of our goal of making 200 hp at the wheels. Check out the chapter on engine builds to see what we did to get even closer to 200 hp at the wheels.

Superchargers: Big Boost Bolt-Ons

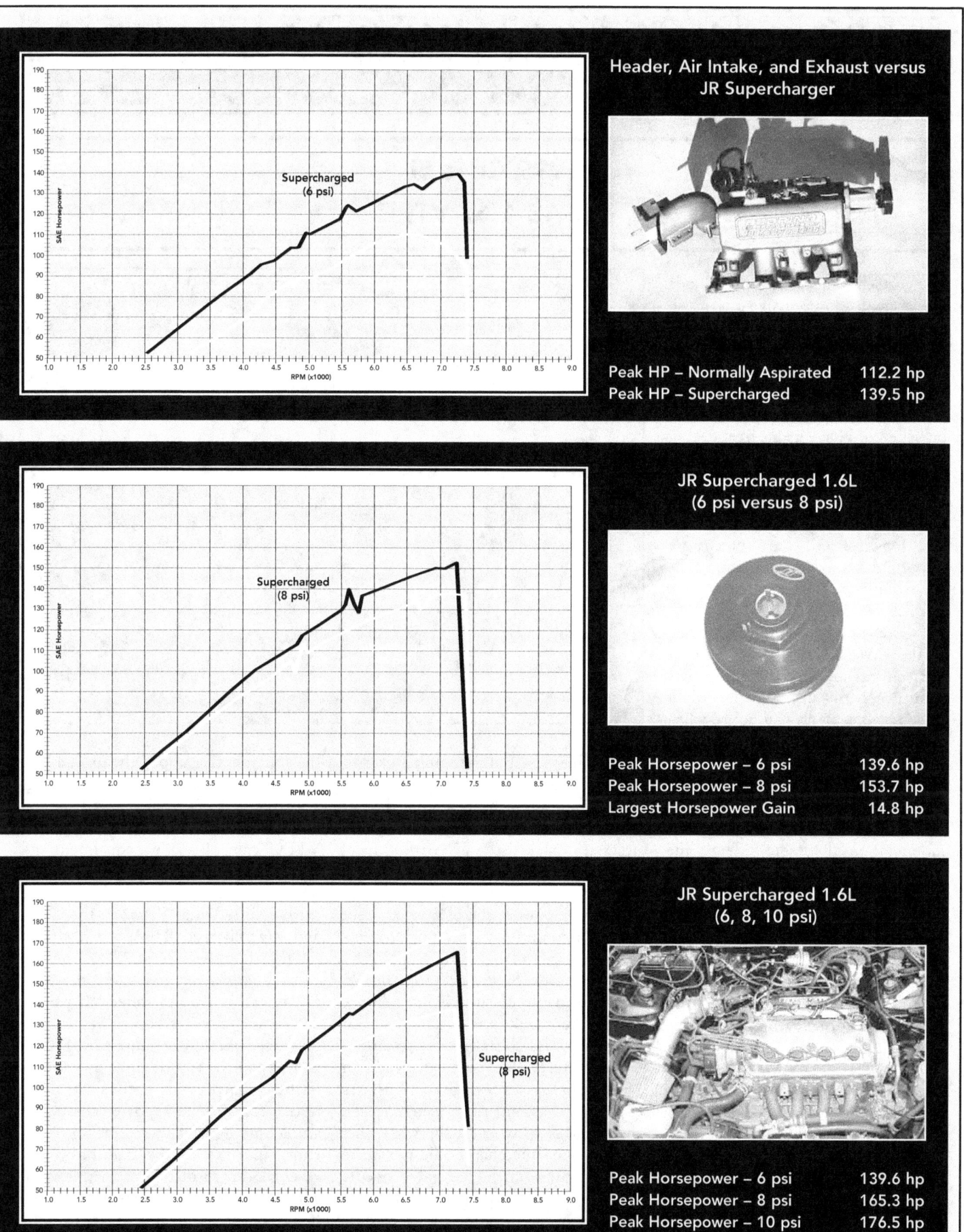

Header, Air Intake, and Exhaust versus JR Supercharger

Peak HP – Normally Aspirated	112.2 hp
Peak HP – Supercharged	139.5 hp

JR Supercharged 1.6L (6 psi versus 8 psi)

Peak Horsepower – 6 psi	139.6 hp
Peak Horsepower – 8 psi	153.7 hp
Largest Horsepower Gain	14.8 hp

JR Supercharged 1.6L (6, 8, 10 psi)

Peak Horsepower – 6 psi	139.6 hp
Peak Horsepower – 8 psi	165.3 hp
Peak Horsepower – 10 psi	176.5 hp

Chapter 5

Test 3: Vortech Supercharged/Intercooled Civic Si

1999 Civic Si
B16A3 1.6L VTEC

Vortech jumped into the Honda market with an impressive offering in their Civic Si kit. Long a favorite of domestic V8s, the gear-driven centrifugal supercharger enjoys excellent efficiency and a surge of top-end power that has to be experienced to be believed. I have had a great deal of experience with Vortech in the past, having owned serial number 001 supercharger for a number of years before returning it to Vortech to be used for display. If that supercharger is any indication, look for thousands of trouble-free miles with your Vortech supercharged Civic Si.

Given the packaging constraints of the Civic Si, it is a wonder that Vortech was able to cram all that performance hardware in such a tight area. The first thing you notice when viewing the installed Si kit is obviously the supercharger and intercooler. Individuals brought up on domestic V8s applications will immediately notice that the supercharger is not mounted on the same side of the motor as the crank pulley. This is important as the supercharger relies on the crank pulley for motivation. Unlike most of the domestic Vortech supercharged applications, this Civic Si kit utilizes a transfer shaft to drive the supercharger. Power is taken from the crank in normal fashion via a drive

(serpentine) belt, but the crank is used to rotate a shaft enclosed inside a safety tube. Inside the tube is a splined shaft attached to the blower. The shaft was necessary to locate the V5 G-trim supercharger in an acceptable location in the engine compartment. There simply wasn't room to mount the blower adjacent to the air conditioner unit, power steering, or alternator.

The Civic Si kit utilized the V5 G-trim capable of supporting 575 hp. While the stock non-intercooled kit provided 6 psi, this aftercooled (air-to-water intercooler) kit allowed an increase in boost pressure to 10 psi. As expected of a centrifugal supercharger, the serious power rush was post VTEC. The supercharger did not make itself known until the tach needle swung past 3,000 rpm, at which point the supercharged motor began to outpower the stock motor. At 4,000 rpm, the supercharger upped the torque ante by some 25 ft-lbs, with similar gains available at 5,000 rpm. By 6,000 rpm, all hell broke loose and the boost and VTEC cams became acquainted and skipped together happily off into horsepower heaven. By 6,000 rpm, the torque differential between the stock and supercharged B16A was a whopping 55 ft-lbs, while at 7,000 rpm the gains exceeded 65 ft-lbs. By the time the boost gauge registered 10 psi (at 8,000 rpm), the aftercooled Vortech kit improved the power output by 130 hp and upped the torque peak by over 80 ft-lbs. Sharp-eyed enthusiasts will notice that the horsepower curve was still climbing at the redline of 8,000 rpm, and the motor had only just reached the torque peak at this rpm. There was definitely more power to be had from this kit by extending the engine speed a bit.

Superchargers: Big Boost Bolt-Ons

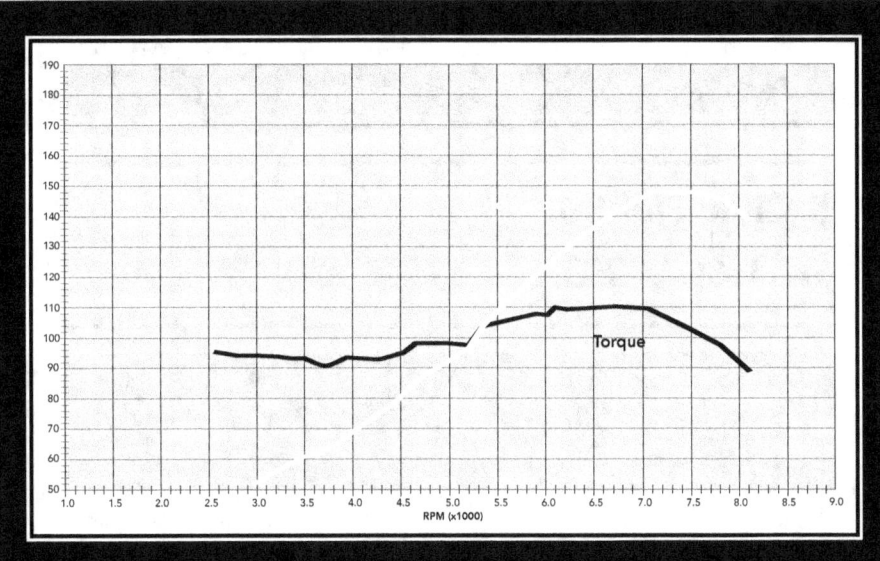

Baseline: B16A3 (Stock)

Any VTEC motor with 8-10 psi of boost will immediately bring a smile to your face, as this Vortech supercharger test shows – blower boost is one of the best ways to add power to a VTEC motor.

Peak Horsepower – Stock	148 hp
Peak Torque – Stock	112 ft-lbs

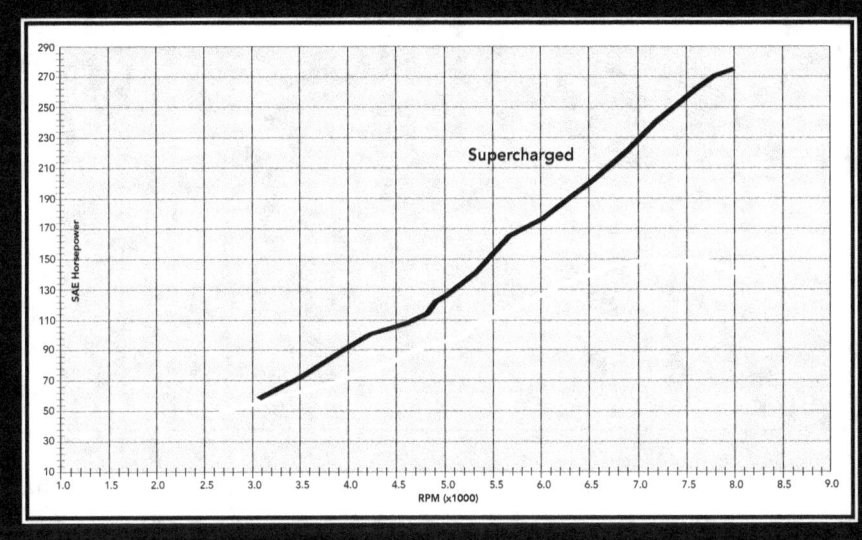

Vortech Aftercooled Supercharger: Horsepower

Peak Horsepower – Stock	148 hp
Peak Horsepower – Supercharged	273 hp
Largest Horsepower Gain	134 hp

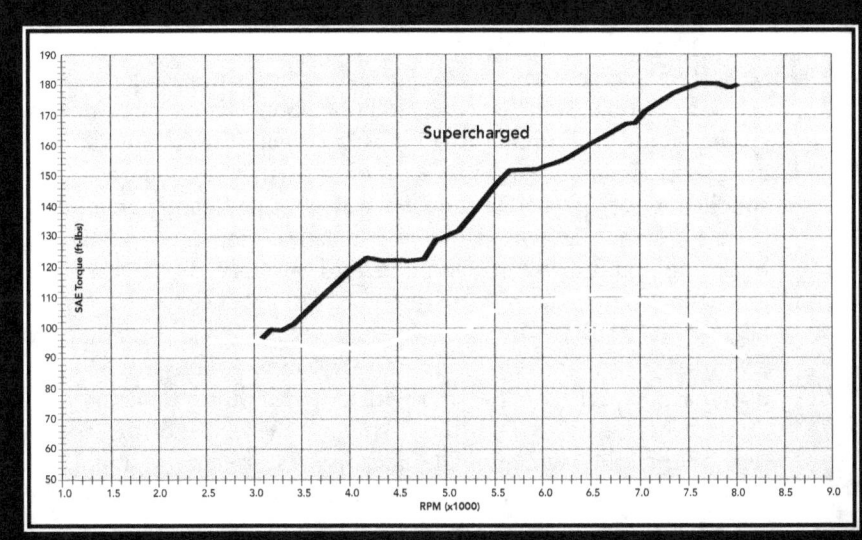

Vortech Aftercooled Supercharger: Torque

Peak Torque – Stock	112 ft-lbs
Peak Torque – Supercharged	180 ft-lbs
Largest Torque Gain	87 ft-lbs

How to Build Honda Horsepower

Chapter 5

Test 4: Vortech SC Civic Si Big Boost

1995 Civic Del Sol
B16A 1.6L VTEC

As impressive as the standard aftercooled kit was for the Civic Si, yours truly could not leave well enough alone. The reasoning behind all the testing was simple. The blower kit added 130 hp to a near-stock B16A. To find out just how much power was available from the Vortech Civic Si kit, I built a dedicated high-performance blower B16A motor. While designated a blower motor, the only real item that differed significantly from the average all-motor buildup was the swap to low-compression Arias forged pistons. The B16A motor was assembled with a set of 9:1 forged pistons from Arias to allow us to safely turn up the boost on the Vortech supercharger. While we were running C16 (116 octane) race fuel to eliminate detonation during the tuning phase (with our Hondata ECU), the lower compression (versus 10.2:1 in stock form) provided another safety margin. Since previous experience (with a turbo motor) had shown us that the stock cast pistons tend to give up at about the 350-hp level (from excess cylinder pressure and not detonation), the forged pistons would allow us to exceed that power ceiling without fear of crushing another ring land.

The remainder of the motor was built with additional airflow in mind. The B16A cylinder head was first treated to Extrude Hone porting and then to a set of Crower valve springs and titanium retainers. Crower also supplied a set of 63402 cams to further improve breathing and allow for extended engine speed beyond 8,000 rpm. A JG Edelbrock header and optional B-pipe took care of the exhaust system while the intake chores were handled by a Killer Bee Racing prototype intake manifold and 68-mm Holley throttle body. The motor was run with 440-cc injectors and an FMU to further increase the fuel supply. Controlling the larger injectors was a Hondata programmable ECU. The basic Vortech Civic Si supercharger was employed, but the testing was performed on a 1995 Del Sol. The only changes to the kit were the fabrication of 6-rib pulleys to eliminated belt slippage as the boost was increased. A larger crank pulley and smaller blower pulley were employed to produce 14–15 psi. The modified B16A produced a whopping 376 hp at the wheels, with belt slippage still a major concern. This test was run later with a revised pulley ratio and produced 413 hp at the wheels on this B16A. The motor was used to establish a Bonneville Land Speed Record with the author behind the wheel of the 1998 Civic.

Superchargers: Big Boost Bolt-Ons

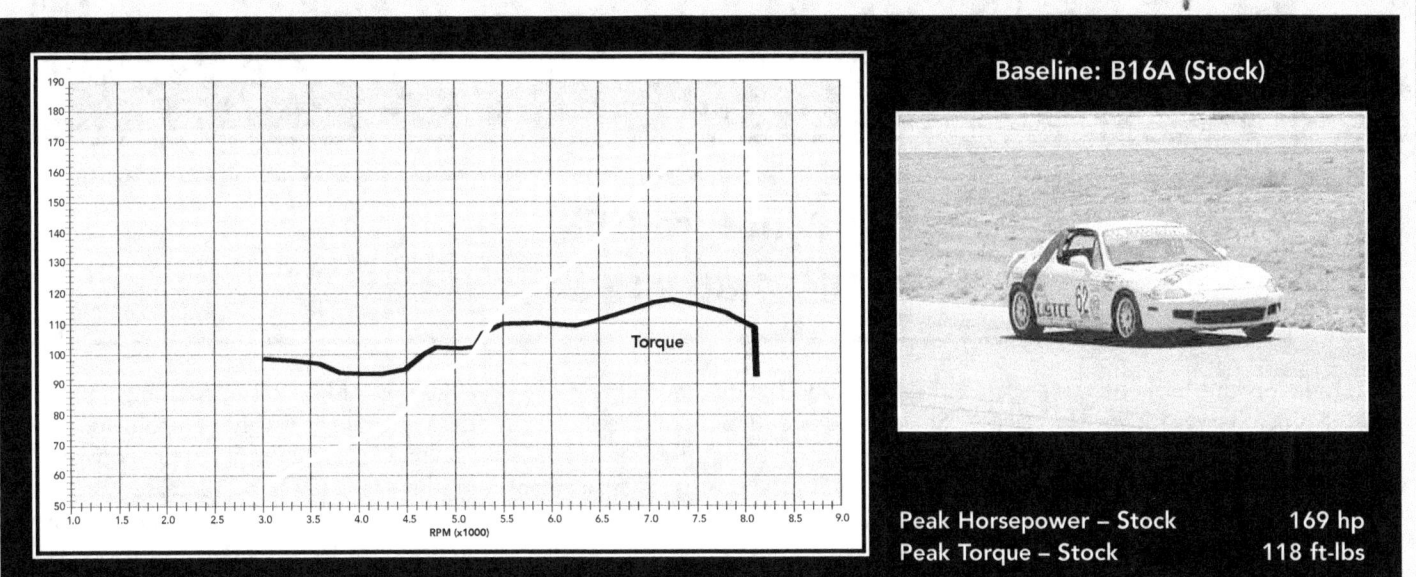

Baseline: B16A (Stock)

Peak Horsepower – Stock	169 hp
Peak Torque – Stock	118 ft-lbs

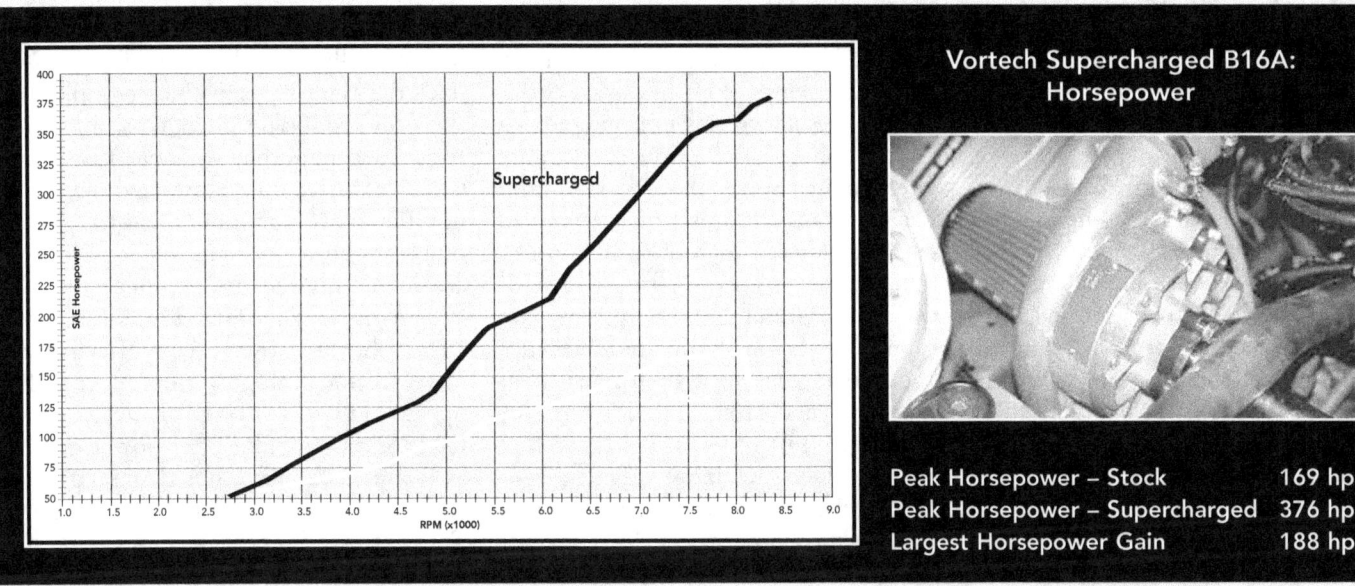

Vortech Supercharged B16A: Horsepower

Peak Horsepower – Stock	169 hp
Peak Horsepower – Supercharged	376 hp
Largest Horsepower Gain	188 hp

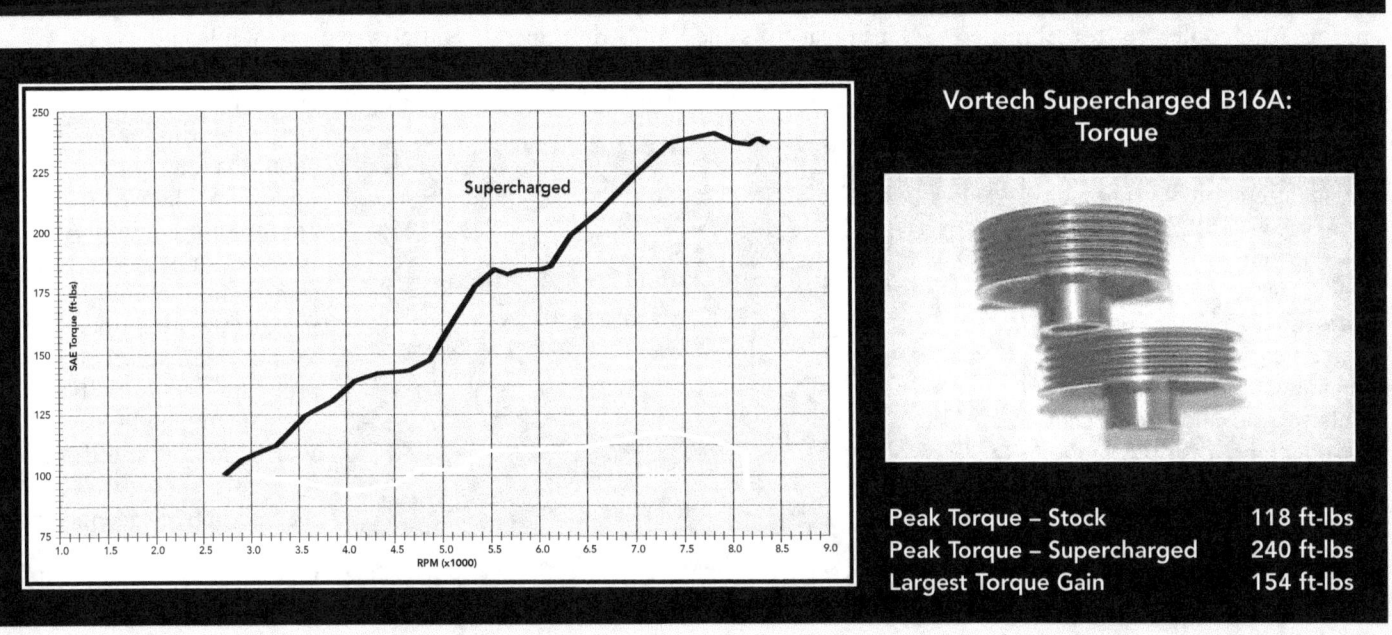

Vortech Supercharged B16A: Torque

Peak Torque – Stock	118 ft-lbs
Peak Torque – Supercharged	240 ft-lbs
Largest Torque Gain	154 ft-lbs

Chapter 5

Test 5: Vortech Supercharged Integra GSR

1999 Integra GSR
B18C 1.8L VTEC

Right on the heels of their successful supercharger kit for the Civic Si, Vortech got to work on a kit for the Integra GSR. The move was an obvious one as the two motors share a great deal of architecture. The major differences between the B16A in the Civic Si (and 1992–1995 Del Sol) and the B18C in the 1994-up GSR are the increased deck height of the 1.8L B18C block (to make room for the longer stroke) and the position of the throttle body on the dual-stage intake manifold. Where the throttle body on the B16A is positioned up high in the traditional location (for easy access), the dual runner GSR intake required the throttle body to be located relatively lower. These differences, though subtle, required major changes to the supercharger kit—meaning that you can't simply bolt a Civic Si kit onto a GSR—although the GSR kit would probably fit the Type R. It would require a change of inlet tube from the supercharger and/or Aftercooler to the throttle body, but by the time you read this, there may well be a kit available for the Type R and LS Integra.

I chose the non-intercooled (aftercooled) version of the Vortech GSR kit, as that was the first to be produced. The non-intercooled kit also represented a change from the intercooled Civic Si kit tested elsewhere in this chapter. Who wants to read about the same test over and over? A good many enthusiasts are interested in the non-intercooled (both Civic Si and GSR) kits as they represent an excellent value (read less expensive than the higher boost aftercooled versions). Since the introduction of the Vortech kits, the Internet is a blaze of comparisons between the positive displacement Jackson Racing supercharger kits and the centrifugal kits offered by Vortech. Since most of the Jackson Racing kits run much lower boost pressures in standard form that the 10-psi aftercooled Vortech kits, comparisons are difficult. While the merits of both kits are excellent, the results of this non-intercooled kit will offer ammunition for a more direct comparison of the 5–6 psi Jackson Racing kit and the 6-psi non-intercooled kit from Vortech. Before rushing off to the Internet to extol the virtues of whichever supercharger system you happen to favor (both are excellent), know that the positive displacement superchargers offer superior low-to-midrange boost response (and therefore power) while the more efficient centrifugal will almost always make more ultimate horsepower.

The GSR kit is quite similar to the Si kit in that the same V5 G-trim supercharger is used to provide boost. The V5 supercharger itself is capable of 575 hp at 20+ psi of boost, so providing 6 psi to the GSR motor was not a problem. The fuel management (enrichment) consisted of the same FMU to increase the fuel pressure in proportion to boost. The signal to the factory map sensor was also diverted to ensure the ECU never registered positive pressure. Running the stock crank pulley and a 3.33-inch blower pulley (the 10-psi Civic Si utilized the same 3.33-inch blower pulley), the GSR produced right at 6 psi at 8,000 rpm. It is important to note that the GSR was tested on a Mustang dyno and not the more common DynoJet. The numbers (both stock and supercharged) are lower on the double-roller dyno. Where the stock motor made 131 hp and 104 ft-lbs of torque, the Vortech kit increased the peak power output to 201 hp and 139 ft-lbs. Note that (like the Civic Si kit) GSR kit offer power gains as low as 3,000 rpm, but the real gains came after the onset of the VTEC cam. The centrifugal supercharger acted like a huge VTEC cam, offering massive top-end power gains. While enthusiasts will continue to debate the merits of the positive displacement and centrifugal superchargers, the best thing about having both is the option to choose. If you are looking for impressive throttle response that transforms your little motor into a big one, then the positive displacement is probably for you. If you bought the high-winding VTEC motor specifically to savors the rewards of the addictive secondary cam profile, then the Vortech GSR is definitely your cup of tea.

Superchargers: Big Boost Bolt-Ons

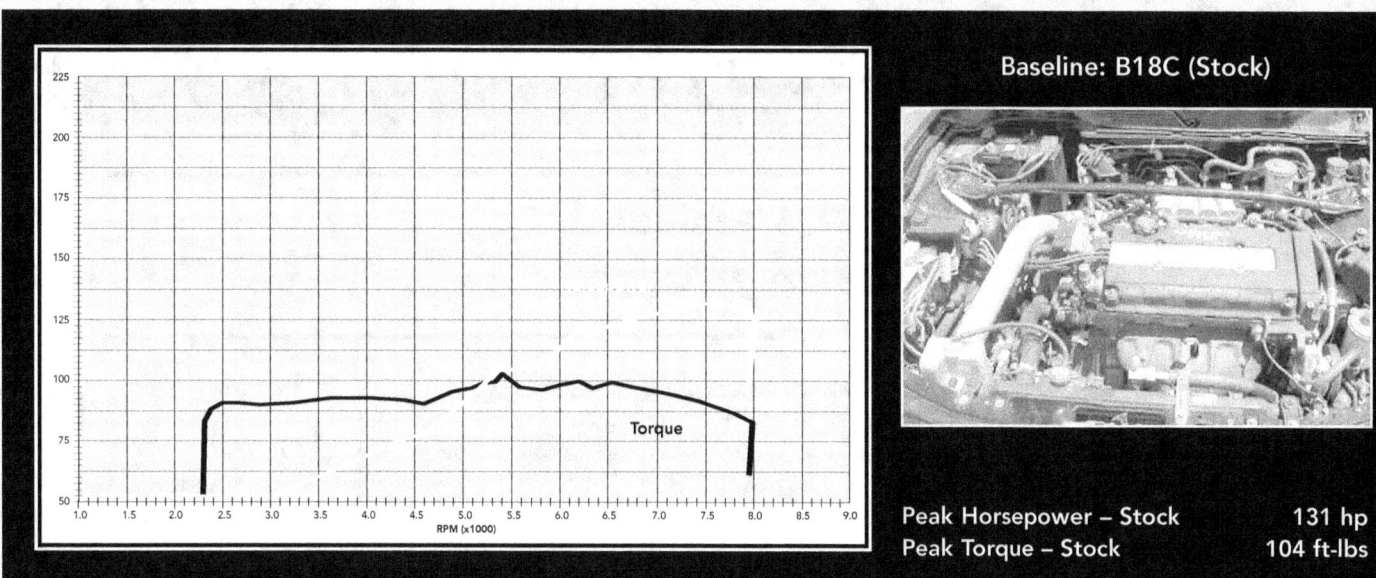

Baseline: B18C (Stock)

Peak Horsepower – Stock	131 hp
Peak Torque – Stock	104 ft-lbs

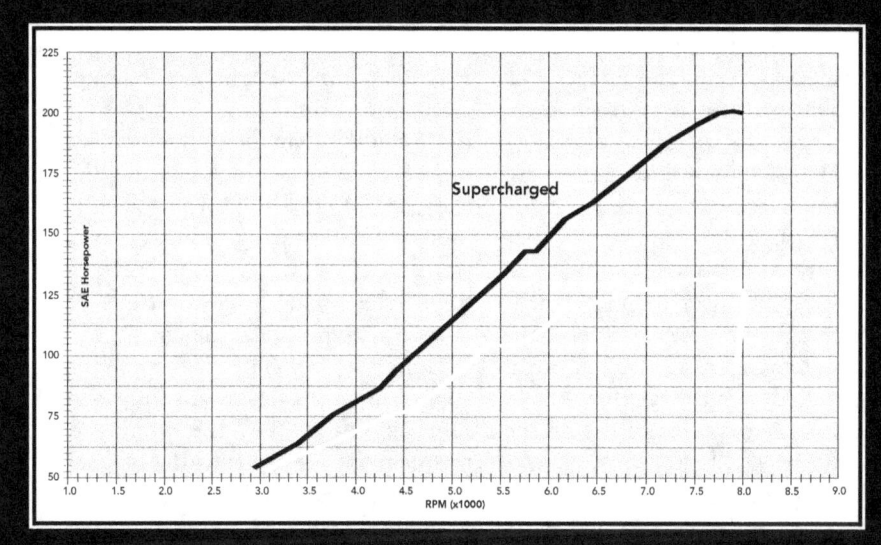

Vortech Supercharger: Horsepower

Peak Horsepower – Stock	131 hp
Peak Horsepower – Supercharged	201 hp
Largest Horsepower Gain	74 hp

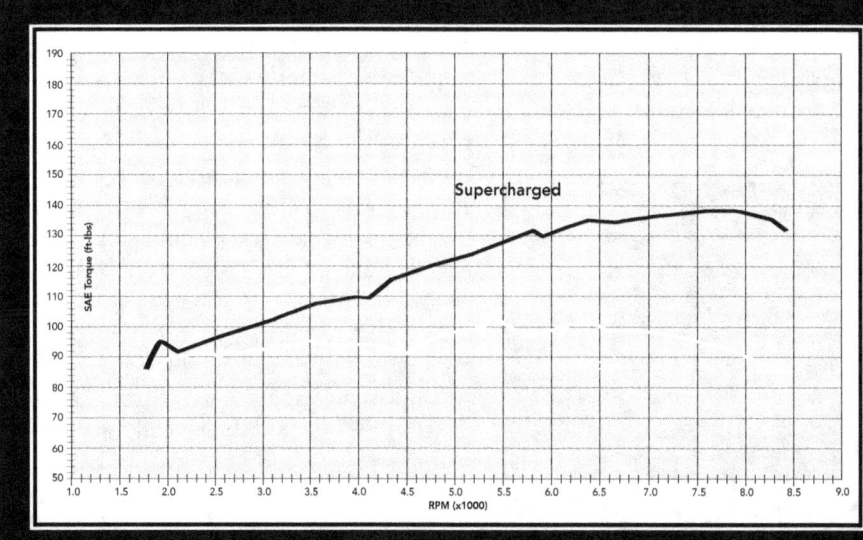

Vortech Supercharger: Torque

Peak Torque – Stock	104 ft-lbs
Peak Torque – Supercharged	139 ft-lbs
Largest Torque Gain	48 ft-lbs

Chapter 5

Test 6: Jackson Racing Supercharged Prelude

1999 Prelude
H22 2.2L VTEC

Take a close look at the Jackson Racing supercharger kit for the H22 Prelude and you will notice something different. The usual cast of characters is present and accounted for, as the kit featured the positive displacement M62 Eaton supercharger, a dedicated intake manifold, and inlet elbow for the throttle body. While all the normal performance gadgets are there, this Prelude kit actually has something in common with the Vortech kits for the GSR and Civic Si. Unlike the other kits tested for this book (as well as the many other kits available for various Honda/Acura applications), this Prelude kit utilized a transfer shaft to direct power from the crank to the supercharger pulley. It is not as long as the lengthy shaft used on the Vortech kit, but the JR Prelude kit utilized a small shaft with a pair of pulleys. The serpentine accessory belt was used to drive one pulley, which in turn (via the shaft) spun the drive pulley on the other end of the shaft. A small drive belt was used to attach the pulley from the transfer shaft to the pulley on the Eaton supercharger. This trick transfer shaft allowed the use of the supercharger where there was insufficient room to drive the blower directly from the crank. It is systems like these transfer shafts that allow Jackson Racing to supercharge applications that would otherwise not enjoy the benefits of boost.

The Prelude kit also required some custom electronics tuning that were eventually applied to all the Honda and Acura kits. On the early kits, a simple vacuum/boost switch was used to alter the value of the air temperature sensor. This provided supplemental fuel enrichment in additional to that provided by the rising rate fuel pressure regulator (FMU). The simple vacuum/pressure switch was replaced by more sophisticated electronics to provide a smoother transition from off-boost to boosted conditions with respect to fuel enrichment. Although the previous fuel management systems employed by Jackson Racing resulted in ideal air/fuel ratios (and timing), the new electronics on the Prelude kit cured a hesitation that was present when lifting off the throttle (transition from boosted conditions back to normally aspirated). This electronics upgrade is another example of the quality (both products and development) put into every Jackson Racing supercharged kit. The continued research and development (extensive dyno, street, and track testing) is the reason why the Jackson Racing superchargers are one of the few systems that look and perform to OE specs.

The Prelude kit is another example of how well Honda/Acura motors take to forced induction. While the positive displacement supercharged motors will never rival the big-boost turbo or centrifugal superchargers for maximum horsepower output, they do provide immediate throttle response and impressive torque production. Nowhere is this more evident than the Prelude kit, as the big block of the Honda/Acura lineup exceeded 133 ft-lbs of torque on this test motor. This torque production is why so many Civic owners want H22 power under the hood. You just can't get a B-series to produce the grunt of the Prelude motor. The Jackson Racing supercharger made an absolute torque monster out of the H22, upping peak torque from 133 ft-lbs to 182 ft-lbs. The baseline power numbers were generated with an air intake, header, and cat-back exhaust. The free-flowing H22 motor took full advantage of the M62 Eaton supercharger by posting a peak power reading of 235 hp. The larger H22 motor required a slightly higher drive ratio (essentially supercharger speed) compared to the B16A, B18C, or B18C5, to produce the same maximum boost pressure of 6 psi. Another interesting trick employed by Jackson Racing was early engagement of the secondary VTEC cam profile. The early engagement of the secondary cam actually improved the low-speed power production, greatly improving full-throttle torque production. While not beneficial on normally aspirated motors, this ultra-early VTEC engagement was excellent with the positive displacement supercharged motors.

Superchargers: Big Boost Bolt-Ons

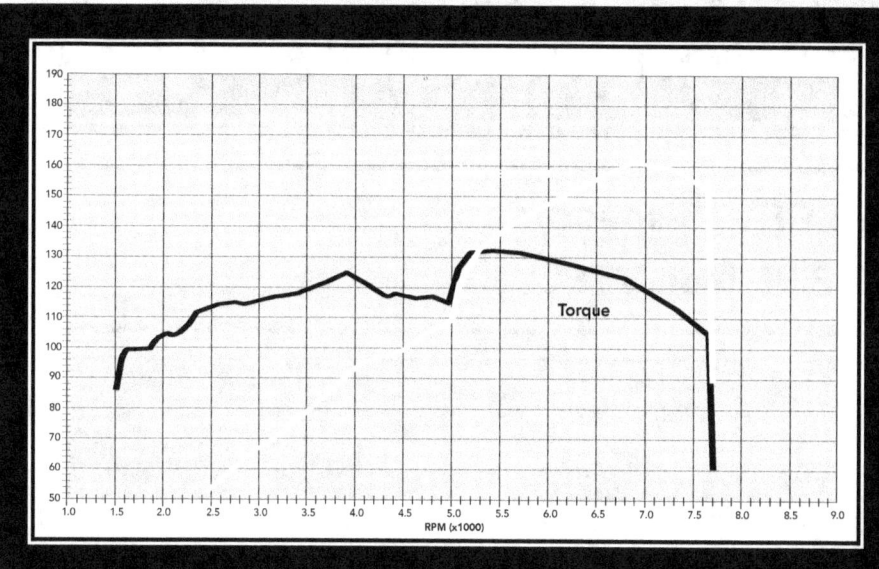

Baseline: H22 (Stock)

The Prelude engine is considered the big block of the Honda family. Nothing compares to the combination of big displacement, VTEC cam trickery, and a gauge full of boost.

Peak Horsepower – Stock	162 hp
Peak Torque – Stock	133 ft-lbs

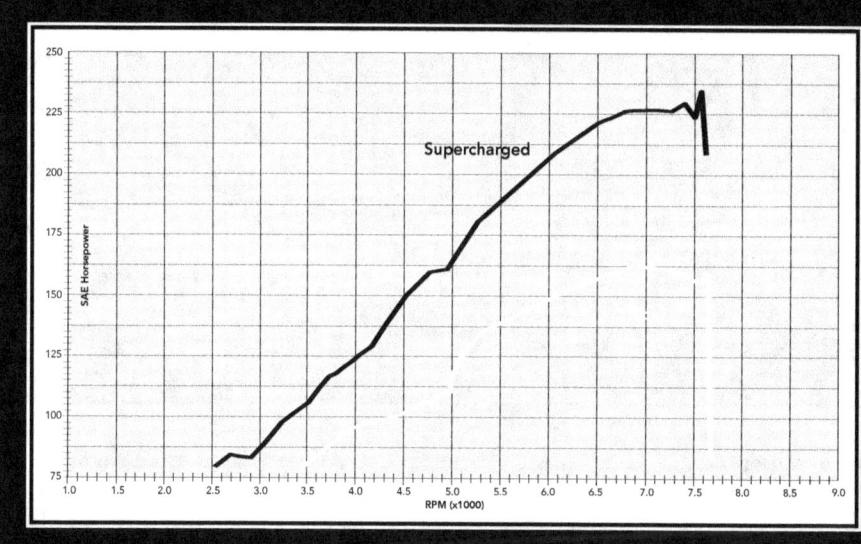

Jackson Racing Supercharger: Horsepower

Peak Horsepower – Stock	162 hp
Peak Horsepower – Supercharged	235 hp
Largest Horsepower Gain	63 hp

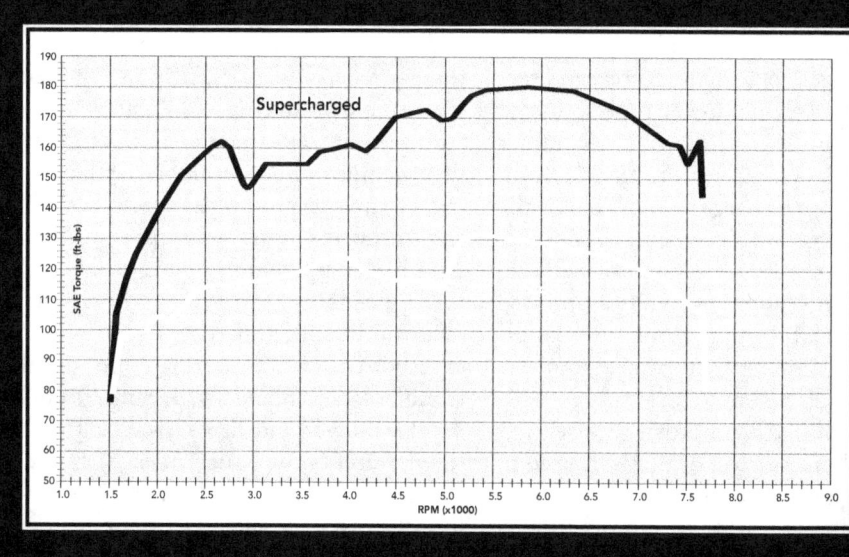

Jackson Racing Supercharger: Torque

Peak Torque – Stock	133 ft-lbs
Peak Torque – Supercharged	182 ft-lbs
Largest Torque Gain	62 ft-lbs

How to Build Honda Horsepower

Chapter 5

Test 7: Jackson Racing Supercharged CRV

1998 CRV (5-speed)
B20 2.0L Non-VTEC

If ever there was an ideal application for a positive displacement supercharged Honda motor, the 2.0L CRV is it. The positive displacement supercharger, like the Eaton units employed by Jackson Racing in their Honda/Acura kits, is characterized by immediate boost response. Essentially a giant air pump, the positive displacement supercharger grabs air from one side of the blower and moves it to the other. Being positive displacement, this amount of air is fixed. In other words, each revolution of the blower grabs a given amount of air (the amount of air is based on the size of the supercharger). The amount of air delivered to the motor is determined by the drive ratio (the size of the crank or drive pulley versus the blower pulley) and therefore blower speed. Obviously, the positive displacement supercharger is able to move (grab and deliver) more air to the motor than it could otherwise ingest. Although no true compression takes place inside a roots-style positive displacement supercharger, providing additional airflow to the motor produces extra power. The buildup of air between the supercharger and the intake (or valves) result is boost pressure.

Unlike a turbocharger, the positive displacement supercharger is coupled directly to the motor via the crankshaft. There is no waiting for sufficient exhaust energy to spool up the compressor side of the turbo, although a turbocharger can be sized to produce near-immediate boost (even better than the typical positive displacement blower), but such a turbo would not be able to support much power as the exhaust turbine would limit ultimate power potential.

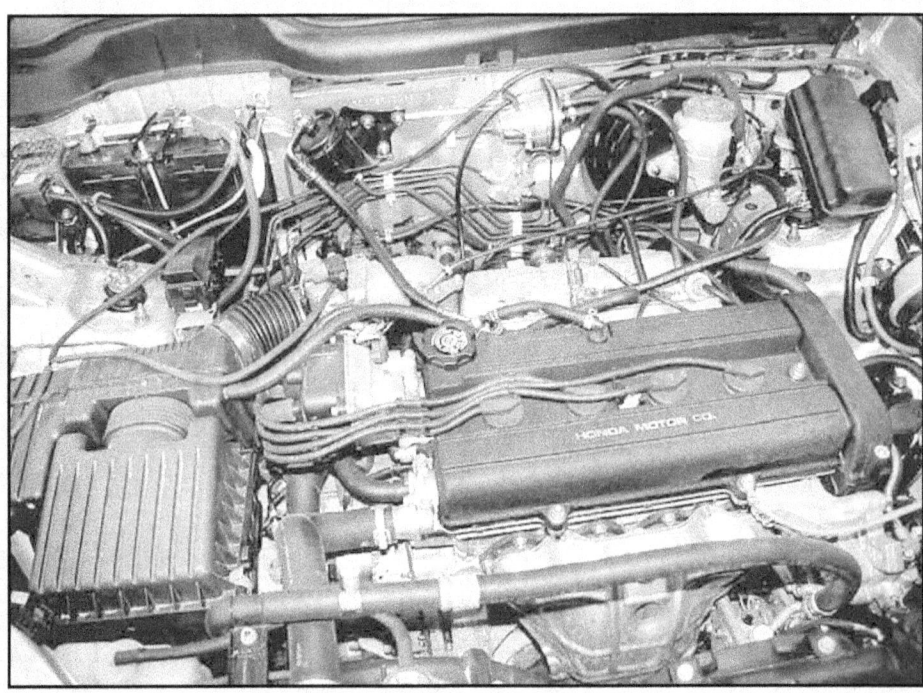

The Eaton supercharger used in the Jackson Racing kit suffers from no such limitation. The positive displacement is not the ideal choice for a maximum effort power producer, but it does excel at torque production. Jackson Racing has discovered that adding a small supercharger to a small motor can literally transform the power production of that motor. In the case of the rather weak 2.0L CRV motor, the Jackson Racing supercharger increased the power output by 50 percent. This power gain made the 2.0L CRV motor perform like a well-tuned normally aspirated 3.0L, with all the part-throttle drivability improvements that come from the added displacement.

The 2.0L CRV motor was essentially a big-bore version of the 1.8L used in the LS (and GS) Integras. Where the 1.8L (actually 1,834-cc) motor utilized an 81-mm bore and an 89-mm stroke, the 2.0L CRV upped the bore diameter to 84 mm. The increase was done to improve torque production, as Honda knew that CRV owners would not be searching for those 8,000 rpm VTEC shift points. What an SUV owners wants and needs is low-speed torque, something even the best 2.0L four-cylinder has trouble producing. Add a substantial curb weight to the picture and you have the makings for a real slug when it comes time to get on the freeway with any authority, never mind passing that 18-wheeler up a long grade. What the CRV needs is a bigger motor. The Jackson Racing supercharger provides exactly that, without having to go to the trouble of an engine swap. Simply pop on the blower and drive away with all the drivability (and fuel mileage) of the smaller 2.0L, but have an extra 30–45 ft-lbs of torque available any time you want, even below 2,000 rpm!

Superchargers: Big Boost Bolt-Ons

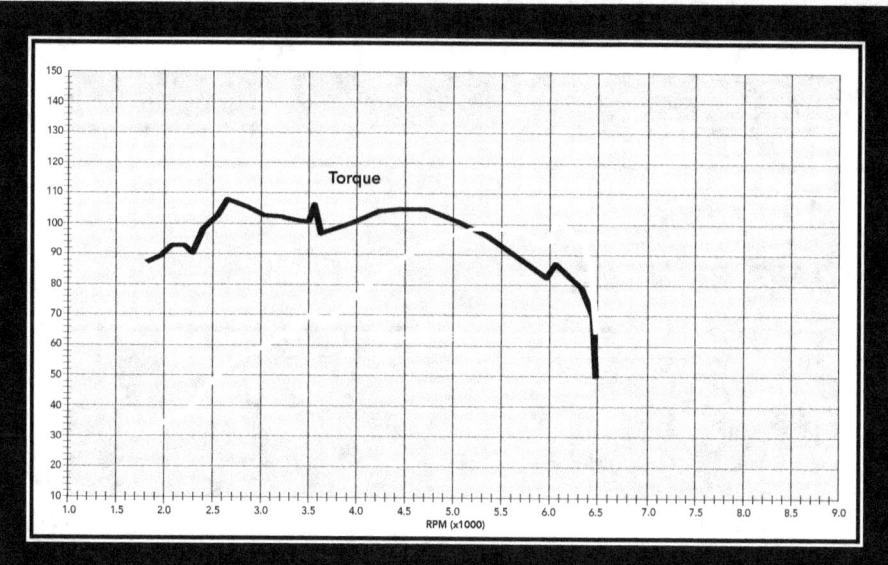

Baseline: B20 (Stock)

The CRV is a capable performer and family hauler, but what the 2.0L four-cylinder really needed to pull those mountain passes was some boost courtesy of Jackson Racing.

Peak Horsepower – Stock	100 hp
Peak Torque – Stock	108 ft-lbs

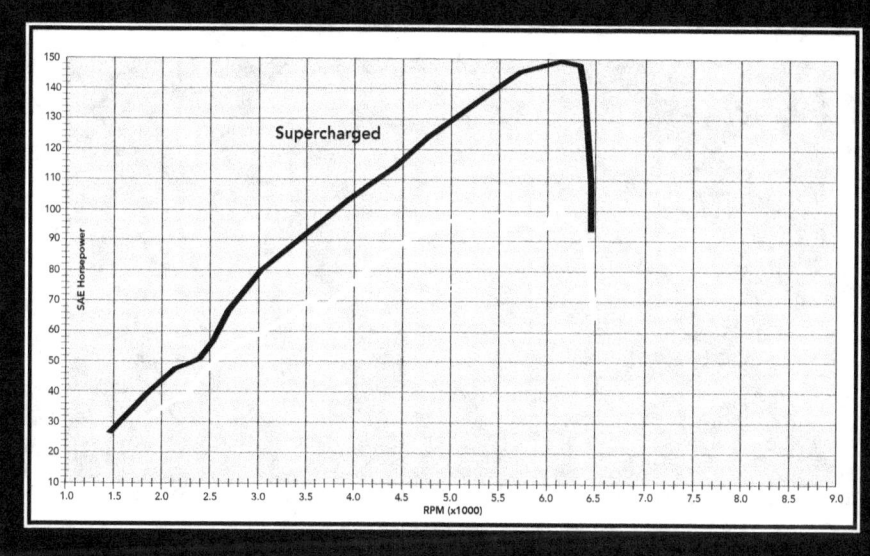

Jackson Racing Supercharger: Horsepower

Peak Horsepower – Stock	100 hp
Peak Horsepower – Supercharged	150 hp
Largest Horsepower Gain	56 hp

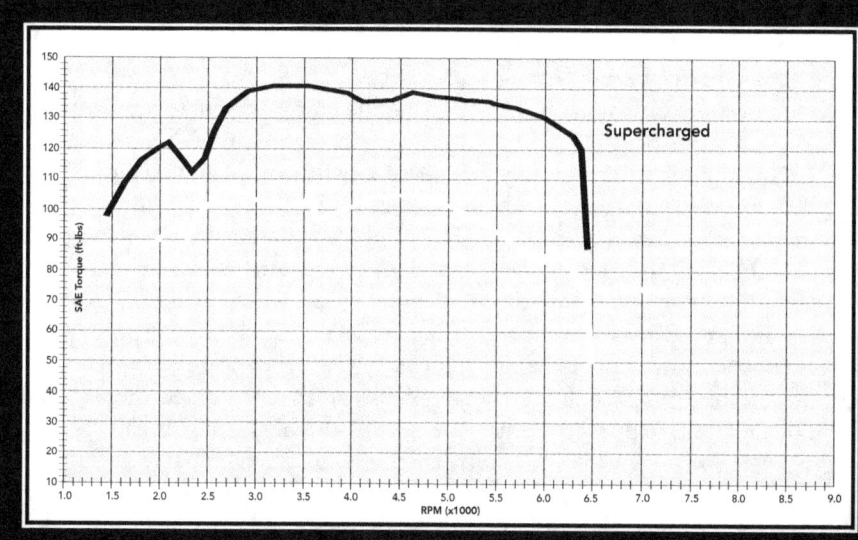

Jackson Racing Supercharger: Torque

Peak Torque – Stock	108 ft-lbs
Peak Torque – Supercharged	144 ft-lbs
Largest Torque Gain	51 ft-lbs

How to Build Honda Horsepower

Chapter 5

Test 8: Comptech Supercharged NSX

1997 NSX
C30A 3.0L VTEC

The NSX is a great car. I speak not just as an admirer but also as an owner. How many cars offer the combination of extreme performance and daily reliability all wrapped up in an exotic (look at me) package? The answer is not very many. Sure there are a number of cars that may equal or even surpass the performance numbers offered up by the stock NSX, but how many can back those numbers up with unparalleled reliability? How short is the list of super-performance cars that you wouldn't think twice about jumping in for a cross-country trip? Which ones could knock down better than 25 mpg without fear of being stranded miles away from the nearest exotic car dealership? The list keeps dwindling. The reality is that not many other cars on the road offer the combination of performance and practicality of the NSX. Is it the perfect car? Probably not, as there are always enthusiasts out there who seek to find fault in near perfection. The major complaint among NSX owners (besides the brakes) is a lack of power.

While the 290 hp (270 for early 3.0L models) 3.2L motors offer plenty of performance in the lightweight chassis, what car wouldn't benefit from an extra 100 hp? That list is indeed short, as we can always use another 100 hp. Luckily for enthusi-

asts, Comptech found a way to provide exactly what NSX owners were looking for—namely 100 extra hp. Finding 100 extra horsepower is no easy feat, especially on the ultra-efficient Honda/Acura motors. While not quite on par with the Type R or S2000 in terms of specific output, the 3.2L NSX motor offered a very respectable 90.6 hp/liter. Comptech took the only route available to them for the additional 100 hp: they added a supercharger. Sure, they also offer an air intake, header, and exhaust (not to mention big brakes) for both the 3.0L and 3.2L versions, the big gains came from the addition of the positive displacement supercharger.

The addition of the positive displacement supercharger to the high-winding NSX motor improved not only the peak power output but also provided something else that was missing, that something called torque. Making 290 hp from just 3.2 liters required that the peak power occur out near 8,000 rpm. While hearing the motor scream to 8,000 rpm is music to the ears of any NSX owner, the high-rpm nature of the motor meant that low-speed torque production suffered. The need for low-speed torque was why Acura increased the displacement from 3.0 liters to 3.2 liters in the first place. They weren't looking for more peak power, (though they were rewarded with 20 extra hp) drivers wanted more grunt for normal driving. The graphs illustrate that the Comptech supercharged kit, especially when combined with the air intake, headers, and exhaust, really wake up the NSX motor.

Superchargers: Big Boost Bolt-Ons

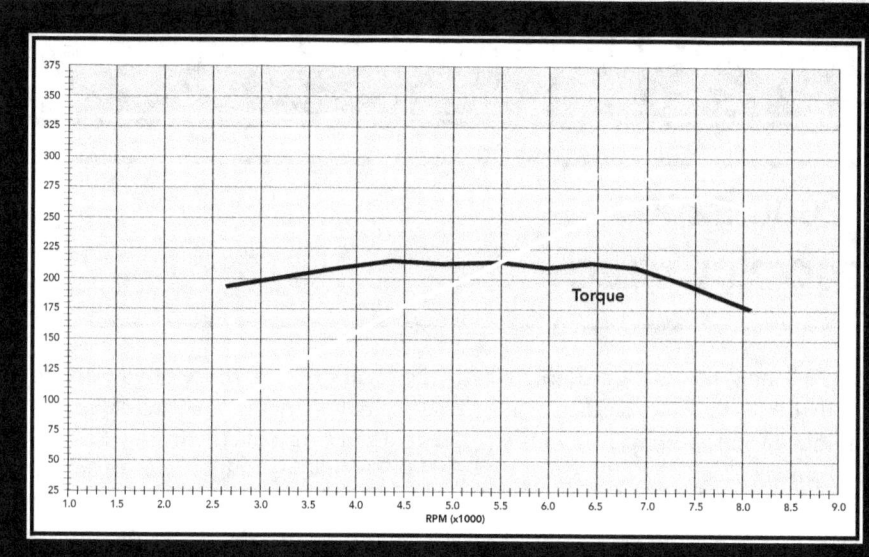

Baseline: C30A1 (Stock)
(with air intake, header and exhaust)

The NSX proved that Honda/Acura had the mettle to stand toe-to-toe with Italy's finest. The NSX was also the first US Honda machine to sport the VTEC system; like all VTECs, the NSX motor responds to boost.

Peak Horsepower – Stock	297 hp
Peak Torque – Stock	230 ft-lbs

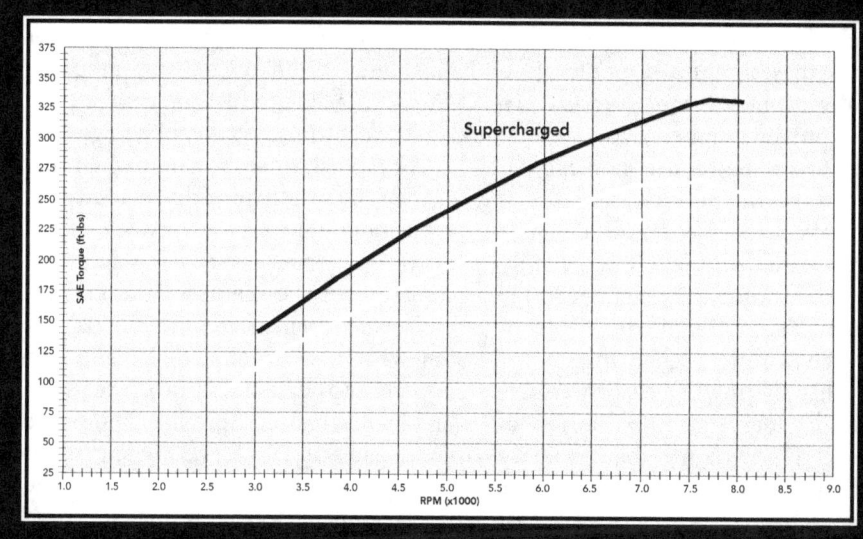

Comptech Supercharger: Horsepower

Peak Horsepower – Stock	297 hp
Peak Horsepower – Supercharged	367 hp
Largest Horsepower Gain	70 hp

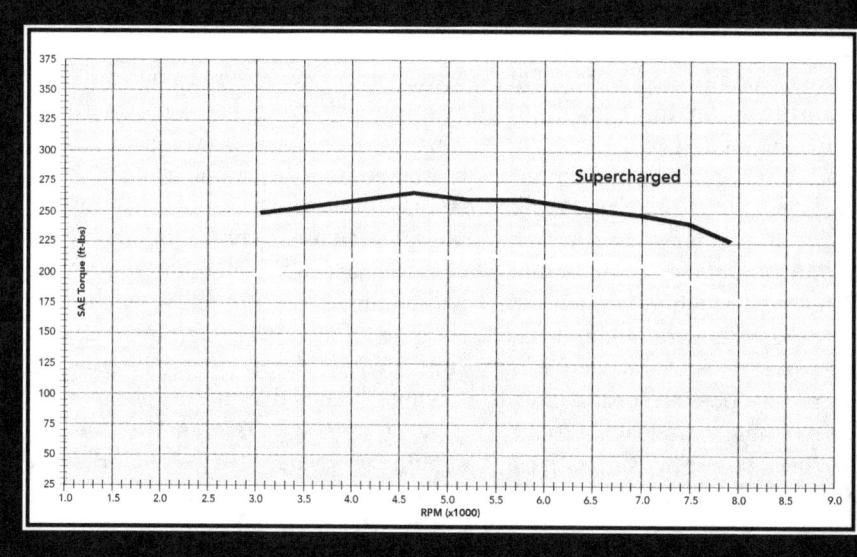

Comptech Supercharger: Torque

Peak Torque – Stock	230 ft-lbs
Peak Torque – Supercharged	268 ft-lbs
Largest Torque Gain	50 ft-lbs

How to Build Honda Horsepower

Chapter 5

 Test 9: Comptech Supercharged S2000

2000 S2000
F20C 2.0L VTEC

Honda/Acura has given us many impressive power plants that post ultra-impressive specific outputs. The specific output of a motor is an efficiency rating based on the power output and displacement. The more power a motor produces for its displacement, the better the specific output. The 170-hp 1.8L GSR motor produces 94.44 hp/liter. It wasn't long ago that any motor that approached 100 hp/liter could only be found on the racetrack. While over 94 hp/liter is an excellent achievement, Honda has a number of motors that exceed even that figure. The 1.6L B16A actually achieves the magical 100 hp/liter by producing 160 hp from just 1.6 liters of displacement. All the more impressive is the fact that all these Honda motors produce these specific outputs while simultaneously achieving the ultra-low emissions standards. Not wanting to merely achieve 100 hp/liter, Honda set out to exceed it, and did so with a pair of Type R-spec motors. The 1.8L B18C5 Integra Type R motors bests the 100 hp/liter by producing 195 hp from just 1.8 liters, topping 108 hp/liter in the process. The high water mark for the front wheel drive motors was the 1.6L Civic Type R motor, which produced 185 hp from just 1.6 liters or a whopping 115.62 hp/liter. While other manufacturers were playing catch up to these marvelous Type R motors, Honda set the automotive world on its ear with a motor that produced an unbelievable 120 hp/liter in the new S2000 convertible.

At just 2.0 liters, the S2000 is the undisputed champ of the specific output arena. While rumors surface about even more power available from this combination, the elevated power has one drawback. There really is only one way to produce these specific output levels in a normally aspirated configuration. To make big power numbers, you have to rev the motor. Since the horsepower output of a motor is nothing more than a mathematical representation of where the motor makes torque, Honda simply extended the torque curve higher in the rev range. The unfortunate effect of shifting the torque higher in the rev range is that the low speed power suffers. Honda does an admirable job of combating this with the mild primary cam timing, but there is only so much a 2.0L can do to make up for power that peaks at 8,400 rpm. The benefit of such a motor is that the excellent intake manifold, cylinder head, and camshaft (especially the secondary VTEC profiles) make for an ultra efficient motor. This efficiency makes a motor that is just begging for a supercharger.

Comptech recognized the need for a supercharger for the S2000 and unlike their positive displacement unit for the NSX, Comptech chose a centrifugal supercharger for the high-winding S2000. While the debate rages on about which supercharger system is better, there is no real answer. The positive displacement (regardless of manufacturer) will produce better low-speed power but suffers at elevated boost levels and engine speeds. A centrifugal will produce better top-end horsepower. Boost for boost, the centrifugal will produce more power due to its efficiency. Any one that tells you different hasn't tested them in the real world. The choice boils down to where you want to improve the power output of the motor. If excellent low-to-medium speed torque production and low levels of boost are desired (with reasonable peak power gains), a positive displacement is the answer. If maximum power gains with emphasis on mid-range to top-end power production are the goal, then the centrifugal is the way to go.

Comptech took the centrifugal route for the S2000, opting for that mad rush of power, not unlike that of the stock motor. It is obvious from the power graphs that discussion of the merits of the positive displacement versus the centrifugal was somewhat over simplified. When sized properly (not unlike a turbo), a centrifugal supercharger can provide impressive power gains as low as 4,500 rpm, about halfway to redline on the S2000. The Paxton supercharger produced torque gains of 25 ft-lbs as low as 4,500 rpm, but thing really started to get out of control after 6,000 rpm. By redline, the power gain was as much as 100 hp, a number not usually associated with positive displacement supercharging. For running around town, the low-speed power gains offered by the positive displacement supercharger may offer more usable performance, but for track use the power offered by the centrifugal is right where the engine will be running when pushed hard through the gears. The added benefit of the Paxton supercharger used in the excellent Comptech kit is that there is plenty more power to be had (at least another 100 hp!) should an owner decide to build the motor with forged pistons. The same cannot be said for most kits using positive displacement superchargers.

Superchargers: Big Boost Bolt-Ons

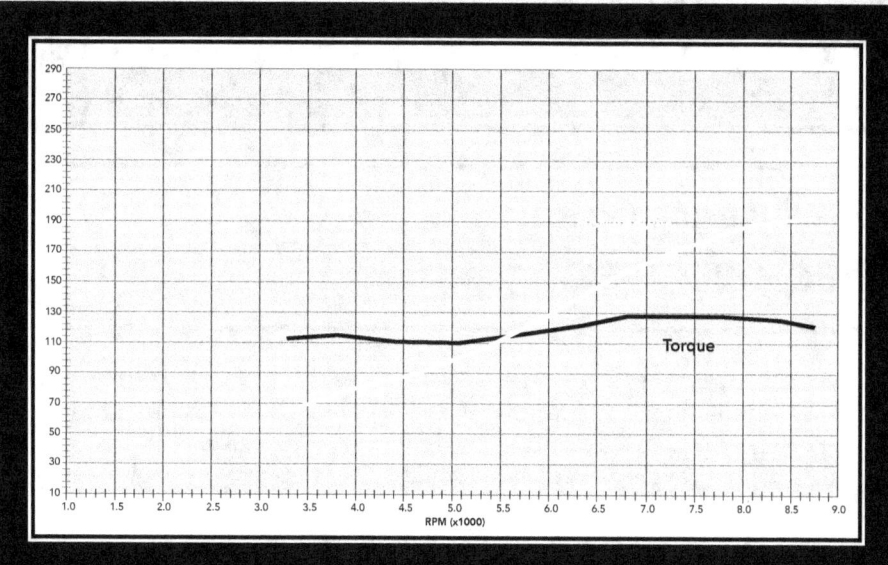

Baseline: F20C1 (Stock)

Are you disappointed with the power of your S2000? The Comptech supercharger system can add an extra 100 horsepower! Can you say Corvette killer?

Peak Horsepower – Stock	194 hp
Peak Torque – Stock	127 ft-lbs

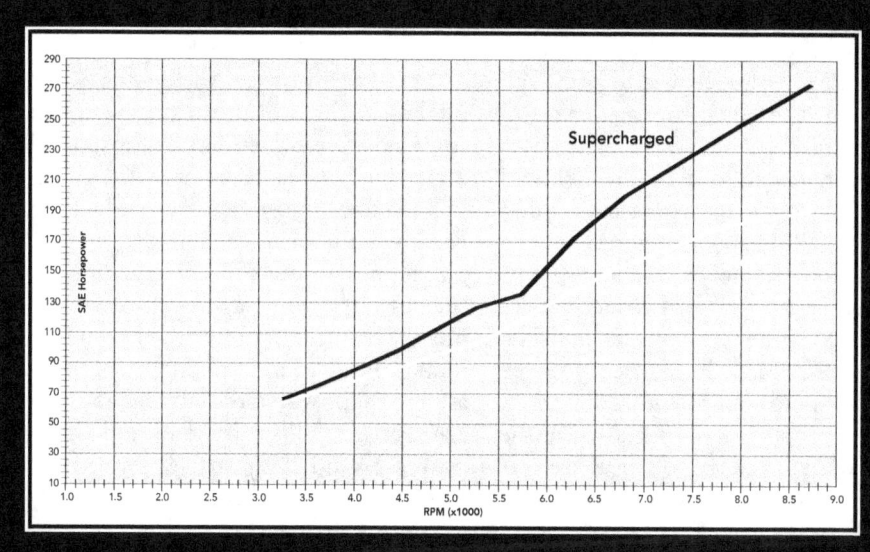

Comptech Supercharger: Horsepower

Peak Horsepower – Stock	194 hp
Peak Horsepower – Supercharged	286 hp
Largest Horsepower Gain	99 hp

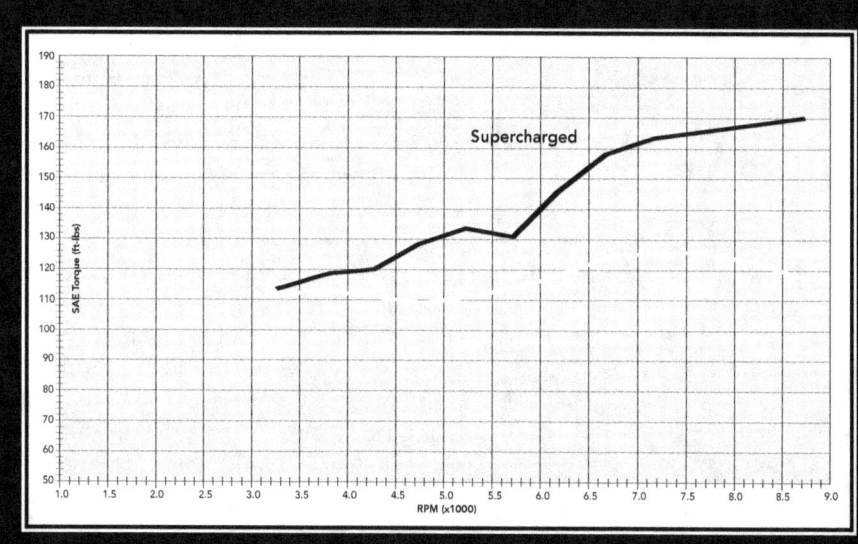

Comptech Supercharger: Torque

Peak Torque – Stock	127 ft-lbs
Peak Torque – Supercharged	172 ft-lbs
Largest Torque Gain	59 ft-lbs

How to Build Honda Horsepower

Chapter 5

Test 10: Jackson Racing Supercharged GSR

2001 Integra GSR
B18C 1.8L VTEC

Until the Type R appeared and showed us just how serious Honda was about performance motors, the GSR was top dog in the B-series camp. With 170 hp, the GSR held a slight edge over the smaller 1.6L B16A. Though the 170-hp GSR was only 10 hp stronger than the B16A, the difference in performance between the two motors was more than the 10-hp deficit might suggest. The reason the B18C GSR motor had little trouble handling a B16A on the street was the additional displacement and a little intake trickery. The longer stroke (87.2 mm versus 77 mm) helped produce much more bottom end torque than the puny B16A, while the dual-stage intake helped produced a broad power band. The long runners worked with the displacement to improve the low-speed power while the short runners worked with the secondary cam timing and free-flowing cylinder head to maximize top-end power. In truth, the dual-stage intake was actually limiting in terms of maximum power output, as the combination actually only produced excellent results in the mid range.

The GSR was and continues to be very popular among racers. Look under the hood of many of the fastest racers on the track and odds are that you will find at least a GSR bottom end and possibly even a GSR cylinder head. Although most ditched the dual-runner intakes in favor of the top-end power offered by the Type-R manifold, the GSR cylinder head is a favorite among racers around the world. While drag racers may seek to optimize top-end power, the key to performance street use is a broad power band. Next time you are behind the wheel, take note of how often you rev your GSR motor out to 8,000 rpm versus how much time you spend down in the 3,000–4,000 rpm range. Chances are that you would spend even less time high on the VTEC cam if you had an additional 25–35 ft-lbs of torque available pre-VTEC. Those banzai squirts through traffic with your exhaust at full song would be history if you could simply flick the throttle and summon up the kind of power rush normally seen only at redline. Such is the benefit of the positive displacement supercharger.

Like most of the B-series motors, even the 1.8L GSR suffers from a lack of low-speed power. All the dual-stage intakes in the world are no match for some positive pressure. For those GSR owners having a hard time imagining what kind of improvement that Jackson Racing supercharger adds (not even taking into account the fit and finish of the kit), try to imagine all the extra power you got from adding your air intake, header, and exhaust. Take that additional power and double it and you are getting close to the additional power provided by just 6 psi at only 2,500 rpm. The torque curve clearly illustrates that the JR supercharger kit substantially improved the power output of the GSR even as low as 2,000 rpm. While the measurable gains offered by the typical array of bolt-ons normally occurs at or near redline, the supercharger adds a chunk of torque not available from any level of normally aspirated modifications short of a sizable hike in displacement (and compression). With a 25 ft-lb gain at 2,000 rpm, you'd think all the fun would be down low, but you'd be wrong. The JR supercharged GSR motor spun happily to 8,000 rpm, where the 1.8L produced right near 200 hp at the wheels (up from a tad over 140 hp). This supercharger GSR would wipe the smile right off that Type R owner's face as you blew by him (once you got traction of course).

How to Build Honda Horsepower

Superchargers: Big Boost Bolt-Ons

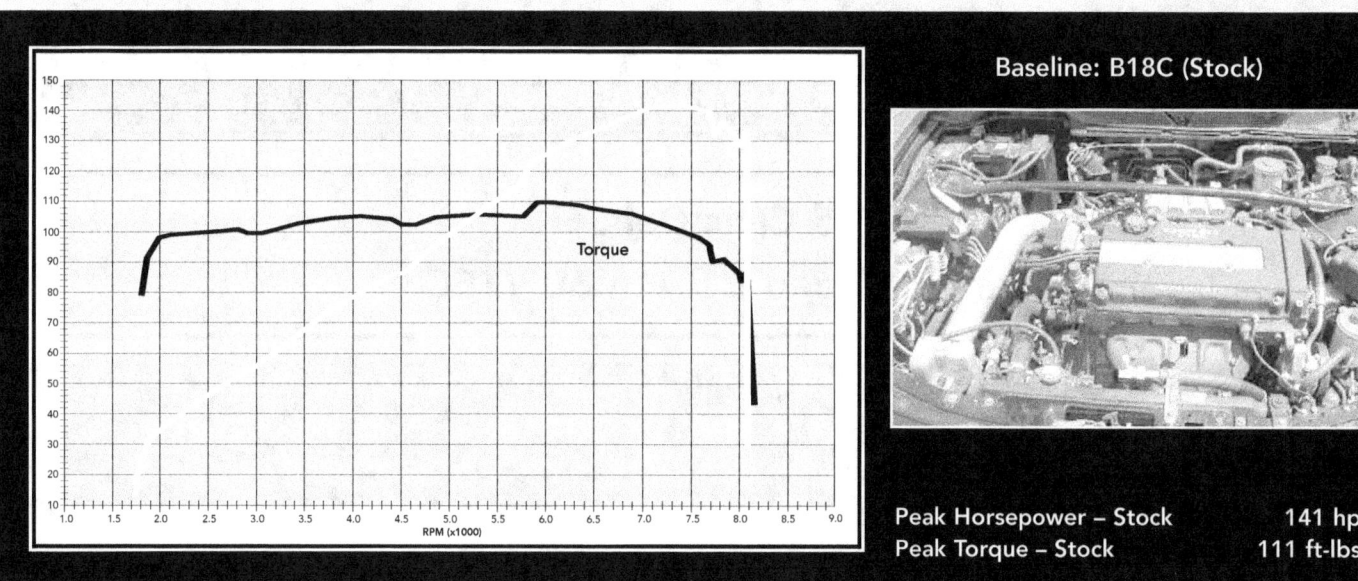

Baseline: B18C (Stock)

Peak Horsepower – Stock	141 hp
Peak Torque – Stock	111 ft-lbs

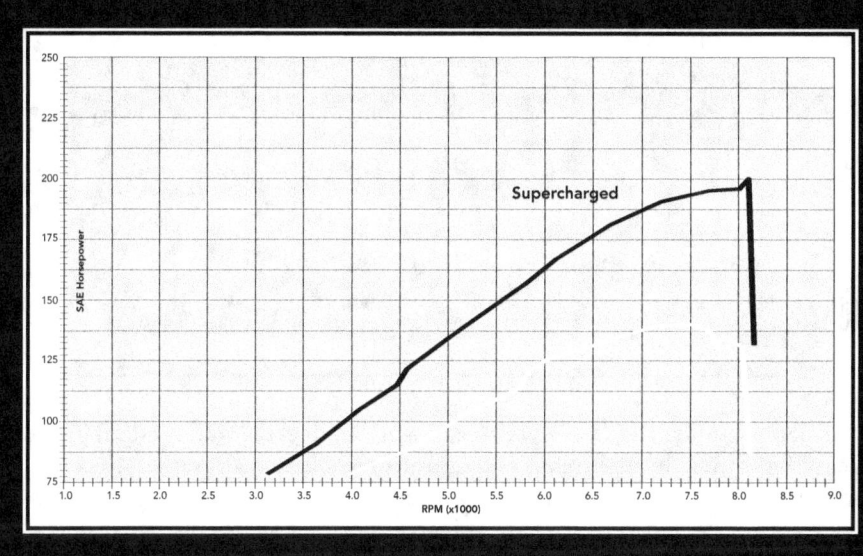

Jackson Racing Supercharger: Horsepower

Peak Horsepower – Stock	141 hp
Peak Horsepower – Supercharged	200 hp
Largest Horsepower Gain	59 hp

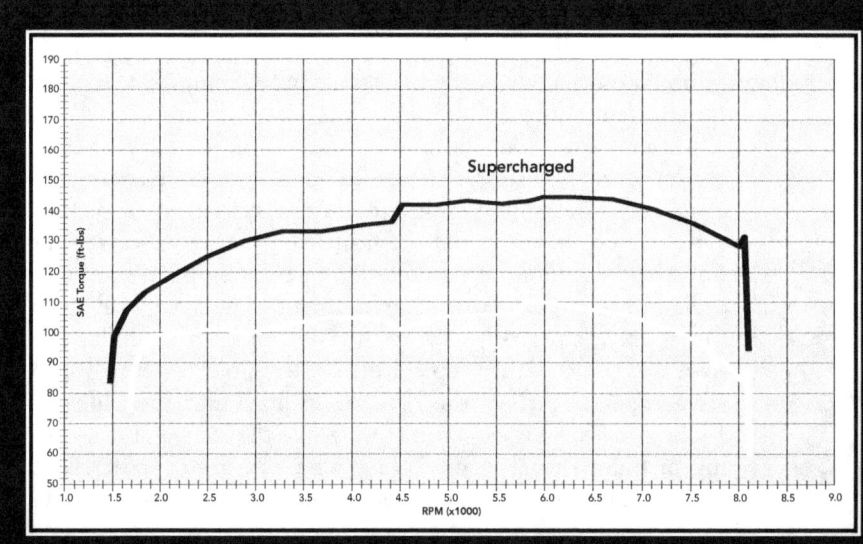

Jackson Racing Supercharger: Torque

Peak Torque – Stock	111 ft-lbs
Peak Torque – Supercharged	145 ft-lbs
Largest Torque Gain	43 ft-lbs

How to Build Honda Horsepower

Chapter 5

Test 11: Effects of Intake Charge Temp: Ice Water versus Ambient

1995 Civic Del Sol
Supercharged B16A 1.6L VTEC

This test was done in an effort to demonstrate the effect of a drop in charge temperature on the power output. The test was also done to help settle the argument between the fans of air-to-air intercoolers and those who favor the air-to-water variety. Like the argument between the proponents of positive displacement and centrifugal superchargers, the air-to-air/air-to-water argument is merely a matter of application rather than of outright efficiency. From a most basic standpoint, the function of an intercooler is to lower the temperature of the compressed air exiting a turbo or supercharger. This compression that occurs in forced induction applications (measured in boost) results in elevated charge temperatures. The laws of nature dictate that any time you compress air you heat it. Unfortunately, cooler air is much better for power production, as the colder air is denser with more power-giving oxygen molecules. Intercoolers re-cool the air after the supercharger (or turbo) heats it up. The result can be additional power and a reduction in the tendency toward detonation.

As the names imply, the two styles of intercooling differ in the manner they cool the air. The air-to-air intercooler runs the heated charge air through a larger heat exchanger exposed to ambient airflow. Think of the coolant in your motor as the charge air from the supercharger. The airflow across the radiator (intercooler) cools the heated coolant (charge air from the supercharger). The efficiency of this system is dependent on the size and design of the cooler. Obviously, an air-to-water has an advantage in the cooling, as the cooling medium (usually water) can be super cooled. The result is that you can get 32-degree water cooling the 250-degree charge air rather than 75-degree (ambient) air cooling the 250-degree air. Of course, the downside is that the ice water will not last forever, so the air-to-water is best used for short runs like drag racing or Bonneville. Or is it? This test demonstrated that while the ice water indeed improved power, the gain was not significant over the ambient water. This Aftercooled-Vortech kit employed a separate heat exchanger in the system to help draw out the heat from the water leaving the Aftercooler, in an attempt to keep it at or near ambient. The heat exchanger used in the Civic Si kit was similar to a typical oil cooler mounted in front of the radiator to maximize the exposure to airflow. While the ice water is a definite plus (who can argue with 12–15 hp), the test shows that the air-to-water aftercooler performed well even with the ambient water.

110　　　　How to Build Honda Horsepower

Superchargers: Big Boost Bolt-Ons

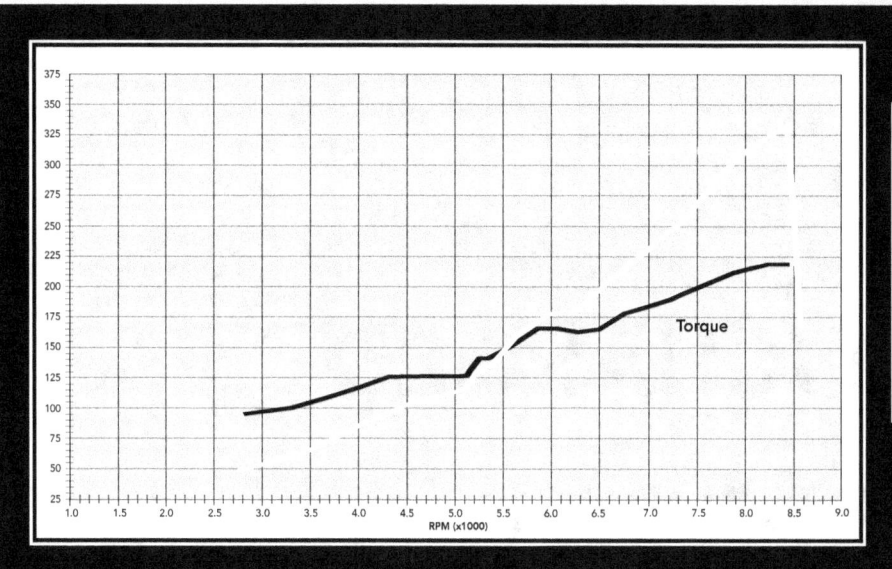

Baseline: Supercharged B16A

Though water at ambient temperature reduces the charge temperature effectively, adding ice water will lower it even more, sometimes even below the ambient air temperature.

Peak HP – Supercharged	332 hp
Peak Torque – Supercharged	219 ft-lbs

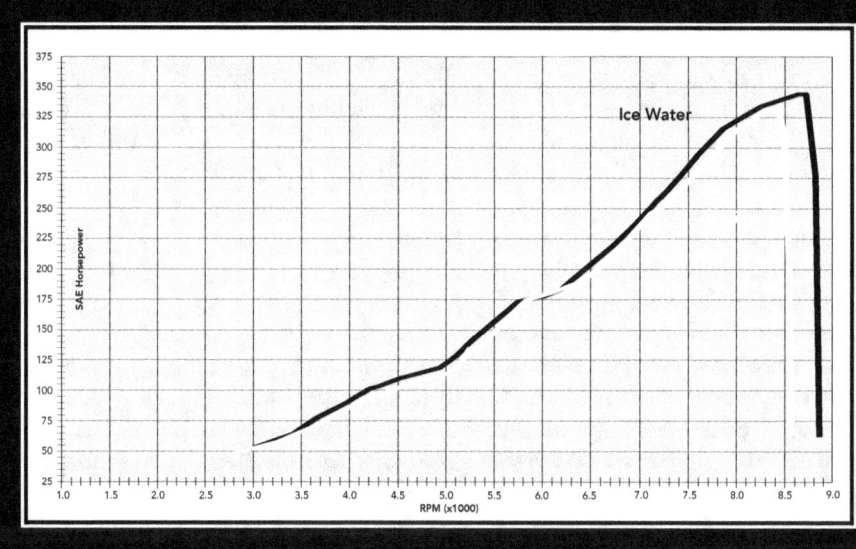

Ambient versus Ice Water: Horsepower

Peak Horsepower – Ambient	332 hp
Peak Horsepower – Ice Water	342 hp
Largest Horsepower Gain	15 hp

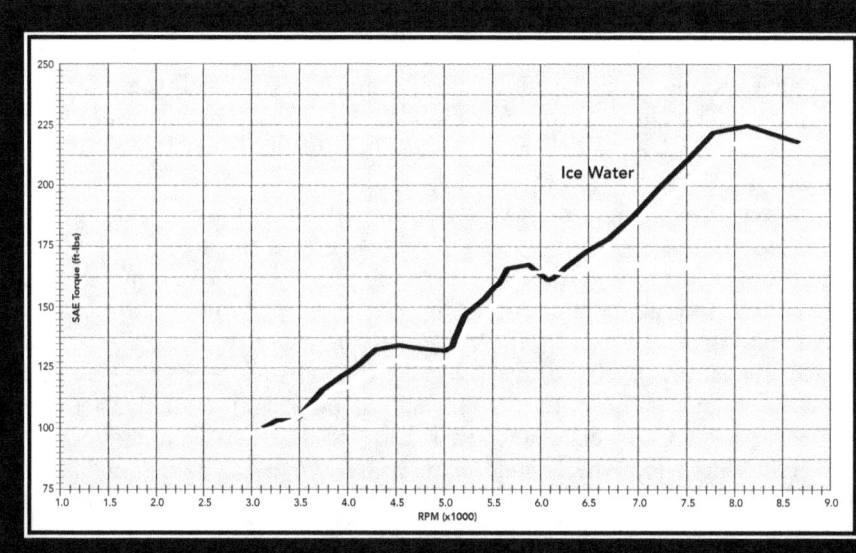

Ambient versus Ice Water: Torque

Peak Torque – Ambient	219 ft-lbs
Peak Torque – Ice Water	224 ft-lbs
Largest Torque Gain	12 ft-lbs

Chapter 6

Turbocharged Terrors

When it comes time to build serious Honda horsepower, there is nothing like forced induction. The most popular form of forced induction, at least the most prevalent at the track, is turbocharging. Nothing wakes up a Honda/Acura motor like the addition of some boost pressure. All the head porting, cams, and even stroker motors in the world will never equal the power potential of a good turbo system. In fact, an argument can be made for the affordability of turbocharging, at least in terms of power gain per dollar spent. You could drop some serious coin (well over $1,000) on an air intake, exhaust system, and stainless header and have just 10–15 hp to show for all your hard work. While you are not likely to find a turbo system for a grand (unless you build it yourself), the power gains are much more inline with the cash outlay. Even the mildest turbo kit running just 5–6 psi will get you 50–60 hp. Contrary to claims you may have seen in various performance magazines, it is damn hard to get an additional 50–60 hp out of your normally aspirated B-series Honda/Acura motor.

Although a 50–60 hp gain will make a noticeable improvement in acceleration on a street Civic or Integra, this is just a starter kit in terms of turbocharging. Add the right turbo, intercooler and fuel management and the sky is the limit in terms of power. The current crop of turbo motors that terrorize the strip are making in excess of 750 hp and four-digit power levels are not far off. Of course, hooking all that power up is another thing entirely, but it is always nice to have an overabundance of power! Obviously, these race motors are not designed for street use and the power levels are commensurate with the price, but it is possible to produce 300, 400 and even 500 hp at the wheels and drive your car on a regular basis. As the power level goes up however, the reliability goes down. Rest assured that a 300-hp (at the wheels) Civic is a serious street machine, a 400-hp version even more so. While the number of Honda/Acuras out roaming the streets with a real 500 hp at the wheels can probably be counted on one hand, it is possible to drive a 10-second VTEC motor on the street.

Turbocharging offers massive power potential, much more than either form of supercharging (centrifugal or positive displacement). The centrifugal supercharger can offer similar (and even better in some cases) peak power but the linear boost curve generally produces lower average power numbers. Positive displacement superchargers can offer rapid boost response but generally lack the absolute power potential in the sizes most commonly used on Honda/Acura kits. The massive power potential available from a good turbo kit is what usually gets enthusiasts in trouble. The key to maximizing the power potential from any turbo kit is in the tuning. Bolt on a kit from Greddy, Drag, or any other source and chances are you will have a nice package, if you remain at the listed boost level. Boost, like any good drug, is addictive and the first thing we do after sampling boost is want more. If 5 psi is good, then 6, 7, or 8 psi must be even better. The problem with this theory is that the fuel and ignition (timing) must work together with

Though small, the impeller of a typical turbocharger can spin as fast as 100,000 rpm to produce exceptional airflow and power.

the turbo to produce safe power. Too much ignition timing and/or not enough fuel and your motor is history. All the decked blocks, forged pistons, and trick rods in the world won't save your bacon if the motor has too much timing or insufficient fuel.

The key to long-term turbo enjoyment is to spend a few extra bucks to have the combination tuned to precision. I won't even touch the throttle of a turbo motor without taking it to a near-by chassis dyno equipped with a real-time air/fuel meter. Even then, the combination is run with very little static timing, a rich air/fuel mixture, and race fuel for the preliminary runs. I shudder to think of a Civic/Integra owner installing a turbo kit and finding out that the waste gate line was unplugged during that first hard run down the street. Same for a failing fuel pump, excessive static ignition timing, or any of several things that can cause a major disaster when you add boost. When it comes to tuning, a conservative approach works best. It is much better to tune 10 hp out of your 350-hp with a reduction in timing and an ultra-safe air/fuel mixture, than to run it on the ragged edge and hope you never get a bad tank of gas. You will probably never miss the 10 hp, but you will miss having your car for a few weeks while the motor is being rebuilt. Ditto for the dent in your bank account! Tuned properly however, a turbo system can provide years of service and more than a few unhappy domestic V8 owners.

There are a myriad of turbo kits available for Honda/Acura owners. Some of the things to look for include a properly sized turbo. In most cases, the kit will be for a specific application, one that the manufacturer has tested. You cannot install just any old turbo on your VTEC motor and expect success. A turbo must be matched to the motor and desired usage. For street application, a cast-iron exhaust manifold is recommended. The cast-iron manifold will offer better long-tem use than popular tubular headers used by the import Racers. Never mind what Gary and Lisa use on their 8-second Civic, your street Integra will work best with a cast-iron exhaust manifold. The last thing you want is to be constantly welding up the cracks that accompany tubular manifolds. If you plan on running more than 6 psi on you turbo kit, think about installing an intercooler. Both air-to-air and air-to-water coolers are available, but the air-to-air is probably preferred on the street. Not that the air-to-air is more effective, but there are more readily available kits for front-mounted air-to-air cores. Keeping the charge temperature down is always a good idea, and the intercooler should allow you to crank up the boost a little—provided there is sufficient fuel to do so.

A few other tips are in order with regard to turbocharging. Most turbo kits rely on some sort of rising rate fuel management system for fuel enrichment. Increasing the fuel pressure under boost increases the fuel flow through the injectors to supply more fuel to the boosted motor. Unfortunately, increasing the fuel pressure also makes things difficult on the fuel pump. Increasing the pressure actually reduces the flow rate of the pump. Many kits come equipped with some sort of inline fuel pump upgrade. This is important, as most stock Honda/Acura fuel pumps are not sufficient to feed the requirements of a turbo motor at the elevated fuel pressure. When it comes to exhaust systems for a turbo motor, bigger is better. The pipe exiting your turbocharger should be free of restrictions and lead to a free-flowing exhaust system of at least 2.5-inches in diameter. We have even seen 3-inch systems work well on high-horsepower motors. The great thing about the turbo motor is that the large exhaust diameter will not dramatically increase exhaust noise. In fact, the turbo motor will likely be much quieter than a like-exhausted N/A motor. The turbo itself acts as muffler to deaden the exhaust note. There is of course a great deal more information, enough so that many books have been written on this subject alone. For now, check out the testing on turbo systems, boost levels and even different turbos, but remember to sneak up on the boost levels before sticking your foot in it.

Add the right turbo (like this 62-1 unit from Turbonetics) to your Honda motor and watch the horsepower numbers climb.

Chapter 6

Test 1: Low Buck B16A Turbo

1995 Civic Del Sol
B16A 1.6L VTEC

Some of the tests run for this book were more fun than others, and the buildup of this low-buck turbo ranks right up near the top. The idea behind the buildup was to see how cost effectively a turbo kit could be built for a Honda/Acura application. Although I chose a B16A for testing purposes, the same basic turbo combination (with the proper exhaust manifold) could be applied to nearly any of the popular Honda/Acura engines. With cost as the major concern, I began the buildup by sourcing the least expensive turbo available. Obviously there was no room for a brand new, custom turbocharger in a low-buck build. While designing or building a turbo to suit the needs of a specific application produces the best results, we were looking to minimize expenditures. Our turbo selection was more a matter of availability and price, and the results were darn impressive considering the turbocharger's humble beginnings. Our low-buck turbo came right from the wrecking yard from under the hood of no less than an SVO Mustang (or T-bird or other turbo 2.3L Ford). The T3 was not THE turbo of choice by any means, but the power available from something that cost only $125 bucks made this purchase the deal of the century.

The entire turbo kit (including the T3 turbo) cost less than $850. This price included the oil feed lines and fittings, an oil return line and even a fuel management system. So, the fuel system upgrades consisted of a simple FMU and a trio of aquarium valves (to stop the map sensor from seeing boost), the air/fuel mixture under boost was plenty safe using the stock 240-cc injectors. The non-intercooled kit also included an inlet tube connecting the T3 turbo to the stock throttle body, an exhaust down pipe, and a cast iron Drag turbo exhaust manifold (the most expensive part in the kit). The T3 turbo utilized an internal wastegate, so there was no need to add an external unit to the cost. We did need to source a suitable wastegate actuator, as the stock SVO actuator was set to open at 9 psi. We found one that opened much earlier

at just 6 psi. Even though we would later increase the boost up to 10 psi using a TurboXS manual wastegate controller, the first tests were run at just 6 psi.

The test motor was nothing more than a stock B16A that was purchased from a local used Japanese engine warehouse. The motor was not rebuilt or even freshened up. Just new oil, a valve and timing adjust, and we were off and running. Equipped with a DC Sports header and AEM intake, the stock B16A motor produced 153 hp at the wheels on a DynoJet. The installation of the low-buck turbo kit provided a maximum of 6 psi (±1 psi) and increased the peak power to 214 hp. The torque gains were equally impressive as the low-buck turbo motor produced 153 ft-lbs of torque, with gains available as low as 2,700 rpm. The T3 added 20–25 ft-lbs of torque below VTEC and 35–40 ft-lbs after the secondary cam actuated. I was pleased with the power potential of the little T3 turbo, as the $850 turbo kit was now making more power than an LS/VTEC stroker at a fraction of the price. The turbo kit was run without an intercooler at 6 psi, but we decided to install an intercooler before cranking up the boost.

In keeping with the low-buck nature of the kit, I sourced a suitable air-to-air intercooler from the wrecking yard. I got lucky and found a core from a late-model Supra turbo. A bit large (physically) for our application, it did allow me to safely increase the boost to 10 psi. The fuel system was also augmented with an inline T-Rex fuel pump. After tuning, the peak power soared to 275 hp and torque right along with it. The little B16A was now thumping out a whopping 201 ft-lbs of torque (all from just 1.6 liters). The new torque curve was indeed impressive as the turbo motor hovered right near 190 ft-lbs from 5,500 rpm all the way to 7,500 rpm. All the power gains weren't post VTEC either. Running 10 psi, the turbo motor improved the torque production by 60–65 ft-lbs all the way down at 4,000 rpm. A good 50 ft-lbs was available as low as 3,500 rpm. The results were indeed impressive considering the cost of the turbo system.

Turbocharged Terrors

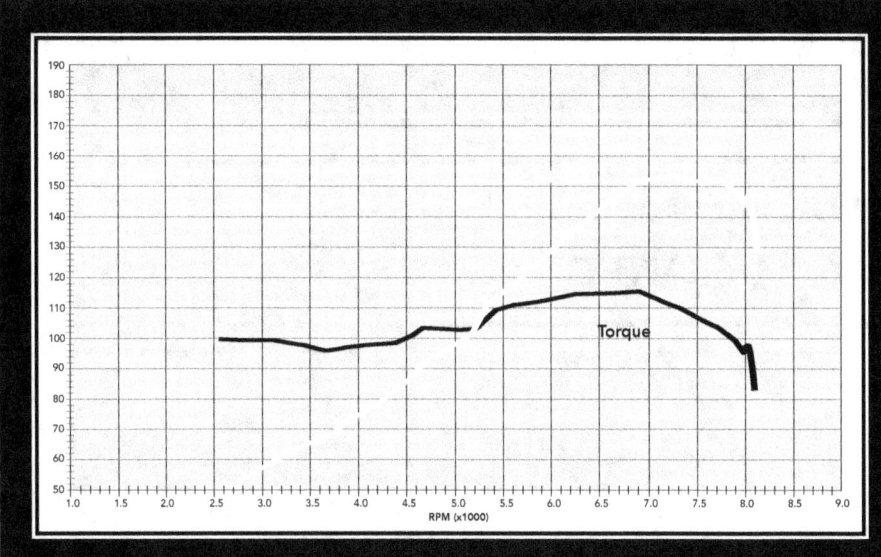

Baseline: B16A (Baseline)

Just because you're on a budget, doesn't mean you have to be slow. This test shows how some junkyard parts and some ingenuity can produce a turbo setup worth more than 100 horsepower.

Peak Horsepower – Baseline	153 hp
Peak Torque – Baseline	115 ft-lbs

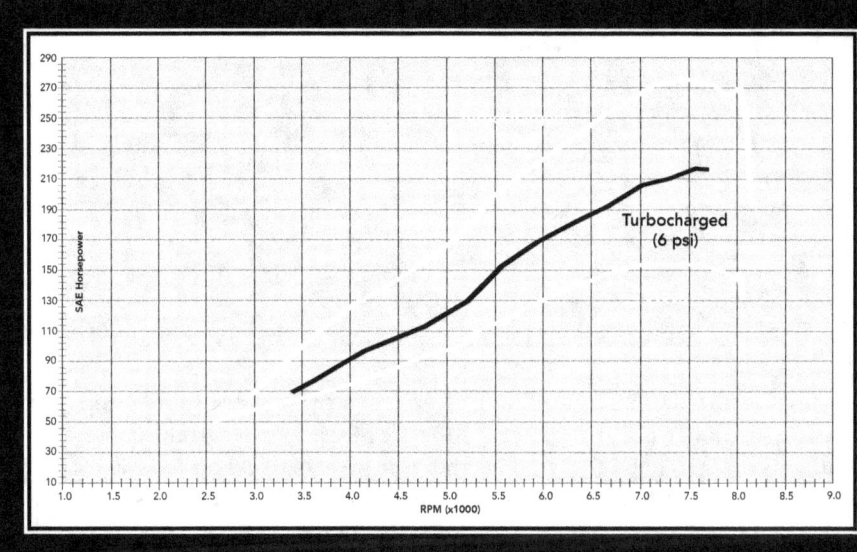

Baseline B16A at 6 psi and 10 psi: Horsepower

Peak HP – Baseline	153 hp
Peak HP – Turbocharged 6 psi	214 hp
Peak HP – Turbocharged 10 psi	275 hp

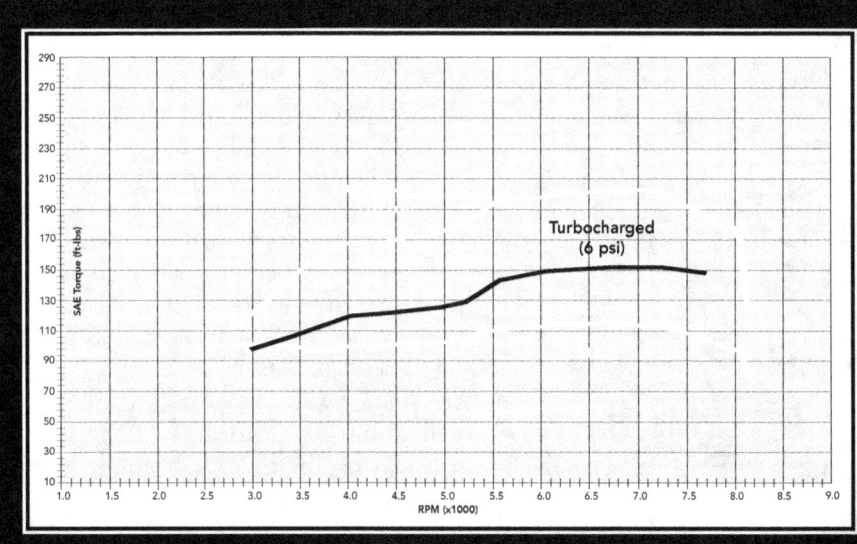

Baseline B16A at 6 psi and 10 psi: Torque

Peak Torque – Baseline	115 ft-lbs
Peak Torque – 6 psi	152 ft-lbs
Peak Torque – 10 psi	201 ft-lbs

Chapter 6

Test 2: Boost Wars: 12 psi versus 15 psi

1995 Civic Del Sol
B16A 1.6L VTEC

As you might have guessed, I did not stop at 10 psi when testing the low-buck turbo kit. Although I would find out through testing that the turbine on the T3 was becoming a major exhaust flow restriction (43 psi exhaust pressure at 15 psi boost pressure), the turbo kit had more to give. The previous tests run at 6 and 10 psi demonstrate what usually happens when you turn up the boost, assuming there is additional flow capability (both compressor and turbine) left in the turbo. When we upped the pressure from 6 psi to 10 psi, we included an intercooler and additional fuel pump. Although the Supra intercooler core was probably good enough for our low-buck booster, we opted to swap in a real intercooler in the form of an air-to-air Spearco core. The larger front-mounted core required some custom tubing to connect the turbo to the core and the core to the throttle body. Additional mods included an external Turbonetics wastegate, larger RC injectors, and a Crane Hi6 ignition amplifier. Also worth mentioning are the Denso Iridium spark plugs.

These test results demonstrate not only the effect of boost (12 psi versus 15 psi), but also what happens when you run out of flow from your turbo. In this case, we had maxed out the exhaust flow of the T3 turbo by increasing the boost from 12 psi to 15 psi. It is easy to see that increasing the boost was providing diminishing returns. Note the big power gains offered after the turbo spooled up, but look closely at the top of the curve. The increase in boost pressure increased the power output by as much as 50 hp in the mid range, but the peak-to-peak power gain was only 20 hp. The reason for the fall off in increased power (even though boost was kept constant) was that boost is not a measurement of mass flow. In short, more boost does not equal more power. More mass flow equals more power, but the little turbo simply had no more airflow available. The installation of a pressure gauge in the exhaust system (before the turbo) indicated that there was as much as 43 psi of backpressure present at 15 psi of boost. The turbine was simply too small and had become a restriction. Still, 329 hp at the wheels combined with 250 ft-lbs of torque is impressive considering the humble beginnings of our junkyard turbo. These tests were all run with 110-octane race fuel to eliminate any chance of detonation.

Turbocharged Terrors

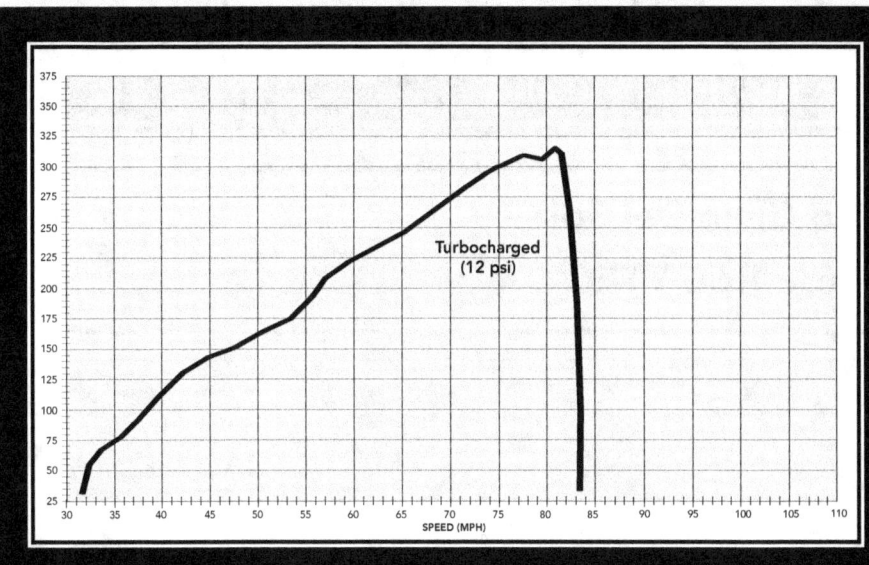

Baseline: 12 psi Boost

Need still more power? Here we dial up the boost on the budget turbo setup – but note that we're starting to see diminishing returns caused by the size of the turbo.

Peak Horsepower – 12 psi   309 hp

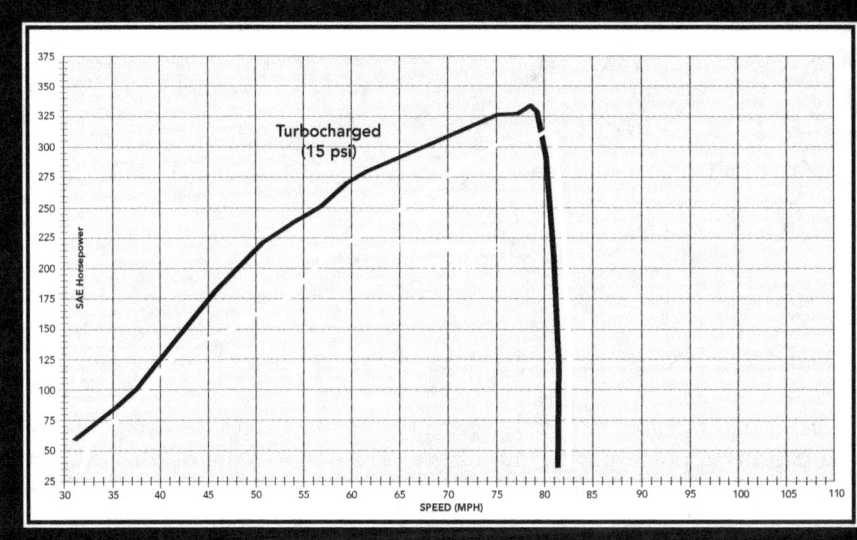

12 psi versus 15 psi: Horsepower

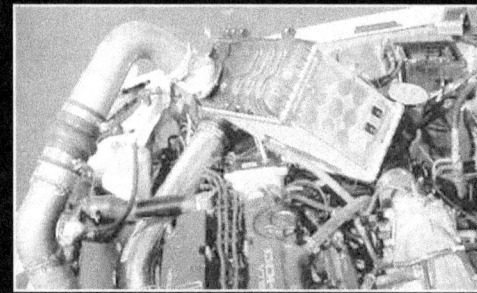

Peak Horsepower – 12 psi   309 hp
Peak Horsepower – 15 psi   329 hp

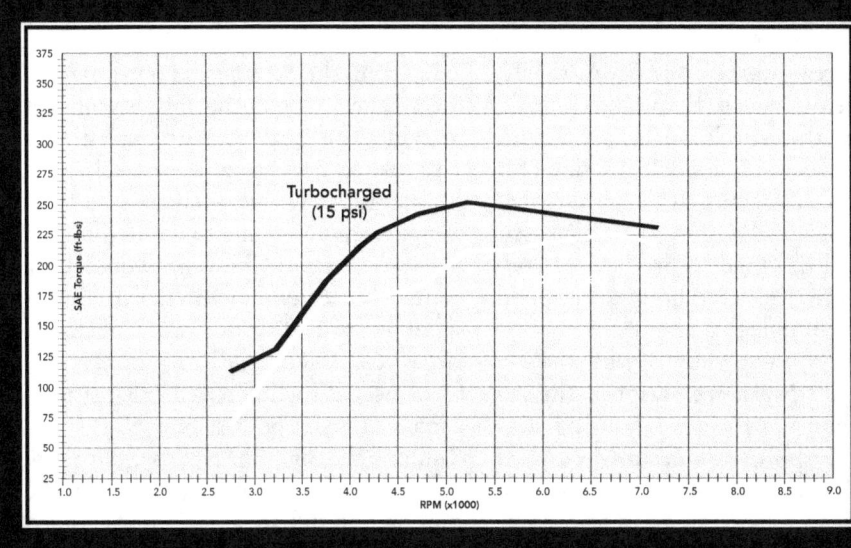

12 psi versus 15 psi: Air/Fuel

Max Air/Fuel – 12 psi   14.1:1
Max Air/Fuel – 15 psi   14.0:1

How to Build Honda Horsepower

Chapter 6

Test 3: .48 A/R Housing versus .63 A/R Turbine Housing

1995 Civic Del Sol
B16A 1.6L VTEC

While we had just about reached the limit of the stock T3 turbo, there was one more test left to perform for this book. Since it seemed that the backpressure was holding back our power production, anything that could decrease backpressure should increase performance. This test was centered on a change in the A/R ratio of the turbine housing. There is insufficient space available for a definition and the necessary detailed explanation of the definition (I suggest reading Corky Bell's Maximum Boost), but know that the A/R ratio is an important element in tuning a turbine section of a turbocharger for a given application. Though we hardly put any science into the selection of our junkyard turbo, it was obvious that we had excessive backpressure and the culprit was the turbine housing. A simple cure (actually more of a crutch than a cure) was to increase (numerically) the A/R ratio of the turbine housing and run back-to-back tests on the effect of the change. If the theory held true, a turbine housing with a larger A/R ratio should soften the spool up but increase maximum power by allowing additional exhaust flow.

The T3 turbo used in this low-buck buildup came with a rather small .48 A/R turbine housing. This small A/R ratio was used to help produce quick spool up on the 2.3L turbo motors. This .48 housing was popular among 2.3L owners equipped with automatic transmissions, who required more torque down low to get the heavy cars moving quickly. The T3 was also available with a larger .63 housing, popular among the 5-speed 2.3L owners, especially the lighter Mustangs (compared to a larger T-bird). The larger A/R ratio reduced backpressure to improve top-end power, but the cost (there is always a tradeoff) was a reduction in low-speed power. The reason for the reduction in low-speed power was that the larger housing required more exhaust energy to spool the turbo. While we thought the .48 housing worked great on the 1.6L B16A, the T3 was never intended to produce nearly 330 hp at the wheels. In fact, the compressor map for the stock T3 signs off well below 300 (crank) hp. I am sure that the Ford engineers never dreamed that the little turbo used to produce a maximum of 205 (flywheel) hp could be good for nearly double that amount.

After running the T3 with the .48 housing at 15 psi, we swapped the .48 turbine housing for a .63 housing supplied by Turbo City. Since it was a Ford part, the .63 housing was a direct bolt on replacement. Once the swap was complete, we ran the turbocharged B16A again with the larger housing. In my haste, I did not monitor the exhaust backpressure, but we were rewarded with a textbook example of a change in A/R ratio. As illustrated by the power and torque graphs, the motor lost power with the larger turbine housing until about 5,000 rpm. From 5,000 rpm past 7,500 rpm, the .63 housing out-powered the smaller .48 housing by a significant margin. The peak power output was now up to 342 hp at the wheels. The peak torque had also taken a healthy jump, from 250 ft-lbs to 269 ft-lbs. On the street, the .48 housing would be a better choice, as most of the driving is spent below 5,000 rpm. For the track, the larger .63 A/R would offer better performance, as the improved exhaust flow produced better power above 5,000 rpm. Running the car at the track would allow you to keep the engine speed above 5,000 rpm, taking full advantage of the added power offered by the .63 housing.

Turbocharged Terrors

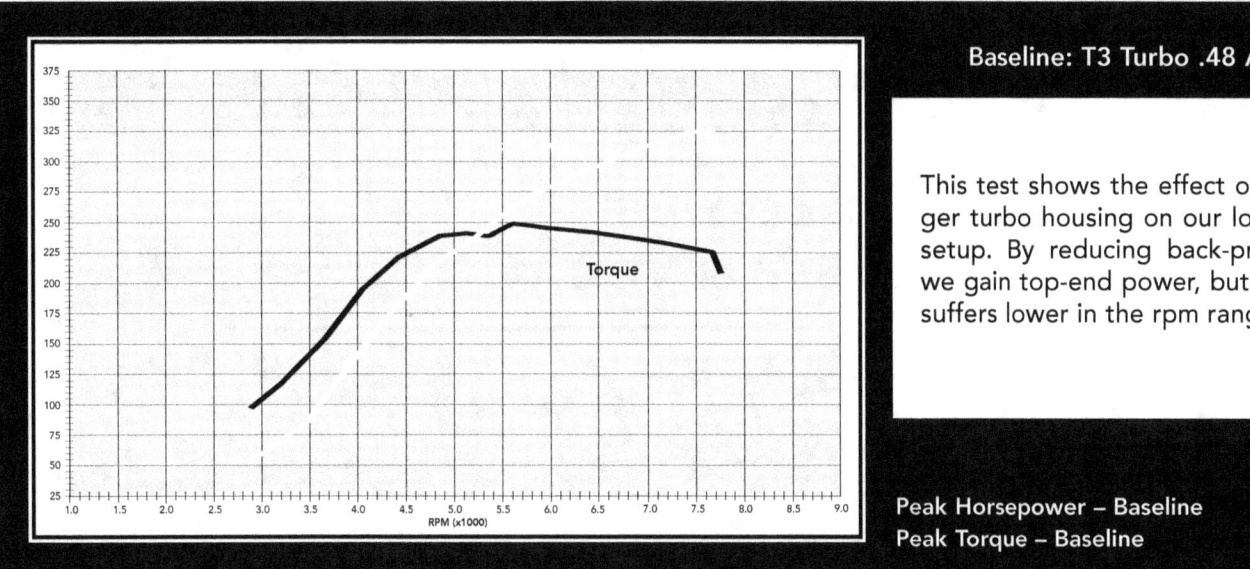

Baseline: T3 Turbo .48 A/R

This test shows the effect of a bigger turbo housing on our low-buck setup. By reducing back-pressure, we gain top-end power, but output suffers lower in the rpm range.

Peak Horsepower – Baseline	329 hp
Peak Torque – Baseline	250 ft-lbs

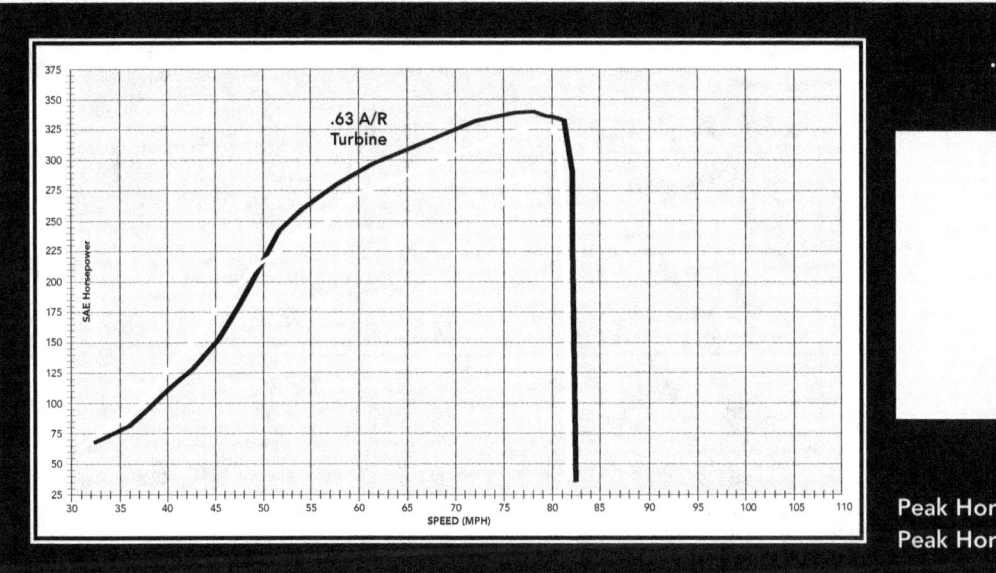

.48 A/R versus .63 A/R: Horsepower

Peak Horsepower – .48 A/R	329 hp
Peak Horsepower – .63 A/R	342 hp

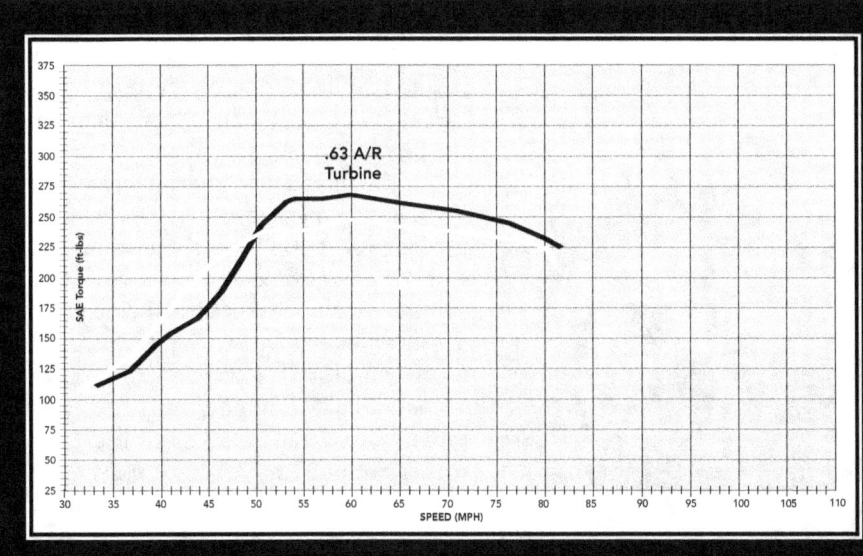

.48 A/R versus .63 A/R: Torque

Peak Torque – .48 A/R	250 ft-lbs
Peak Torque – .63 A/R	269 ft-lbs

How to Build Honda Horsepower

Chapter 6

Test 4: Greddy Civic Si at 5.5-psi Boost

2000 Civic Si
B16A 1.6L VTEC

The Greddy turbo kit for the 1999–2000 Civic Si should not be compared to other kits available in the aftermarket, especially those without emissions certification. Sure, it is possible to produce more power with a larger turbo and/or more boost pressure, but the Greddy kit was designed as a legal bolt-on kit allowing an Si owner to increase the power output of a B16A without resorting to something as radical as an LS/VTEC hybrid swap. The problem with the B16A in the Civic Si is that it is already impressive to begin with. Rated at 160 hp, the little 1.6L produces 100 hp/liter. It is hard to find big chunks of power going the bolt-on route, as Honda did not leave much on the table. The usual array of headers, air intakes, and exhaust will only get you about 10-15 hp, a little more if you choose wisely. Gains of 50 hp or more take some serious engine work, or just a little forced induction.

The Greddy kit comes with everything you need to bolt on 40–50 extra hp (at 5–6 psi), all without breaking either the bank or your precious VTEC motor. When regulated to just 5.5 psi, the Greddy kit (with optional air-to-air intercooler) produced peak readings of 186 hp and 135 ft-lbs of torque at the wheels. In typical VTEC fashion, the torque curve was relatively flat from 3,500 rpm to nearly 8,000 rpm. Adding 5.5 psi of boost simply elevated the entire boost curve, but did not alter the shape dramatically. This is not surprising as the turbo kit retained the factory intake manifold, one of the major factors that determine the overall shape of the power curve.

It is interesting to note that the horsepower peaked at 7,500 rpm and then fell off slightly thereafter. The stock B16A horsepower curve has a similar dip in power after 7,500 rpm. This particular Greddy Si kit was tuned using the Hondata system and a set of 440-cc (RC Engineering) injectors rather than the usual FMU or fuel controller supplied by Greddy. The post-VTEC air/fuel hovered a hair above 12.0:1, but more tuning was necessary on the primary cam.

Turbocharged Terrors

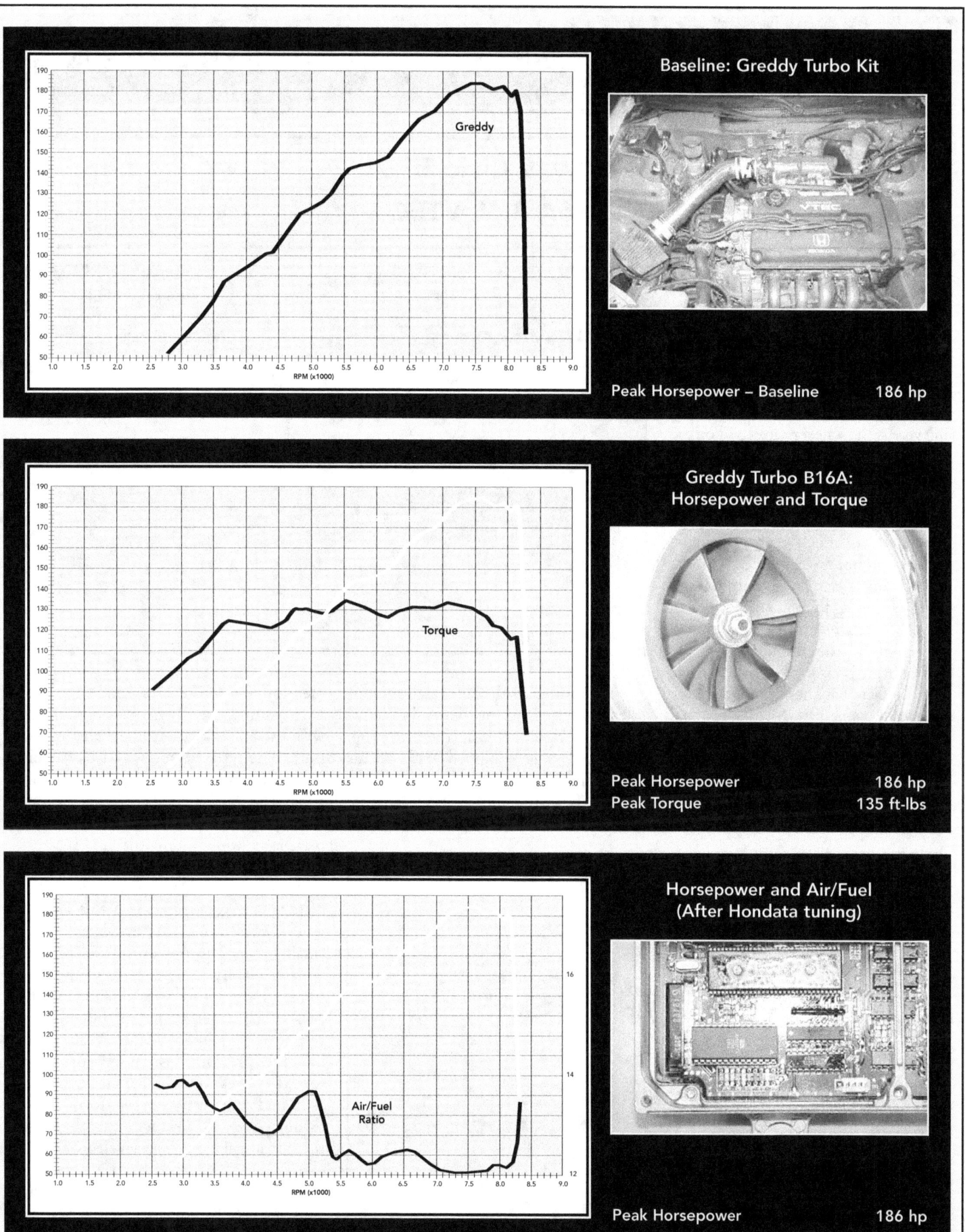

Baseline: Greddy Turbo Kit

Peak Horsepower – Baseline — 186 hp

Greddy Turbo B16A: Horsepower and Torque

Peak Horsepower — 186 hp
Peak Torque — 135 ft-lbs

Horsepower and Air/Fuel (After Hondata tuning)

Peak Horsepower — 186 hp

How to Build Honda Horsepower

Chapter 6

Test 5: Greddy Civic Si at 7.1-psi Boost

1999 Civic Si
B16A 1.6L VTEC

The information for this second test was supplied by Greddy. The test involved running their turbo kit on a 1999 Civic Si at 7.1 psi. Obviously the power was up compared to the test run at just 5.5 psi, but the big difference in power is attributed to the flywheel rating versus the wheel rating used on the previous test. These power numbers were generated on a loaded dyno and then converted to flywheel numbers. As such, the flywheel power numbers generated are much higher than the power numbers generated at the wheels on a typical DynoJet. The important thing to remember with this test is the relative difference in power generated by the addition of the Si turbo kit. It is also important to point out the fact that these numbers were generated using the Si kit, optional front-mounted air-to-air intercooler, and B-Spec boost controller. The controller allows much more consistent control over the boost pressure than a simple bleed orifice.

According to the information supplied by Greddy, the B16A in the Si produced right at 170 (flywheel) hp. The B16A was equipped with an air intake and EVO exhaust system, making the 170 hp number seem accurate given the factory rating of 160 hp. No mention was made of a header, so we will assume the B16A was equipped with the factory cast-iron exhaust manifold. The peak torque was a hair over 120 ft-lbs, again a reasonable amount given the minor mods to the motor. Installing the Greddy turbo kit at 7.1 psi, the air-to-air intercooler and B-Spec boost controller resulted in an increase in peak power to 244 hp and 188 ft-lbs of torque. Again, remember this is flywheel horsepower. As expected of a small turbo, the power was increased approximately 10 hp per pound of boost. Larger turbos will show even greater gains per pound of boost, but response will likely suffer. Note that like the previous test at 5.5 psi, the torque curves were similar in normally aspirated and turbocharged form. The torque curve had a rather steep climb as the boost came on, then leveled off and carried over 180 ft-lbs from 4,100 rpm to 6,700 rpm. It is this average power gain that really improved acceleration, not the peak power number.

Turbocharged Terrors

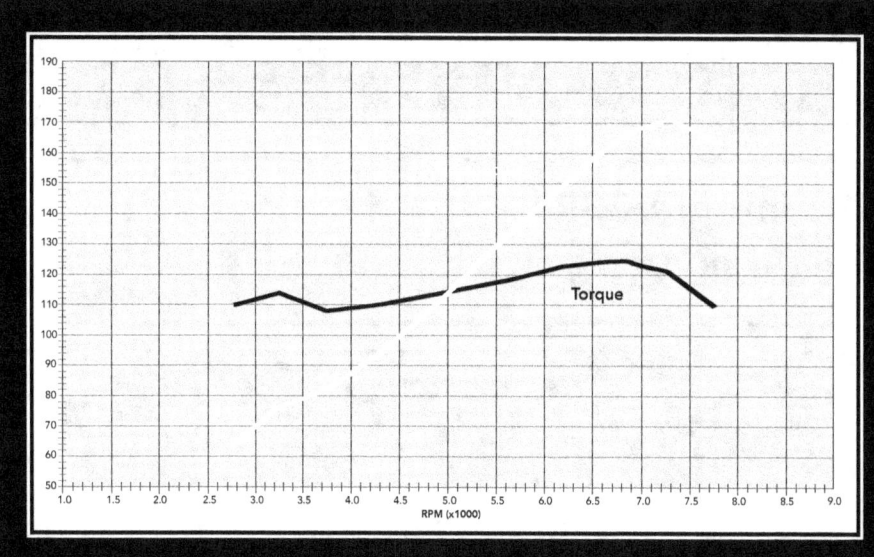

Baseline: B16A (Stock)

Peak Horsepower – Stock	170 hp
Peak Torque – Stock	122 ft-lbs

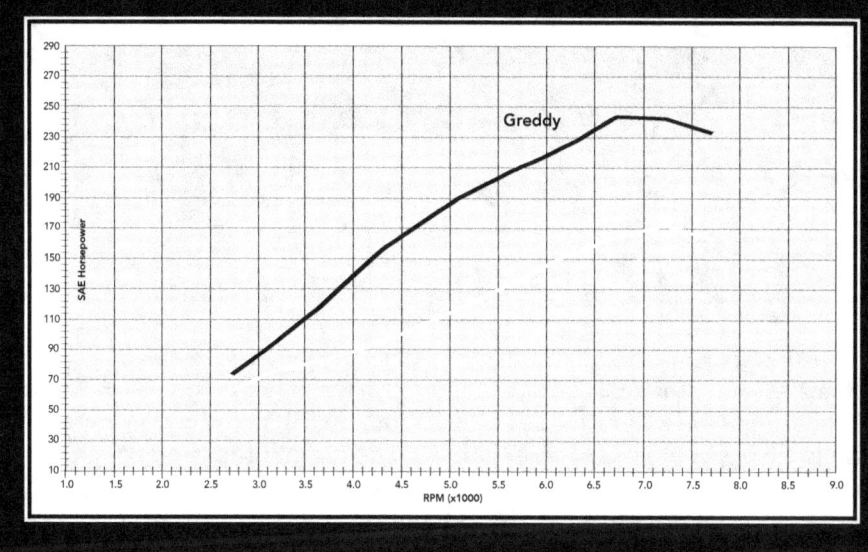

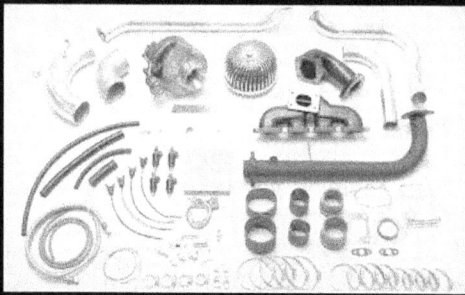

Greddy Turbo B16A (7.1 psi): Horsepower

Peak Horsepower – Stock	170 hp
Peak Horsepower – Greddy Turbo	244 hp

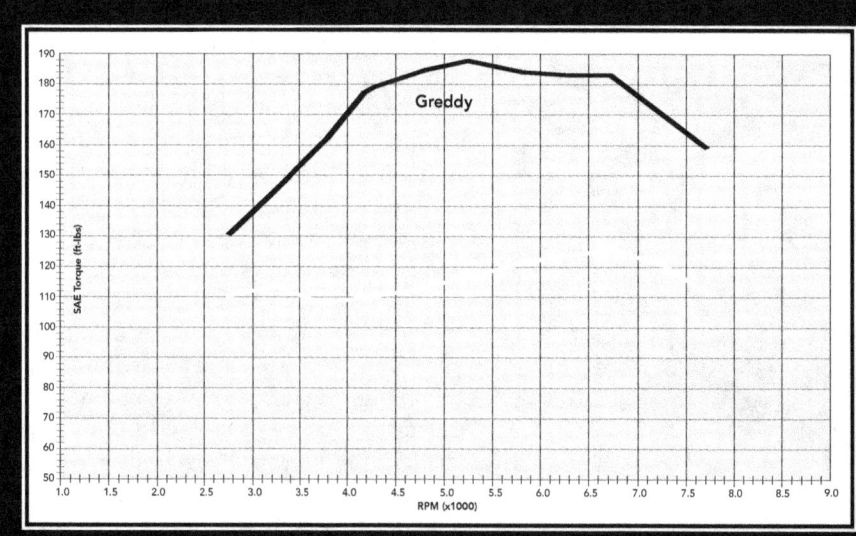

Greddy Turbo B16A (7.1 psi): Torque

Peak Torque – Stock	122 ft-lbs
Peak Torque – Greddy Turbo	188 ft-lbs

How to Build Honda Horsepower

Chapter 6

Test 6: Greddy GSR at 8.5-psi Boost

1995 Integra GSR
B18C 1.8L VTEC

Like the data on the Civic Si run at 7.1 psi, Greddy supplied this information on the turbocharged GSR. This kit was also run with a front-mounted air-to-air intercooler and a B-Spec boost controller. No doubt, the B-Spec controller allowed much finer control of the boost curve (limiting spikes and surges in boost pressure), allowing a much more refined power curve. Eliminating spikes in the boost curve can also help prevent detonation, as elevated boost pressure can promote detonation. Like the Civic Si run at 7.1 psi, this GSR was run on the same Bosch chassis dyno with the numbers converted to flywheel power outputs. Apparently, the conversion from wheel to flywheel horsepower is reasonably accurate, as the stock GSR motor was tested to produce 170 flywheel hp, right at the factory rating for the B18C. It seems odd that the larger displacement GSR motor produced near-identical torque numbers compared to the smaller B16A tested on the Civic. In fact, the smaller Si motor actually out-torqued the larger GSR motor by 2 ft-lbs. Possibly the slight modifications to the Si motor helped the power output, but the larger B18C motors are generally good for a substantial torque gain in the lower rev ranges.

Once Greddy added the turbo kit, intercooler, and boost controller to the equation, the B18C really came into its own. The turbo kit increased the peak power to 254 hp (up from 170 hp), with significant gains posted from below 3,000 rpm. Note that the power peaked just past 7,000 rpm. This can be attributed to the dual-runner GSR manifold. Swapping on a B16A or Type R intake can yield some substantial power gains, but there will be tradeoffs in power at certain points. The dual-runner intake is effective for most street motors. The torque curve tells a similar story, as boost really woke up the B18C. Sure, 256 hp is impressive, but what you will feel most on the street is the steady 200 ft-lbs of torque. The turbo motor exceeded 200 ft-lbs of torque way down at 2,800 rpm, a point nearly devoid of power production on the stock GSR motor. The Greddy turbo kit nearly doubled the torque output at 3,000 rpm, something that will definitely bring a smile to your face.

Turbocharged Terrors

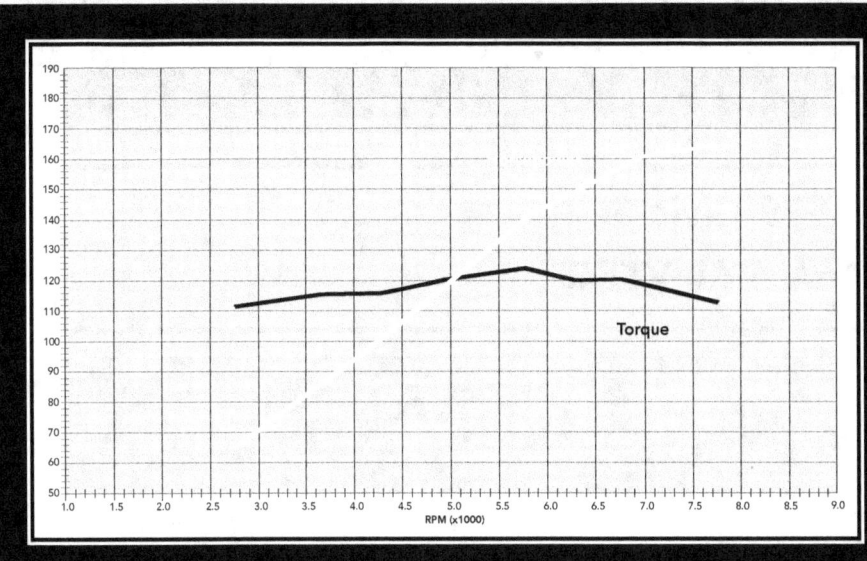

Baseline: B18C (Stock)

Peak Horsepower – Stock	170 hp
Peak Torque – Stock	120 ft-lbs

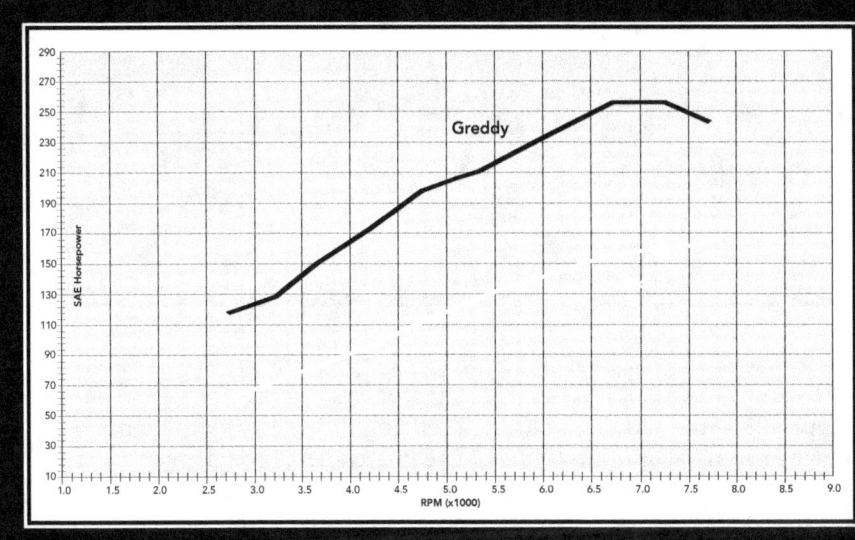

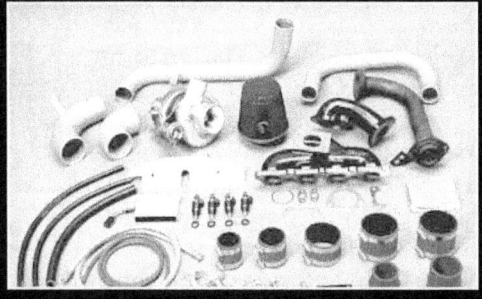

Greddy Turbo B18C (8.5 psi): Horsepower

Peak Horsepower – Stock	170 hp
Peak Horsepower – Greddy Turbo	254 hp

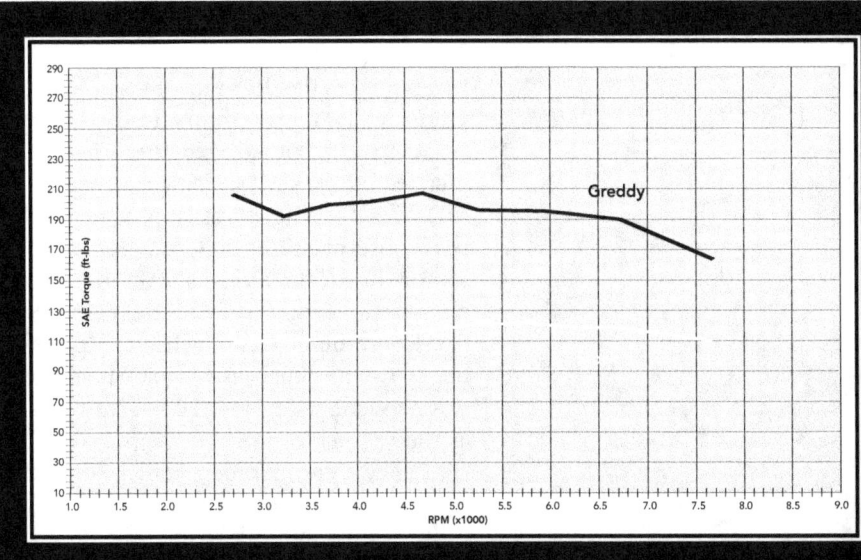

Greddy Turbo B18C: Torque

Peak Torque – Stock	120 ft-lbs
Peak Torque – Greddy Turbo	208 ft-lbs

How to Build Honda Horsepower

Chapter 6

Test 7: Drag Civic Si at 8.9-psi Boost

1999 Civic Si
B16A 1.6L VTEC

Unlike the Greddy kit for the 1999–2000 Civic Si, the turbo system offered by Drag was not (as of this writing) 50-state legal. While not emissions legal, the Drag kit is capable of pumping out some serious horsepower thanks to the use of a larger (compared to the Greddy kit) T3/T4 hybrid turbo. The Drag kit comes with a cast-iron exhaust manifold, something that is a big plus for sustained street use, as the welded tubular turbo manifolds are much more susceptible to cracking. The cast-iron exhaust manifold included a provision for mounting a Turbonetics Deltagate wastegate to control the boost pressure of the system. In kit form, the Drag system utilized a rising-rate fuel-pressure regulator for fuel enrichment, though we have seen a number of these kits converted to larger injectors and stand-alone fuel management system when searching for more serious power levels. According to Drag, the T3/T4 turbo selected for use in the kit is capable of over 20 psi and 400 hp at the wheels, believable levels given

the power produced by the smaller T3 on a stock B16A.

As supplied for the Civic Si (Drag offers other Honda/Acura kits), the Drag kit included a healthy air-to-air intercooler and all the necessary piping. The intercooler is a nice addition and should be considered mandatory if boost levels exceed 5–6 psi on the relatively high-compression B16A. Without the intercooler, timing retard (and the attending power loss) will be necessary. The intercooler allows higher boost levels to be run (assuming adequate fuel delivery) at a given (charge temperature-induced) detonation threshold. Basically, by dropping the inlet charge temperature, you can run more boost pressure. The Drag system also included an inline fuel pump, as the flow rate of the stock Si pump will fall off dramatically when asked to run the elevated fuel pressure dictated by the FMU (rising rate regulator). When testing, we attempted to keep the boost pressure at 8 psi, but some minor boost creep was present that pushed the ending pressure to nearly 9 psi. The result of pumping nearly 9 psi of boost to the otherwise stock Si motor was an increase of over 120 hp, from 142 at the wheels to nearly 270 hp at 8,000 rpm. The dyno numbers indicated that the torque peak occurred at nearly 7,500 rpm, a sure indication that there was more left in the combination.

Turbocharged Terrors

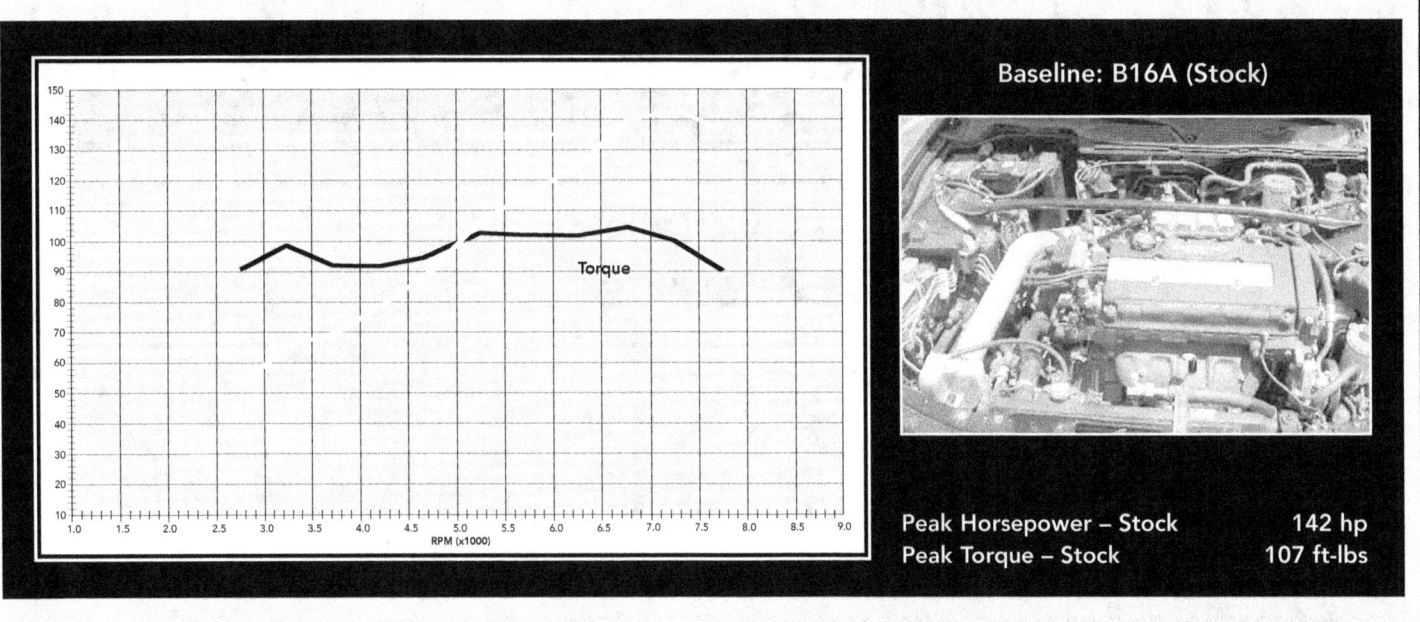

Baseline: B16A (Stock)

Peak Horsepower – Stock	142 hp
Peak Torque – Stock	107 ft-lbs

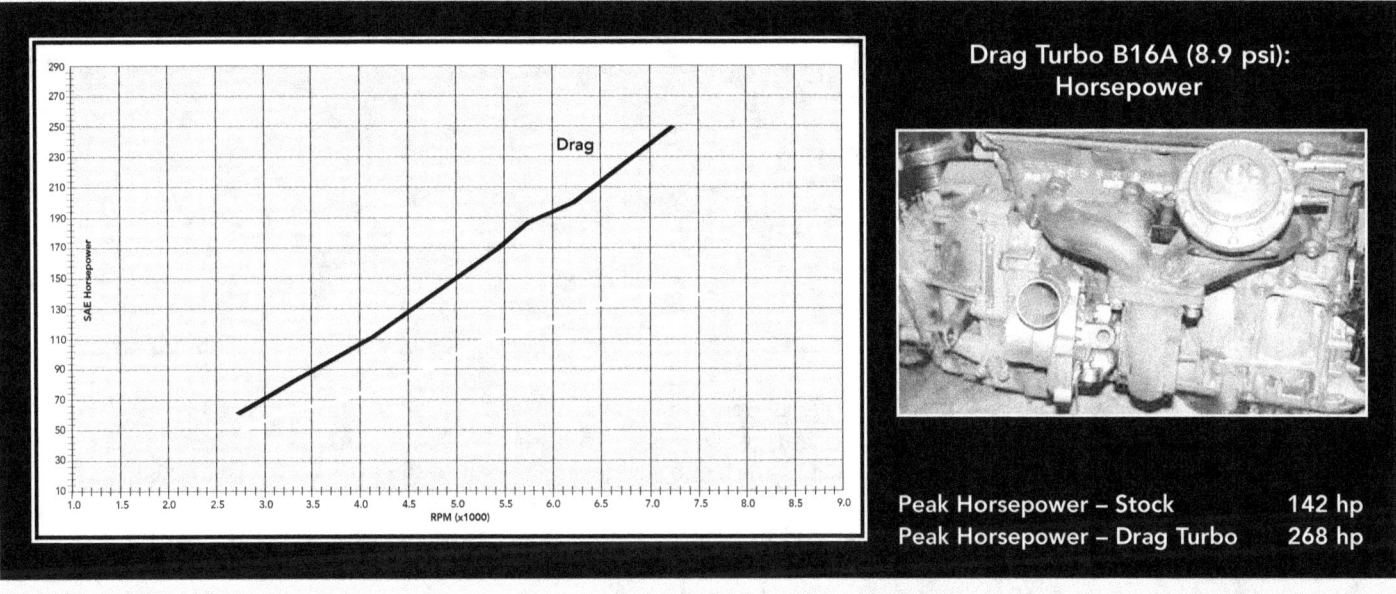

Drag Turbo B16A (8.9 psi): Horsepower

Peak Horsepower – Stock	142 hp
Peak Horsepower – Drag Turbo	268 hp

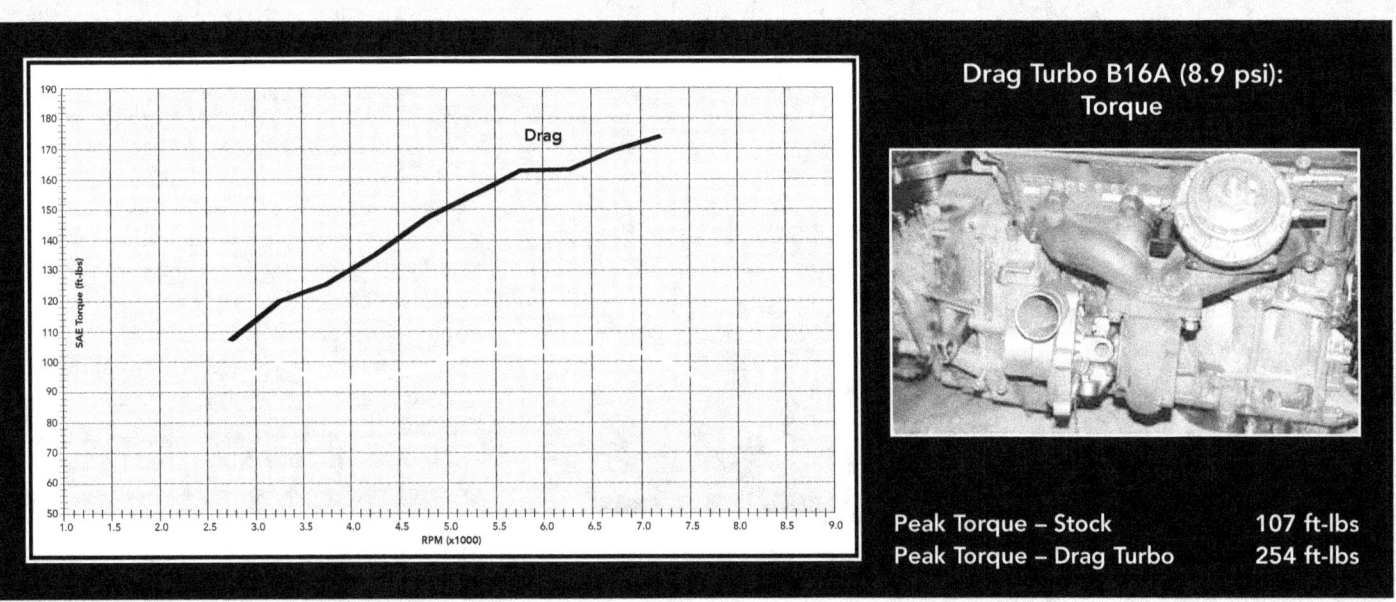

Drag Turbo B16A (8.9 psi): Torque

Peak Torque – Stock	107 ft-lbs
Peak Torque – Drag Turbo	254 ft-lbs

Chapter 6

Test 8: T3 versus T3/T04B Hybrid on B16A Motor

1995 Civic Del Sol
B16A 1.6L VTEC

This test was run to demonstrate what happens when you select the wrong turbo for your application. In previous testing with this particular stock B16A, we found that a T3 pirated from a 2.3L SVO Mustang (from the local wrecking yard) worked very well on the smaller 1.6L VTEC motor. The small T3 turbo worked so well, that many in the turbo industry were reluctant to believe the results of the tests run on this B16A motor. They questioned the ability of the relatively small T3 turbo to support in excess of 340 hp at the wheels. Their concerns were genuine, as the compressor map for this particular turbo showed nowhere near this flow potential. Regardless of what the books and maps say, the reality is that the turbo did indeed produce these power levels on this B16A and not just once. The motor was subjected to dozens of passes exceeding 300 hp at the wheels using the T3 turbo. The boost pressure was varied (see previous test on effect of boost pressure), but the turbo seemed all done at about 15

psi. We could increase the power curve before the horsepower peak, but the peak remained the same—a clear indication that the turbo was spent in terms of maximum flow.

Since the small T3 was all done at 15 psi and 342 hp at the wheels, we attempted to run a slightly larger compressor in hopes of increasing the peak

power output of the B16A test motor. What we found out instead was that installing the wrong turbo size on your motor can have a dramatic effect on the overall power curve. The turbo selected was a T3/T04B hybrid, something common in the industry. Combining the larger T04B with the smaller T3 turbine allowed the turbo to produce additional intake flow, while retaining the response of the T3 turbine—at least in theory. The reality is that the B16A did not respond well to the larger T04B compressor, regardless of what the theories said. In fact, the motor lost power everywhere (at an identical boost level). Since both turbos featured identical .63 A/R turbine housings, the change in power has to be the different compressor. We did not have enough time to pinpoint the problem, but this test demonstrates the importance of choosing the right turbo for your application. For the B16A, the standard T3 works great up to and beyond 300 hp at the wheels.

Turbocharged Terrors

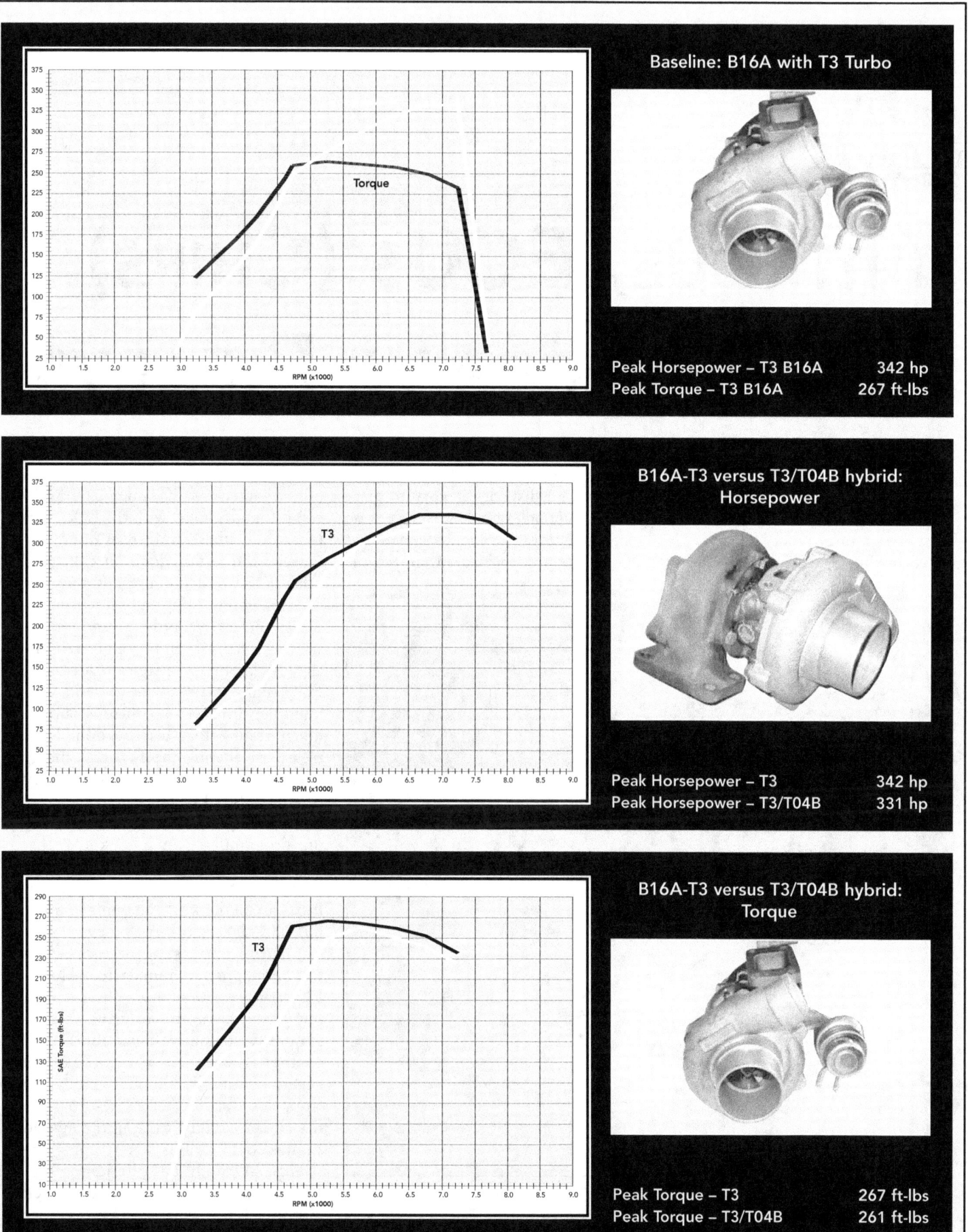

Baseline: B16A with T3 Turbo

Peak Horsepower – T3 B16A   342 hp
Peak Torque – T3 B16A   267 ft-lbs

B16A-T3 versus T3/T04B hybrid: Horsepower

Peak Horsepower – T3   342 hp
Peak Horsepower – T3/T04B   331 hp

B16A-T3 versus T3/T04B hybrid: Torque

Peak Torque – T3   267 ft-lbs
Peak Torque – T3/T04B   261 ft-lbs

How to Build Honda Horsepower

CHAPTER 7

NITROUS, ECUs (CHIPS), AND UNDERDRIVE PULLEYS

This chapter was originally scheduled to include only ECU and related testing. As it turned out, I included a great many non-ECU related tests, as there was no distinct category to place them in. A good example was the test on synthetic lubricants. The Redline oil test did not seem to belong in any of the other chapters, so (like a number of others) it found a home with the ECU testing. Adding these misfit tests in no way reduced the testing done on chips and other ECU-related tuning. Rather, the addition of the testing on synthetic lubricants, underdrive pulleys, and power steering removal simply enhanced the already important chapter. Obviously, ECU tuning plays a major role in optimum performance, but there is only so much testing that can be done with regard to altering the fuel and timing tables in either a programmable factory or aftermarket ECU. If you come away with nothing else from the dyno testing on programming ECUs, know that without the proper fuel and timing, all the best turbo, supercharged, or nitrous hardware in the world amounts to nothing more than a broken motor.

During the testing performed for this book, programming factory Honda ECUs was at its infancy. There were a few manufacturers offering reprogrammed computer chips for OBD1 computers, but these were more of the generic brand. It should be obvious from this chapter that a one-program-fits-all chip cannot work in the myriad engine combinations out roaming the streets. A modified program (chip) designed to enhance an otherwise stock motor can be beneficial if for no other reason than to raise the rev limit and/or

Unorthodox Racing makes a complete line of underdrive pulleys like this race version. Less parasitic loss means more horsepower.

Nitrous, ECUs (Chips), and Underdrive Pulleys

slightly enhance (usually make more aggressive) the timing curve. These changes, while beneficial on a stock motor, may be too aggressive on a motor equipped with a header, exhaust, and air intake. The problem resides in the fact that Hondas rely on a speed-density engine management system. Unlike the more adaptive mass air meter management systems (for example Ford), the speed density systems do not compensate (very well) for the additional airflow provided by the aftermarket components. The added airflow (and hopefully power) offered by an air intake, header, and/or exhaust goes unnoticed by the Honda ECU in terms of additional fuel. No added fuel can mean a dangerously lean mixture. The cure is to alter the fuel (and timing) curve to optimize the air/fuel ratio for the new performance modifications. Enter reprogramming the ECU.

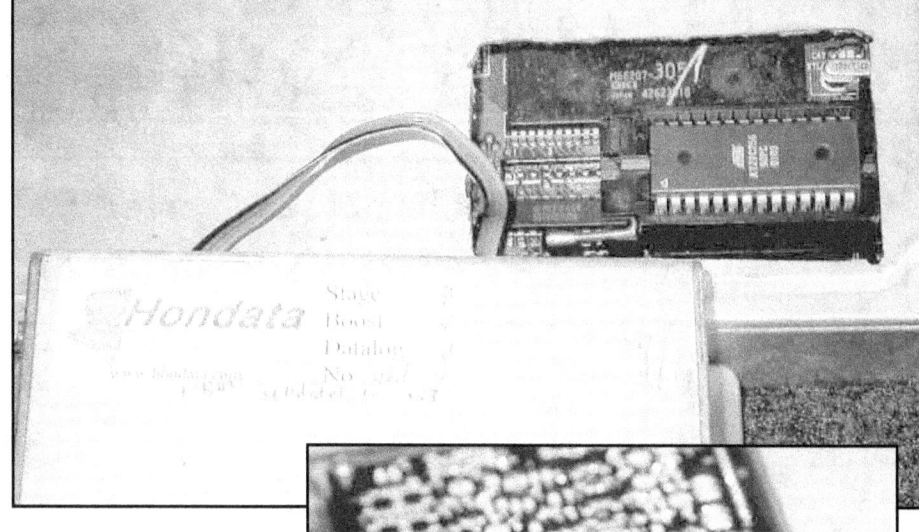

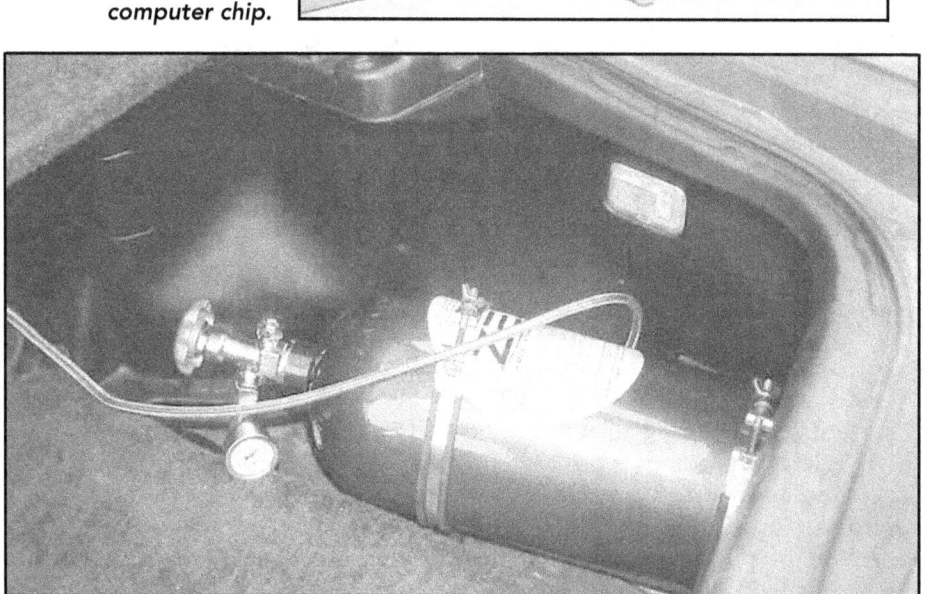

Whether you run "all motor" or "force fed," the key to maximum safe performance is proper tuning. This Hondata system gave us the ability to run massive 77 lbs./hr. injectors in a daily driven Si (that made 500 supercharged horsepower). All that is necessary to change the air/fuel and timing curve of any motor was a simple computer chip.

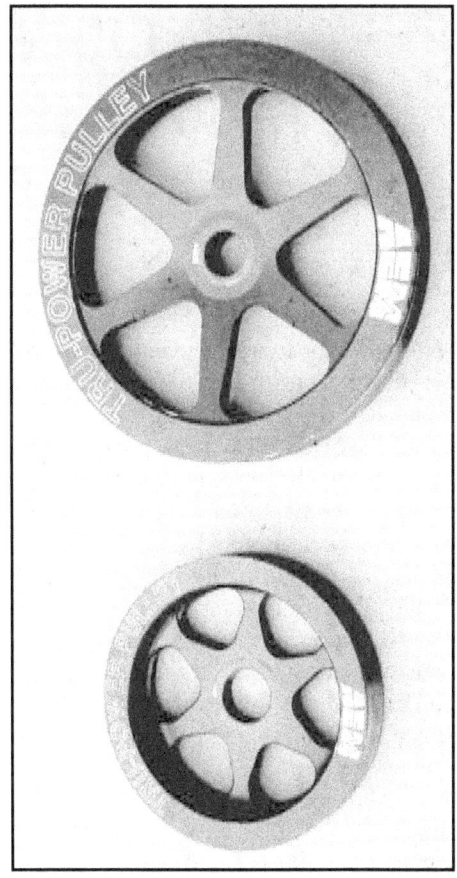

AEM is a household name in Honda Performance, offering trick bolt-ons like these aluminum underdrive pulleys.

Made famous by the movie "The Fast and the Furious", nitrous oxide can give your stock motor a serious boost in power. This Zex system takes nitrous systems to the next level.

How to Build Honda Horsepower

Chapter 7

Test 1: June ECU versus Mugen ECU

Civic Si (Converted EX)
B20 2.0L CRV Short Block with B16A Cylinder Head

Any performance fuel-injected motor is only as good as the computer programming. Take your average B16A-equipped Honda Civic Del Sol or Si for instance. There is no doubt that the Honda programming is spot on for their stock VTEC motors. The problem arises when performance (hardware) modifications are made, especially major ones. Many companies offer computer (software) upgrades to compliment their performance hardware modifications. After all, the stock Honda Civic Si or Del Sol computer was never intended to operate the fuel and timing on a motor that is 25 percent larger and 50 percent more powerful. Although Honda computers do surprisingly well on mild and even wild combinations, the speed density system is simply not quite as adaptable as other fuel injection systems that employ a (hot wire) mass air meter. On such systems, the changes in airflow brought about by the performance modifications are taken into account by the mass air meter. Thus, the MAF-equipped computer recognizes the additional airflow (and changes in load) and reacts accordingly with additional fuel.

Unfortunately, the Honda ECUs are not so equipped and are not quite as forgiving to changes. Sure, they will tolerate your basic bolt-ons and even a low-boost supercharger or turbo kit (provided fuel enrichment is part of the package), but maximum power is best achieved via modifications to the programming. Taking it to an extreme, the motors that power the vast majority of the mega-boost, 9-second import drag racers are equipped with stand-alone fuel injec-

tion systems. The stock ECUs are simply ill-equipped (programmed) for a motor that produces (in the case of the import Racers) 3 to 4 times the power of a stock VTEC motor. These motors really benefit from the tuning ability provided by the DFIs and TEC IIs of the computer world. As we see from the results of this test, even milder combinations desire the proper programming for maximum power.

The motor used for this ECU shootout was a 2.0L stroker equipped with a B16A cylinder head, Type R cams, and a ported Type R intake manifold (see chapter on engine buildups for complete details). Obviously the motor was pretty far removed from a stock B16A or even a modified B16A. It should be noted that neither of the aftermarket computers used in this comparison were specifically programmed for the 2.0L, but rather for modified B16As. Even more unfortunate was the fact that we were unable to coax the programming specifics from either manufacturer. Both June and Mugen are pretty tight-lipped about their programming. Those minor problems aside, the test clearly illustrates that the high-compression 2.0L favored the June programming over the programming offered by the Mugen ECU. The peak power numbers were similar, but check out the power difference at 6,000 rpm! The June computer was a good 15 hp stronger at 6,000 rpm than the Mugen on this modified 2.0L. While the power difference was significant, it is important to realize that in no way does this mean that the power produced by June computer will always better than the Mugen. The Mugen was worth a sizeable amount over the stock Del Sol computer on the author's USTCC Del Sol. The programming is obviously application specific and the test result would no doubt vary on a different engine combination. Note how the air/fuel mixture leaned out with the additional power produced by the June ECU.

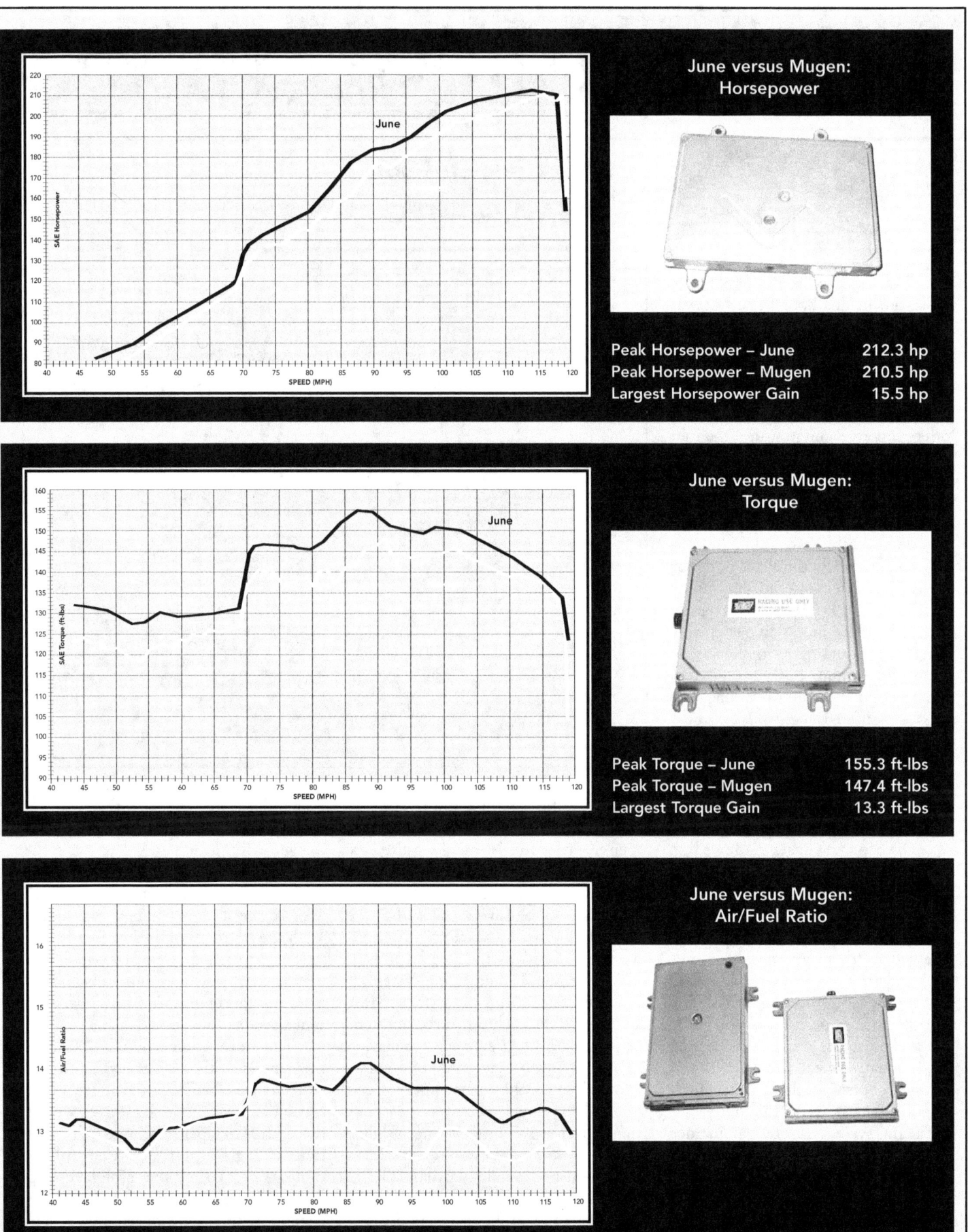

June versus Mugen: Horsepower

Peak Horsepower – June	212.3 hp
Peak Horsepower – Mugen	210.5 hp
Largest Horsepower Gain	15.5 hp

June versus Mugen: Torque

Peak Torque – June	155.3 ft-lbs
Peak Torque – Mugen	147.4 ft-lbs
Largest Torque Gain	13.3 ft-lbs

June versus Mugen: Air/Fuel Ratio

Chapter 7

Test 2: Stock ECU versus Hondata ECU

1995 Civic Del Sol
B16A 1.6L VTEC

This test is a little different than most run in this book. The test was run to demonstrate the critical link between tuning and horsepower. Obviously, other chapters deal with tuning from the standpoint of optimizing efficiency. The cam chapter offers test runs on adjusting the cam and ignition timing, which is, in effect, tuning the combination as opposed to changing it with the installation of hardware (performance components).

When enthusiasts think of tuning, they generally think about minor gains in power offered by minor adjustments to either the air/fuel mixture or ignition timing. In part, that is correct. This tuning example was all about fine-tuning both the air/fuel mixture and the ignition timing, but this test differed slightly from most you may have read about. While power gains are indeed available from tuning, this test (motor) literally could not have been run without the aid of the Hondata computer.

The Hondata system allowed us total control over the factory Honda spark and timing tables. Just like your average stand alone engine-management system, the Hondata allowed us to program the desired fuel and timing curves for our turbocharged combination. Even the use of much larger than stock (440-cc) fuel injectors did not throw off the Hondata system. On par with the aftermarket stand-alone fuel injection systems as far as tunability, the Hondata system offered a distinct advantage over the typical stand-alone management system. Unlike the stand alones, the Hondata comes with base (factory Honda) files, so there is usually little or no need to spend countless hours tuning the idle and part-throttle tables. Tuning a wide-open throttle table is actually quite easy on most systems (including the Hondata), but tuning the part-throttle stuff can take forever. Credit the Hondata for being a factory programmable ECU with all the nice features of both a stock and stand-alone system.

The test was run on a stock B16A equipped with a custom turbo kit. The kit featured a Drag exhaust manifold, a 2.3L Ford turbo, and a Spearco intercooler. Feeding the turbo motor was a set of 440-cc fuel injectors from our friends over at RC Engineering. While a 310-cc injector is about the limit of a stock (non-programmable) B16A ECU (originally designed for 240-cc injectors), the Hondata allowed us to use step up to the 440-cc injectors. The first graph illustrates the fact that using a stock ECU and an FMU resulted in a dangerously lean condition once the motor revved past 3,400 rpm. In fact, the motor was so lean that the run was aborted until more tuning was done. With a few strokes of the keyboard and a new chip installed in the Hondata ECU, the mixture came back to a realistic level. With a little tuning, we finally managed to make some full-throttle passes.

The motor soon produced 292 hp at the wheels with a nice air/fuel curve. While it was possible to produce a perfectly flat curve if we so desired, we left the air/fuel to taper off (in the rich direction) as engine speed increased to keep things safe. Using the Hondata (and more boost), this turbocharged B16A engine eventually produced 335 hp and 245 ft-lbs of torque.

Nitrous, ECUs (Chips), and Underdrive Pulleys

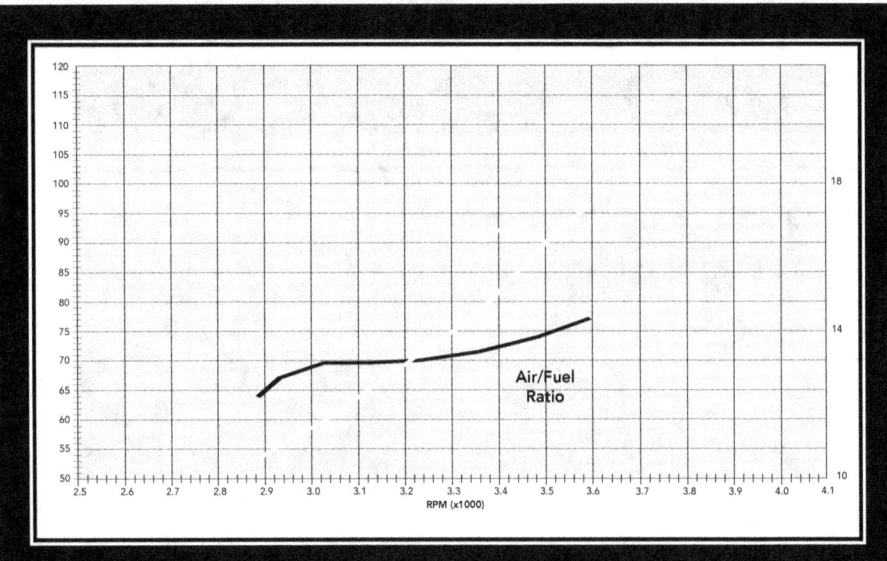

Baseline: B16A (Stock)

The Hondata programmable ECU has made performance life so much easier, especially when we are trying to tune high-horsepower Hondas.

Peak Horsepower – Stock	97 hp
Peak Air/Fuel – Stock	14.4:1

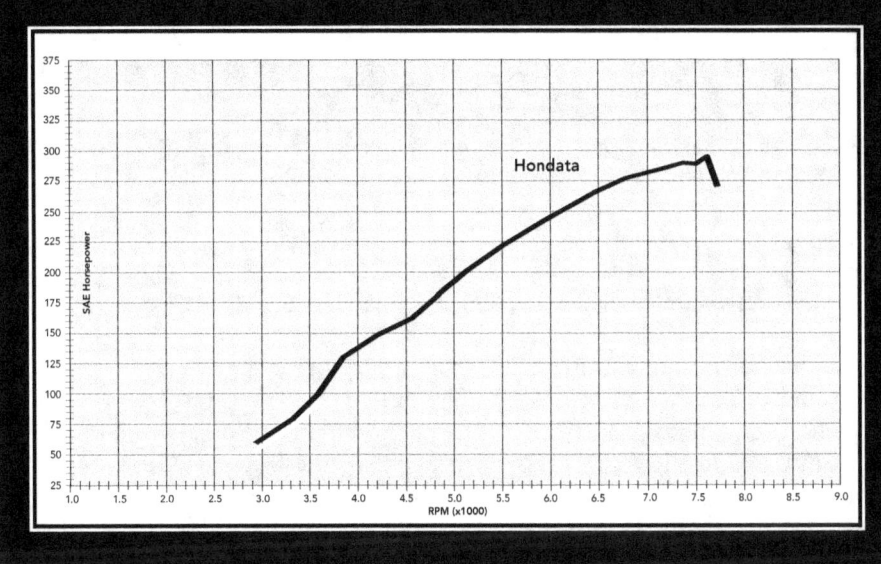

Stock versus Hondata: Horsepower

Peak Horsepower – Stock	97 hp
Peak Horsepower – Hondata	292 hp
Largest Horsepower Gain	195 hp

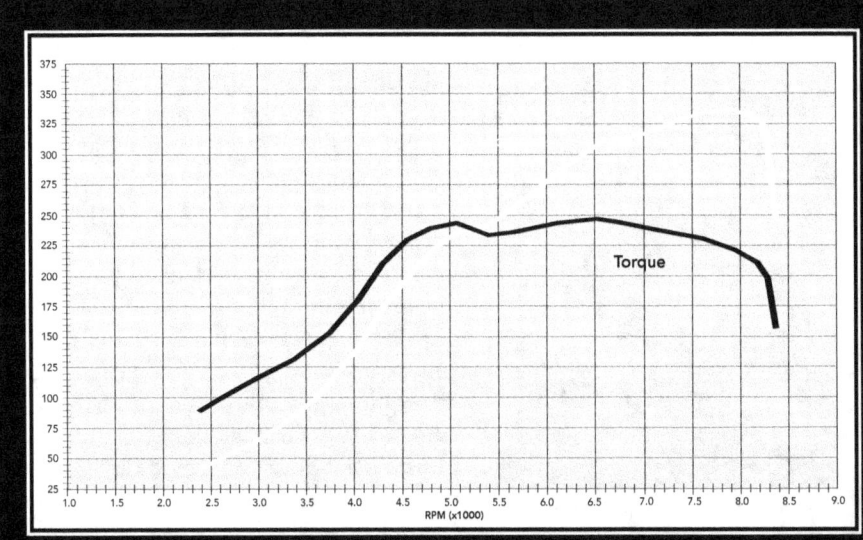

Max Power After Tuning

Peak Horsepower – Hondata	335 hp
Peak Torque – Hondata	245 ft-lbs

How to Build Honda Horsepower   135

Chapter 7

Test 3: APEXi VTEC Controller versus Stock

1990 Integra GS (Engine Swap)
B16A 1.6L VTEC

The Honda VTEC engines are now legendary. The sophisticated system that allows the use of a pair (there are actually three distinct cam lobes) of different cam profiles to maximize low-speed and top-end power is a real work of art. The critical part of the system is obviously to provide a smooth transition between the two different cam profiles. The transition onto VTEC would obviously be much easier if the cams were not dramatically different, but that would defeat the whole purpose of having a VTEC system in the first place. Having two vastly different cam profiles requires a transition point. Anyone who has ever driven a Honda equipped with VTEC, especially one with a healthy aftermarket exhaust system, will attest to the fact that it is no secret when the secondary cam (or cams) comes into operation.

One of the areas where gains can be made, especially on a modified motor, is the VTEC switchover point. It is quite easy to tell if additional power is available from an aftermarket VTEC controller. By

looking at the power curve generated by a dyno run, it is quite easy to determine whether your motor will benefit from a VTEC controller. Pay close attention to how quick the power increases once the VTEC cam is activated. If the power curve has a dramatic increase in power (indicated by a line perpendicular to the bottom of the graph), then your motor will benefit from a change in the activation point. This means that the motor was ready for the switch to the bigger cam profile earlier than the factory ECU allowed. When the proper switchover point is programmed (using a VTEC controller such as this VFC from APEXi), the transition from the primary to the secondary (VTEC) cam should be a smooth line. Too early and the power will fall off slightly before rising; too late and the power will jump dramatically. On our B16A test motor, the activation point was too late—indicated by the sharp rise in power at 5,600 rpm.

By lowering the activation point down to 5,200 rpm, we picked up a significant chunk of power from 5,200 rpm to 5,700 rpm. This APEXi VTEC controller also allowed the author to dial in the required amount of fuel to maintain a safe air/fuel ratio, as the activation of the cam itself does not provide any additional fuel. The additional fuel also provided a power gain across the board, especially near 7,500 rpm.

Nitrous, ECUs (Chips), and Underdrive Pulleys

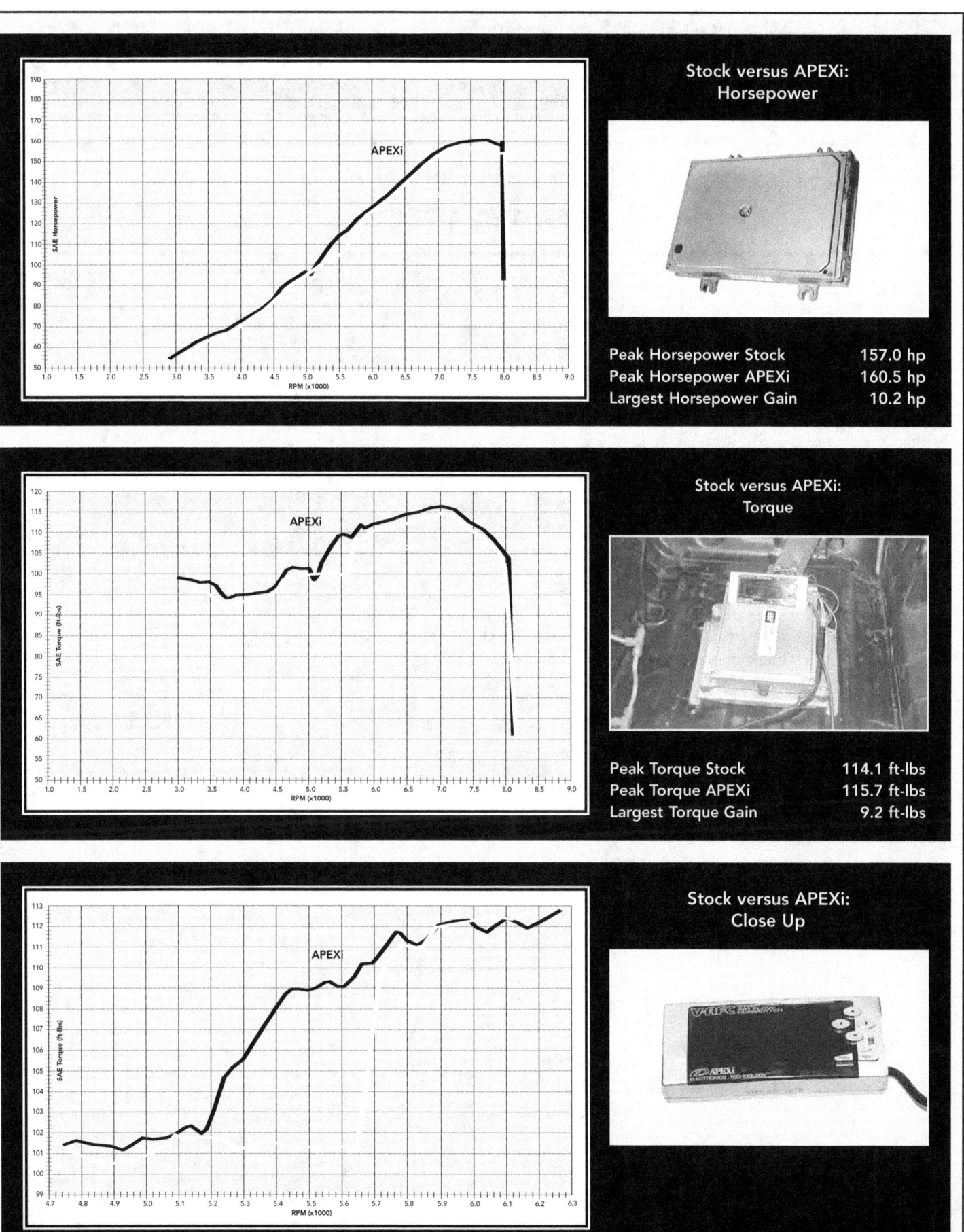

Stock versus APEXi: Horsepower

Peak Horsepower Stock	157.0 hp
Peak Horsepower APEXi	160.5 hp
Largest Horsepower Gain	10.2 hp

Stock versus APEXi: Torque

Peak Torque Stock	114.1 ft-lbs
Peak Torque APEXi	115.7 ft-lbs
Largest Torque Gain	9.2 ft-lbs

Stock versus APEXi: Close Up

Chapter 7

Test 4: Remove Power Steering Pump

1995 Civic Del Sol
B16A 1.6L VTEC

Necessity really is the mother of invention. While searching for additional performance from the author's very own USTCC-championship winning Del Sol, we came across a way to both increase power and remove weight (the enemy of performance and the second critical element in power-to-weight ratio). Knowing that underdrive pulleys work well to reduce parasitic losses in the accessories (see the test on the Unorthodox Racing crank pulley), we decided to go that step one better by completely eliminating the entire power steering system. By removing the power steering pump, we eliminate a considerable chunk of weight off the nose-heavy Del Sol and increased the power output of the B16A race motor all in one fell swoop.

The B16A "race" motor was actually nothing more than a used B16A from one of the local wrecking yards that specialize in the used motors from Japan. The B16A was equipped with a header from APEXi, an AEM air intake, and an open exhaust. Some tuning with the static ignition timing, an adjustable fuel pressure regulator, and the Mugen ECU resulted in a power output of 154 hp to the wheels. The removal of the power steering pump dropped a few precious pounds off the nose while increasing power across the board. The power gains were most pronounced as engine speed increased—typical of an underdrive-pulley type modification. The loss of power steering was not missed, as the Honda Civic steering seems to be over-boosted for my taste. The new manual steering resulted in more power, less weight, and improved road feel. What more could you ask for from a performance modification?

Nitrous, ECUs (Chips), and Underdrive Pulleys

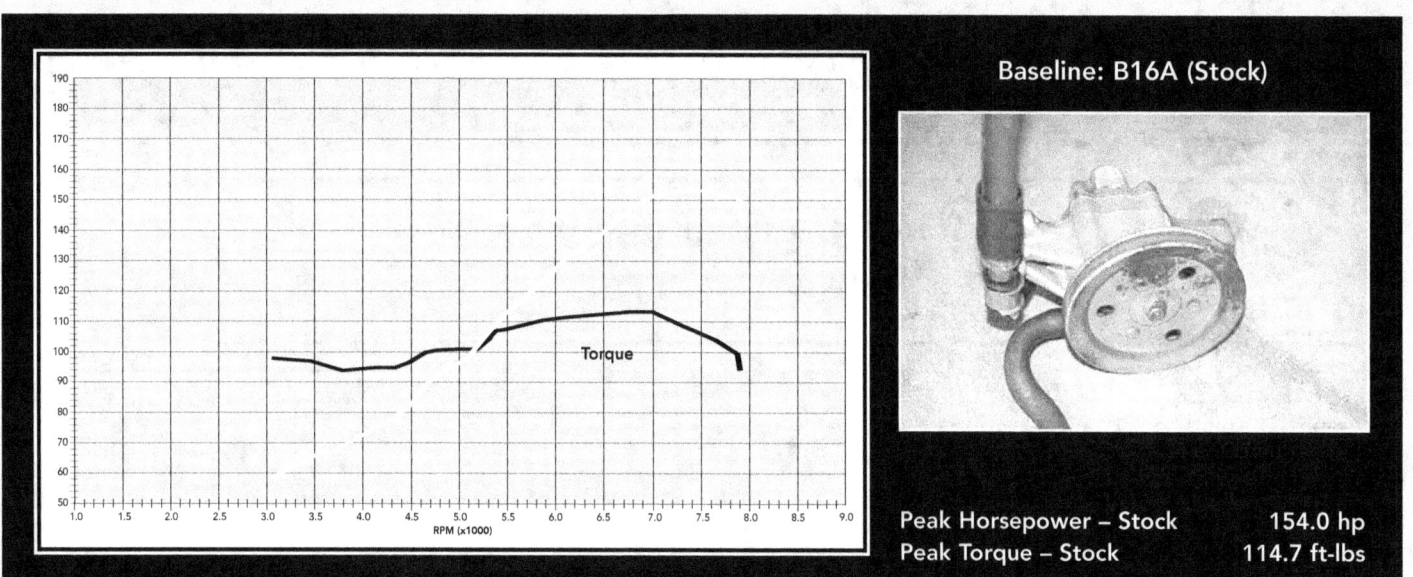

Baseline: B16A (Stock)

Peak Horsepower – Stock	154.0 hp
Peak Torque – Stock	114.7 ft-lbs

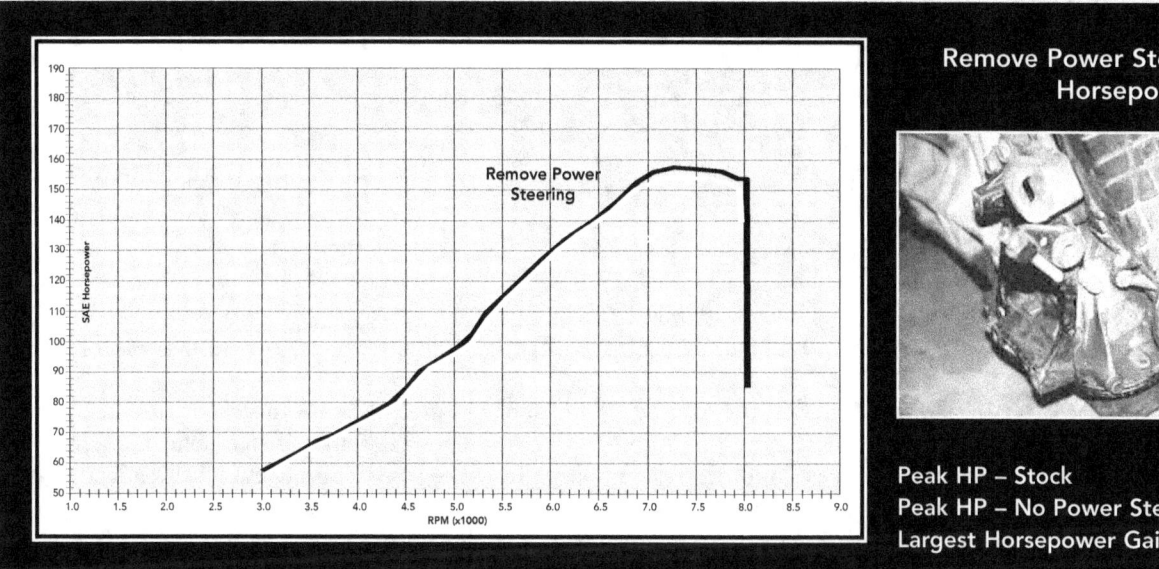

Remove Power Steering Pump: Horsepower

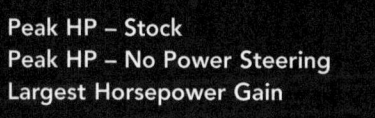

Peak HP – Stock	154.0 hp
Peak HP – No Power Steering	158.2 hp
Largest Horsepower Gain	4.2 hp

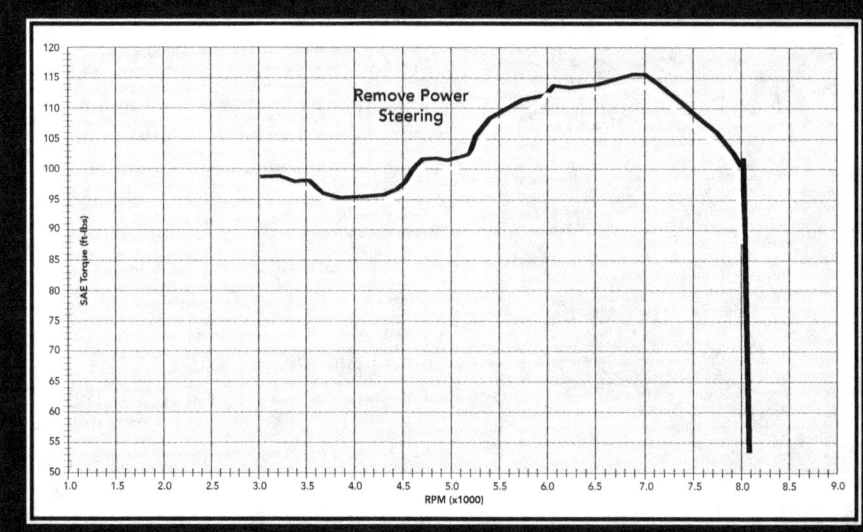

Remove Power SteeringPump : Torque

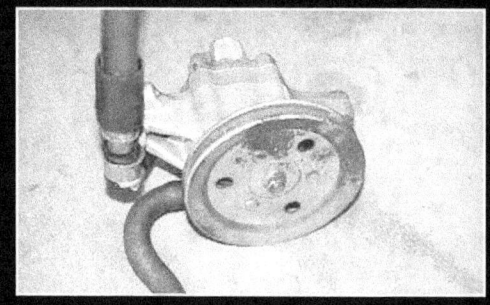

Peak Torque – Stock	114.7 ft-lbs
Peak Torque – No P/S	116.2 ft-lbs
Largest Torque Gain	3.4 ft-lbs

How to Build Honda Horsepower

Chapter 7

Test 5: Unorthodox Racing Underdrive Pulley

1990 Integra GS (Engine Swap) B16A 1.6L VTEC

Having run both AEM underdrive power steering and alternator pulleys along with dyno testing the removal of the power steering pump, I was anxious to see the results of this test. The Unorthodox Racing underdrive crank pulley was not only significantly lighter (net weight difference) than the heavy factory B16A crank pulley, but also smaller in diameter. The combination resulted in both a change in parasitic loss from slowing the speed of the other accessories (in this case just an alternator), but also the reduction in mass. The smaller diameter and weight reduction both decreased the moment of inertia, making it much easier for the motor to spin the new aluminum crank pulley. Making it easier on the motor resulted in the freeing up of power that was lost to spinning the factory crank. The underdrive pulleys don't add power in the same way as a header or camshaft; they simply reduce the amount of power that is lost. Of course, the result is the same—an improvement in power output.

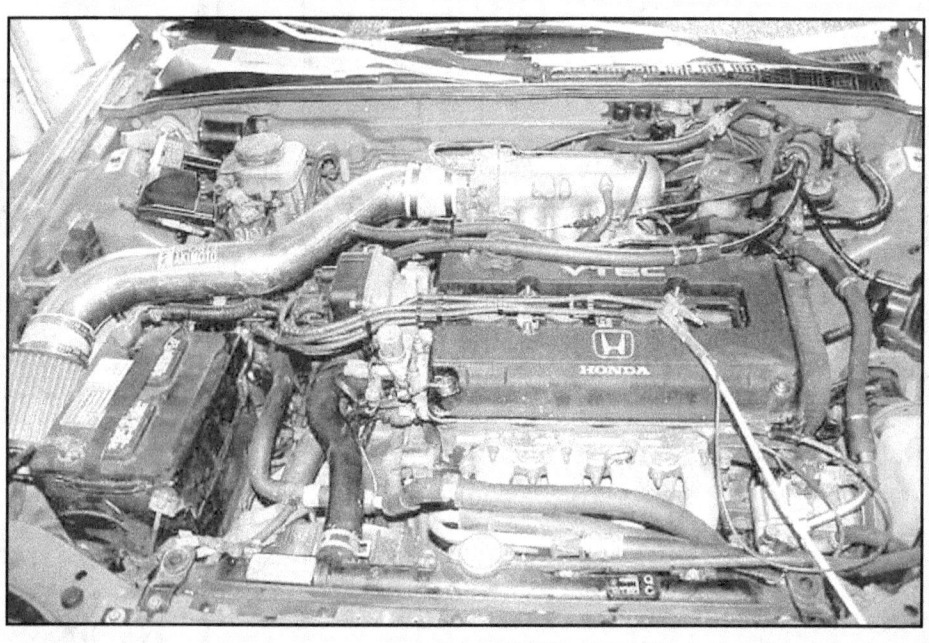

The test motor resided in the author's 1990 Acura Integra. The tired B18A had long since been swapped out in favor of the little VTEC motor. The B16A was equipped with a DC Sports header, RS Akimoto air intake, and Thermal stainless steel exhaust system. The Integra also featured a Hondata programmable ECU, though no timing or fuel changes were required or performed between test runs. We simply ran the B16A motor on the DynoJet with the factory steel crank pulley running the alternator only and then swapped it in favor of the UR aluminum pulley. Obviously, care was taken to ensure the correct oil and coolant temps and the two tests were run within minutes of each other—negating any change in ambient temperature. The installation of the UR underdrive crank pulley increased power from as low as 3,000 rpm all the ay to 7,300 rpm. Oddly enough, the power gains diminished after the motor reached peak power. Although the power gains offered by underdrive pulleys typically increase with engine speed, the gains on this test diminished after 7,200 rpm. Backup runs produced the same results.

Nitrous, ECUs (Chips), and Underdrive Pulleys

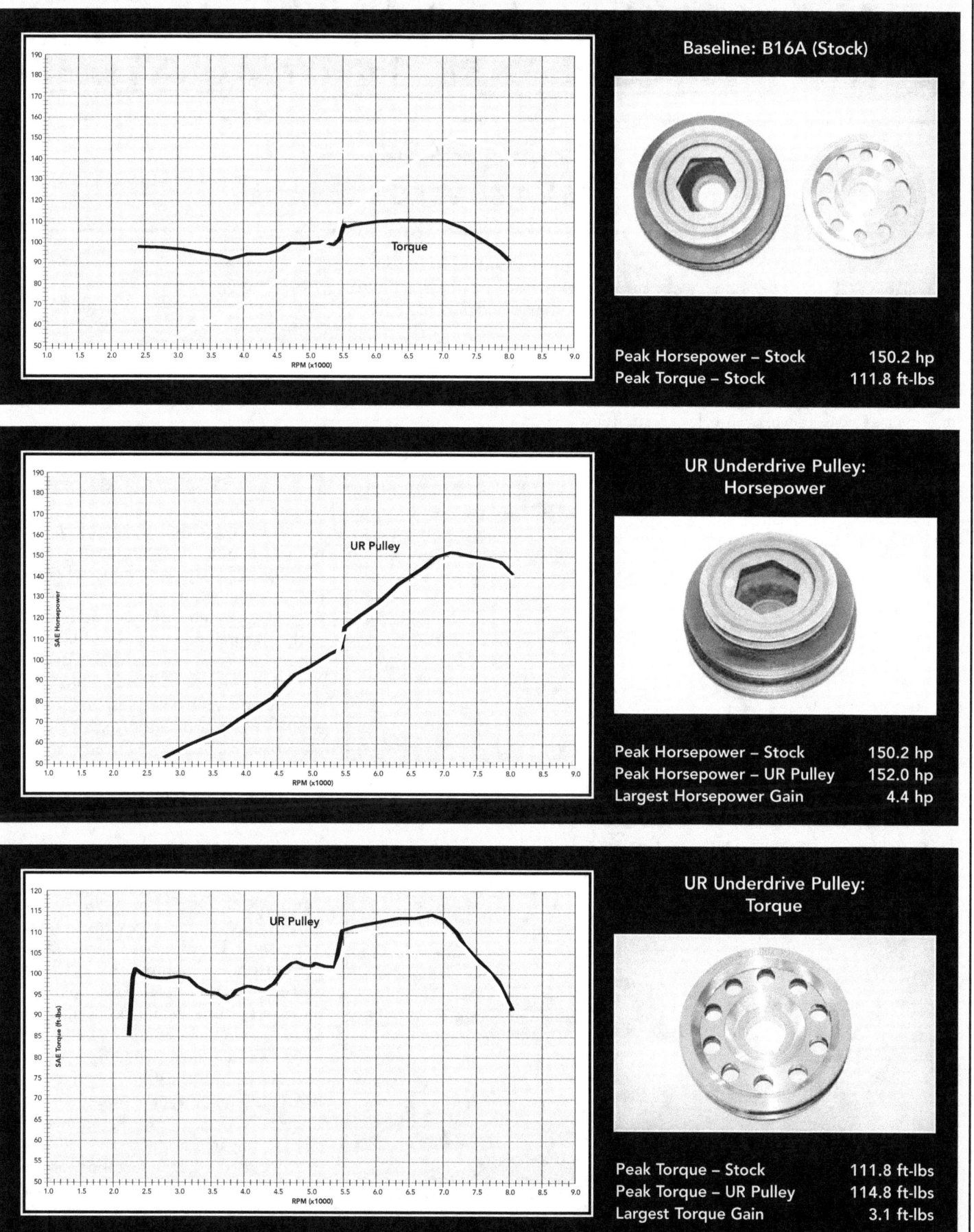

Baseline: B16A (Stock)

Peak Horsepower – Stock	150.2 hp
Peak Torque – Stock	111.8 ft-lbs

UR Underdrive Pulley: Horsepower

Peak Horsepower – Stock	150.2 hp
Peak Horsepower – UR Pulley	152.0 hp
Largest Horsepower Gain	4.4 hp

UR Underdrive Pulley: Torque

Peak Torque – Stock	111.8 ft-lbs
Peak Torque – UR Pulley	114.8 ft-lbs
Largest Torque Gain	3.1 ft-lbs

How to Build Honda Horsepower

Chapter 7

Test 6: Stock ECU versus Mugen ECU

1995 Civic Del Sol
B16A 1.6L VTEC

Before we had the Hondata programmable ECU at our disposal, we ran the Mugen ECU in our USTCC Del Sol (2000 season). The factory ECU had (among other undesirable qualities) an 8,000-rpm rev limiter. While the near stock B16A "race" motor made peak power well below that engine speed, we needed the ability to increase engine speed in a race to do what is referred to as "stretch a shift." When running on a section of the track, often we run into a situation where we hit the rev limiter just a second or two before we have to downshift for the turn. There is not enough time to shift into the next gear, but it is annoying, not to mention bad for the motor, to run it on the rev limiter for a second or two. Although we shift right at 8,000 rpm during the race, having the ability to run to 8,200 rpm or 8,300 rpm would allow us to stretch the shift for that one corner.

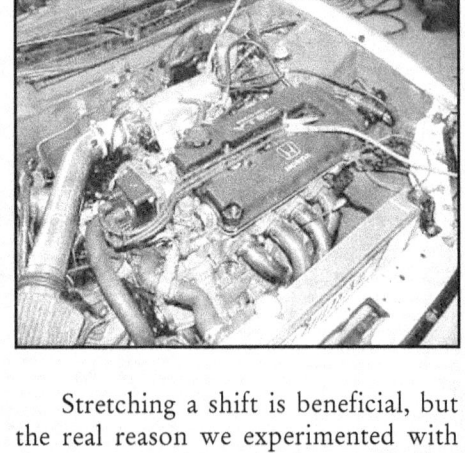

Stretching a shift is beneficial, but the real reason we experimented with the Mugen ECU was in hopes of gaining performance over the factory ECU. As we have demonstrated in other tests in this chapter, power is available from tuning the combination. The installation of the Mugen ECU was proof positive that the motor will respond to the proper ECU program. Neither King Motorsports nor Mugen directly would comment on the programming changes, and we suspect a more aggressive timing and fuel curve curves were responsible for the added power. With the stock P30 (Del Sol) ECU, the B16A produced 151.8 hp and 111.4 ft-lbs of torque. With just the addition of the Mugen ECU, the peak power increased to 155.0 hp. The Mugen ECU increased power from the onset of the VTEC cam profile (which came at 5,600 rpm) all the way to our self-imposed redline of 8,200 rpm. Given enough motor, the ECU would allow 9,500 rpm—well beyond the rpm capability of a factory B16A. It is important to note that the Mugen ECU gave up a big chunk of power compared to the stock ECU due to the raised VTEC operation point. We used the APEXi VTEC controller to cure this situation in the racecar to provide the best of both worlds.

Nitrous, ECUs (Chips), and Underdrive Pulleys

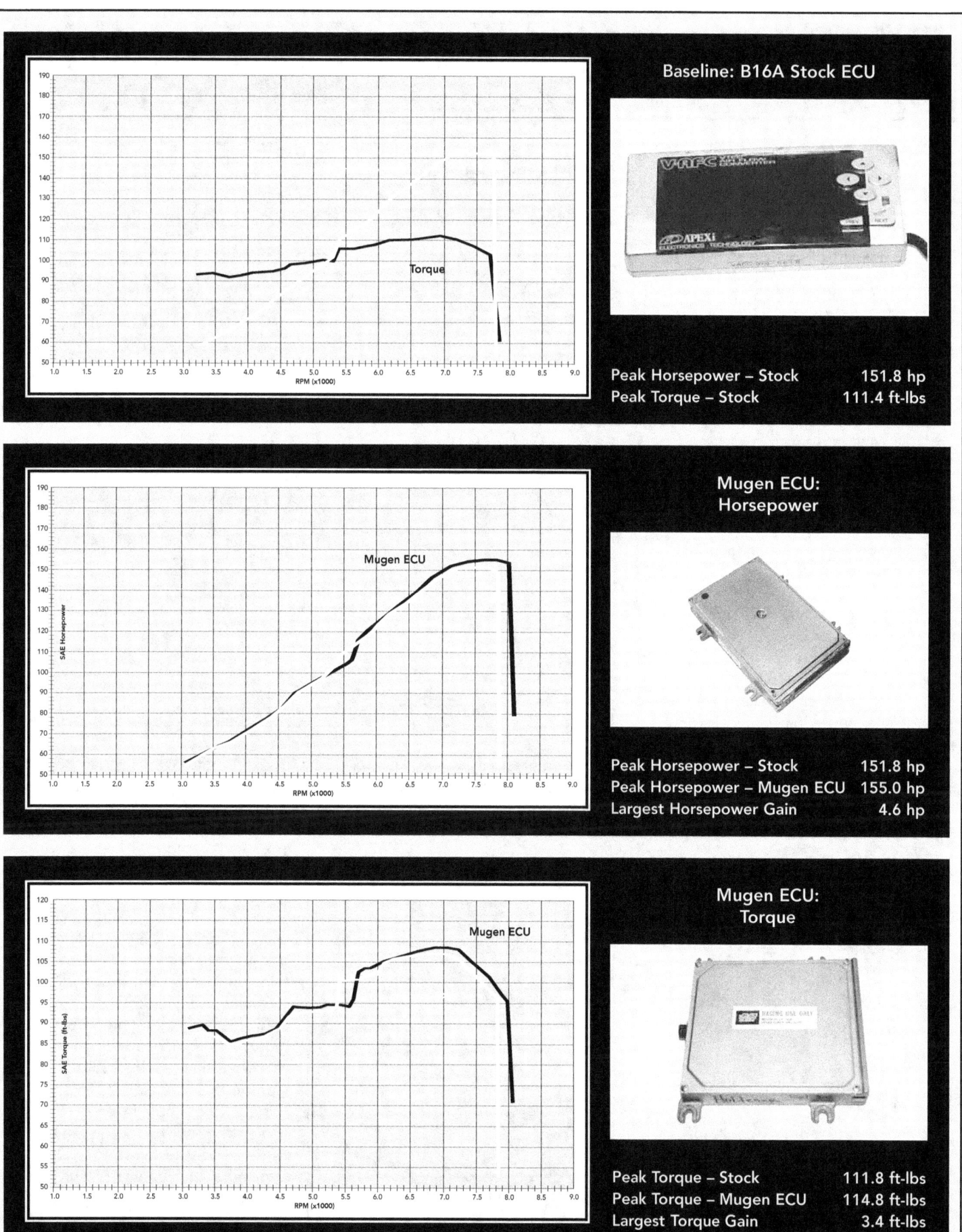

Baseline: B16A Stock ECU

Peak Horsepower – Stock	151.8 hp
Peak Torque – Stock	111.4 ft-lbs

Mugen ECU: Horsepower

Peak Horsepower – Stock	151.8 hp
Peak Horsepower – Mugen ECU	155.0 hp
Largest Horsepower Gain	4.6 hp

Mugen ECU: Torque

Peak Torque – Stock	111.8 ft-lbs
Peak Torque – Mugen ECU	114.8 ft-lbs
Largest Torque Gain	3.4 ft-lbs

How to Build Honda Horsepower

Chapter 7

Test 7: Stock ECU versus Comptech ECU

1999 Integra Type R
B18C5 1.8L VTEC

This was one of the few dyno test not actually run directly by the author. As you might imagine, the logistics of getting dozens of cars to dozens of different dynos for testing is a difficult proposition. Having had experience both with the Comptech products and personnel, I can attest to the fact that the power numbers presented here are representative of what to expect when installing one of their ECUs on your Type R. Unlike many aftermarket performance products offered for the Hondas and Acuras, the Comptech lineup has a serious racing history. While the Indy and IRL affiliation is certainly enough to brag about, what really impressed me the most was the fact that the Comptech products are used on the Real Time World Challenge Integra Type Rs. In my opinion, the World Challenge championship-winning Real Time cars are the Integras that all others are measured by.

The Comptech ECU test demonstrated that not only do they have a handle on proper programming but also that the factory ECU was an area where Honda/Acura left a lot on the table. This is very unusual for Honda/Acura, especially on a motor that already makes 108 hp/liter like the impressive Type R. According to their test results, the Type R ECU offered power gains from 2,000 rpm all the way to the redline. A close examination of the curve reveals a smooth transition from the primary to the secondary cam, indicating the proper VTEC activation point. The test motor was equipped with a header, cat-back, and drop-in filter (all from Comptech of course). It is impressive that the motor made over 180 hp at the wheels, although the Integra was tested on a Dyno Dynamics Dynamometer and the raw numbers can't be compared to those generated by another car on the DynoJet.

Nitrous, ECUs (Chips), and Underdrive Pulleys

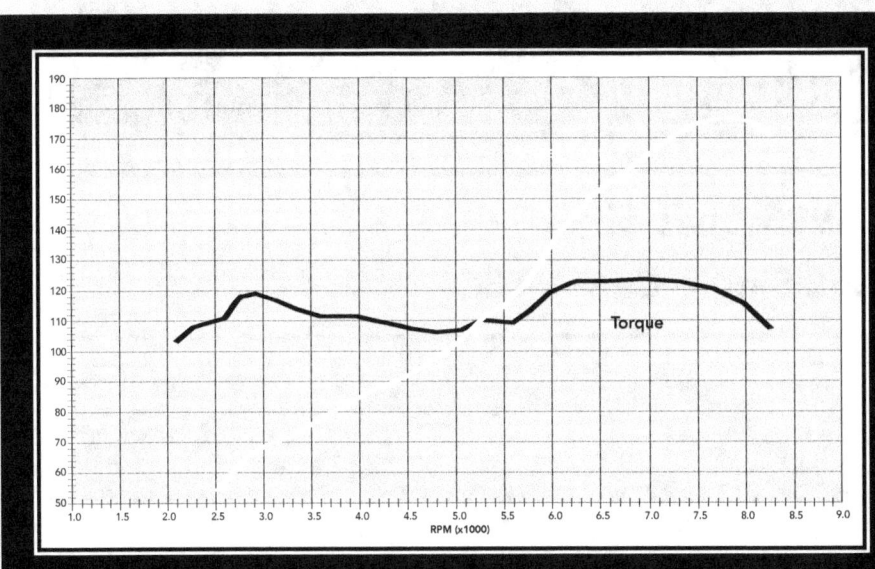

Baseline: B18C5 (Stock ECU)

A Comptech ECU picked up a sizable chunk of power, even on the already impressive Integra Type R. It comes as no surprise that the company with a true racing heritage would offer so much power from ECU tuning.

Peak Horsepower – Stock	151.8 hp
Peak Torque – Stock	111.4 ft-lbs

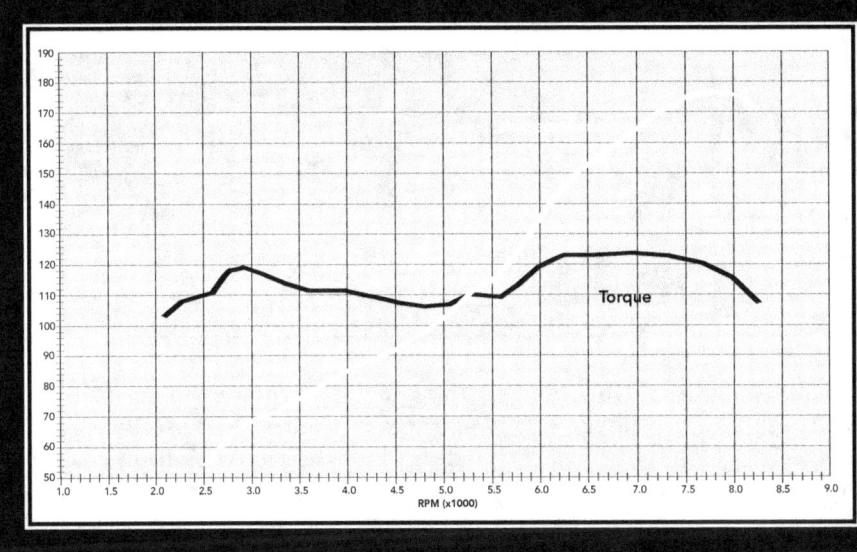

Comptech ECU: Horsepower

Peak HP – Stock	151.8 hp
Peak HP – Comptech ECU	155.0 hp
Largest Horsepower Gain	4.6 hp

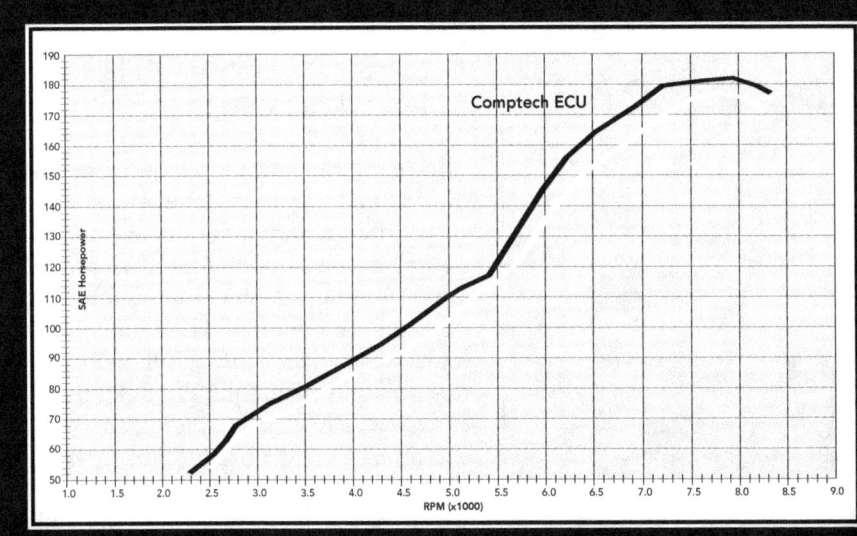

Comptech ECU: Torque

Peak Torque – Stock	111.4 ft-lbs
Peak Torque – Comptech ECU	114.8 ft-lbs
Largest Torque Gain	3.4 ft-lbs

How to Build Honda Horsepower

Chapter 7

Test 8: Horsepower from an Oil Change
Redline Synthetic Oil

1993 Civic Si
D16Z 1.6L Single-Cam VTEC

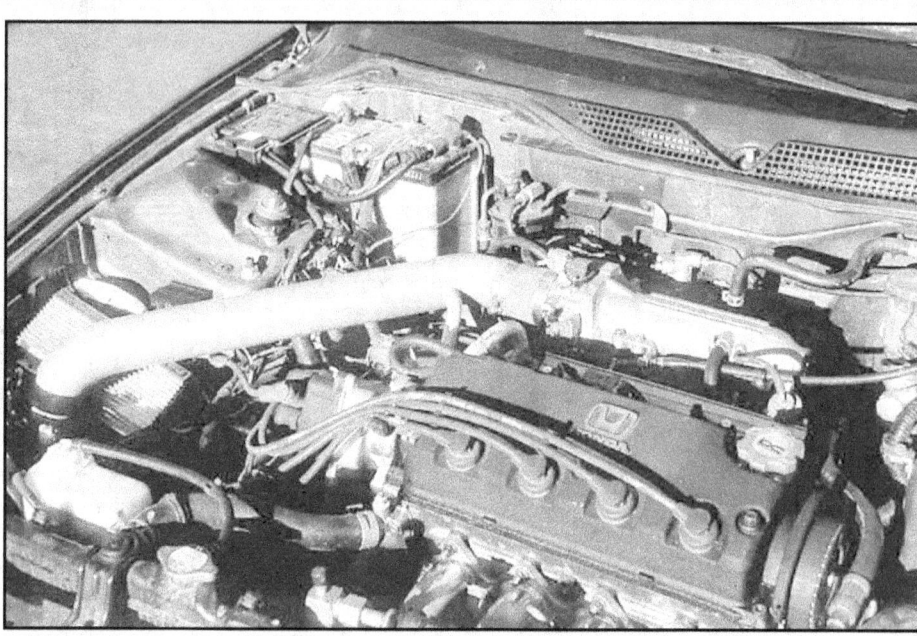

This test was run to demonstrate the effectiveness of synthetic oil. The most impressive benefits offered by synthetic lubricants are not demonstrated by a simple dyno test, but the addition of synthetic oils, especially lightweight synthetic oils can result in power gains. To put the theory to the test, we subjected Redline Synthetic Oil to a series of dyno tests. The testing was run on a DynoJet chassis dyno, with the output measured at the wheels. Since we would be looking for only minor power gains, we made sure to include backup runs to duplicate the power curves generated with each oil. Lucky for us, the single-cam VTEC D16Z Civic motor was dead repeatable (varied by less than 1 hp run to run). The first step was to establish a baseline using a conventional petroleum based oil. We employed a major brand of 20W-50, pouring in fresh oil and using a new oil filter. The car was driven for several miles before running on the chassis dyno. The oil and water temps were logged before each run. Using the conventional petroleum-based 20W-50, the mildly modified D16Z motor produced a peak power reading of 113 hp at the wheels.

Next up was the switch to Redline Synthetic Oil. Out came the major brand of petroleum oil and in went 10W racing oil. This test was obviously more than a simple synthetic oil test, as we altered the viscosity as well. Even though this represented a pair of changes in one test (not usually a good idea), the basic test was an oil change. Before getting to the results, I must stress here than it is not a good idea to run extended miles on 10W racing oil. As the name implies, racing oil was designed with racing (and therefore frequent oil changes) in mind. Synthetic oil should be in the crankcase of every performance Honda/Acura on the road today, but stick with either a multi grade offered by Redline and leave the racing oil for track events or trips to the drag strip. After installing the Redline oil and new filter, we subjected the Civic to the same 10-minute drive before strapping it back on the DynoJet. The results were impressive, as the Redline Oil increased the power output by a good 4 hp. As expected, the gains increased with engine speed, but a backup run repeated the increase perfectly. Synthetic oil works, so use it. Your engine will thank you with years of trouble-free miles.

146   How to Build Honda Horsepower

Nitrous, ECUs (Chips), and Underdrive Pulleys

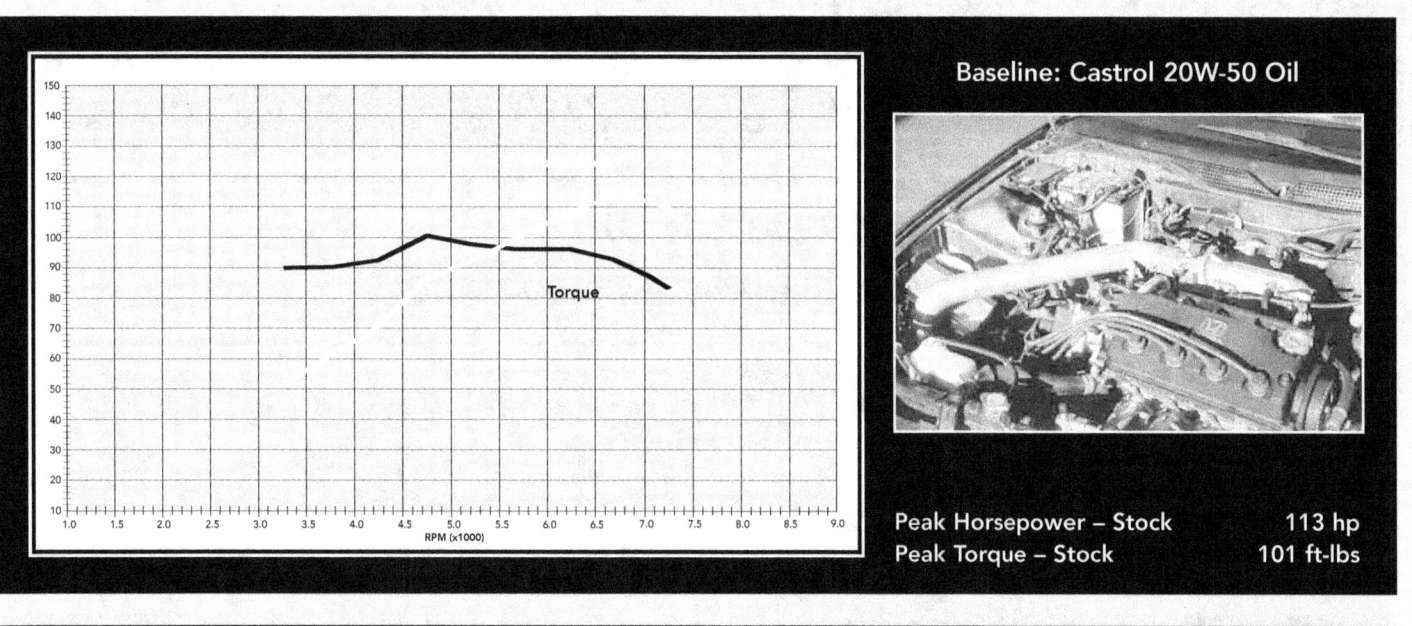

Baseline: Castrol 20W-50 Oil

Peak Horsepower – Stock	113 hp
Peak Torque – Stock	101 ft-lbs

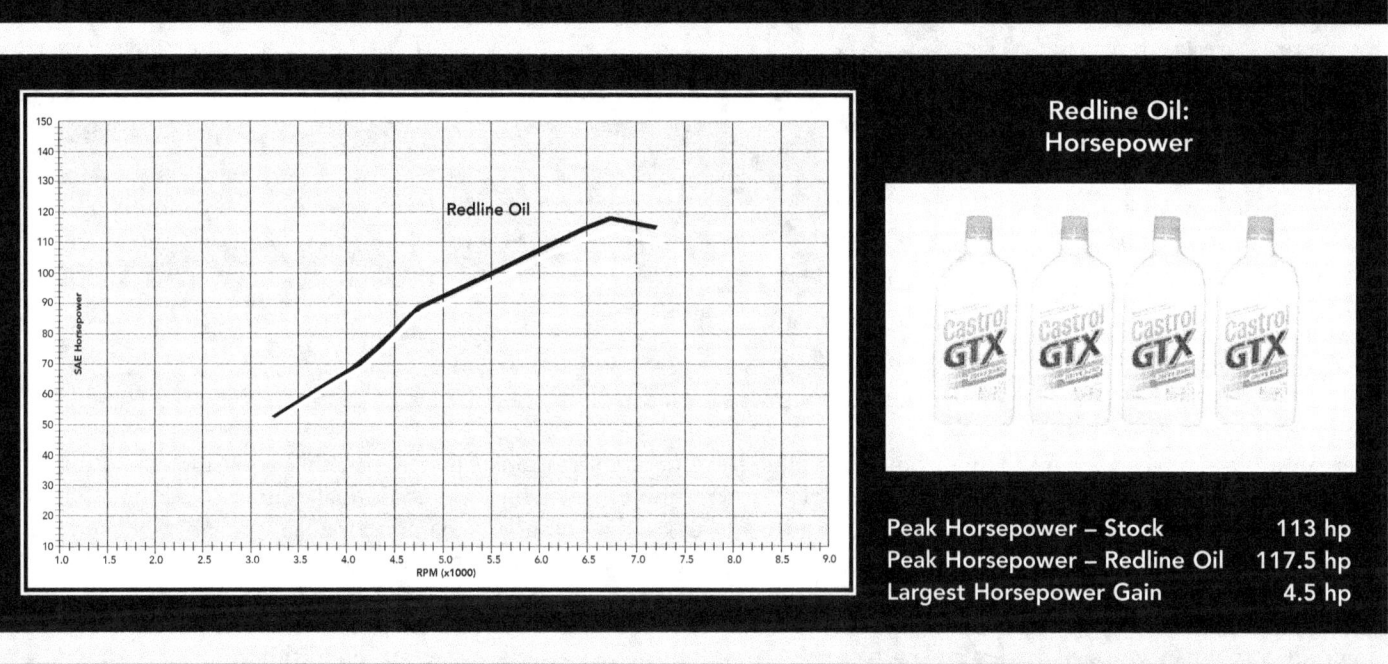

Redline Oil: Horsepower

Peak Horsepower – Stock	113 hp
Peak Horsepower – Redline Oil	117.5 hp
Largest Horsepower Gain	4.5 hp

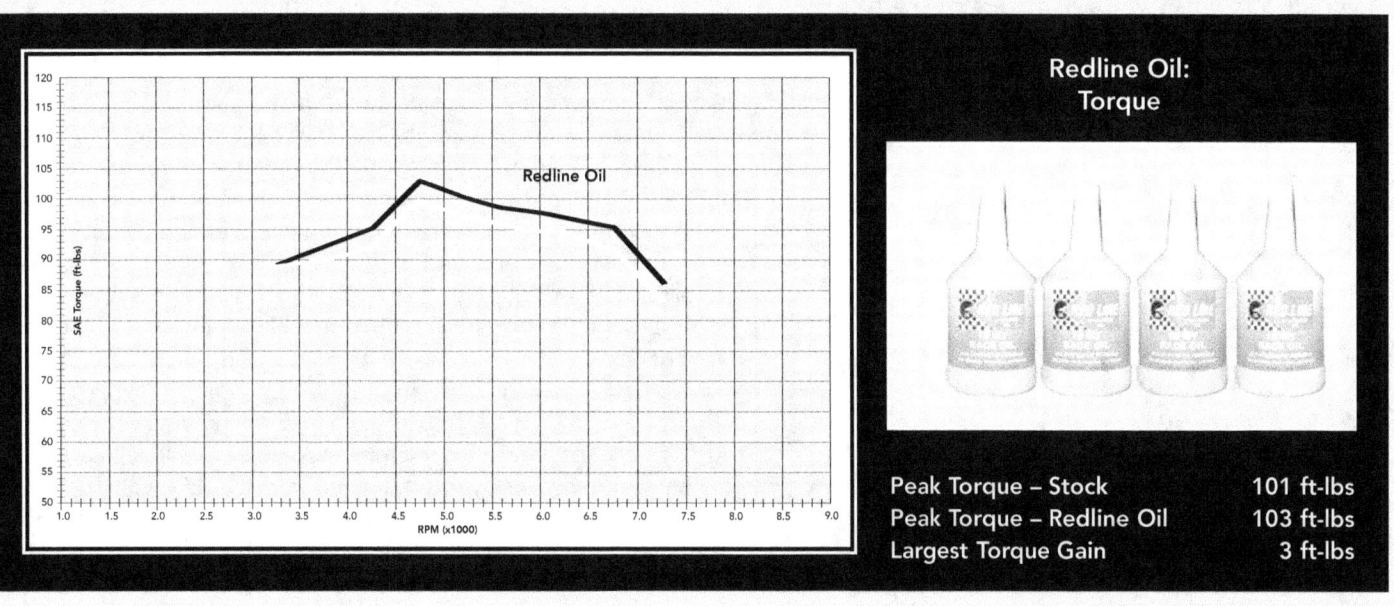

Redline Oil: Torque

Peak Torque – Stock	101 ft-lbs
Peak Torque – Redline Oil	103 ft-lbs
Largest Torque Gain	3 ft-lbs

How to Build Honda Horsepower

Chapter 7

Test 9: Air Conditioning and Lights

1995 Civic DX
D15B 1.5L Single-Cam Non-VTEC

One of the problems associated with testing Honda/Acura motors has always been one of repeatability. The problem is not that the motors don't repeat a given power curve, but rather dyno operators (tuners) don't take the necessary precautions when testing to assure accurate results. The usual method of testing is to run a baseline run in stock or unmodified trim and then again, once a certain modification has been performed. The potential problem with this method is that the temperature of the motor and/or ambient air can change not to mention a number of other factors. This test was run to demonstrate the effect of both heat and the accessories, namely the air conditioner, and field generated by the alternator. No changes were made to the car other than allowing the motor to run warm (after a few hard dyno pulls) and then to switch on the air conditioner. This was done in an effort to demonstrate how much power is lost when you are driving around on those hot summer days.

The car chosen for this test was a 1995 Civic DX, although the relative differences would be similar for just

about any model/engine combination. The test was rather simple, involving just running the motor on the DynoJet in cool condition (intake cool to the touch) and then again after a few hard dyno runs to get things nice and warm. The baseline (cool) run netted a peak power reading of 100.8 hp. Although the hot run netted an almost identical power reading (100.6), the power loss from the change in engine temperature was very evident throughout the curve. Note that the motor lost power across the board, the largest difference approaching 5 hp. This test clearly illustrates the importance of consistent engine temperature. Given that some of the performance test components in this book did not result in an additional 5 hp, it is easy to see how temperature can dramatically skew the results of a dyno test.

The second test illustrated how much power was lost through driving the air conditioning and headlights. Actually, the headlights produced only a minor amount of additional drag from the alternator, as they required additional voltage from the charging system. Once again, the results speak for themselves, as driving the accessories cost power. The air conditioner and lights combined to reduce peak power by 1.5 hp, but the loss was consistent from 2,000 rpm to 6,500 rpm (shown as road speed on the graph). Is the air conditioner worth a few ponies? If you live somewhere where the summer months produce 100+ degree heat then the answer would probably be yes. At least you know to turn off the air conditioner when rolling up to the light next to a potential match race.

Nitrous, ECUs (Chips), and Underdrive Pulleys

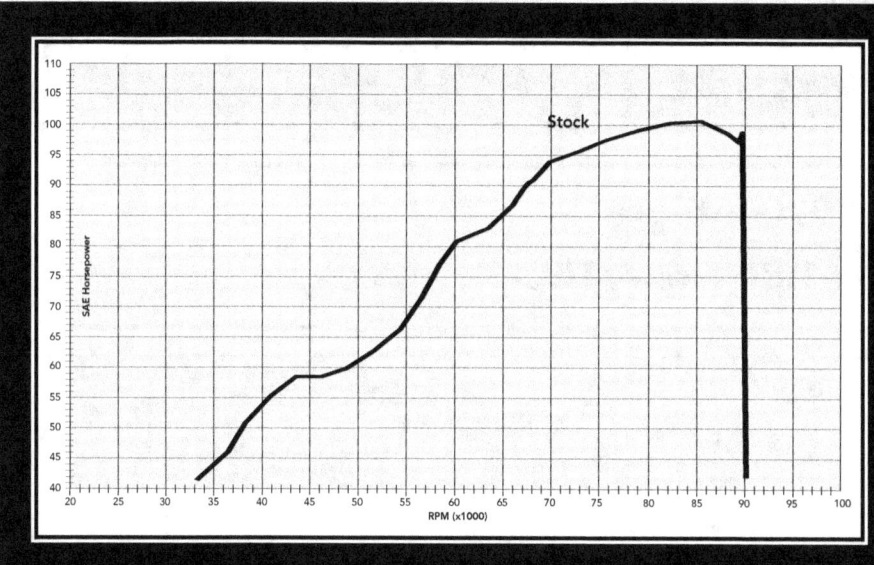

Baseline: D15B (Stock)

Does turning on your A/C and headlights cost you performance? The extra drag placed on the motor by the A/C compressor and the alternator do, in fact, sap performance from your Honda motor.

Peak Horsepower – Stock	100.8 hp
Peak Torque – Stock	N/A

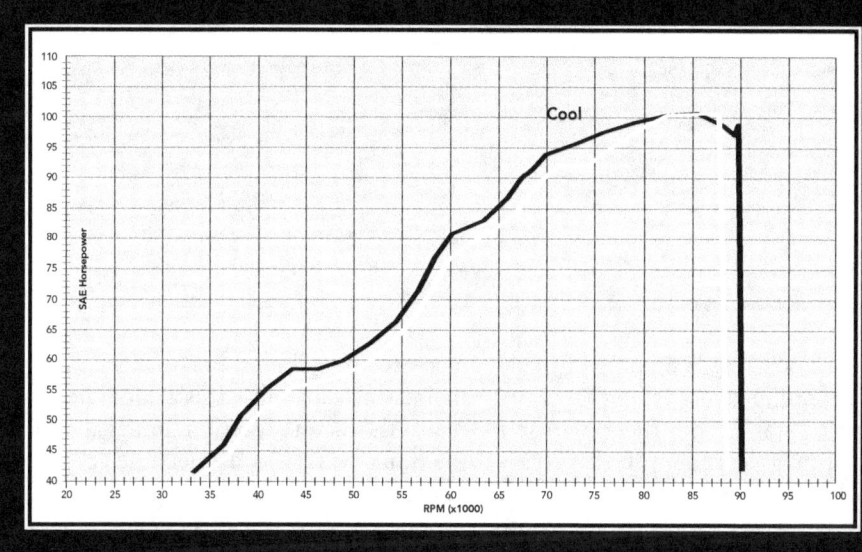

Hot versus Cold: Horsepower

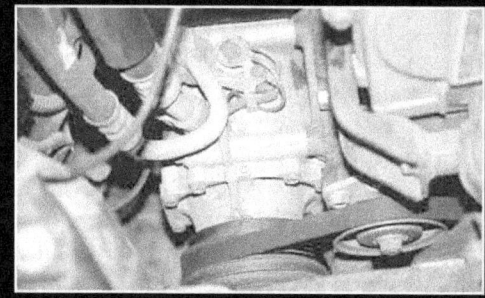

Peak Horsepower – Cool	100.8 hp
Peak Horsepower – Hot	100.6 hp
Largest Horsepower Gain	4.8 hp

Air Conditioner and Lights: Horsepower

Peak HP – Stock	100.6 hp
Peak HP – A/C and Lights	99.2 hp
Largest Horsepower Gain	2.3 hp

How to Build Honda Horsepower

Chapter 7

Test 10: ZEX Nitrous Oxide

1990 Integra
B18A 1.8L Non-VTEC

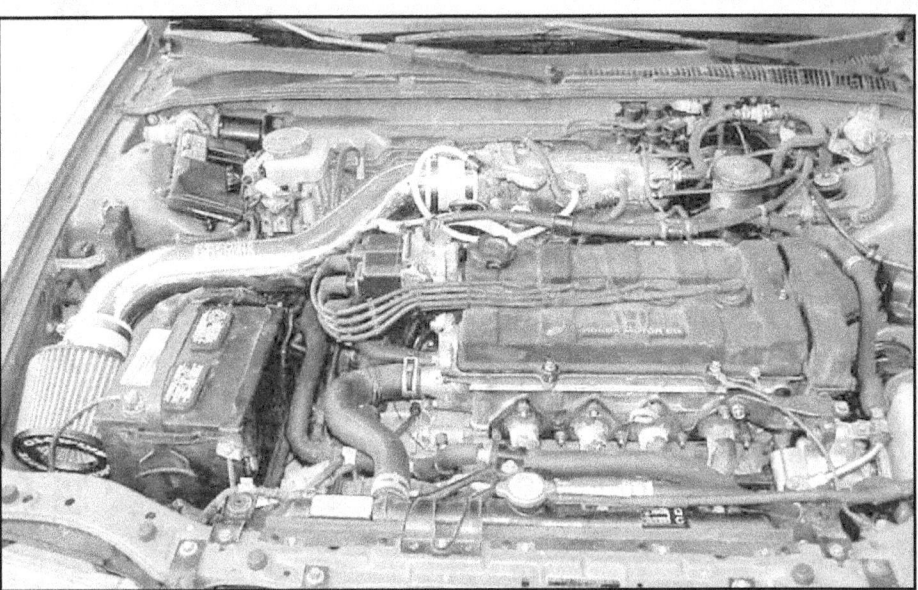

The VTEC motors have all the street rep, but that doesn't mean that you can't make a non-VTEC motor run just as strong. While you are not likely to get a non-VTEC B18A to pull strongly to 8000 rpm without the help of a VTEC head swap or some seriously aggressive (not streetable) cam profiles, you can help it pull much stronger to the realistic redline of 6500 rpm. The answer is nitrous oxide. Much like forced induction, nitrous oxide fools the motor into thinking it is much bigger and badder than it really is. Just like turbo or superchargers, it is possible to feed the motor too much nitrous oxide and bang, your day is over quick. Like boost, if applied correctly, your car ingest bottle after bottle of the laughing gas and go on to live a strong (rebuild-free) life.

Just like installing a turbo kit on your motor, the installation of nitrous oxide like the ZEX system installed on this 1990 Integra GS requires proper operation of your fuel and ignition timing sub systems. Adding nitrous (or boost) with a failing or inadequate fuel pump is just asking for trouble with a capital T. Your fuel pump and filter must be able to supply the necessary additional fuel (pressure) to work in conjunction with the nitrous oxide. The same goes for your ignition system. High mileage spark plugs will likely not provide optimum performance, as the increase in cylinder pressure may tax their firing capability. It is a good idea to retard the factory ignition timing and fill the tank with good fuel and octane booster before your first squeeze. ZEX supplied a set of nitrous-friendly spark plugs for this test, and the stock fuel pump (pressure) checked out while running on the dyno. We filled the tank with 91-octane premium unleaded and then threw in a can of octane booster as a hedge against detonation. The results were impressive, as the ZEX system pumped up the power output of the lowly non-VTEC GS motor from 118 horsepower to 153 horsepower. The peak torque was up as well, from 115 lbs. ft. to 157 lbs. ft. The impressive part of the ZEX system, and the reason for the huge gain in _-mile times is the increase in average torque across the rev range. The ZEX system elevated the torque curve by a good 35-40 lbs. ft. across the board. You can really feel the difference on the street and so can that pesky VTEC Civic in the next lane.

Nitrous, ECUs (Chips), and Underdrive Pulleys

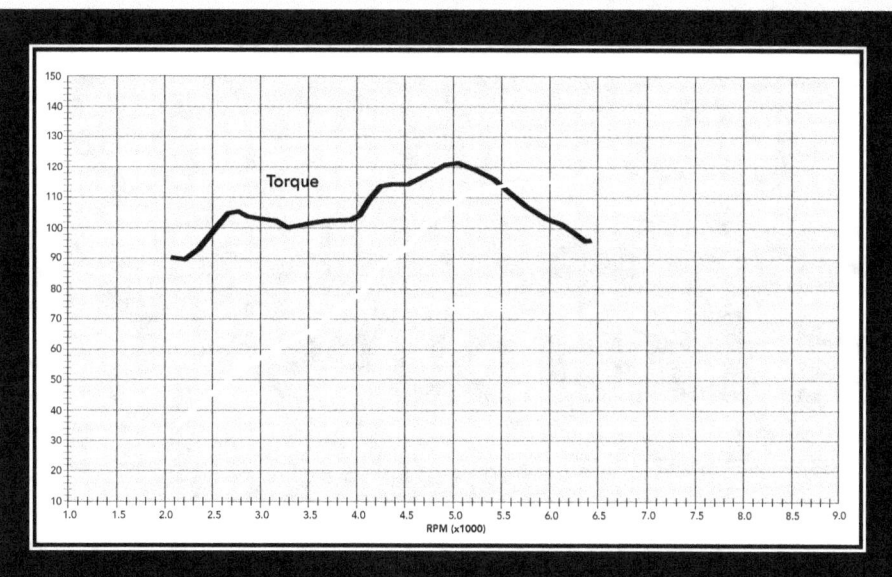

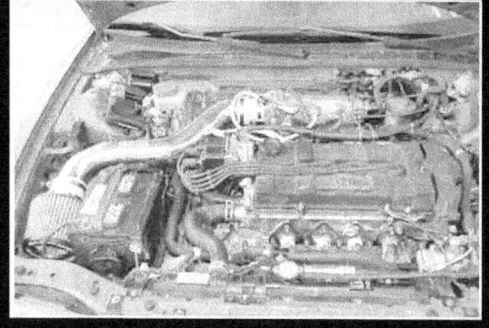

Baseline: B18A (Stock)

Peak Horsepower – Stock	118.2 ft-lbs
Peak Torque – Stock	114.6 ft-lbs

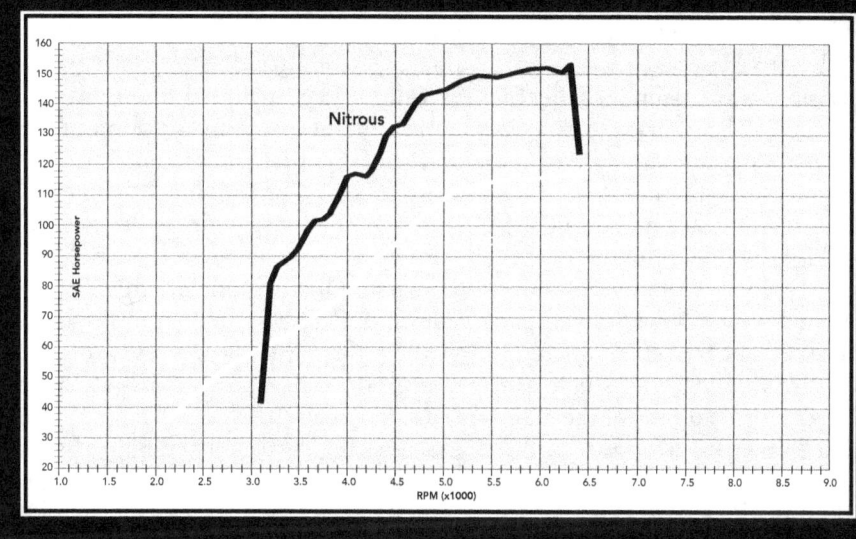

Stock versus ZEX Nitrous: Horsepower

Peak Horsepower – Stock	118.2 hp
Peak Horsepower – ZEX	152.9 hp
Largest Horsepower Gain	37.4 hp

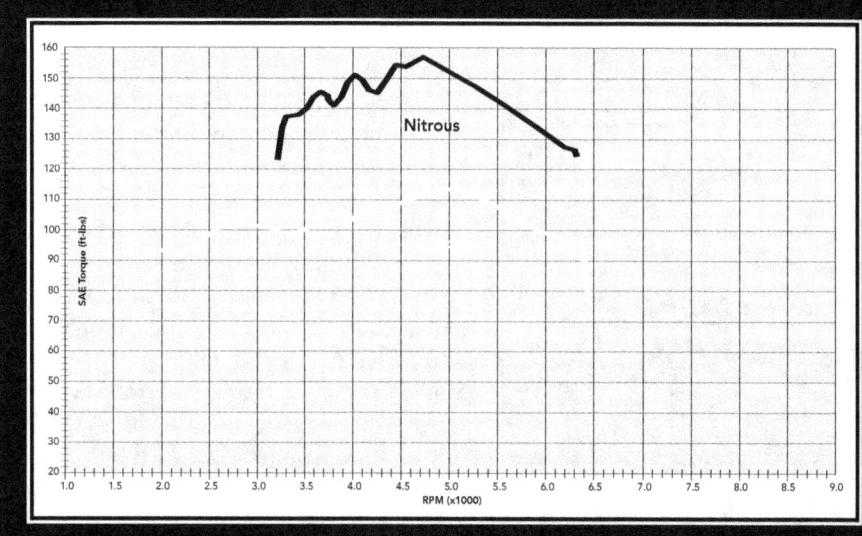

Stock versus ZEX Nitrous: Torque

Peak Torque – Stock	114.6 ft-lbs
Peak Torque – ZEX	156.7 ft-lbs
Largest Torque Gain	40 ft-lbs

How to Build Honda Horsepower

CHAPTER 8

ENGINE BUILDUPS

Since the majority of this book is dedicated to dyno testing individual components, I thought it would be a good idea to include a chapter in which a number of these components were brought together. It is always helpful to discover what effect an individual component will have on a particular engine combination, and it is useful to find out what happens when you build a particular combination. While we all long for big horsepower, the reality is that most enthusiasts would not want to live with the headaches associated with most race motors. Sure, they are great when running at full throttle down the quarter-mile, but can you really live with a 13.0:1 stroker motor on a daily basis? How would such a motor survive the daily commute or those long holiday trips to visit the family? How much of that Honda/Acura reliability would be sacrificed in our quest for ultimate power? The truth is that race motors and street motors are completely different animals. A 500-hp turbo motor has no more business in a daily driver than a stock motor has at the strip. Sure, both may survive quick trips, but neither would provide optimum results. For that reason, I have included buildups that cover both street and strip motors. The coverage includes everything from mild D16Z single cam VTEC street motors to one of the many JG Engine Dynamics turbo race mills.

A great many more (literally thousands) combinations exist, some even more powerful and successful in their respective fields. It is obviously impossible to include every possible combination and many worthwhile combinations were omitted due to space considerations. The included buildups do cover a broad spectrum, including street performance, road racing, and 9-second strip terrors. The buildups can be followed to the letter with results comparable to those printed in the book, or simply used as a guideline to tailor to your specific application. You should be warned that altering the components used in the buildup could just as easily cause a reduction in performance as the intended improvement. Frankly speaking, it is difficult to improve upon something like the JG Engine Dynamics turbo race motor. Javier and the gang know more about Honda/Acura engine combinations than anyone I came across while gathering the information for this book. I thank them for providing some of their secrets behind their motors and helping us with my own record-setting Bonneville project. A motor such as the Killer Bee Racing motor used in the author's USTCC winning Del Sol is another story, as the rules required mainly stock components that could easily be improved upon. Killer Bee Racing now offers affordable crate motor assemblies for those wanting to take the guesswork out of buildups. From mild street to all-motor madness, from supercharged to turbocharged, this chapter should have a little something for everyone.

Equipped with a supercharged D16Z, this little Civic Si motored to the tune of nearly 200 wheel horsepower and 143 miles per hour.

Engine Buildup 1
Supercharged D16Z

One way to improve power output is by force-feeding more air into the motor than it can ingest of its own accord. Forced induction has been around for some time and the Honda motors seem to take to the notion like the proverbial duck to water. This little forced induction adventure became necessary when the author went looking for a way to propel a 1992 Civic Si hatchback to a top speed of 150 mph. The so-called 150-mph Hot Hatch was featured in a series for one of the more popular import (sport compact) performance magazines. The idea was quite simple: build up a Civic Si to prepare it to travel to the far side of 150 mph. The car was given a complete performance makeover, including aerodynamics, suspension, safety, interior, and, of course, the VTEC engine. The single-cam VTEC motor was treated to numerous upgrades that eventually nearly doubled the factory power output. Although the best (radar-verified) speed the car would eventually run was shy of 150 mph (143 mph), the exercise was considered a success. We generated a considerable amount of data on supercharged single-cam motors, not to mention providing the opportunity to experience my very first Honda engine rebuild under the watchful eye of the experts at Jackson Racing.

To reach 150 mph, we selected a target horsepower goal of 200 hp at the wheels. Given that our stock Si motor produced 105 hp at the wheels, we figured that doubling the power output would allow us to safely reach 150 mph. While we could have simply thrown everything we had at the D16Z motor in one fell swoop, we chose a slow, methodical route by installing and testing each individual component. This provided us with documented data on the affect of each performance component. Rather than simply bolt on all manner of performance hardware and guess which ones really helped, we tested every single component individually and documented the results. This way we could eliminate those parts that were just along for the ride. We wanted every

Engine Buildup 1
Supercharged D16Z

Car	*1992 Civic Si*
Block	D16Z
Bore	D16Z
Sleeved	No
Solid Deck	No
Stroke	D16Z
Piston Type	Stock Cast D16Z
Manufacturer	Honda
Rod Length	Stock D16Z
Manufacturer	Honda
Head Type	Stock D16Z
Ported	Yes, Mild
Valve Sizes in./ex.	Stock D16Z
Injector size	
Cam(s)	Stock D16Z
Adjustable Cam Sprocket(s)	No
Intake Type	Jackson Racing for Supercharger
Ported	No
Throttle Body Type	Stock D16Z
Size	Stock D16Z
Air intake	Jackson Racing
Header	Kamakazi 4-1
Exhaust	RSR
Turbo/Supercharger	Jackson Racing Supercharger
Type	Eaton Positive Displacement
Maximum Boost Pressure	12 psi
Intercooler Type	None; did employ JR water injection
Fuel/Timing Management	Stock ECU

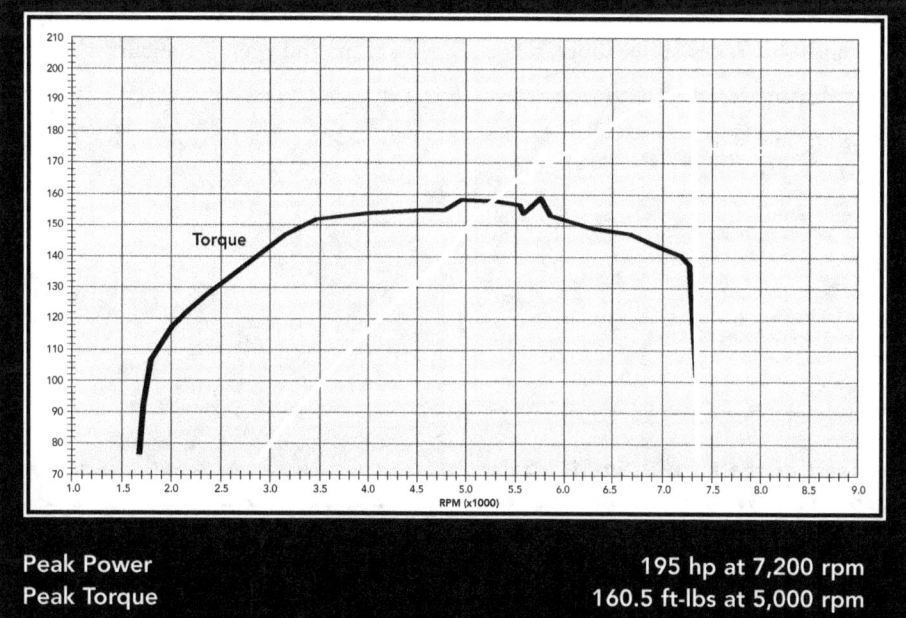

Peak Power	195 hp at 7,200 rpm
Peak Torque	160.5 ft-lbs at 5,000 rpm

If there is one thing that really wakes up a single-cam VTEC motor, it's a Jackson Racing supercharger.

performance piece to offer some kind of performance.

The single-can D16Z didn't stay stock for very long. First came the usual array of bolt-on performance parts including an AEM air intake and RSR exhaust system. After running some comparisons between different air intake systems, the Si was taken to Jackson Racing for some boost. The first step was to install the M45 supercharger and related hardware. The installation included a fuel pump upgrade, fuel management unit, and the roots-style supercharger. Though the 5-psi kit did not require a fuel pump upgrade, we knew that we would be upping the boost at a later date and that meant more fuel flow would be required. With the addition of the Jackson Racing supercharger, peak power jumped from 112 hp to 140 hp. The torque was up as well, from 98 ft-lbs to 119 ft-lbs. The motor was off to a good start, but the power output was nowhere near where it had to be to propel our Civic to 150 mph. We needed more.

One of the great things about forced induction (and one of the curses) is that additional power is usually a matter of simply running more boost. If 5 psi is good, then 8 psi must be even better. Obviously, boost (like all good things) should be taken in moderation. With the additional boost pressure comes added heat, a need for additional fuel, and the increased change of detonation. Producing more boost pressure (and increasing the flow) out of the M45 supercharger was easy enough. We simply had to increase the blower speed relative to the engine speed. This was accomplished by switching to either a smaller supercharger pulley or by installing a larger crank pulley. We went the crank pulley route to begin with and increased the boost pressure up to 8 psi. In addition to the increase in blower speed, we also installed a Kamakazi 4-1 header, removed the catalytic converter, and adjusted the valves. Adjusting the valves and a subsequent spark plug change had no effect on power, but the other modifications surely made themselves known. The new (higher boost) combination netted us 165 hp and 128 ft-lbs of torque. (See the chapter on supercharging for detailed graphs on the changes in boost)

Sure, we had another 25 hp, but we were still quite a way from our goal of 200 hp at the wheels. In the previous exercise where we increased the boost pressure from 5 psi to 8 psi, we did so using the stock 240-cc fuel injectors. The increase in fuel flow came via the 5:1 FMU supplied with the Jackson super-

The heart of the kit was an M45 Eaton supercharger. We pushed the little M45 to the limit and managed to coax nearly 200 hp at the wheels. Had spaced allowed, installing the M62 would have made life much easier for us.

A 3-inch air intake was employed on the supercharged motor, although a number of configurations were tested.

The fuel management system on the stock JR supercharger kit consisted of a rising rate fuel regulator.

Engine Buildups

After experimenting with 5 psi, we upped the boost by swapping both the blower and crank pulleys to increase the boost pressure up to 12 psi.

charger kit. The FMU increases the fuel pressure by 5 psi for every 1 psi of boost pressure. Thus, our fuel pressure changed from 43 psi (at idle) up to 68 psi under 5 psi of boost. We increased the boost pressure to 8 psi, and the fuel pressure jumped up to 83 psi. The added pressure supplied the necessary enrichment under boost. The fuel pump upgrade was necessary to supply the required fuel while running such elevated fuel pressures. It is important to note that the flow rate of a fuel pump goes down with an increase in the system pressure. Simply put, an electric fuel pump will flow more at 40 psi than it will at 80 psi.

While our FMU-enhanced fuel system worked well at 8 psi, we had reached the limit of the stock 240-cc injectors. Before increasing the boost pressure any further, we first sent off for a set of 270-cc injectors. RC Engineering came to our rescue with a set of squirters and we were ready for more boost. The added boost came via a change to a smaller blower pulley while retaining the larger crank pulley. The combination netted us 11 additional hp, bringing the peak power to 176 hp and 141 ft-lbs. This run was achieved using a mixture of race fuel and premium-unleaded pump gas. Unfortunately for us, the combination hurt one of the factory pistons while top-speed testing (running near 140 mph). We took the opportunity to not only rebuild the motor but also upgrade a few of the major components.

The D16Z was rebuilt using factory pistons (.010 over). The cylinders were bored and the new slugs installed. Although we went the inexpensive route, it would be preferable to run a set of forged (Arias or JE) pistons on any motor running forced induction. While our test motor was down, we sent the cylinder head to Joel at Competition Heads for a valve job and some porting. The ported head was installed on the fresh short block followed by the Jackson supercharger. During the subsequent testing, we employed the use of an Extrude Hone–ported intake and S inlet tube (between the throttle body and supercharger) along with the installation of 310-cc fuel injectors. Right on the edge as far as drivability (with the stock

During the course of the buildup, it became necessary to rebuild the D16Z motor.

ECU), the 310s offered plenty of fuel to meet our intended goal of 200 hp at the wheels. Knowing that we experienced elevated charge temperatures during our last top-speed runs, we opted to install an ERL water injection system to help keep the inlet air charge temperature down to a reasonable level. After all, we were spinning the daylights out of the little Eaton supercharger. With the water injection and a race fuel mixture, the fresh motor running 12 psi netted peak power numbers of 195 hp and 161 ft-lbs of torque. Had we been able to exceed the factory rev limit of 7,200 rpm, we feel that 200 hp was in our grasp. Unfortunately, the series of articles ended with 195 hp and a best run of 143 mph before the Civic was sold and I went on to other projects.

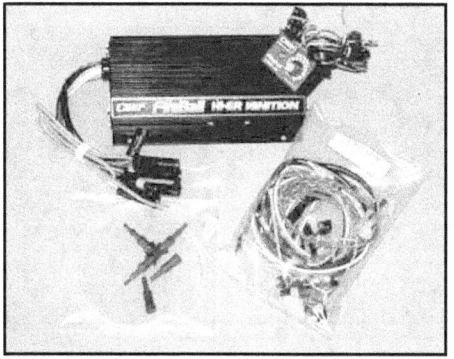

The supercharged motor required an ignition amplifier to properly ignite the plugs under the elevated cylinder pressure. We installed a Crane Hi6 amplifier to ensure adequate spark energy for our boosted motor.

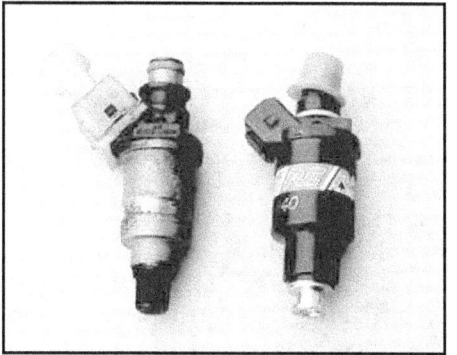

Going from 112 hp at the wheels to 197 hp at the wheels eventually required larger fuel injectors. RC Engineering supplied a set of 270-cc injectors and then a set of 310-cc injectors for the D16Z project.

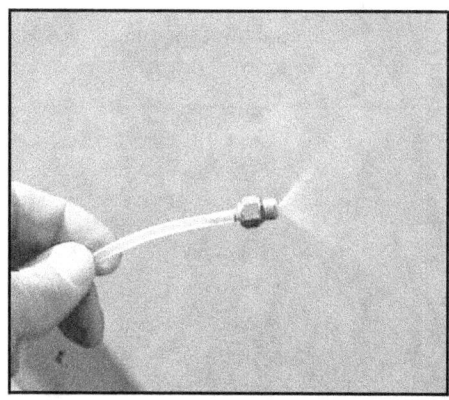

We even employed water injection (and race fuel) during the top speed runs to ward off detonation. The combination was successful, even at 12 psi and 143 miles per hour.

How to Build Honda Horsepower

Chapter 8

Engine Buildup 2
USTCC B16A 1.6L

This engine buildup was done out of necessity. After driving a 1995 Civic Del Sol in the Motorola Cup professional road racing series, the author decided to purchase the car to compete in the then-new, NASA-sanctioned United States Touring Car Championship (USTCC). The series was similar in concept to the Motorola Cup, but the new series allowed a few more modifications to the motor. In the Motorola Cup series, the motor had to remain stock, including the exhaust manifolds and factory air box assembly. By comparison, the USTCC series allowed competitors to run aftermarket air intake systems (but no ram air intake setups), headers, and modifications to the management system (chips). Obviously, the competitors were going to take advantage of the additional power available from these modifications, so the Del Sol motor was modified for the new racing series. The B16A motor used in the Del Sol provided plenty of information for this book, as endless hours were spent at PowerTrain Dynamics on their DynoJet in an effort to coax every last ounce of horsepower out of the limited modifications.

According to the rules, the internal components of the motor had to remain stock. That eliminated the use of stroker cranks, high-compression pistons, and even aftermarket camshafts. The rules did allow a cleanup overbore of .010, which we took advantage of. The overbore not only provided a fresh cylinder

In route to winning the USTCC road racing championship, the B16A in our Del Sol was subjected to hundreds of dyno sessions.

The B16A was surprisingly stock, but produced impressive (and winning) power with minimal modifications.

wall pattern to maximize sealing and cylinder pressure, but also a slight increase in both displacement and compression. In a series in which modifications are limited, it is important to take advantage of every last allowable modification that will provide an advantage over the competition. We knew that nothing we could (legally) do would give us a huge gain in power. Rather than search for that big increase, we went looking for a bunch of small ones. This route was more time consuming and expensive, but the results were well worth the effort. The break-in procedure was as important as the overbore. Both the engine speed and load were minimized during the break in, as was the use of synthetic oil. The friction saving (and power increasing) synthetic oil was reserved for use after the rings had time (and miles) to seat completely.

The short block was assembled with care using factory B16A (Del Sol) pistons featuring 10.2:1 compression. The short block was topped off with a factory fresh B16A VTEC cylinder head. The head was treated to a 3-angle valve job as per the rules. Since no porting was allowed by the USTCC rules, the head was installed as cast. B16A cams were also used. We made sure to utilize the 5-speed B16A camshafts, as the automatic cams offer less lift and duration and will restrict the eventual power output of the motor. As no cam adjustable sprockets were allowed, the factory (non-adjustable) sprockets were utilized. It is doubtful that the motor would have adjustable cam sprockets given the use of so many stock components (cams, head, and so forth).

With our stock long block finalized, we began the legal modifications to the motor. The first modification allowed was minor port-matching of the throttle body entry in the B16A intake manifold.

Both AEM and RS Akimoto air intake were used during the 2000 season, but both were eventually covered with an aluminum housing to direct ambient air to the motor at speed. The short air inlet length was critical to top-end performance.

---

156   *How to Build Honda Horsepower*

The throttle-body entry on the B16A intake manifold was port-matched to the 64.5-mm throttle body from RC Engineering. The USTCC rules allowed larger throttle bodies and minor port matching to provide a smooth transition for the airflow from the larger throttle entry to the manifold. RC Engineering took a stock throttle body and treated it to boring and a larger throttle plate. The result was a new throttle body that significantly out-flowed the stock unit. Although the benefits of such a larger throttle body are rather limited on a near-stock motor, we opted to try it in hopes of just a few extra ponies.

The test numbers available in the chapter on air intake systems indicate that the air intake design has a dramatic effect on the power curve of a VTEC motor. The full-length air intakes that position the filter in the fenderwell produce significant pre-VTEC power gains and even offer sizeable gains over a stock filter assembly. By contrast, the short-length air intakes provide a dramatic increase in post-VTEC power. The tuning of the air intake positively affects cylinder filling. While the short-runner air intakes lose out to the full-length intakes down low, they really make up for it after the motor comes on the VTEC cams. Knowing that our motor would almost never see engine speeds below the onset of the VTEC cams, we opted for the big power gains offered by the short-style air intake. We successfully ran systems from both AEM and RS Akimoto; the motor preferred the 3-inch RS Akimoto system.

One of the problems associated with running an open element cone filter on any car, especially a racecar, is that heat is the enemy of power and performance. While the free-flowing cone filter is the way to go in terms of minimizing airflow restrictions, having it suck hot air certainly isn't optimum for getting that cold, dense air that really makes power. The cure was to enclose the open-element filter in a large box with an opening that only allowed the motor to breathe cold air from the fenderwell. The aluminum box wasn't the most impressive thing to look at but it did work perfectly by providing a dedi-

Engine Buildup 2
USTCC B16A 1.6L

Car	*1995 Civic Del Sol USTCC*
Block	B16A
Bore	81 mm
Sleeved	No
Solid Deck	No
Stroke	77 mm
Piston Type	Stock Cast B16A
Manufacturer	Honda
Rod Length	5.290 inches
Manufacturer	Honda
Head Type	Stock B16A
Ported	No
Valve Sizes in./ex.	Stock B16A
Injector size	24 lbs/hr Ford Racing
Cam(s)	Stock B16A (Late model)
Adjustable Cam Sprocket(s)	No
Intake Type	Stock B16A Del Sol
Ported	No
Throttle Body Type	RC Engineering
Size	64.5 mm
Air intake	RS Akimoto (Also used AEM short version)
Header	APEXi Type R Integra
Exhaust	Custom 2.5-inch with glass-pack muffler
Turbo/Supercharger	NA
Type	NA
Maximum Boost Pressure	NA
Intercooler Type	NA
Fuel/Timing Management	Mugen Reprogrammed ECU

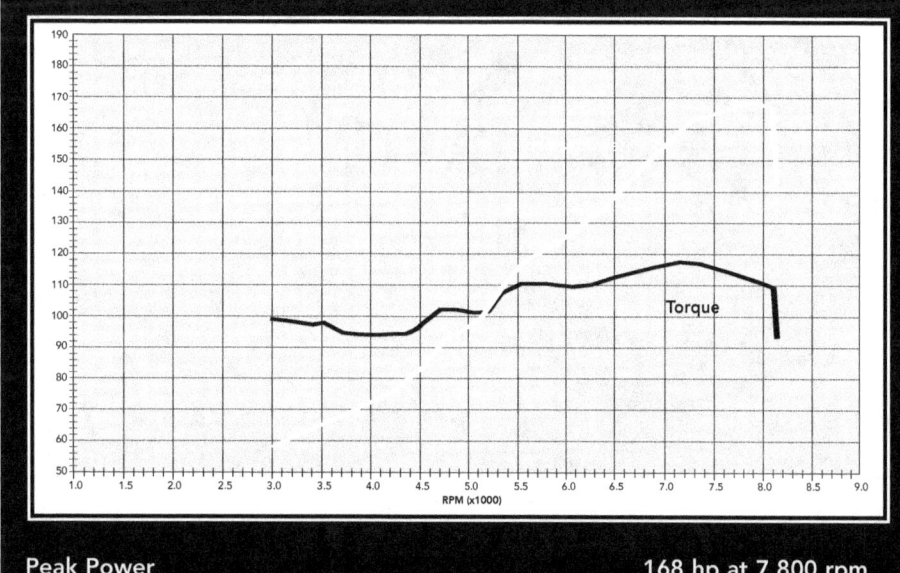

Peak Power	168 hp at 7,800 rpm
Peak Torque	118 ft-lbs at 7,000 rpm

The rules allowed a larger throttle body, so we had RC Engineering bore and reblade the factory Del Sol throttle body to improve airflow.

cated cold air source for our race motor. The difference between a true cold air intake and the hot air from an open element filter in an engine compartment can be as much as 7–10 hp. That represents a huge difference in power in a road racing class that allows limited engine modifications. The cold air also makes the motor less susceptible to the harmful affects of detonation.

With plenty of air getting into our motor, we turned our attention to the exhaust portion of the equation. The rules allowed us to replace the factory cast-iron exhaust manifold with a tubular header. The question was—which one? We obviously wanted the header that performed best on our motor, not simply one of the generic off-the-shelf models. The header choice took several weeks of testing; no less than seven different configurations were tried. Running both 4-into-1 and Tri-Y designs, long primaries and short primaries, big tubes and small tubes, we finally settled on a header from APEXi. Oddly enough, our choice was a header designed for the 1.8L JDM Integra Type R. We tried their offering for the smaller-displacement JDM Civic Type R, but the larger model for the 1.8L Integra offered more power (see exhaust chapter for power curves) on our test motor. The header choice is a perfect illustration of why testing is so important. Sure, any of the headers would have offered a few extra horsepower over the stock exhaust manifold setup, but a little experimentation provided us with even more power. Experimentation that pointed to a header we would likely not have chosen if we had not tested it ourselves.

The APEXi Type R header was run into a free-flowing exhaust system that consisted of 2.5-inch tubing and a tubular muffler that offered little or no restriction. We tested the combination versus an open pipe and found that the exhaust combination actually made 1–2 more peak horsepower and offered a few extra ft-lbs of torque. The exhaust was modified for one of the races at Laguna Seca. The maximum decibel level was specified at this facility that required the use of yet another muffler. We simply installed a second muffler behind our first and headed off to the track. The dyno told us that the only thing missing from the new combination was noise, as the dyno curve was identical with the addition of our new muffler. We wound up winning that race, dual mufflers, and all.

One of the competitors (fighting us tooth and nail for the lead, no less) was not so lucky, as his muffler fell off during the race and he was black flagged for a noise violation.

Additional modifications to the B16A race motor included an APEXi VTEC controller and an adjustable fuel pressure regulator from Killer Bee Racing. The controller was used to adjust the onset of the VTEC operation point. This was important as we also used a reprogrammed Mugen ECU. The Mugen ECU offered an extra 5 hp, but raised the VTEC operation point to 5,700 rpm. We found (by testing) that the ideal VTEC point was 5,200 rpm. This provided the ideal power curve that resulted in a minimal change (drop or increase) during the switchover. If the VTEC was set too low, there would be a drop in power when the secondary cams activated. If the VTEC was activate too early, there would be a drop in power as the primary cams fell off, followed by a sharp increase when the motor was given the cam profile it needed. The adjustable regulator was used along with the fine-tuning in the VTEC controller to optimize the air/fuel mixture under wide-open throttle.

We also employed a few other tricks to maximize the power output. The power steering pump was removed for three reasons. The stock power steering was over-boosted which offered less road feel. The power steering also represented a sizeable weight penalty, something critical on a road racecar with a minimum weight (2,080 pounds). The final reason to ditch the pump was to

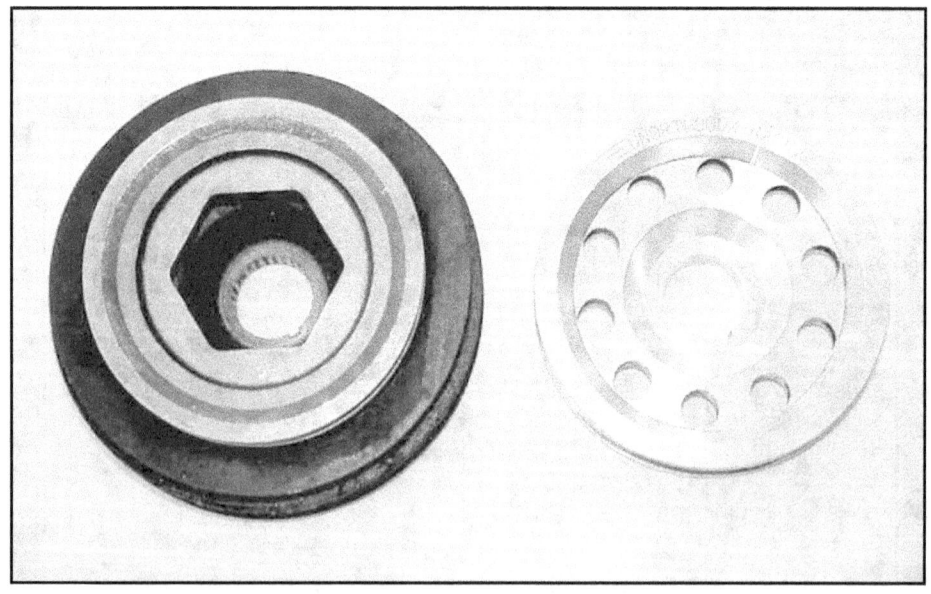

An Unorthodox Racing underdrive crank pulley was also used on the B16A to minimize parasitic losses and improve power. Ditching the power steering and installing the underdrive pulley netted some impressive power gains. A little here and a little there starts to add up.

Engine Buildups

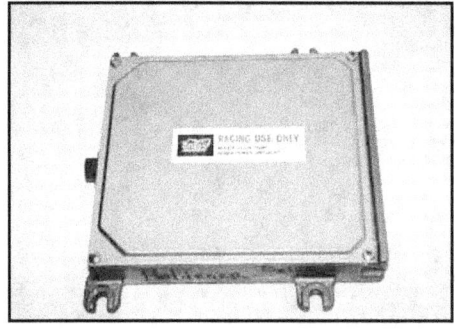

A Mugen ECU provided a few additional horsepower and allowed unrestricted engine speed, although we kept the shift points at or near 8,000 rpm.

free up some power. Not having to spin the steering pump resulted in a gain of 3–4 hp. Like we said, a little here and a little there. It was all starting to add up. The ignition timing was optimized on the PowerTrain DynoJet along with the proper fuel type. We found that by running a mixture of premium unleaded and 100 octane race fuel, we could pick up some power by advancing the distributor 4 degrees. Any more and the motor lost power. We found the sweet spot, but the motor sure could have benefited from the tuning available from the Hondata system. Just advancing the distributor changes the whole curve. It might be that a motor needs more timing down low and less up top or some combination of both. Testing is the only way to tell for sure.

After breaking the motor in, we changed from the conventional oil to a synthetic. We even ran an ultra-low viscosity 0W-30 to minimize losses associated with driving the oil pump. The ultra-thin oil resulted in a few extra horsepower. One of the critical elements in the success of the USTCC-winning B16A was the addition of an aluminum radiator from Fluidyne. In the first race, the water temps soared to 225 degrees, requiring some slowing on our part to save the motor. The new radiator dropped the temps to 185 degrees in racing conditions. The motor makes much better power at 185 degrees than 225 degrees, not to mention being able to last the full length of a race. The lower water temperature allowed us to tune the motor to the edge without concern for elevated race temperatures. Tuning to the edge brought us a few more horsepower, something that would not have been available without the Fluidyne radiator.

We tried a number of unsuccessful performance upgrades as well, including different range and style spark plugs, different ignition wires, and different fuel injectors. None of these changes resulted in any measurable power increase, although testing them was still a worthwhile proposal as it is just as important to find out what doesn't work as what does. Eliminating the unsuccessful upgrades leaves the successful ones. When all was and done, the B16A used in the USTCC road race managed a peak power reading of 168 hp at the wheels. This is an impressive figure considering the use of stock cams, pistons, and unported cylinder head. This power output compares nicely to a stock Integra Type R, equipped with a larger 1.8L motor. Even with the increased displacement, higher compression and high-performance Type R components, a stock 195-hp 1.8L B18C5 will only generate about 165–168 hp at the wheels. Think about that. The B16A is a pretty impressive package, especially when you consider that the little VTEC motors can be bought all day long for less than 1/10 of the cost of a used Type R motor. Even without a whole slew of aftermarket bolt-ons, the B16A can be made to produce serious horsepower—enough in fact, to propel a 1995 Del Sol to the 2000 USTCC road racing Championship. Killer Bee Racing now offers this championship-winning motor in crate form.

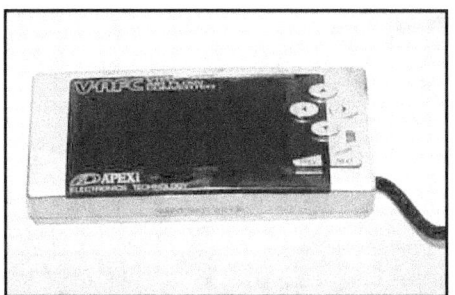

The APEXi VTEC controller allowed us to tailor the actuation of the secondary cam. This was helpful as the Mugen ECU engaged the VTEC cam too late-costing us power.

Engine Buildup 3
Bonneville/El Mirage
2.0L LS/VTEC

Motorsports seem to bring out the best in engine combinations and this 2.0L B20/VTEC hybrid was no exception. This particular engine was built for the express purpose of setting land speed records at Bonneville and El Mirage. The 1998 Civic was converted to run as a 1999 Civic Si in a class that restricted engine displacement to under 2.0L. Attempts were made at the records using a modified B16A but the power output was simply insufficient to propel the Civic to the required speeds. The original B16A produced approximately 170 hp at the wheels, but the combination resulted in a peaky motor that offered little in the way of average torque production. A record attempt at El Mirage resulted in a top speed of near 133 mph. Unfortunately, the record speed for the class was a hair over 137 mph. The B16A simply did not produce adequate power to reach the required speed. The situation was compounded at El Mirage, as the course required the Civic to accelerate from a standing start up to speed in 1.3 miles. All this was accomplished on dirt, which limited traction in the first two gears. While the peak power number is important for absolute top speed (providing ideal gearing), the relatively short course at El Mirage would require a much more meaty power curve. The answer was found in displacement.

Since the Civic was running in an under 2.0L class, it seemed foolish to attempt the records with a Civic packing

This converted 1998 Civic Ex eventually set records at both Bonneville and El Mirage.

Chapter 8

Engine Buildup 3
Bonneville/El Mirage 2.0L

Car	1998 Civic Si (Converted Ex)
Block	B20
Bore	84 mm
Sleeved	No
Solid Deck	No
Stroke	89 mm
Piston Type	Forged 12.5:1
Manufacturer	Arias
Rod Length	5.394-inch
Manufacturer	Eagle
Head Type	Stock B16A
Ported	No (Not for this test; was later ported)
Valve Sizes in./ex.	Stock B16A
Injector size	310-cc RC Engineering
Cam(s)	Integra Type R
Adjustable Cam Sprocket(s)	Yes, AEM
Intake Type	Extrude Hone–ported Type R and Killer Bee
Ported	No
Throttle Body Type	RC Engineering
Size	64.5 mm
Air intake	Hosetech
Header	Custom-Hytech
Exhaust	Custom 2.5-inch with no muffler
Turbo/Supercharger	NA
Type	NA
Maximum Boost Pressure	NA
Intercooler Type	NA
Fuel/Timing Management	June Reprogrammed ECU

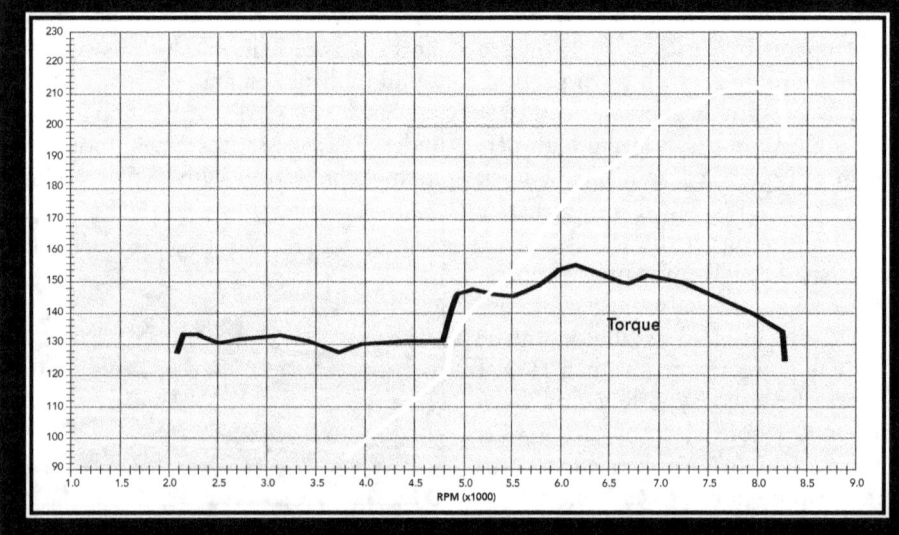

Peak Power	212 hp at 8,000 rpm
Peak Torque	155 ft-lbs at 6,100 rpm

Again, RC 310-cc injectors were used on this race motor.

only a 1.6L. The 2.0L started out life as a B20 short block from a CRV. The B20 is very similar to the 1,834-cc non-VTEC motors used in 1990–2001 Integras. Designated a 1.8L by Acura, the (so-called) LS motors actually pack 1,834 ccs. The B20 shares the 89-mm crank with the LS Integra motors. The added displacement comes courtesy of an increase in bore size from 81 mm to 84 mm. The combination of the 84-mm bore and 89-mm stroke put the final displacement just a shade under the 2.0L limit for the SCTA class. The unfortunate thing about the big-cube 2.0L was that it was saddled with a non-VTEC cylinder head set up. Obviously if the motor, even at nearly 2.0Ls of displacement, was to make any real power, it would have to be retrofitted with some VTEC headgear.

Before being subjected to the VTEC conversion, the stock 89-mm crank in the B20 was outfitted with a quartet of Eagle (LS-length) forged connecting

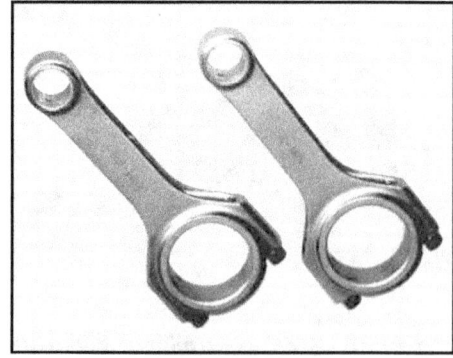

The 2.0L short block included JE pistons (later with Arias slugs) and Eagle forged rods.

Engine Buildups

Combining the non-VTEC B20 block with the B16A (VTEC) head required a dedicated oil feed line for the VTEC solenoid.

rods and a set of custom forged JE pistons. The combination of the domed pistons and B16A combustions chambers resulted in a static compression of 12.5:1. The compression really gave the 2.0L motor some much-needed snap. The 12.5: short block was topped off with an un-ported B16A cylinder head. Although there was certainly more power to be had from proper porting, we simply ran out of time and had to install the stock head that was run on the B16A used for the previous record attempts. The head was milled to help achieve the proper compression ratio and sported a set of trick June valve springs, titanium retainers, and Integra Type R cams. Again, there was certainly more power to be had with more aggressive cam profiles, but the time frame for the buildup dictated a set of tried-and-true Type R cams. The cam timing was finalized using a set of AEM adjustable cam gears. The ideal combination with the milled cylinder head worked out to be 2 degrees of retard for both cams. Anything different resulted in a loss of power.

Since breathing is critical to power production, the big motor was run with an Extrude Hone–ported Type R intake, a 64.5-mm throttle body, and Hosetech air intake system. As with the USTCC Del Sol, a number of intakes were tried on the 2.0L Civic. The Hosetech seemed to give the best overall (usable) power curve. If you look at the chapter on intake manifolds, you will see that results of an interesting comparison between the ported Type R intake and a ported Del Sol manifold. You might expect the smaller Del Sol intake to out-perform the bigger Type R on a relatively small B16A motor, but we did not expect the same to happen on this larger 2.0L. For street use, the Del Sol intake (at least in ported form) should be the clear choice for 1.6L, 1.8L, and even 2.0L VTEC variants. The Killer Bee Racing intake manifold was also tested on this 2.0L combination and dramatically out-performed the ported Type R. The 2.0L made best average and overall power with the Killer Bee Racing intake manifold.

One thing we discovered during testing was that the stock 240-cc injectors were too small for the power output of this modified 2.0L. The stock squirters were nixed in favor of a set of larger 310-cc injectors from the injection experts at RC Engineering. The 310-cc injectors were run using a June-modified ECU. We tried the Mugen ECU (see ECU chapter) on this motor but the combination worked best with the programming in the June computer. Along with the June ECU, we also employed an APEXi VTEC controller to tailor the VTEC operation. As with the Del Sol, the APEXi was worth a few extra horsepower at the onset of VTEC. The fuel system was also upgraded with a Kenne Bell Boost-a-Pump and an adjustable fuel pressure regulator. The Boost-a-Pump

AEM cam sprockets and Integra Type R cams allowed us to set a number of early records, even though the cams were later upgraded to wilder specs.

was installed to increase the flow rate of the stock pump by increasing the supply voltage. The adjustable fuel pressure regulator allowed us to make global adjustments to the fuel curve to dial in the air/fuel mixture at wide-open throttle.

One of the key ingredients to making big power on this 2.0L hybrid was the trick header designed by John at Hytech. Known for his work on exhaust systems for open-wheel racecars, John welded up a work of art for the 2.0L stroker in the Civic. The header featured all the tricks including stepped tubing, Burns merge collectors, and even adjustable secondary lengths. The header was built so we could adjust the sec-

The 2.0L LS/VTEC Hybrid utilized a Hosetech air intake. A number of different combinations were tried, but the Hosetech worked the best on this motor.

Chapter 8

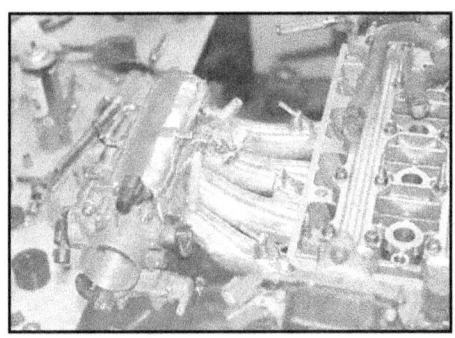

A number of different intakes were run on the 2.0L, but we eventually settled on a dedicated intake from Killer Bee Racing.

ondary length to tune the motor to meet our (power curve) needs. The header dumped into a section of tubing but no muffler. This 2.0L must be heard to be believed—it was plain loud at wide-open throttle and almost painful when the VTEC switches on. The combination resulted in a motor that produced 212 hp and 155 ft-lbs of torque at the wheels. Loud or not, the combination obviously worked as we managed to set a pair of records at El Mirage and Muroc; the faster was 139.5 mph. Given sufficient room to run to maximum speed, the car would top 155 mph and was timed (with a radar gun) at 157 mph on the dry lake bed. This Civic also set a land speed record at Bonneville in G production running just over 153 mph.

Engine Buildup 4
1834-cc LS/VTEC

The Honda/Acura lineup is full of street/strip motor choices ranging from the economy minded 1.5L DX to the ultra-sophisticated S2000 2.0L. Obviously neither of these choices would be high on any Civic/Integra owners list as swap candidates, as the DX would hardly be a good starting point for ultimate performance. The 240-hp S2000 mill on the other hand, while offering excellent performance even in stock trim, would require major modifications for installation in a front-drive application. The S2000 motor is one of the first 4-cylinders to rotate clockwise, with the remainder of the four-cylinder lineup running counter-clockwise. While the 240-hp output would sure make for one heck of a Civic motor, a modified B-series would make life much easier. The world is full of B-series powered Civics and Integras originally equipped with D16Zs (or worse) and B18A (Non-VTEC 1.8Ls). Most step up to the easiest engine swap on the list, installing a B16A in place of a single-cam VTEC D16Z or the 1.8L Non-VTEC B18A. Of course, there are more than a few Civic/Integra owners who have stepped up to the B18C level; a few brave souls have opted for the high-ticket B18C5 Type R motor.

While the 160-hp B16A is worlds better than the 125-hp D16Z, the performance gap narrows slightly compared to the 140-hp (later) version of the B18A. The gap narrows even more than the 20-hp differential might suggest, as the B18A offers something lacking in the B16A—namely torque. Although listed as a 1.8L (same as the B18C family), the B18A actually displaces 1,834 cc. This compares nicely to the 1,797-cc displacement offered by the B18C family (GS-R and Type R) and even more so to the mere 1,587 ccs offered by the B16A. The additional displacement of the B18A provides plenty of bottom-end grunt. Compared stock-to-stock, the B18A can offer as much as 12–15 ft-lbs from 2,000–3,500 rpm, right where most (normal) street driving takes place. Unlike the B18A, the B16A does not fall on its face at 5,500 rpm, and is in fact just jumping onto the secondary (VTEC) cam profile to produce some stellar top-end horsepower numbers. Credit the VTEC cylinder head and valve train for the impressive high-rpm power offered by the little VTEC motor.

The combination was run on the Shop DynoJet. The dyno time allowed us to dial in the cams using the cam sprockets.

There must be those of you who are reading this book who are asking why not simply install a B18C or B18C5 motor that will provide the bottom end of the B18A with the top end of the B16A? Good question, but one with a good answer. The B18C motor offers excellent performance, especially the B18C5 Type R unit. With 195 hp, the 1.8L Type R has plenty of potential, but there are two things holding it back from extensive street use—namely, price and availability. Certainly full of performance, the 1.8L Type R motors are both difficult to locate and costly to purchase. Compared to the low $375 cost of a 160-hp B16A, a used 195-hp B18C5 will set you back every bit of $6,000. The lower performance 1.8L GS-R motors are somewhat cheaper at around $3,500 (but hardly any easier to locate). Besides, the GS-R motor only offers an additional 10 hp for the 10-fold price increase (but a significant torque increase throughout the power band.) Is there any alternative? Enter the LS/VTEC Hybrid!

As the name suggests, the LS/VTEC hybrid combines the torquey displacement of the non-VTEC B18A with the top-end charge of the B16A. The added benefit of this hybrid is that it accomplishes the feat of out-performing even the mighty Type R motor at a fraction of the cost. It is not hard to understand how a typical LS/VTEC can provide both a much better average power curve as well as better peak torque and horsepower numbers than the Type R. Credit the longer stroke (89 mm versus 87.2 mm) for the additional displacement 1,834 cc versus 1,797 cc) of the B18A. The B16A, B18A, and B18C all share a common bore size of 81 mm. The longer stroke provides plenty of low-speed torque. When was the last time you heard anyone extol the virtues of the torquey nature of the Type R motor? The additional displacement adds power all the way through the power band, especially once the VTEC kicks in. Is it surprising that the VTEC head, designed to work on a 1.6L, has no trouble feeding a 1,834-cc motor? Not really, since the same B16A head is also used on the 1.8L Type R, albeit with mild porting. Don't go thinking that the Type R motor will out-power an LS/VTEC on the big end due to its exotic Type R cams and intake, as the typical LS/VTEC, even those equipped with nothing more than B16A cams and intake, will easily produce more power than a stock Type R. Add the Type R cams and intake to the LS/VTEC and you have a serious piece of performance hardware, all at a fraction of the cost of a genuine Type R motor.

Holeshot Racing was responsible for the buildup of this LS/VTEC hybrid motor. The hybrid combined the B18A bottom end with the B16A cylinder head, valve train, and intake system. The motor was built for installation in a 1995 Civic. Making the LS/VTEC swap even easier was the fact that the Civic was already equipped with an LS motor from a previous swap. Like most Honda/Acura enthusiasts, the owner wanted more power after sampling the additional torque and horsepower offered by the LS motor (compared to the smaller D16Z). The B18A bottom end was rebuilt using factory Integra Type R pistons. The reason for the choice of pistons was primarily price, as the Type R slugs are considerably less expensive than either the B16A factory pistons or aftermarket forged equivalents. Although cast, the Type R pistons offered plenty of compression (more than the stock B18A but less than those from a B16A). The motor was not to see boost or nitrous, so the cast pistons were deemed fine for the buildup.

The remainder of the bottom end consisted of the stock B18A block, crank, and rods, but the rods were treated to a polish job on the beams. The magazines are full of buildups that include aftermarket rods, but the factory stuff has worked well on even my road race motors where engine speed is kept reasonable (below 8,200 rpm). This LS/VTEC hybrid was designed as a street motor, so most of its life would be spend out of VTEC. The B18A bottom is plenty strong for those occasional (even frequent) trips to the 8,000-rpm redline, as long as there are no missed shifts or back holes. Since the stock B18A block offered no provision for the

Engine Buildup 4
1834-cc LS/VTEC

Car	1993 Civic (Engine Swap)
Block	B18A
Bore	81 mm
Sleeved	No
Solid Deck	No
Stroke	89 mm
Piston Type	Integra Type R (cast)
Manufacturer	Honda
Rod Length	5.394 inches
Manufacturer	Honda
Head Type	Stock B16A
Ported	No, milled .030
Valve Sizes in./ex.	Stock B16A (Type R Springs)
Injector size	240-cc B16A
Cam(s)	B16A auto
Adjustable Cam Sprocket(s)	Yes, AEM
Intake Type	B16A
Ported	No
Throttle Body Type	Early B16A
Size	60 mm
Air intake	Monster Flow
Header	DC Sports
Exhaust	Custom 2.25-inch with RSR muffler
Turbo/Supercharger	NA
Type	NA
Maximum Boost Pressure	NA
Intercooler Type	NA
Fuel/Timing Management	Reprogrammed Factory P28

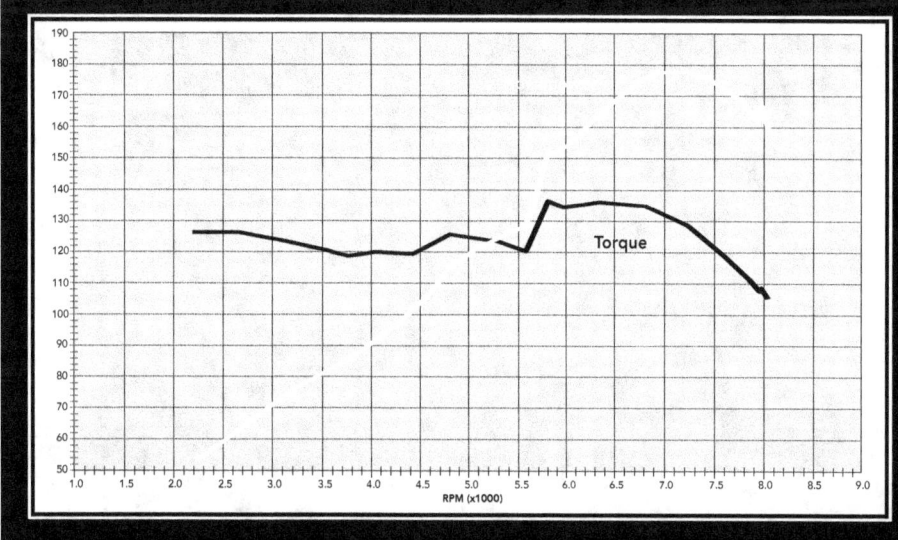

Peak Power	178 hp at 7,200 rpm
Peak Torque	136 ft-lbs at 6,500 rpm

Chapter 8

A Monster Flow air intake allowed plenty of breathing.

VTEC (an oiling source), it was necessary to take oil from the oil sending unit. A T fitting was installed (adjacent to the oil filter) to provide a VTEC oil source and retain the factory oil sending unit. Since the non-VTEC B18A head and VTEC B16A head have head dowels in different locations, holes were drilled in the block to allow for the VTEC head-dowel orientation. It was also necessary to tap the factory oil feed in the B16A head (original oil source for VTEC solenoid) and to install a pipe plug. The final mod was to utilize the fitting in the side of the B16A head as the new oil feed (feed line from the oil sending unit).

The mechanical modifications of the installation were not difficult, especially considering the potential power gains. Since cost was a major consideration, most of the components from the B16A donor motor were used on the hybrid. This list of components included the head, injectors, and throttle body. The list did not include the mild stock B16A cams. As the donor motor was originally teamed with an automatic transmission, the stock B16A cams were especially tame (much smaller than those run on the 5-speed cars). The owner of the motor desired the wilder (and more powerful) Integra Type R cams, but the significant step up the performance ladder was a bit more than his wallet could bear. While the automatic B16A cams were not the first choice for optimum performance, the B16A intake manifold should be. If you doubt this, look at the chapter on intake manifolds. The B16A intake (especially Extrude Hone ported) provided the best overall power curve of all the manifolds tested. The lone exception was the Killer Bee Racing intake—although a dedicated casting, it was originally based on the runner and plenum profiles in the B16A. Apparently, the owner had read some of my previous articles for the import magazines and wisely chose to retain the B16A intake.

The spent gases were handled by a DC Sports Tri-Y feeding a custom 2.5-inch exhaust.

Feeding the motor was a high-flow fuel pump. Obviously, a pump designed to feed the wimpy D16Z has no place supplying fuel for an LS/VTEC hybrid. Oddly enough, stock 240-cc fuel injectors were used on the motor. According to the math, the stock injectors are good for about 200 hp (at 100 percent duty cycle and .45 BSFC) at the flywheel. Reduce that figure down 11–12 percent for a DynoJet number and you have 175–178 hp, or right what this hybrid put out at the wheels. This motor might well have benefited from a set of either 270-cc or even 310-cc injectors. The stock throttle body was employed, as was a reprogrammed P28 (single-cam VTEC) computer. The ECU was reprogrammed with modified twin-cam VTEC fuel and timing tables along with actuation of both the intake and exhaust VTEC cam profiles. A Hondata system would be optimum, but again, cost was the major buildup concern. A DC Sports header and Monster Flow intake system were also used on the Hybrid, along with a set of adjustable cam sprockets. The sprockets were necessary due to the milled (.030) cylinder head. Once optimized, the LS/VTEC hybrid posted power numbers of 178 hp and 136 ft-lbs a the wheels (measured on a DynoJet). Even saddled by the wimpy cams, these numbers compared nicely to the 162–165 hp normally thrown down by a stock B18C5 Type R motor. Holeshot has run a number of these LS/VTEC hybrids at or near 195 hp at the wheels with a good set of cams (Type R or better).

The LS/VTEC hybrid combined the torque of 1,834 cc and the high-rpm power of a VTEC cylinder head. The only thing missing was more cam timing.

EngineBuildup 5
Street Performance D16Z

This motor was a good example of what is possible from a good street D16Z. Built with daily drivability in mind, the buildup was not done to optimize maximum performance. The difference between street (and even dual purpose) motors and those dedicated for quarter-mile assaults is the level of compromise. While a strip-only, single-cam VTEC motor buildup might include 12.5:1 or even 13.0:1 high-compression forged pistons, this street version was assembled with just 10.0:1. The compression was upped slightly by milling the D16Z aluminum head, but given that most B-series motors run over 10.0:1 compression in stock form, this D16Z motor was nowhere near overboard on the static compression. The reason for the concern in terms of static compression is that ultra-high compression motors are much more susceptible to detonation. Since detonation can ruin a motor in just one cycle, it should be avoided at all costs. Building a street D16Z motor with 10.0:1 compression is plenty safe, as long as ignition timing is kept at a reasonable level and the owner is prepared to run a strict diet of premium unleaded pump gas.

To further improve flow, the stock cylinder head was treated to a thorough port job. Given that the power band differs between a street motor and a race motor, so too should the porting. While a race motor may seek to trade low-

Although the B-series twin cams get all the press, the single-cam VTEC motors greatly out-number the twin cammers. This Civic is a perfect example of a single-cam street buildup.

Engine Buildup 5
Street Performance D16Z

Car	1995 Civic Si
Block	D16Z
Bore	D16Z
Sleeved	No
Solid Deck	No
Stroke	D16Z
Piston Type	10.0:1 Forged (Flat top)
Manufacturer	JE
Rod Length	Stock D16Z
Manufacturer	Honda
Head Type	Stock D16Z (milled .030)
Ported	Yes, Mild
Valve Sizes in./ex.	Stock D16Z
Injector size	240-cc GSR
Cam(s)	Custom Rubens
Adjustable Cam Sprocket(s)	Yes
Intake Type	Stock D16Z
Ported	No
Throttle Body Type	Bored D16Z
Size	60 mm
Air intake	Jackson Racing
Header	DC Sports Tri Y
Exhaust	Greddy Evo
Turbo/Supercharger Type	None
Maximum Boost Pressure	NA
Intercooler Type	None
Fuel/Timing Management	Stock ECU

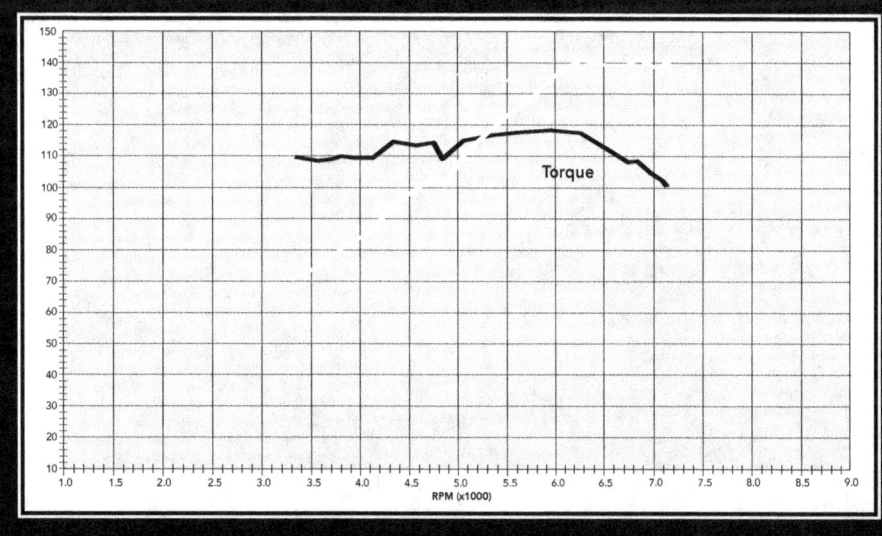

Peak Power	141.2 hp at 6,300 rpm
Peak Torque	118.1 ft-lbs at 6,000 rpm

Chapter 8

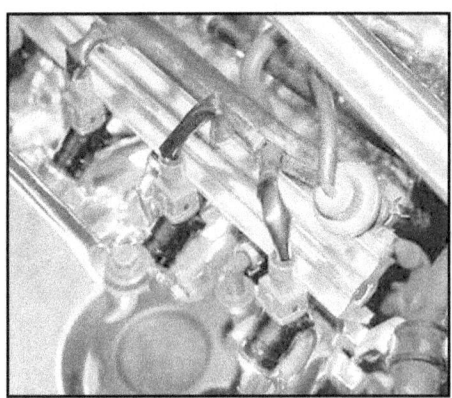

The owner installed a set of 240-cc GSR injectors to ensure the motor had plenty of fuel.

To optimize the power band of the modified B16Z, the owner opted for a Tri-Y header from DC Sports.

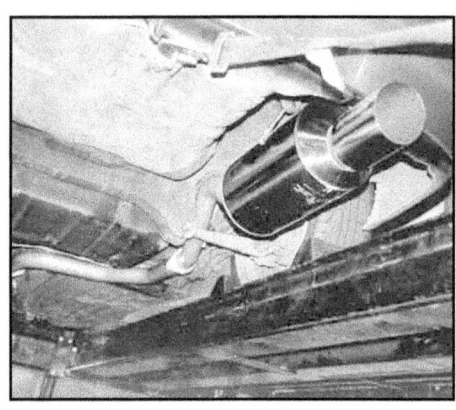

The remainder of the exhaust included a stock catalytic converter and an all-stainless steel Greddy Evo system.

speed torque for maximum top-end power, any performance street motor should concentrate on maintaining a broad torque curve. When it comes to impressive street performance, torque production is king. Given the relatively long stroke (compared to the bore size) of the D16Z, Honda purposely designed the combination for torque production. The VTEC (intake only) valve train simply added top-end power to a motor otherwise designed for torque production. The head porting included a good cleanup and removal of a minimal amount of material. It is just as easy to ruin the factory flow numbers on a Honda head as it is to improve them. The phrase "hogging out" has no place in a good Honda head porter's vocabulary. The head was also treated to minor milling (.030) to help further increase the compression. Although not done for this buildup, it is a good idea to polish the combustion chambers to reduce hot spots that can lead to detonation.

The short block was kept pretty much factory fresh. If engine speed is kept reasonable, the stock crank, rods, and even pistons are fine for performance street use. If there is one item that can be considered a weak spot in the combination, it is the factory cast pistons. While adequate for most normally aspirated buildups, a forged piston will tolerate more abuse (minor detonation). The forged JE pistons also provided the opportunity to up the compression, so the installation of the new slugs was a win-win situation. The assembly was rebalanced using a lightened factory flywheel. The flywheel was taken to a local machine shop where material was removed to reduce the reciprocating weight. Less rotational weight means that it is easier for the motor to accelerate (less power taken away from the output). When having a flywheel lightened, make sure not to remove too much mate-

Even in normally aspirated trim, the single cam VTEC motors can be made to produce impressive horsepower and torque figures.

An adjustable cam sprocket allowed fine-tuning of the Rubens performance cam. Unfortunately for the single cam crowd, the intake and exhaust cannot be adjusted individually to optimize and given combination.

rial, as a thin flywheel is more prone to warping and you don't want to see what happens when an improperly machined flywheel comes apart.

With a bottom end featuring forged pistons and a milled and ported cylinder head, the D16Z was ready for some bolt-on power producers. The long block was augmented with a custom Rubens cam featuring additional lift and duration. The cam was dialed in with a matching adjustable cam sprocket. The milled cylinder head made the adjustable cam sprocket a necessity, as lowering the cams relative to the crank pulley retards the cam timing. An adjustable cam sprocket allows the cam timing to be brought back into proper orientation after the milling, not to mention dialing in the cam for optimum power. Additional modifications included a set of 240-cc (GSR) fuel injectors, a DC Sports header, and Greddy Evo exhaust system. A short-length air intake and cone filter ensured plenty of airflow to the bored (stock) throttle body and stock (polished externally) intake manifold. A factory ECU ensured proper fuel and timing calibrations. Once broken in, the performance street D16Z buildup produced peak numbers of 141.2 hp and 118.1 ft-lbs of torque. Note the flat (post-VTEC) torque curve, something the owner gets to enjoy much more often than the also impressive 141 hp number. Chances are that some additional cam/ignition timing and air/fuel tuning could have coaxed more power from this combination, especially past 6,300 rpm where the power leveled off.

Engine Buildup 6
JG Engine Dynamics
2.0L Drag Motor

When the talk turns to race motors, one name is always mentioned—JG Engine Dynamics. The name is certainly familiar to anyone who follows import drag racing—you need look no further than their web site (www.jgenginedynamics.com) to see that Javier Guiterez and the gang have built some impressive motors. The listing of dyno results is impressive, especially considering that it represents but a fraction of the motors

that have seen dyno action at JG. With both engine and chassis dynos available, it is no wonder that some of the quickest and fastest import drag racers are wearing the JG logo. You know you must be doing something right when a prestigious company such as Edelbrock comes to you to help design and test their new line of Sport Compact components.

One of the difficulties with including JG Engine Dynamics in this chapter on engine buildups was choosing which combination to include. Surf through the dyno results on their web site—any one of them would be welcome under the hood of an enthusiast's ride. If you're wondering what it takes to make serious power from your single-cam D16Z, JG has dyno tests on everything from 160+ hp (at the wheels) all-motor applications to 450-hp turbo race versions. They even have results on a stroker version equipped with a Jackson Racing supercharger that pumped out a hair over 200 hp at the wheels. If single cam VTECs aren't your bag, how about 1.8L non-VTEC LS motors making over 600 hp at the wheels. Not enough? Top off the LS short block with a VTEC head and wind up with anything from a mild street stormer (about 200 hp at the wheels) to a full-on race motor that can exceed 700 hp at the wheels. Of course, there are always straight B16A, B18C, and even H22/23 motors, some of which exceed 800 hp.

As you can see, the sheer number of choices made it difficult to select just two. The first JG Engine Dynamics motor was based on a B18C GSR block. Though the eventual displacement was to wind up at 2 liters, the starting point was a tried and true GSR block and crank. Since the motor was to see serious strip action, the GSR block was given the full Pro-Series treatment. The weak link in the Honda motor is the open deck block, even though it is possible to make serious street power with a stock block. Under the stress of serious horsepower and rpm, the stock cylinders can distort and even crack. At the very least, the shifting can cause sealing problems for the head gasket. If the wick is really turned up, the weak cylinders can actually crack. The Pro series treatment eliminates the weak link with the installation of stronger (and thicker) cylinder sleeves. The block also receives a deck insert (not

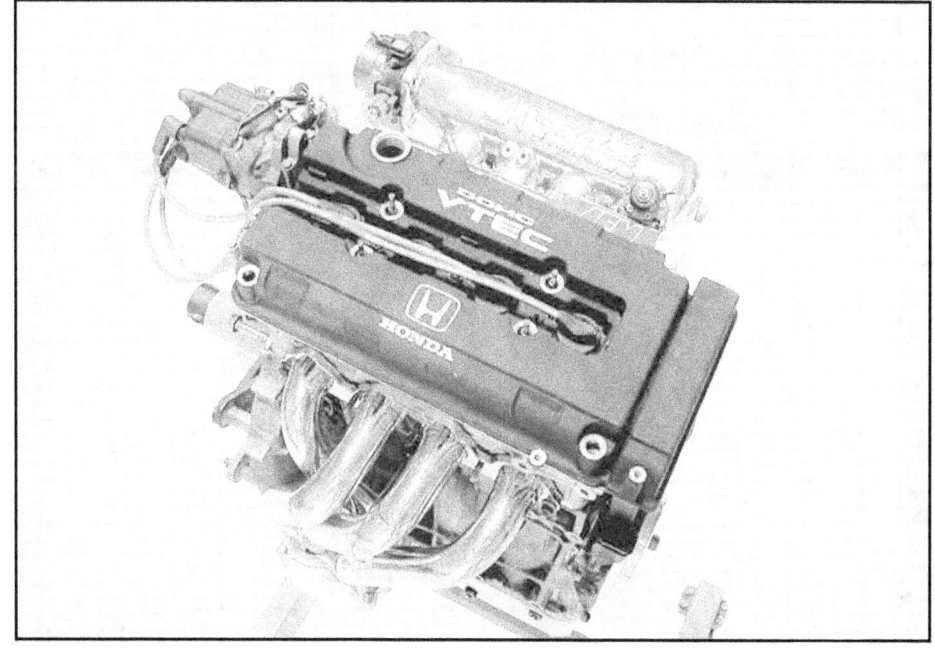

JG Engine Dynamic teamed up with Edelbrock to produce a wide variety of Honda/Acura performance components including a trick (high-rpm) intake manifold and tubular race header. These components were used to produce 256 horsepower at the wheels.

Engine Buildup 6: JG Engine Dynamics 2.0L Drag Motor

Car	*Drag Civic Racer*
Block	GEN2 Pro series B18A block with B16A head
Bore	85 mm
Sleeved	Yes
Solid Deck	Yes
Stroke	89 mm
Piston Type	Forged (High Compression) 13.0:1
Manufacturer	JE
Rod Length	140 mm
Manufacturer	Saenz
Head Type	B16A with welded chamber
Ported	Yes, Pro Race
Valve Sizes in./ex.	34-mm intake and 29-mm exhaust
Injector size	4) 500 cc
Cam(s)	JG 308 316
Adjustable Cam Sprocket(s)	Yes, JG
Intake Type	JG Edelbrock prototype
Ported	Yes
Throttle Body Type	Honda bored out to 64 mm
Size	64 mm
Air intake	JG Edelbrock custom
Header	JG Edelbrock
Exhaust	JG Edelbrock racing B pipe
Turbo/Supercharger	None
Type	Normally aspirated
Maximum Boost Pressure	NA
Intercooler Type	None
Fuel/Timing Management	Motec M4 SEQUENTIAL

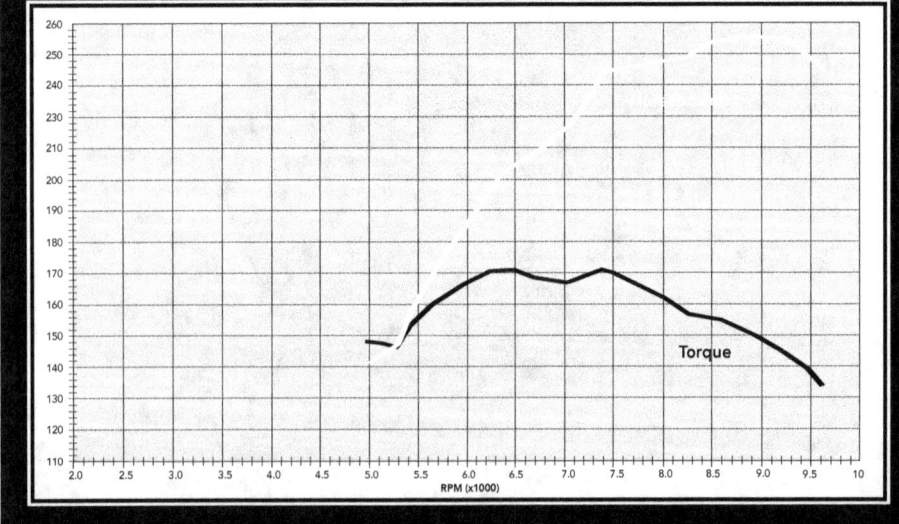

Peak Horsepower	256 hp
Peak Torque	172 ft-lbs

one of the cheapy press-in varieties). JG machines both the block and insert to ensure a slight interference fit, then welds and machines the deck surface to achieve an ultra strong, leak-free block.

The 2.0L race motor was built using a stock B18C steel crank. The stock Honda/Acura cranks are nearly perfect and will take just about any amount of abuse as long as detonation is kept in check. Even the lowly LS cranks have been run at the 700-hp level with out any trouble. Obviously, the stock cast pistons were ditched in favor of a set of forged (high-compression) slugs. This motor was built with a set from Arias to JG specs. The same goes for the rods. The Saenz forged connecting rods measured 140 mm. When teamed with the welded B16A head, the Arias pistons produced a race-only 13.0 compression ratio. Although the block, crank, rods, and pistons make up the majority of the bottom ends, a great deal of time, energy, and experience went into producing this JG race motor. Critical clearances, meticulous assembly procedures, and attention to detail are why JG motors almost always wind up in the winners circle and not scattered across lane one.

The Pro-series short block ensured that the bottom end was plenty stout for racing use, so it was time for the power producers, namely the head, cams, and intake manifold. While the static compression does have an effect on the power output of a motor, the major contributors are those that determine the airflow. First up was the cylinder head. The GSR bottom end might suggest a GSR head (which work very well), but JG chose a B16A cylinder head. There is obviously a great deal of potential in the B16A casting, as Acura saw fit to use this casting for the Type R motors. The B16A head was brought up to Redline series specs, including full porting, extensive chamber work, and larger valves. Not simply hogged out heads (it is just as easy to ruin a Honda head as it is to improve one), the heads from JG are application specific. Of course, a full-race turbo motor will require different flow levels than a mild or even-built all-motor application. The Redline series

Engine Buildups

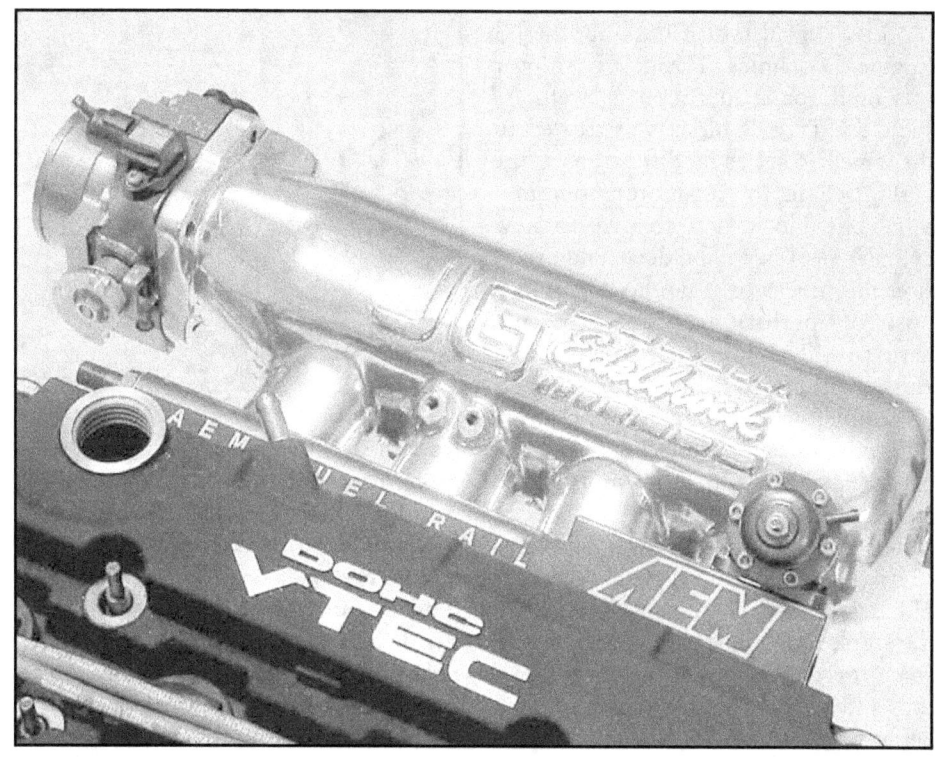

This Victor X manifold was designed with high-rpm breathing in mind.

head was ported to achieve maximum power over a given rpm range, not to achieve a big (max lift) airflow numbers. JG is one of the few tuners out there who understands that it is important to maximize air speed in addition to flow.

Cam specs are another important consideration when porting a cylinder head. Big flow figures at .600 valve lift are of minimal value (actually detrimental) to a motor equipped with .500 lift cams. The same goes to matching the intake manifold to the duration specifications (that determine operating rpm) on the cam. Simply put, a cam that wants to make efficient power at 9,000 rpm will be limited by an intake designed to make peak power at 7,500 rpm. The 2.0L race motor was equipped with a cam/intake combination designed to maximize power at high rpm. Where a stock GSR might make peak power at 7,600 rpm, this 2.0L was equipped with cams and intake to produce peak power at a lofty 9,200 rpm. The 308/316 (a duration designation) JG cams were installed along with a custom fabricated sheet metal intake to optimize top-end power. You will note from the dyno figures that power numbers were not even taken below 5,000 rpm, as the shifts will never allow the motor to drop much below 6,500 rpm.

The final element in the 2.0L buildup by JG Engine dynamics was use of the JG Edelbrock Pro Flow header and optional B-pipe. The Pro Flow header was teamed with the optional B-pipe—essentially a racing exhaust section consisting of merge pipe and long collector extension. The 2.0L race motor was run on the DynoJet chassis dyno with a MOTEC M4 stand-alone fuel injection system and 550-cc fuel injectors. The 2.0L produced peak readings of 256 hp and 172 ft-lbs. While the motor is a race only piece, note the exceptional torque production even down as low as 5,000 rpm. Credit the displacement and compression for the impressive grunt down low, while the big cams, intake and head flow are responsible for the impressive peak power numbers. This motor has produced a best of 11.0 at 123 mph in all-motor configuration. These runs were even more impressive considering that the car was more than 100 pounds over the minimum weight for the class. All motor kicks ass!

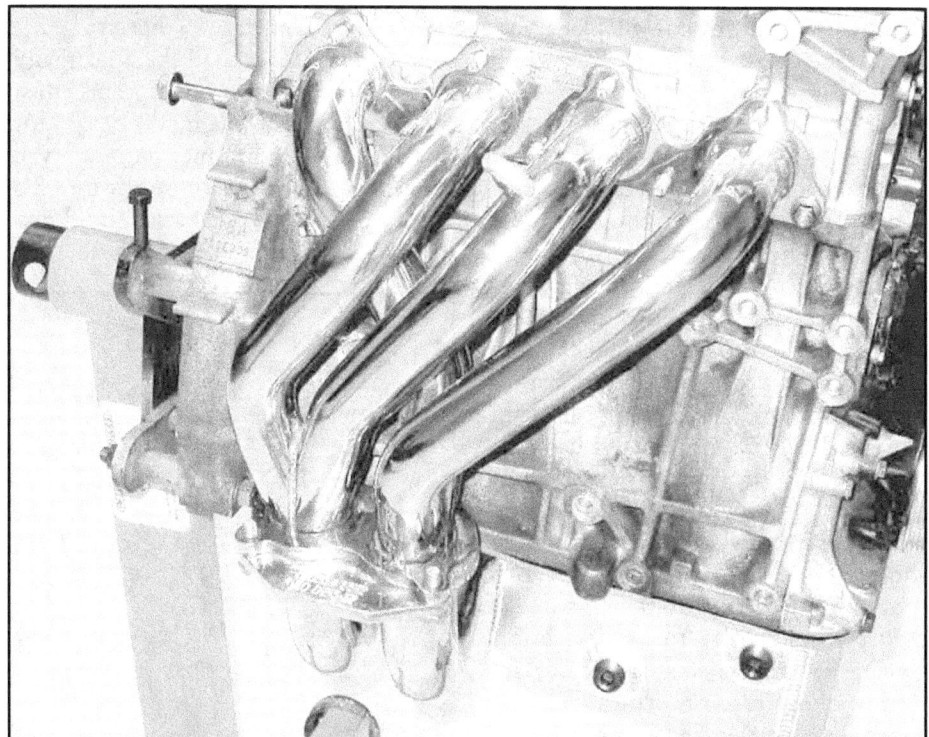

Whether you run the standard down pipes or the optional B-pipe, these Edelbrock headers are a surefire way to increase performance. Not many "All-Motor" B-series engines produce 250+ wheel horsepower!

EngineBuildup 7
JG Engine Dynamics
B18C Turbo Race Motor

When it comes to big torque figures, there is nothing like combining displacement with forced induction. In fact, this motor goes the combination one better by adding the broad power band of the VTEC system to the mix. While a B16A can be made to produce big power, it is simply easier to reach a given power level with a larger motor. The added benefit of displacement is a broader power curve or more power under the curve. Imagine, dual cam profiles, near 2 liters of displacement and big boost all in one motor! The displacement came in the form of a big bore Type R motor. While LS/VTEC motors are all the rage, it is hard to beat the bore and stroke combination of a B18C5, especially when you take into consideration the ability to run a longer connecting rod. The longer rod provides a more favorable rod to stroke ratio, allowing better top-end power production. According to Javier at JG Engine Dynamics, the rod ratio is critical in high-rpm, high-horsepower applications. Apparently, high-rpm race motors favor the shorter B18C 87.2-mm crank and a longer rod over the larger LS 89-mm crank and a shorter rod. Having built so many different, successful combinations, Javier should know what works.

Like the all-motor buildup, the JG Engine Dynamics Turbo race motor was built for strip action as well. As such, the Type R block was treated to the same Pro series modifications as the GSR used in the all-motor combination. The block was treated to new cylinder sleeves, a solid deck, and precision machine work, not to mention a host of performance reciprocating hardware. The JG Pro Series bottom end consisted of 11.0:1 compression JE forged pistons, 137-mm Saenz connecting rods, and the stock B18C5 steel crank. As with all B-series motors, the stock forged steel cranks are ideally suited to high-horsepower applications. The recipe for high-horsepower Hondas is to beef up the block, ditch the stock rods and pistons, and toss in some forged units. Adding forged pistons and rods to the steel crank and Pro Series block makes for one stout foundation. The bottom end is now ready for some serious abuse, whether in the form of boost or nitrous, a well-prepped block is necessary if you plan on dipping into the nines.

We mentioned that one of the beauties of additional displacement (versus the more common B16A) is the added torque production. The extra displacement (and low-speed power production) actually makes life easier in terms of choosing the power producers. While things like cam timing, intake choice, and head porting are ultra critical on small displacement race motors, things get easier with added inches. The reason is that the added cubic inches make power production much easier. Not only does a bigger motor make more power, but also the added low-speed torque provides exhaust energy to the turbo much sooner, allowing the use of an otherwise larger turbo. The added displacement provides an earlier spool up for the turbo, taking some of the pressure off turbo selection. Getting exhaust energy to the turbine section of the turbo is critical. The big cubes just get the boost party started sooner.

The cam choice is critical to a turbo motor, as excessive overlap can kill performance. The cams that run on turbo motors are usually smaller than those run on most all-motor applications of similar displacement. While a typical all-motor LS/VTEC or B18 would require a JG 308/316 cam combo, the turbo motor made 769 hp using the smaller 296/300 cams. Like a normally aspirated combination, the cams must work closely with the intake design for optimum power production in a given rpm range. The turbo motor featured a custom fabricated intake manifold and big-valve Pro series cylinder head.

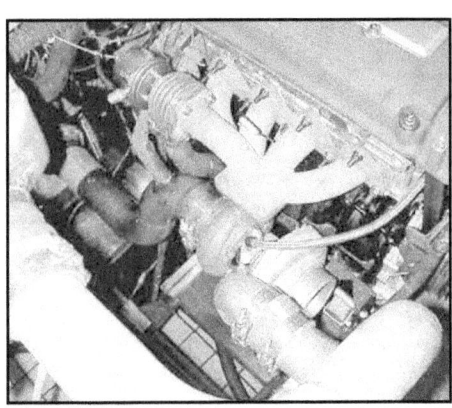

Note the position of the wastegate on the exhaust manifold. Centrally mounting the wastegate reduces exhaust backpressure evenly in the manifold. Some manifolds rely on an offset position that eliminates pressure from the pulses of just one cylinder. It is never a good idea to alter the pulses of just one cylinder, never mind that it makes the wastegate less effective at controlling boost pressure.

What more can you say about a B-series motor that pumps out 769 hp and 525 ft-lbs of torque, at an altitude of 7,000 feet no less?

This shot illustrate the generous size of the turbo compressor and the plumbing to the intercooler.

Working with the cam profiles, the intake design helps determine the effective rpm range of the motor. Since no factory Honda/Acura intake was designed to produce in excess of 750 hp at 9,000+ rpm, JG took it upon themselves to make one that did. They came up with a hand-fabricated combination that employed the ideal runner size, length, and plenum volume to match the cam profiles.

Obviously, the cylinder head has a great deal to do with the power production of the motor. While it does not affect the effective operating range of the motor to the same extent as the intake or cam timing, a cylinder head must be capable of supporting over 750 hp worth of flow. How is it possible to coax a cylinder head originally intended to support just 160 hp to flow sufficient air to feed a motor that makes 769 hp? Of course, the turbocharger is part of the answer, as the boost pressure forces air into the motor at an alarming rate. While the turbo might be responsible for greatly improving the efficiency of the intake ports, what happens to the exhaust ports? Those same ports that flow 160 hp are now subjected to an additional 600 hp worth of exhaust flow. Credit a great deal of research and development for optimum head porting. It is important to mention that optimum head porting might not result in the largest flow figures on a flow bench (no one races flow benches), but the combination of air flow and air speed (velocity through the ports) is what really fills those cylinders. JG topped the turbo motor off with a Pro Series head that featured turbo-specific porting along with larger valves made of high-strength stainless steel. The high-strength valves should be considered mandatory for extreme turbo applications, as the elevated heat can burn lesser valves in less time that it takes to miss a shift.

The key to any good turbo motor is obviously the turbo. Exact turbo specs are a close-guarded secret, and for good reason. A turbo is much more than a conglomeration of a turbine and compressor wheels in high-flow housings. Using this 769-hp B18C motor as

Engine Buildup 7: JG Engine Dynamics Turbo Race Motor

Car	(Dyno Engine)
Block	B18C-5
Bore	82.5 mm
Sleeved	Yes
Solid Deck	Yes
Stroke	87.2 mm
Piston Type	11.0 Forged (Flat Top or High Compression)
Manufacturer	JE
Rod Length	137 mm
Manufacturer	Saenz
Head Type	B16A with welded chamber
Ported	Yes, Pro Race Series
Valve Sizes in./ex.	34-mm intake and 29-mm exhaust
Injector size	4) 1,600 cc
Cam(s)	JG 296/300
Adjustable Cam Sprocket(s)	Yes, JG
Intake Type	JG Edelbrock prototype
Ported	Yes
Throttle Body Type	Billet RC
Size	65 mm
Air intake	Turbo
Header	JG Turbomanifold
Exhaust	JG downpipe
Turbo/Supercharger	Turbo
Type	T4
Maximum Boost Pressure	22 psi
Intercooler Type	XS air to air
Fuel/Timing Management	Motec M4 Pro

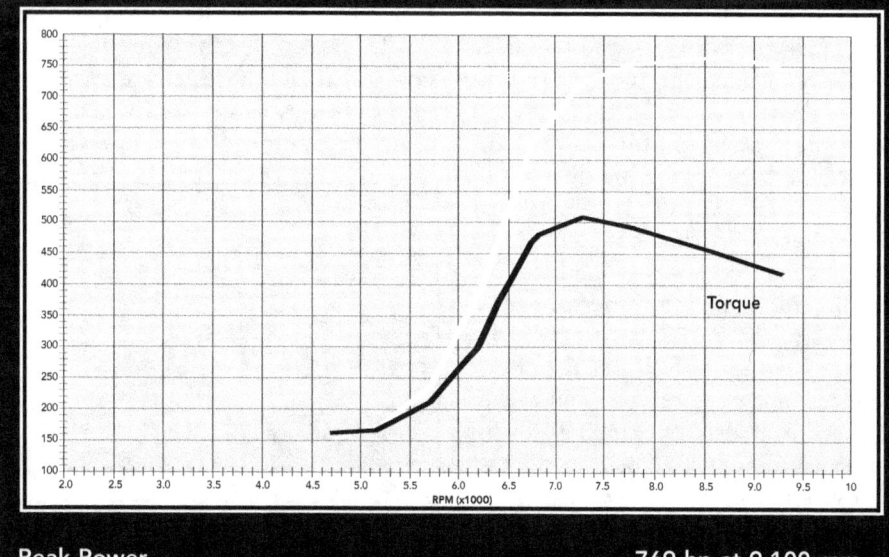

Peak Power	769 hp at 9,100 rpm
Peak Torque	525 ft-lbs at 7,200 rpm

Chapter 8

an example, the compressor side of the turbo must be able to flow sufficient air at a given pressure ratio to feed 769 hp. Choosing a compressor (both wheel and housing) is actually quite easy, as maps are available from the various turbo manufacturers to get you close. Actual performance depends mostly on experience, as the maps aren't always a true indicator of real-world performance. Once a compressor is chosen, it is necessary to choose a matching turbine section. The turbine must provide enough energy to the shaft to spin the compressor sufficiently to produce the boost and flow to feed the 769 hp motor, but not restrict exhaust flow (produce excessive back pressure) to the point where performance suffers.

The problem is actually even more complicated, as a compressor section capable of pushing 769-hp worth of air requires a healthy turbine section. The high-flow turbine section requires plenty of exhaust flow to provide energy to the compressor shaft. A turbo capable of supporting 769 hp needs enough exhaust energy to energize the turbine. This energy comes from the power of the motor—which comes from the compressor side of the turbo.

The compressor needs exhaust energy, while the exhaust gets energy from the extra power created by the boost pressure (actually airflow) from the compressor. This cycle, where the compressor feeds the turbine and vice versa, makes turbo selection critical, especially when the power output reaches the levels seen by this B18C.

While a street motor can get reasonable performance from just about any small turbo such as a T25, T28, or T3, absolute performance motors must have matched compressor and turbine sections for maximum performance. Obviously, the turbo on this 769-hp B18C was sized perfectly as the motor produced not only big top end power numbers but also over 500 ft-lbs of torque, running just 22 psi.

Even more impressive is the fact that these power numbers were generated at an elevation of 7,000 feet! JG has since built combinations that exceed 900 hp.

Engine Buildup 8
Killer Bee Racing Supercharged B18C Stroker Motor

This particular motor was built by the author to run in what would become the World's Fastest Honda Civic. The motor was built in an effort to be the first to officially reach 200 mph in a Honda Civic. Rather than go the usual turbo route, I elected to run a somewhat unconventional (and untested) centrifugal supercharger. Although the design has been around for ages, the centrifugal superchargers were somewhat new to the Sport Compact market at the time of this writing. The Vortech kit for the Civic Si and Integra GSR had recently been released and while we expected the Vortech guys to penetrate the market even further, the Honda/Acura kits were just getting into the hands of the enthusiasts. While the Civic/Integra kits were new, Vortech was not. They had been offering superchargers for domestic applications for years. I proudly wore serial number 001 under the hood of my 1988 Mustang for many years before retiring it back to Vortech for display. Before you laugh at the domestic machinery, know that the daily driven Mustang was timed at 193 mph and spent much of its life running top speed events in excess of 175 mph. By the time this reaches the hands of enthusiasts, both the Mustang and the Civic will have officially exceeded 200 mph.

The reason for the Mustang discussion is that all that supercharger experience gained over the years was put into Civic. The motor for the Civic was built

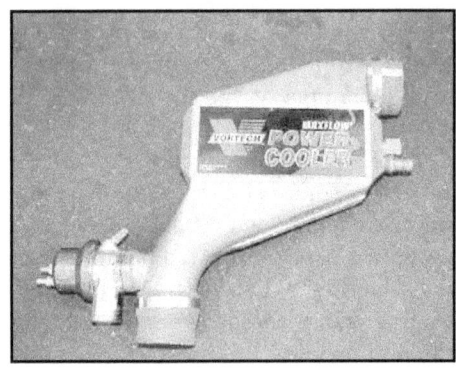

A Vortech Aftercooler was used to minimize the charge temperature at 20 psi.

with reliability as a major goal and power as a minor one. While the specific power needs of the record run were important, the approach to the motor was much different than a typical drag race application. Unlike a drag strip, where a motor need only survive brief 10-second blasts at full throttle, a record run at Bonneville would require the motor to run at full song (against an aerodynamic load no less) for up to 5 miles. Imagine Jojo, Steph, or Adam not shutting down their drag motors after running through the lights and continuing to accelerate for another 4.5 miles. To say that it is a little tough on the motor is an understatement. The motor must be tough enough, not to mention well tuned enough to survive 5 miles of foot-to-the-floor and 20 psi. Talk about a torture test.

Knowing that the motor would have to be stout, I turned to the experts at JG for block prep. They treated the B18A (1.8L non VTEC block) to the Pro Series treatment including high-

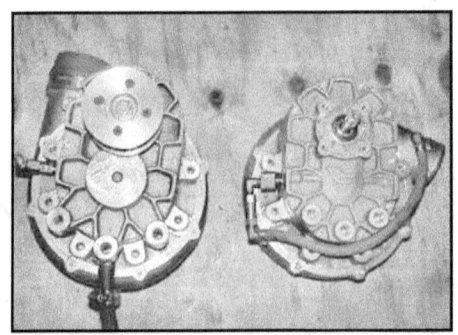

The V2 E-trim was much larger than the V5 G-trim used on the Vortech kits for the Civic Si and GSR.

Note the solid deck block on the B18A. The bores were machined to accept the 84-mm Arias pistons.

strength ductile iron sleeves, a solid deck (welded), and precision machine work. The new sleeves were bored to accept the 84-mm Probe Racing pistons. The combination of the 84-mm bore and the 89-mm stroke produced a displacement of just under 2.0 liters. The remainder of the short block included Probe Racing forged connecting rods and Probe Racing forged 9.0:1 pistons. The pistons featured eyebrows that provided plenty of piston-to-valve clearance for our larger-than-stock camshafts. Originally, we planned to run a set of 296/308 JG cams, but were forced to make the preliminary runs with Crower 63402 cams. The Crower cams were larger than a set of Integra or Civic Type R cams, but I feel that more testing is necessary to optimize the cam profile for a centrifugal supercharger. The Crower cams helped make the supercharged motor efficient to 8,500 rpm.

The motor was topped off with a ported B16A cylinder head. The head featured Extrude Hone porting, which improved the flow rate of the stock intake and exhaust ports, without dramatically increasing the port size. Killer Bee Racing supplied one of their prototype intake manifolds that was optimized for our combination. The casting was further improved by Extrude Hone porting. The intake was fed by a Holley 68-mm throttle body and custom air intake system. A high-flow header from APEXi handled the exhaust chores. The header design was necessary to provide clearance for the Vortech supercharger, which was mounted down where the air conditioner normally resides in a stock Civic. The V2 E-trim Vortech supercharger was much larger than the supercharger used in the 1999–2000 Civic Si and 1994–2001 Integra GSR kits. The V5 G trim used in the kits was good for over 400 hp, but we wanted to make sure we had plenty of flow potential to produce as much as 500 (wheel) hp if necessary. While the calculations told us that 500 (wheel) hp was not necessary to exceed 200 mph, it is always nice to have some in reserve.

Since compression causes heat and our motor was likely to see 20 psi, we elected to not only run race fuel, but also

Engine Buildup 8: Killer Bee Racing Supercharged B18C Stroker Motor

Car	*2000 Civic Si*
Block	B18A
Bore	84 mm
Sleeved	Yes
Solid Deck	Yes
Stroke	89 mm
Piston Type	9.0:1 Forged
Manufacturer	Arias
Rod Length	5.394
Manufacturer	Eagle
Head Type	B16A (milled .030)
Ported	Yes, JG Pro Series
Valve Sizes in./ex.	34-mm intake and 29-mm exhaust
Injector size	77 lbs/hr
Cam(s)	Crower 63401
Adjustable Cam Sprocket(s)	Yes, AEM
Intake Type	Killer Bee Racing Custom
Ported	Yes
Throttle Body Type	Holley
Size	68 mm
Air intake	Custom
Header	Custom Hytech
Exhaust	Straight Pipe
Turbo/Supercharger	Supercharger
Type	Vortech V2 E-trim
Maximum Boost Pressure	20 psi
Intercooler Type	Air-to-water (Vortech Aftercooler)
Fuel/Timing Management	Hondata

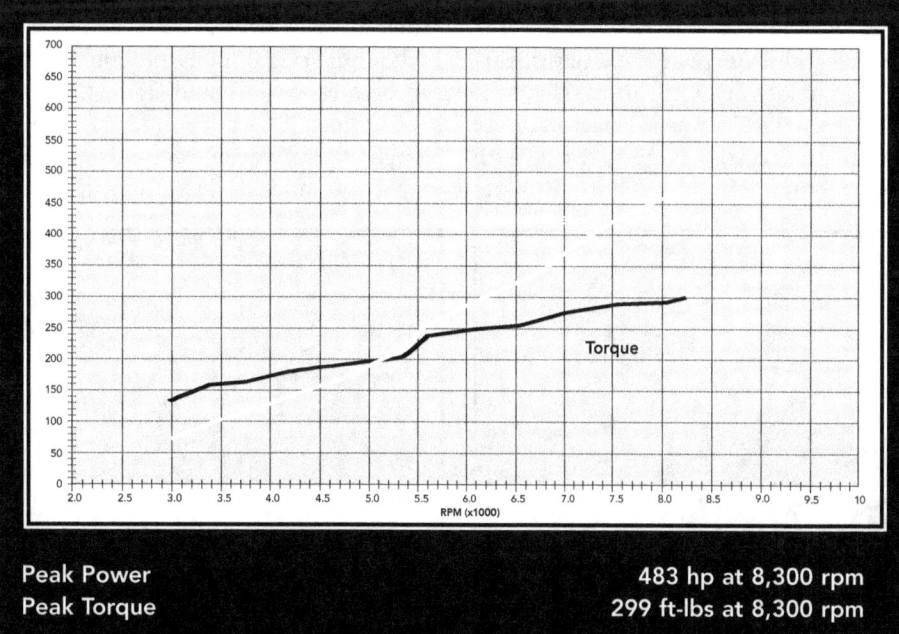

Peak Power	483 hp at 8,300 rpm
Peak Torque	299 ft-lbs at 8,300 rpm

an intercooler. Actually, we ran a Vortech Aftercooler. The air-to-water intercooler utilized ice water (from a 10 gallon cell) to cool the heated charge air during the runs. The fuel for our thirsty motor came from a set of 77-lbs/hr Ford Mustang injectors (actually modified 36 lbs/hr). The injectors (not to mention most of the dyno time for this book) came from Steve Rideout over at PowerTrain Dynamics. Thanks again! Since it was necessary to fire all that air and fuel, we also employed a Crane Hi6 ignition amplifier and a set of Denso Iridium spark plugs. The plugs were critical to performance, as they allowed us to increase the plug gap without fear of misfires. Credit for the power production of the Iridium plugs goes to a combination of the unique properties of the rare metal (very long lasting, even in a harsh environment) and ultra-fine electrode. In our testing, the Iridium plugs allowed us to run 3 to 4 more pounds of boost than a conventional plug before misfiring occurred (tested with a stock ignition). It should also be noted that the motor and tranny were run with Redline synthetic oil products exclusively. Having run Redline in all my (street and race) motors, I saw no reason to mess with the power and security offered by the quality Redline Oil products.

The engine management system consisted of a programmable factory ECU. The Hondata modified P30 (Del Sol) ECU allowed us to fine tune the air/fuel and timing curves at part throttle and wide open throttle. This was critical as the 77-lbs/hr injectors were obviously way too large to work with the factory ECU. The Hondata employed a 3-bar (GM) map sensor that allowed the factory computer to recognize as much as 29 psi. We had no intention of running that much boost, as we felt that our power needs would be met with much lower boost levels. The Hondata was slick in that it provided fuel and timing tables for both the primary cam and secondary VTEC cams. Each table had columns for different engine speeds versus the map readings (basically load).

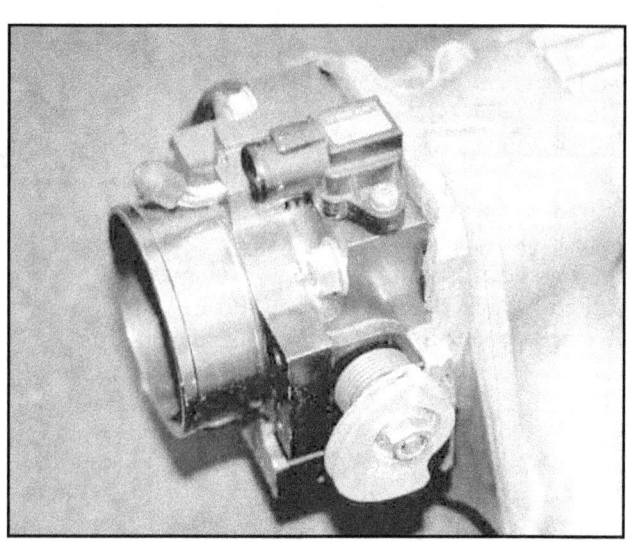

Once again, we employed a 68-mm Holley throttle body.

The values of each can be changed as well as entire columns or even the entire table (a global 10 percent increase for example). The system also featured a starting point that allowed us to select a specific size injector, although it was still necessary to make adjustments once selecting our rather large injectors.

The buildup was a success, as the supercharged 2.0L pumped out nearly 500 hp at the wheels at 19 psi of boost. The Civic Si managed to exceed 185 mph on its first voyage and then sneak into the 190-mph bracket, with a clocking of 191 mph, making it the World's Fastest Honda Civic. Remember too, that this Civic was not a racecar, but rather a street-driven 1999 Civic Si. The author put several thousand miles on the car before, during, and after the top-speed runs. At one point, the supercharged Civic was my daily driver, logging 2,000 miles in just a month's time.

Once tuned properly, the Vortech supercharged 2.0L also managed to exceed 30 mpg on the freeway. Although the supercharger replaced the air conditioner unit, the Civic still featured all of the comforts of home including a killer stereo, sunroof, and power windows. By the time you read this, the Civic will have posted the first 200-mph speed ever seen by a Honda Civic. Imagine that, a 200-mph street Civic!

Probe Racing pistons and rods were used in the supercharged 2.0L buildup.

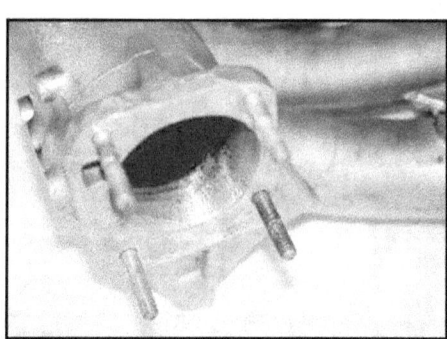

This Killer Bee Racing prototype intake was used during the top-speed runs.

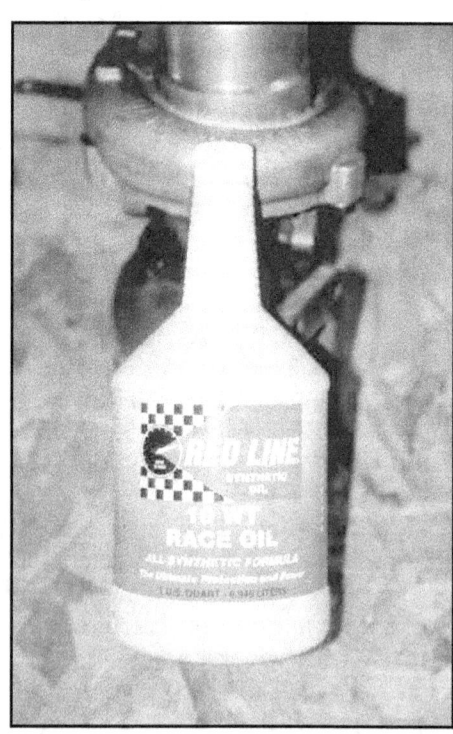

The only oil I ran in the top-speed motor was Redline synthetic.

Appendix A

Source Guide

Advanced Clutch Technology
P.O. Box 903425
Palmdale, CA 93590
(661) 947-7791

AEM
2205 126th St. Unit A
Hawthorne, CA 90250
(310) 484-2322
www.aempower.com

APEXi
330 West Taft
Orange, CA 92865
(714) 685-5700

Arias
13420 S. Normandie Ave.
Gardina, CA 90249
(310) 532-9737
www.ariaspistons.com

ARP
531 Spectrum Circle
Oxnard, CA 93030
(805) 278-7223

Best Products/ProM
21890 Meyers Rd.
Oak Park, MI 48237
(248) 399-9223

Borla Performance Industries
5901 Edison Dr.
Oxnard, CA 93033
877-Go Borla
www.Borla.com

Coast High Performance/Probe
1650 W. 228th St.
Torrance, CA 90501
(310) 784-2977
www.347streetfighter.com

Chikara-Hedman
16410 Manning Way
Cerritos, CA 90703
(562) 921-0404

Comp Cams
3406 Democratt Rd.
Memphis, TN 38118
(901) 795-2400

Comptech
4717 Golden Foothills Pkwy
El Dorado Hills, CA 95762
(916) 933-1080

Crane Cams
530 Fentress Blvd.
Daytona Beach, FL 32114
(904) 252-1151
www.cranecams.com

Crower Cams & Equipment
3333 Main St.
Chula Vista, CA 91911
(619) 422-1191

DC Sports
1451 East 6th Street
Corona, CA 92879
(909) 734-2030
www.dcsports.com

Denso
3900 Via Oro Ave
Long Beach, CA 90810
(888) 511-4312
www.densoiridium.com

Drag
2168 S. Atlantic Blvd. #219
Monterey Park, CA 91754
(213) 721-9689

Eagle
8530 Aaron Lane
Southhaven, MS 38671
(662) 796-7373

JG/Edelbrock
2700 California St.
Torrance, CA 90503
(310) 781-2222
www.edelbrock.com

Extrude Hone
8800 Somerset Blvd
Paramount, CA 90723
(562) 531-2976

Fel Pro
One Equation Blvd.
Ashland, MS 38603
(662) 224-8972
www.federal-mogul.com

Ford Racing Performance Parts
P.O. Box 51394
Livonia, MI 48151
(586) 468-1356

How to Build Honda Horsepower

Appendix A

Greddy Performance Products
9 Vanderbilt
Irvine, CA 92618
(949) 588-8300
www.greddy.com

Holeshot Racing
1525 N. Endeavour Pl Unit M
Anaheim, CA 92801
(714) 772-VTEC

Hondata, Inc.
2341 West 205th St
Torrance, CA 90501
310 782 8278
sales@hondata.com

Holley/Hooker
1801 Russellville Rd.
PO Box 10360
Bowling Green, KY 42102
1 (800) Holley 1

HyTech Exhaust
12 Hammond Drive Suite 202
Irvine, CA 92618
(949) 581-2181

Iceman
(909) 875-1600
www.ice-man.com

Innovative Turbo Systems
845 Easy Street, Unit 102
Simi Valley, CA 93065
(805) 526-5400
www.innovativeturbo.com

Jacobs
500 N Baird St.
Midland, TX 79701
(915) 685-3345
www.jacobs.com

Jackson Racing
440 Rutherford St.
Goletta, CA 93117
(888) 888-4079
www.jacksonracing.com

JG Engine Dynamics
(626) 281-5326
www.jgenginedynamics.com

JE Pistons
15312 Connector Ln
Huntington Beach, CA 92649
(714) 373-5530

K&N Engineering
P.O. Box 1329
1455 Citrus Ave.
Riverside, CA 92502
(909) 826-4000
www.knfilters.com

Kenne Bell
10743 Bell Ct.
Rancho Cucamonga, CA 91730
(909) 941-6646

Killer Bee Racing
15561 Product Ln. Suite D1
Huntington Beach, CA 92649
(714) 901-9101

King Motorsports/Mugen
(262) 593-2800
www.kingmotorsports.com

Magnaflow
(800) 959-9226
www.magnaflow.com

Moroso Performance Products
80 Carter Dr.
PO Box 1470
Guilford, CT 06437
(203) 453-6571
www.moroso.com

MSD
1490 Henry Brennan Dr.
El Paso, Texas 79936
(915) 857-3344

Pacesetter
2841 W. Clarendon
Phoenix, AZ 85017
(602) 266-3154

PowerTrain Dynamics
15628 Graham St.
Huntington Beach, CA 92649
(714) 373-0068

RC Engineering
1728 Border Ave.
Torrance, CA 90501
(310) 320-2277
www.rceng.com

Redline Oil
(800) 624-7958
www.redlineoil.com

RS Akimoto
18239 S. Figueroa St.
Gardena, CA 90248
(310) 532-6617

Skunk 2
(510) 781-0538
www.skunk2racing.com

Stillen
3176 Airway
Costa Mesa, CA 92626
(800) 576-2177
www.stillen.com

Thermal Research
7624 Winnetka Ave.
Canoga Park, CA 91306
(888) 2 Thermal

TurboXS
267 Kentlands Blvd #3043
Gaithersburg, MD 20878
(877) 887-2679

Turbonetics/Spearco
2255 Agate Ct.
Simi Valley, CA 93065
(805) 581-0333
www.turboneticsinc.com

Turbo City
1137 West Katella Ave.
Orange, CA 92867
(714) 639-4933
www.turbocity.com

Toucan Industries
(877) 598-6000
www.californiastylin.com

Unorthodox Racing
11 Brandywine Dr.
Dearpark, NY 11729
(631) 253-4909
www.info@unorthodoxracing.com

Venom
(714) 828-1406
www.venom-performance.com

Vortech
1650 Pacific Ave
Channel Islands, CA 93033
(805) 247-0226

Zex
(888) 817-1008
www.Zex.com

www.ingramcontent.com/pod-product-compliance
Lightning Source LLC
Chambersburg PA
CBHW051407070526
44584CB00023B/3325